GERMANISTIK
IN IRELAND

Jahrbuch der / Yearbook of the
German Studies Association
of Ireland (GSAI)

Volume 7
2012

Special Issue:

Adaptation: Text into Film and Beyond

Editors: Rachel MagShamhráin (University College Cork)
Sabine Strümper-Krobb (University College Dublin)

D1719062

TABLE OF CONTENTS

Introduction

In the opening article of this volume, Thomas **Leitch** offers a critique of a recently published and controversial collection of essays on adaptation studies, Colin MacCabe, Kathleen Murray and Rick Warner's (eds.) *True to the Spirit: Film Adaptation and the Question of Fidelity* (OUP, 2011). Finding many glaring omissions and erroneous assumptions about adaptation study there, Leitch sees this as an opportune moment for a stock-take of the field of adaptation studies as it actually is, which includes asking if the much-beleaguered subject area fulfils what he considers to be the essential criteria of an academic discipline. As such, the essay provides the general reader with a useful map of the field, including what one might call its foundational debates. On the great fidelity debate, for example, which, it is claimed, haunts adaptation studies, catching it in a nefarious binary from which it valiantly tries to but cannot escape, Leitch's essay exposes much tilting at windmills here, suggesting that the field is not so much haunted by the fidelity question than that the arrière-garde of criticism is seeing ghosts. The crucial matter of film and literary studies' attitude to the young pretender discipline of adaptation studies is also addressed – crucial because it marks the intellectual politics in many institutions, in turn, perhaps, explaining the attitude of some criticism. The article proposes that, rather than seeing it as an intruder, we see adaptation studies as provocatively useful, a kind of benign and beneficial trespasser, an impulse transecting and reinvigorating the various disciplines upon whose 'territory' it seems to encroach. Leitch also articulates the specific burdens that face the adaptation studies scholar, who must ever "make it new," and has to be a keen amateur of many non-native fields and their idioms. In addition to the article's clarification of the somewhat pernicious position in which the "anti-discipline" of adaptation studies finds itself, it also propounds and practices, by way of moving things forward from redundant and reductive debates, a productive paradigm of scholarship that might also fruitfully be adopted by many other disciplines: adaptation studies as a communicating, interconnected (inter- or trans-) disciplinary network that is, if not utterly democratic, then aware of its own inclusionary and exclusionary practices and their consequences. Emphasizing the importance of ongoing vibrant dialogue to any would-be discipline, the article criticizes the MacCabe volume's refusal to engage with adaptation scholarship as it actually is, but this criticism is deliberately productive, reopening discourse where it had been closed off. This willingness to (re)engage is precisely Leitch's point, and places his article in counter-point to the approaches with which he takes issue here.

Continuing the vigorous debate that, according to Leitch's typography, is one of the hallmarks of a discipline's establishment, Graham **Allen's** contribution argues against a practice of adaptation studies that he sees as concentrating excessively on "the critical enumeration and analysis of kinds of adaptive practice," recommending instead an approach that sees all texts, both "originals" and their adaptations ("adaptative texts"), as well, indeed, as analytical texts, as intertexts. By "reviving our perception of the intertextual nature of the intertext," Allen argues, we are forced beyond purely metatextual investigations and their failed attempts at categorization, and into acts of interpretation. The analyst, according to this scheme, is no longer a "metacommentator on generic kinds of adaptation practice," but an "interpreter of a shifting, unstable intertext." As an example of this approach, according to which "adaptative texts" are read as existing in an unfixed triadic (or indeed, presumably, tetradic, pentadic, hexadic, and so on and so forth) interpretative relationship with one another, Allen offers a reading of the tetrad Burgess, Kubrick (*A Clockwork Orange*), Beethoven, and Shelley (*Prometheus Unbound* and *The Triumph of Life*), tracing for us a network of intertextual linkages that are brought to light by specific interpretative acts. This approach, Allen suggests, offers a corrective to a blind-spot in adaptation studies, namely the tacit insistence on, if not an original, then a kind of ground-zero anchor text "upon which the adaptational activity is founded." Allen's suggestion of a *blind-spot* in the practice of adaptation study is particularly interesting in the context of Leitch's reference to *panoptic* disciplines which "internalize what Foucault has called 'the power of the Norm' and so police their own, and each others' discourse," and which he distinguishes from a network model of disciplinary activity that "attaches greater importance to the questions – some perhaps foundational and enduring, others ever-changing – that drive the conversation that keeps the network humming," and which, Leitch suggests, is an appropriate paradigm for a discipline such as adaptation studies which "emphasizes the relations among different texts above features specific to the texts themselves," and therefore seems to have "obvious affinities to a network model of disciplinary authority."

Siobhán **Donovan's** analysis of a performance of Alban Berg's "Literaturoper" [literature opera / literary opera] *Wozzeck*, and of a recording of that performance for television, reveals that, despite Berg's claims of fidelity for himself and for future productions, a complex network of intertexts are at work in this piece: the Frankfurt production directed by Peter Mussbach is shown to be an intertext that sometimes refers back to the Büchner 'original' (itself based on a true story, as well as liberally overwritten by overzealous editors), and sometimes takes its direction from Berg's libretto choices (his restructuring of the sequence of the source text is read here as a pragmatic adaptation demanded by the parameters of the opera genre), but also is forced to make its own new interventions as required by the medium of television. Donovan's analysis shows the curious mixture of fidelity and innovation required to remain "true" to core ideas as they are transposed across time and into different media. The analysis also reveals that even the simple act of recording a performance for television does not achieve the 1:1 fidelity we might imagine, as the act of framing as well as the addition of visual effects constitute adaptive interventions.

Taking the example of Matthias Müller's film *Nebel* (2000), based on a poetry cycle by Austrian poet Ernst Jandl, Stefanie **Orphal** turns to a topic that is, she suggests, often overlooked in adaptation studies: the adaptation of poetry into or in film. Rather than applying unproductive and outmoded ideas of fidelity, Orphal suggests that a more fruitful approach is offered by examining the interaction between the poem – which is often fully integrated into filmic adaptations – and the audio-visual techniques that film employs. This, she argues, expands the concept of adaptation in a way that might productively be adopted in the study of more traditional cases of literature-to-film adaptation, as it breaks away from various binary oppositions that have dominated the analysis of adaptations in the past.

In the context of the anti-war film genre, Christiane **Schönfeld** looks at two adaptations of Manfred Gregor's autobiographical novel *Die Brücke* (1958), the story of a group of boys who, at the end of the Second World War, are ordered to defend a bridge in their home town, in the course of which defence most of them are killed. The two films enjoyed very different degrees of critical success: Bernhard Wicki's 1959 film, considered to be one of the best anti-war films ever made, met with both national and international acclaim, while the 2008 television production by Wolfgang Panzer was robustly criticized and then largely forgotten. Schönfeld seeks to explain this by examining the processes of adaptation in each case, paying close attention to the way in which the two directors frame their shots. While Wicki uses close-ups to emphasize the violence experienced by the young boys, thereby giving clear visual expression to the film's anti-war stance, Panzer uses close-ups and music in a much more conventional way, making the events on screen more comfortably digestible for the audience, resulting, ultimately, in *Kitsch*.

Ates **Gürpinar** expands the concept of adaptation in an article that looks at Sergej Eistenstein's notes on a possible film adaptation of Karl Marx' *Das Kapital*, and Alexander Kluge's film *Nachrichten aus der ideologischen Antike: Marx – Eisenstein – Das Kapital*. Rather than viewing adaptation as the transfer of a particular subject matter or material into a different medium, Gürpinar focuses on the adaptation of the forms conventionally used by the receiving medium to accommodate the forms of the medium in which the work originated. In the case of Marx' *Kapital*, this resulted, he argues, in attempts by both Eisenstein and Kluge to create a filmic language adapted to the scientific language and methods employed in Marx' work.

Andreas **Musolff's** contribution analyses the 1940 propaganda film *Der Ewige Jude* through the lens of "conceptual blending theory," a version of cognitive metaphor theory developed by Mark Turner and Gilles Fauconnier according to which concepts are viewed as "input spaces" which can combine (as at times incongruous elements) to form an entirely new conceptual whole. Musolff sees a blending of this kind at work in *Der Ewige Jude* which merges what are in themselves not inoccuous but certainly individually less lethal ideas into a devastating new entity, and one which, cunningly, shifts final interpretative and, with it, moral responsibility onto the film's audience. The only inference the film allows, Musolff argues, if one accepts the individual elements used in the blend, is the inevitability of a Final Solution. So, although the "film left no doubt about what the Nazis were planning for the Jews, [...] the responsibility for 'accepting' this knowledge was left to the spectators." The "input spaces" or individual elements involved here (the long-standing anti-Semitic trope of Jews as parasites, and Hitler's January 1939 prophecy of Jewish extermination in the event of a war, an eventuality that at the time of the film's release had come about) are re-contextualized and blended, as well as presented in a specific order that portrays "the mass murder of all European Jews [...] as a 'natural' solution and as the coming-into-being of the Führer's prediction without spelling it out literally."

Claudia **Buffagni** takes a socio-linguistic approach in her examination of the 1965 film adaptation of the novel *Das Kaninchen bin ich* (1963) by East German author Manfred Bieler. Both the novel and the film (the screenplay of which was written by Bieler in collaboration with DEFA-co-founder and director Kurt Maetzig) were banned in the GDR. Buffagni argues that this rejection by GDR-authorities was a result of specific features in the speech of the main characters which suggested a social identity at odds with what was considered acceptable by the prevailing political system. While Buffagni identifies similar features in the speech of the main characters in both the novel and the film, the film, she argues, uses media-specific means to create a sense of immediacy and authenticity that further emphasizes the ultimately critical nature of the discourse, and thereby manages to circumnavigate to a certain extent the various deletions and changes demanded by party officials.

Bernadette **Cronin's** contribution looks at the special case in adaptation studies presented by postdramatic theatre, a theatre that departs from the conventions of traditional drama and in which "staged text (*if* text is staged) is merely a component with equal righs in a gestic, musical, visual, etc., total composition," to borrow Hans-Thies Lehmann's definition. Cronin takes the example of *POLA*, a stage production based on the short story "Pola" by Polish author and journalist Hanna Krall, which in turn was based on the real life and death of Apolonia Machczyńska, murdered by members of the infamous Reserve Police Batallion 101 for having hidden persecuted Jews under the floorboards of her home in Lublin. Created by a team of collaborators at the Projekttheater Studio, Vienna, this "devised performance," while based on other texts, including Beckett's dance or movement piece for television, the "Fernsehballett" *Quad* or *Quadrat 1+2*, and foregroundedly intertextual to the point that the *Ur*-text is actually pasted to the walls of the performance space, uses the devices of postdramatic theatre to enact its main concerns, which include Austria's refusal to confront its National Socialist past. Cronin's examination of this performative adaptation of Krall's "Pola," which eschews ideas of audience-performer separation as well as directorial and authorial authority, reveals the transpositions involved in the process of staging a prose piece, transpositions demanded by the specificities of different media as well as by the non-hierarchical, collaborative and experimental impulses central to postdramatic theatre production.

Nadine **Nowroth's** contribution analyses the documentary play *Staats-Sicherheiten* (2008) in which former political prisoners from the GDR tell their stories, and the film version of the play produced for German television in the wake of the play's enormous success. As both productions are based on the narratives of contemporary witnesses, using, for example, material previously published in the autobiography of one of the prisoners, Nowroth applies the concept of 'remedialization' – the re-use of already mediated stories and narratives in a new medium – in her analysis, investigating how media-specific features and techniques in the two productions allow the construction of authenticity and, thus, a re-enactment of history.

Una **Carthy's** contribution to the volume's General Contributions section discusses the findings of a two-phase study carried out in Letterkenny Institute of Technology to establish actual student attitudes towards language learning in an institutional environment which, contrary to overwhelming evidence demonstrating the importance of languages to the economy, increasingly saw language learning as low priority and an unpopular subject choice. While the majority of students surveyed did at first seem disinclined to study languages, further investigation in the form of semi-structured interviews found that students actually saw the value of foreign language competence, but were discouraged by negative experiences of language learning in secondary school and by a lack of awareness about the foreign study and work placement options available to them. The study therefore also sheds some light on the relatively low numbers of Irish students who avail of international mobility programmes compared to other European countries.

Antje **Hartje's** article compares the works of W.B. Yeats and Stefan George, proposing a method of 'understanding' their hermetic poetry, poems that replicate the incantatory quality of prayers, and in which formal, structural elements become the meaning-carriers, imparting their content to an initiated group of "worshippers" at the altar of aestheticism by visceral as opposed to cognitive appeal. Applying a modified form of reader-response theory allows, Hartje claims, the strategic gaps in these works to be "read."

A selection of papers from the Women in German Studies (WiGS) conference 2012, hosted by University College Dublin, will be published in the thematic section of the next volume of *Germanistik in Ireland* (volume 8, 2013). For this issue, we are delighted to welcome on board as guest co-editor Gillian Pye of University College Dublin. As always, articles on other subjects are also welcome for the General Contributions section.

The editors would like to thank the Austrian Embassy, Dublin, for its generous sponsorship of this volume. In particular, we would like to express our gratitude to Karin Fichtinger-Grohe, former Deputy Head of Mission, for her support not just of this issue, but also of the Yearbook enterprise and the Association generally, during her term of office in Ireland.

Rachel MagShamhráin and Sabine Strümper-Krobb (editors)

ADAPTATION:
TEXT INTO FILM AND BEYOND

Thomas Leitch

Is Adaptation Studies a Discipline?

Adaptation scholars puzzled or outraged by *True to the Spirit: Film Adaptation and the Question of Fidelity* should acknowledge that they are only eavesdropping on this new collection of essays, edited by Colin MacCabe, Kathleen Murray, and Rick Warner, for it is assuredly not addressed to them. Both its Introduction by MacCabe and its Afterword by Fredric Jameson are roundly dismissive of what Jameson calls "the expanding casebooks of 'adaptation studies.'"[1] Recent scholarship on adaptation, they agree, is fatally compromised by its "denunciation of the notion of fidelity to the original text,"[2] which renders it "ill equipped and unwilling to sketch that particular form of productivity that preserves identity at the same time it multiplies it"[3] – the form that promises to be the leading subject of the essays the volume collects.

The adaptation scholars whose work is so briskly marginalized have responded in one of two ways. Laurence Raw, reviewing the volume in *Literature/Film Quarterly,* represents the first way when he retorts that "the book shows little awareness of recent developments in adaptation theory."[4] It would be hard to dispute this judgment. True, the earliest contributions to the new volume, first submitted as papers for a graduate course MacCabe taught in Spring 2005, were not in a position to consider such recent volumes as Linda Hutcheon's *A Theory of Adaptation,* Julie Sanders's *Adaptation and Appropriation,* Christine Geraghty's *Now a Major Motion Picture: Film Adaptations of Literature and Drama,* the important anthologies edited by Robert Stam and Alessandra Raengo, Mireia Aragay, Peter Lev and James M. Welsh, Deborah Cartmell and Imelda Whelehan, and David L. Kranz and Nancy Mellerski, or anything that appeared in the journals *Adaptation* and *Journal of Adaptation in Film and Performance,* both of which commenced publication in 2008. Though several of them have added references to some of this more recent material in their notes, none of their essays has been shaped or reshaped by it.

What is more surprising is how little use any of the volume's other contributors – from Dudley Andrew, Tom Gunning, Laura Mulvey, and James Naremore, the headliners whose work supplements that of MacCabe's students, to MacCabe and

---

[1] Fredric Jameson: Afterword. Adaptation as a Philosophical Problem. In: Colin MacCabe, Kathleen Murray and Rick Warner (eds.): True to the Spirit. Film Adaptation and the Question of Fidelity. New York: Oxford University Press, 2011, p. 215-33, here p. 232.

[2] Jameson: Afterword, p. 215.

[3] Colin MacCabe: Introduction. Bazinian Adaptation. *The Butcher Boy* as Example. In: MacCabe et al. (eds.): True to the Spirit, p. 3-25, here p. 5.

[4] Laurence Raw: The Death-Rattle of "Fidelity" Studies? In: Literature/Film Quarterly 40/1 (2012), p. 77-78, here p. 77.

Jameson, whose essays were written several years after the class – make of recent adaptation scholarship. Jameson's throwaway reference, in his discussion of the "split subject which is the object of adaptation studies," to the "well-nigh Derridean vigilance to the multiple forms difference takes in the object of such studies,"[5] would have been considerably enriched by an acquaintance with Rochelle Hurst's more rigorously argued essay on adaptation as a Derridean undecidable.[6] When he describes the hypothesis that "Shakespeare's original script (or scenario) is not an original in our sense, nor could it ever be," as "distressingly subversive,"[7] he is presumably unaware of earlier essays that are far less distressed by this possibility.[8] The bold new law he proposes – "the novel and its film adaptation must not be of equal quality. A great film can be made from a mediocre novel; most great novels only yield second-rate movie adaptations"[9] – has been a cliché of cinema studies since at least 1979, when Stanley Cavell alluded to "the familiar fact that mediocre novels often make good film scripts and that great novels almost never do."[10] His blithely essentialist characterization of "film and literature" as "the visual and the verbal"[11] would not have survived engagement with Kamilla Elliott's extended demonstration that "[v]isual/verbal categorizations break down at every level in the hybrid arts of illustrated novels and worded films: at the level of the whole arts, at the level of whole signs, and at the level of pieces of signs."[12] And his injunction to adaptation scholars to move beyond "the universal repudiation of 'fidelity'" which betokens "some initial commitment to Difference" to a more searching exploration of the "philosophical emphasis on antagonism and incompatibility" ignores a decade of adaptation scholarship that has already been doing exactly that.[13]

MacCabe has an equally limited view of the field whose tenets he is so quick to characterize and dismiss. Citing André Bazin's prophecy that "we are moving toward a reign of the adaptation in which the notion of the unity of the work of art, if

---

[5]   Jameson: Afterword, p. 215.
[6]   Rochelle Hurst: Adaptation as an Undecidable. Fidelity and Binarity from Bluestone to Derrida. In: David L. Kranz and Nancy Mellerski (eds.): In/Fidelity. Essays in Film Adaptation. Newcastle: Cambridge Scholars Publishing, 2008, p. 172-96.
[7]   Jameson: Afterword, p. 216.
[8]   See for example Deborah Cartmell: The Shakespeare on Screen Industry. In: Deborah Cartmell and Imelda Whelehan (eds.): Adaptations. From Text to Screen, Screen to Text. New York: Routledge, 1999, p. 29-37; and Elsie Walker: Pop Goes the Shakespeare. Baz Luhrmann's William Shakespeare's *Romeo + Juliet*. In: Literature/Film Quarterly 28/2 (2000), p. 132-49.
[9]   Jameson: Afterword, p. 217.
[10] Stanley Cavell: The World Viewed. Reflections on the Ontology of Film. Enlarged edn. Cambridge, MA: Harvard University Press, 1979, p. 178.
[11] Jameson: Afterword, p. 226.
[12] Kamilla Elliott: Rethinking the Novel/Film Debate. Cambridge: Cambridge University Press, 2003, p. 16-17.
[13] Jameson: Afterword, p. 230, 231. Compare especially the wide range of attitudes toward fidelity argued by the contributors to Kranz and Mellerski (eds.): In/Fidelities.

not the very notion of the author himself, will be destroyed,"[14] McCabe observes: "Given the importance of this conception of adaptation in the history of the cinema, it is surprising that it has not given rise to a whole series of critical studies."[15] But in fact adaptation studies had already drawn repeatedly and fruitfully on such classics of poststructuralism as Roland Barthes's "From Work to Text"[16] and Michel Foucault's "What Is an Author?"[17] A recognition of the power of adaptation to call into question the apparent stability of texts and their authors is central to Robert Stam's invitation to "see filming adaptations as mutations that help their source novel 'survive,'"[18] to Linda Hutcheon's *A Theory of Adaptation,* which argues that "[s]tories […] evolve by adaptation and are not immutable over time,"[19] and to my own assertion "that texts remain alive only to the extent that they can be rewritten and that to experience a text in all its power requires each reader to rewrite it."[20] When MacCabe claims that "this collection perhaps reveals a new category altogether when the film is produced from a close engagement with the original novel but where the aim of the adaptation is not to develop and enhance but to discard and contradict so as to produce a version which has little to do with the source text,"[21] he does not notice that this category has already been discussed by Hutcheon, who observes that "the urge to consume and erase the memory of the adapted text or to call it into question is as likely as the desire to pay tribute by copying,"[22] and still earlier by Kamilla Elliott in her analysis of "ventriloquist," "trumping," and "looking glass" models of adaptation.[23] Elliott's "de(re)composing" model of adaptation, whereby "novel and film decompose, merge, and form a new composition at 'underground' levels of reading"[24] is a particularly precise echo of Bazin with which MacCabe seems unfamiliar.

So it is hard to escape Raw's conclusion that MacCabe and Jameson, and to a lesser extent MacCabe's students, two of whom he enlisted as co-editors, are not

---

[14]   André Bazin: Adaptation, or the Cinema as Digest. In: Bert Cardullo (ed.): Bazin at Work. Major Essays and Reviews from the Forties and Fifties. New York: Routledge, 1997, p. 49.

[15]   MacCabe: Introduction, p. 6.

[16]   Roland Barthes: From Work to Text. In: Image–Music–Text. Trans. Stephen Heath. New York: Hill and Wang, 1977, p. 155-64.

[17]   Michel Foucault: What Is an Author? In: Paul Rabinow (ed.): The Foucault Reader. London: Penguin, 1991, p. 101-20.

[18]   Robert Stam: Introduction. The Theory and Practice of Adaptation. In: Robert Stam and Alessandra Raengo (eds.): Literature and Film. A Guide to the Theory and Practice of Adaptation. Malden: Blackwell, 2005, p. 1-42, here p. 3.

[19]   Linda Hutcheon: A Theory of Adaptation. New York: Routledge, 2006, p. 31.

[20]   Thomas Leitch: Film Adaptation and Its Discontents. From *Gone with the Wind* to *The Passion of the Christ.* Baltimore, MD: Johns Hopkins University Press, 2007, p. 12-13.

[21]   MacCabe: Introduction, p. 23.

[22]   Hutcheon: Theory, p. 7.

[23]   Elliott: Rethinking the Novel/Film Debate, p. 143-50, 173-81, 209-15.

[24]   Elliott: Rethinking the Novel/Film Debate, p. 157.

only victims of a field that has developed more swiftly than they acknowledge, but are also cavalier researchers who have not done their homework. In a fundamental sense, it would be unfair to reproach them for their ignorance of a field to which they are clearly not directing their work. But it is not at all unfair to reproach them for their reckless summary judgments of that field in order to characterize their own work. Their offense is rendered particularly serious by what is presented as the framing premise of the collection: to defend the virtues of fidelity in the face of the "endless attacks on fidelity" that are "common to almost all the new literature on the subject,"[25] for to enter such a charge implies a comprehensive knowledge of recent developments in a field with which MacCabe and his contributors are manifestly unfamiliar.

It is particularly unfortunate that neither MacCabe nor most of his contributors ever indicate exactly who has been responsible for the unrelenting attacks on fidelity to which they feel compelled to respond. Tom Gunning's summary of the field is typical: "For years, essays on filmic adaptations began by indicating that previous writers have got it all wrong. The discussion of adaptations makes up a history of errors, it would seem." These errors include "ignor[ing] the unique language of cinema," "restrict[ing] adaptation to serious canonical literary works," and of course "claim[ing] films have a duty to be faithful to a literary source."[26] No specific offenders are indicted, either because these attacks are so indiscriminate as to be universal or because Gunning is too polite to quarrel directly with any offender.[27]

This courtesy, however, comes at a high cost. When Jarrell D. Wright, the only one of MacCabe's contributors who addresses directly specific attacks on fidelity criticism by George Bluestone, Stam, and myself, characterizes Bluestone's remark that "fidelity analysis is, if not irrelevant, then at least uninteresting,"[28] as a predecessor to the "more virulent arguments against fidelity analysis"[29] represented by assertions like this one – "Fidelity to its source text [...] is a hopelessly fallacious measure of a given adaptation's value because it is unattainable, undesirable, and theoretically possible only in a trivial sense"[30] – both his glosses on the passages he cites and the ensuing analysis of Stanley Kubrick's film adaptation of Stephen King's novel The Shining focus the terms of the debate and help readers choose their

---

[25] MacCabe: Introduction, p. 7.
[26] Tom Gunning: Literary Appropriation and Translation in Early Cinema. In: MacCabe et al. (eds.): True to the Spirit, p. 41-57, here p. 41.
[27] Simone Murray, who is considerably less polite than Gunning, has provided a useful list of specific commentators' attacks on fidelity criticism. See Murray: The Adaptation Industry. The Cultural Economy of Contemporary Literary Adaptation. New York: Routledge, 2012, p. 7-8.
[28] George Bluestone: Novels into Film. Baltimore, MD: Johns Hopkins University Press, p. 5.
[29] Jarrell D. Wright: Shades of Horror. Fidelity and Genre in Stanley Kubrick's The Shining. In: MacCabe et al. (eds.): True to the Spirit, p. 173-93, here p. 176.
[30] Thomas Leitch: Twelve Fallacies in Contemporary Adaptation Theory. In: Criticism, 45/2 (2003), p. 149-71, here, p. 161.

own positions. But when scholars who dissent from earlier scholars' positions decline to identify the scholars with whom they are arguing, they lose any sense of the historically specific context that considers why the earlier scholars would have made such wrongheaded arguments in the first place, and any hope of engaging the specifics of these earlier arguments. Had Gunning or any of MacCabe's other contributors specified the critics of fidelity to whom they were taking exception, they might have felt obliged, for example, to take account of Robert Stam's genuinely ambivalent attitude toward fidelity:

> When we say an adaptation has been "unfaithful" to the original, the term gives expression to the disappointment we feel when a film adaptation fails to capture what we see as the fundamental narrative, thematic, and aesthetic features of its literary source. The notion of fidelity gains its persuasive force from our sense that some adaptations are indeed better than others and that some adaptations fail to 'realize' or substantiate what we most appreciated in the source novels. Words such as *infidelity* or *betrayal* in this sense translate our feeling, when we have loved a book, that an adaptation has not been worthy of that love.[31]

In order to quarrel instead with Dudley Andrew's 1980 essay on adaptation, they would have needed to cite the following highly influential passage, as Wright briefly does:

> Unquestionably the most frequent and most tiresome discussion of adaptation (and of film and literature relations as well) concerns fidelity and transformation. Here it is assumed that the task of adaptation is the reproduction in cinema of something essential about an original text. Here we have a clear-cut case of film trying to measure up to a literary work, or of an audience expecting to make such a comparison. Fidelity of adaptation is conventionally treated in relation to the "letter" and to the "spirit" of the text, as though adaptation were the rendering of an interpretation of a legal precedent.[32]

Although Andrew goes on to characterize the arguments spun out of the dichotomy of letter and spirit as "strident and often futile,"[33] MacCabe never indicates the relation of his own volume, whose title takes its cue from this heresy, to Andrew's attack on it thirty years earlier.

Andrew's own recent position is more nuanced. Observing that "all films, but adaptations most notably, float to their audiences secured by that slender line of credits that allows us to trace their genesis," he contends that "[e]ven in our

---

[31]   Robert Stam: Beyond Fidelity. The Dialogics of Adaptation. In: James Naremore (ed.): Film Adaptation. New Brunswick, NJ: Rutgers University Press, 2000, p. 54-76, here p. 54.

[32]   Dudley Andrew: Adaptation. In: Concepts in Film Theory. Oxford: Oxford University Press, 1984, p. 96-106, here p. 100. See Wright: Shades of Horror, p. 173.

[33]   Andrew: Adaptation, p. 101.

skeptical age, this lifeline – call it fidelity – just won't be easily cut. Fidelity is the umbilical cord that nourishes the judgments of ordinary viewers as they comment on what are effectively aesthetic and moral values."[34] Here Andrew is both mitigating his earlier attack on fidelity criticism and echoing Stam's ambivalence toward it, even though he gets credit for the ambivalence while Stam does not. Hence Andrew has recently argued elsewhere that "the leading academic trend has ignored or disparaged this concern with fidelity. [...] Scholars today dare to detach the films they write about from their anchors and let them float free."[35] If Andrew named me as one of these academics, I would respond that his formulation is a serious mischaracterization of my work, which, acknowledging that "filmmakers occasionally, and adaptation theorists more frequently, have made fidelity central to their enterprise," attempts "to study it rather than attacking or defending it."[36] If he identified Stam as his target, I would argue that it is an even more egregious misreading of Stam, whose monograph *Literature through Film* is studded with value judgments (e.g., "mediocr[e]," "pedestrian," "hackneyed"[37]) based on specific films' relations to their sources.

But the real problem with these rebuttals of attacks on fidelity by unnamed assailants, as with Gunning's remark that "discussion of filmic adaptations seems to me to remain stuck in a defensive posture set by earlier generations of film critics anxious to maintain the value of cinema against the cultural hegemony of literary studies,"[38] and MacCabe's assessment that "it is conventional wisdom within much adaptation studies that the question of the aesthetic primacy of literature or film is the key debate,"[39] is not that they largely misread the consensual wisdom of contemporary adaptation scholarship – though this they certainly do – but that the rebuttals adopt exactly the same overgeneralizing strategy they condemn in their unnamed targets. So it is impossible to argue with their generalizations, since no one in particular has been attacked, and no one can cite contextual chapter and verse in defence. More generally, MacCabe and his contributors' decision to dismiss theoretical positions instead of engaging them prevents them from generating exactly the kind of productive discourse MacCabe claims to want. Instead, they construct a history in which a defensiveness about literature and a concomitant suspicion of adaptation breed a countervailing defensiveness about cinema and cinematic adaptation, but fail to note that their own defensiveness about fidelity is equally reflexive and undiscriminating.

---

34   Dudley Andrew: The Economies of Adaptation. In: MacCabe et al. (eds.): True to the Spirit, p. 27-39, here p. 27.
35   Dudley Andrew: What Cinema Is! Bazin's Quest and Its Charge. Chichester: Wiley-Blackwell, 2010, p. 127.
36   Thomas Leitch: Film Adaptation, p. 20.
37   Robert Stam: Literature through Film. Realism, Magic, and the Art of Adaptation. Malden: Blackwell, 2005, p. 3, 37, 68.
38   Gunning: Literary Appropriation, p. 42.
39   MacCabe: Introduction, p. 7.

Instead of accepting the invitation to continue this endless cycle of recrimination, as Raw's review does, David T. Johnson's response is marked by a resourcefulness and generosity that seem to me far more characteristic of recent work in adaptation studies. He calls *True to the Spirit* a "highly engaging volume" that offers "a window into the way cinema studies views what happens in adaptation studies." Characterizing the collection's defence of fidelity as "largely go[ing] against what adaptation studies has argued in recent years," Johnson describes this defence as "assuming a centrality (and even a novelty) [fidelity] has not seen in some time." To his wish that "the provocative volume [...] had discussed the history of adaptation studies more than it does," Johnson adds: "But this, of course, depends in part upon a recognition of adaptation studies as a *field* – a recognition [...] I am not at all sure is certain, at least within cinema studies more generally."[40] For Johnson, the principal value of MacCabe's collection is a series of questions about the institutional and intellectual status of adaptation studies it more or less unwittingly raises:

> Is adaptation studies a discipline? Or might we characterize it a bit more loosely, as a subspecialty that recognizes traditional disciplinal boundaries, even while it frequently crosses them? Or, perhaps, is it something even more mercurial than this – at heart, an impulse that understanding the way meaning, narrative, or otherwise, moves across and through media might have something to contribute to our collective knowledge?[41]

Instead of following the example of MacCabe and his contributors, who either ignore or misconstrue recent developments in adaptation studies, by exposing their errors of fact and omission, it would be altogether more tonic to follow Johnson's invitation, provoked however inadvertently by MacCabe's collection, to consider whether adaptation studies is a discipline, what the responsibilities of its proponents would be if it were or were not, and what relation *True to the Spirit* would have to those expanding casebooks of adaptation studies either way.

Certainly adaptation studies today has many hallmarks of a discipline. For many years it has been the subject of annual academic conferences that have multiplied on both sides of the Atlantic over the past decade. It supplies the material for not one but three journals whose orientations are sufficiently distinct to promote lively dialogue. Although most scholars who write about adaptation do not work in a dedicated field of adaptation studies, they generally act as if there is such a field by repeatedly citing the same central theorists (George Bluestone, Dudley Andrew, Brian McFarlane, Robert Stam, Kamilla Elliott, Linda Hutcheon) and interrogating the same foundational questions (what is adaptation? what is adaptation studies? is it a discipline, a field of force, or a more general transdisciplinary impulse? if all texts

---

[40]   David T. Johnson: Editorial. Windows onto Disciplines. In: Literature/Film Quarterly 39/3 (2011), p. 162-64, here p. 162.

[41]   Johnson: Editorial, p. 162.

are intertexts, what are the legitimate boundaries of adaptation studies? what is the relation between Anglo-American comparative studies of adaptation and Continental theories of intermediality? what is the relation between adaptation and translation? and, for better or worse, what is the proper place of fidelity in the analysis and evaluation of adaptations?).

Attempting a few years ago to determine whether Hitchcock Studies was a disciplinary field, I sketched out four rules for the emergence of any new discipline:

1. The field is defined and developed by a series of productive debates. [...]
2. The field gains strength from its subject's receptiveness to reinterpretation and regeneralization. [...]
3. The most influential interventions in the field are those that present the subject in ways that provoke further debate rather than those that seek to close off debate. [...]
4. The more vigorous these debates are, the more firmly established the field becomes.[42]

According to these rules, adaptation studies would certainly seem to be a viable discipline.

Even so, the field lacks key features essential to academic disciplines. Outside of the Centre for Adaptations at De Montfort University, it does not have the departmental or program status necessary for academic disciplines that wish to be recognized as disciplines. Instead, it is a poor relation of both literary studies and film studies, neither of which has accepted the sporadic claims of adaptation studies to institutional independence. Although courses in adaptation are widely taught in European and American universities, they remain peripheral to the missions of the English and Cinema Studies departments in which they are typically lodged, and the field of adaptation studies has "seemed always hamstrung by its insider-outsider status and [been] tolerated rather than embraced by medium-specific disciplinary rivals."[43] The general line of *True to the Spirit* is clearly that adaptation studies is at best a wayward subspeciality that needs to be recalled to the central program of film studies. Given its continued marginalization by both the disciplines from which it has most often claimed descent, it might seem more accurate to call it an analytical impulse that cuts across disciplines rather than a discipline in its own right.

Is it possible for adaptation studies to constitute itself a discipline in the absence of such things as departmental status and dedicated grant opportunities with which academic disciplines are typically endowed? My work on Hitchcock studies[44] has

---

[42] Thomas Leitch: Hitchcock and Company. In: Sidney Gottlieb and Richard Allen (eds.): The Hitchcock Annual Anthology. Selected Essays from Volumes 10-15. London: Wallflower, 2009, p. 237-55, here p. 243.
[43] Murray: The Adaptation Industry, p. 186.
[44] Leitch: Hitchcock and Company, p. 249-52.

indicated at least three additional models of disciplinary authority that might be relevant.

These models can best be defined in contradistinction to an academic model in which disciplines rooted in the retrospective acknowledgment of canonical texts (the *Iliad,* Aristotle's *Poetics,* Edward W. Said's *Orientalism,* Eve Kosofsky Sedgwick's *Between Men*) are consecrated by institutional affiliations – departments, tenure-track lines, conferences, and journals – designed to preserve their central mission even as they encourage further exploration and debate. This model, which especially in the early stages of its development places a high priority on the centripetal energy that pulls disparate contributions together into a vital centre, depends on a critical mass of consensual wisdom that allows some contributions (e.g., Robin Wood's *Hitchcock's Films* and *Hitchcock's Films Revisited*) to become canonical at the price of leaving other equally interesting contributions (e.g., Peter Conrad's *The Hitchcock Murders*) on the margins. It is everywhere marked by evaluative discriminations. Because some universities, programs, journals, and grants are more prestigious than others, some academics will inevitably acquire greater authority than others who are equally industrious but less influential.

Although academic disciplines thrive on debate, they require certain foundational questions to be settled as a condition of dialogue within the discipline, and even recognition of who belongs within the discipline. For this reason, the word "discipline" is peculiarly appropriate to academic models of authority, for they acknowledge that healthy disciplines require certain very particular kinds of institutional and dialectical discipline if they are to flourish. One might well argue that MacCabe and his contributors considered their charge to bring greater discipline to the discipline of adaptation studies – if only their volume did not make it so clear that they had limited knowledge of that discipline, were not addressing its practitioners, and did not consider it a discipline.

In a theological model of authority like the Roman Catholic Church, authority is even more centralized and hierarchical than in the academy. The texts in which the discipline's foundational truths are enshrined are not merely canonical but sacred, debates about these texts are encouraged only to the extent that they do not challenge the central tenets of the faith, and radical challenges are read out of the discipline as heresies. This model places even more emphasis than the academic model on centripetal energy and views centrifugal initiatives with suspicion. Much as MacCabe and his contributors might seem to adopt this attitude toward contemporary adaptation studies, the authoritarian tone of this theological model seems remote from the current organization or conceptualization of adaptation studies.

A panoptic model preserves the theological model's authoritarian attitude in the absence of any specific figures or texts in which definitive authority is incarnated. Instead, contributors to panoptic disciplines internalize what Foucault has called "the power of the Norm,"[45] and so police their own, and each others' discourse in order to protect themselves and their discipline from error. It is tempting to ascribe this attitude to either the fidelity police or their critics. But the self-censorship this model stipulates seems exactly what is missing from contemporary adaptation scholars' view of the fidelity police and from MacCabe and Jameson's view of those scholars.

One final model, however, is more promising: a decentered network in which power flows not from a centralized authority, actual or hypothetical, but through the relations commentators on adaptation establish with each other through their dialogue. These relations may involve agreement, extension, qualification, correction, or warfare. In every case, however, authority depends on maintaining rather than severing communications with other commentators. The result is an ongoing conversation in which individual speakers and utterances gain, enlarge, retain, or lose authority by their ongoing connection to other utterances and speakers. Refusal to engage other utterances directly amounts to a failure of the network, with unfortunate consequences both for one's own contributions, which are read out of the network, and for the network as a whole, which loses any benefits that might arise from continuing engagement.

This network has obvious similarities to the academic tabulation of scholarly citations in determining a candidate's fitness for promotion and tenure. In a network model, however, the prizes to be won are not those that institutions award individuals but those that foster the development and vigour of the discursive network, and the number of citations of any given scholar, or the prestige of the articles in which that scholar is cited, is less important than the entire network's success in keeping the conversation vital and vigorous. The network model of disciplinary authority, to put it another way, attaches less importance than the academic, theological, or panoptic models to the centripetal force of canonical texts, obligatory citations, and obeisance to duly constituted authority. Instead, it attaches greater importance to the questions – some perhaps foundational and enduring, others ever-changing – that drive the conversation that keeps the network humming.

The very nature of adaptation studies, which emphasizes the relations among different texts above features specific to the texts themselves, would seem to give it obvious affinities to a network model of disciplinary authority – if not as a mutually exclusive alternative to the academic model, then as a supplement and corrective to it. The question is whether adaptation studies under this model would be a discipline in any recognizable sense or rather an interdisciplinary or transdisciplinary impulse, an anti-discipline. Can an anti-discipline that challenges the rules and boundaries of all the borders it crosses and interrogates – literary studies, cinema studies, theatre studies, translation studies, picture theory – constitute a discipline in any meaningful sense?

---

[45]   Michel Foucault: Discipline and Punish. The Birth of the Prison. Trans. Alan Sheridan. New York: Pantheon, 1978, p. 184.

This question might be less paradoxically reframed by asking how adaptation scholars' responsibilities change under a network model of adaptation studies, and indeed whether these scholars have any responsibilities at all. If they had no responsibilities, then their field could hardly claim to be a discipline. On reflection, however, it is clear that their responsibilities, if anything, have multiplied. As members of a decentered field, they are not required to master any given set of canonical texts. But they must read much more widely across all the fields their work subtends, if not as experts, then certainly as competent amateurs. The reluctance to do this kind of immersive reading outside one's own field, especially when adaptation studies has yet to establish itself as a full-fledged academic discipline, goes a long way toward accounting for the proliferation of novel-to-film case studies that require little reading because they are content to apply consensual theories, in the limiting case, to a single novel and a single film.

In addition to acquiring a working knowledge of literature, cinema, television, radio, opera, ballet, oral narrative, easel painting, book illustration, or whatever other media happen to claim their interest, adaptation scholars must observe due humility toward the disciplines on which they trespass, observing, for example, the very different conventions for discussing ekphrasis, graphic novels, and bumper stickers. Nor are they required simply to follow the rules of the varied disciplines in which they are guests, for their charge is to renew those disciplines by bringing to bear new perspectives on intertextual relations that would be unlikely to emerge from within the disciplines themselves. They must raise questions capable of either reinvigorating specific narrative and representational disciplines or transcending their boundaries.

The incessant demand to raise questions can seem puzzling or perverse to analysts who perceive themselves as outside the network. In her discussion of the utility and the limitations of contemporary adaptation theory, novelist Mary H. Snyder criticizes its obsessive focus on such questions. Summarizing my argument that a given film adaptation's precursor texts should not be limited to the texts explicitly identified in its credits, she notes that I draw on Mikhail Bakhtin,

> implying that Bakhtin's argument that "the real task of stylistic analysis consists in uncovering all the available orchestrating languages in the composition of the novel" (10) should be applied to adapted texts as well, or lit-to-film adaptations. However, what he doesn't offer is a way to do this, and we need to move beyond detection of the problem to solution of the problem. This is a common problem I have found in reading many of these scholars. They have detected the so-called problems but have offered little in the way of solutions, which makes the problems they've detected suspect. Are the problems they've uncovered really problems?[46]

---

[46]   Mary R. Snyder: Analyzing Literature-to-Film Adaptations. A Novelist's Exploration and Guide. New York: Continuum, 2011, p. 206. The passage Snyder is discussing is in Leitch: Twelve Fallacies, p. 165, which in turn cites M.M. Bakhtin: The Dialogic

Putting aside the question of whether any adaptation scholars have actually begun work on solving the problem of broadening the field of languages relevant to any given adaptation,[47] Snyder seems here to confuse the mission of investigators of a field (like experimental scientists) with that of practitioners in that field (like engineers). Although many citizens deny that global warming, overpopulation, and HIV are problems at all, no one to my knowledge has argued that the evidence that they are not really problems is that investigators have not solved them. Quite the contrary, the intractable nature of such problems is the condition most likely to constitute a field as a discipline along the lines of a network because it guarantees that commentators will share both unresolved questions to interrogate and a common set of concepts and analytical tools for discussing them.

The constant charge to raise and renew these questions, as every classroom teacher knows, is no easy task. Adaptation scholars are, or should be, ceaselessly driven by Ezra Pound's dictum: make it new. Their work, which may seem to allow escape from the rules of more established disciplines, actually requires a more stringent, almost a panoptic discipline of its own. Whether adaptation studies is conceived and organized within or between disciplines, it cannot establish itself without enforcing its own discipline.

If we define adaptation studies as a discipline on the model of an academic network that combines features of the first and fourth of these models, then there are several possibilities for situating *True to the Spirit* within that network. One position is that of Laurence Raw: We can read MacCabe and his contributors out of the discipline as amateurs and trespassers, echoing their own stance toward adaptation studies as an ill-informed upstart. Another would be to congratulate the field of adaptation studies on having developed so rapidly in the brief period since MacCabe taught his class that it has left his students and colleagues in the dust. Another would be to acknowledge that strong critics like MacCabe, Jameson, Gunning, and Mulvey can trump weak disciplines, perhaps even remaking them in their own image. Finally and most commonsensically, adaptation scholars could join Johnson in reviewing *True to the Spirit* critically but not dismissively, looking for the insights and provocations that might be most valuable and incorporating them into the network, even though MacCabe and his cohort seem unlikely to reciprocate. In so doing, they can seek to discipline *True to the Spirit* even as they accept the volume's intention of disciplining them.

In this context, it makes sense to propose a hypothetical narrative of the volume's gestation in order to indicate its relation to the field. MacCabe explains that "it was only as a film producer in the eighties that I became aware of the

---

Imagination. Four Essays. Trans. Caryl Emerson and Michael Holquist. Austin: University of Texas Press, 1981, p. 416.

[47]   See for example Thomas Leitch: The Texts Behind *The Killers*. In: R. Barton Palmer (ed.): Twentieth-Century American Fiction on Screen. Cambridge: Cambridge University Press, 2007, p. 26-44; and Kathleen Murray: *To Have and Have Not*. An Adaptive System. In: MacCabe et al. (eds.): True to the Spirit, p. 91-113.

importance of adaptation to the business of film."[48] This experience gave him the idea of teaching a graduate course in the subject, but this dream languished for nearly twenty years: "By then I had read and reread Bazin's texts [...]. There had also been a veritable explosion of academic work on adaptation. But almost none of that work was devoted to illuminating the particular form of adaptation that is so peculiar to the cinema."[49] It seems clear that Bazin became the lodestar first for MacCabe's course, then for his collection – eight of the thirteen contributors cite Bazin, all of them approvingly – and the theological model against which all other work in adaptation studies would be measured. It seems likely that the reading MacCabe assigned to his class may have included Andrew's 1981 essay on adaptation, Stam's "Beyond Fidelity: The Dialogics of Adaptation," an early draft of his Introduction to the 2005 collection *Literature and Film* that appeared in James Naremore's 2000 anthology, and perhaps my own 2003 essay "Twelve Fallacies in Contemporary Adaptation Theory." In general, however, most of MacCabe's students show little more interest in recent adaptation theory than their teacher. Even in Kathleen Murray's "*To Have and Have Not*: An Adaptive System," which develops the most original and penetrating theoretical model of adaptation in the volume, such citations, most of them evidently added to an earlier version of the essay, remain extraneous to the essay's richly rewarding argument. And apart from Jarrell D. Wright's "Shades of Horror: Fidelity and Genre in Stanley Kubrick's *The Shining*," most of the essays by MacCabe's students take no more interest than Laura Mulvey's "Max Ophuls's Auteurist Adaptations" in entering debates about fidelity. After searching for a common theme that would link the essays together, therefore, MacCabe seems to have squeezed them into a Procrustean bed that fits some of them better than others, and in the process announced a quarrel with adaptation studies into which most of his contributors had not chosen to enter.

It is no surprise that MacCabe's contributors were more interested in examining case studies of their own than in providing ammunition for his attack on adaptation studies, for the account of Neil Jordan's *The Butcher Boy* that occupies the greater part of his own Introduction, condensed from his 2007 monograph on the film, neither requires nor reinforces that attack either. Although the essay pretends to move from general principles to specific illustrations, it was evidently constructed backwards, with the generalizations designed retrospectively to introduce a reading of *The Butcher Boy* that had already stood very well on its own. And MacCabe's attack on what he takes to be the heretical orthodoxy of adaptation studies proceeds not by calling for liberation but by reasserting the older orthodoxy of Bazin, a canonical figure in contemporary film studies, and threatening to discipline anyone who departs from his rule.

Jameson's reading of Andrei Tarkovsky's film adaptation of *Solaris* does no more to support his own assertion that if "the two texts – novel and film – really are

---

[48]   MacCabe: Introduction, p. 6.
[49]   MacCabe: Introduction, p. 7.

of equal quality and merit," then "the film must be utterly different from, utterly unfaithful to, its original."[50] But that is no disgrace, both because no single reading could possibly provide compelling evidence for such a sweepingly categorical assertion, and because the highly suggestive insights about "the usefulness of interpretation as such"[51] that emerge in the course of Jameson's allegorical reading of Stanislaw Lem's novel and Tarkovsky's film, though they do not support the assertion either, are worth the price of admission.

The danger to which the volume most commendably calls attention is the parochialism of adaptation studies, even if its insularity does not involve the wholesale rejection of the virtues of fidelity MacCabe and Jameson claim it does. When Jameson criticizes adaptation studies' indiscriminate embrace of Difference, he may have been able to reach his insight, whether or not it is justified, only to the extent that he has remained in his own poststructuralist orbit and refused to enter the gravitational field of the discipline he is taking to task. The line he takes, and the question of whether his argument is strengthened or weakened by his position outside adaptation studies, invites adaptation scholars to consider more closely not only the disciplinary status of their field but the problematic relation between the inside and the outside of adaptation studies, cinema studies, literary studies, textual studies.

More generally, the limitations of *True to the Spirit*'s engagement with the discipline of adaptation studies confirms Jameson's Oedipal, albeit essentialized, theory of the inevitably conflictual relations between texts and disciplines and empires. The volume suggests an answer to one of its leading questions – what place does evaluation have in a textual universe conceived in Bazinian terms, a network in which the unity and essentiality of every work, author, genre, and presentational mode are under the constant threat of dissolution by the arrival of the other texts to which every text hopes to give birth? – that is more judicious than anything its contributors propose. For just as some texts are richer, more interesting, and more valuable than others, so are some textual, critical, theoretical, and methodological conflicts. If the challenge *True to the Spirit* mounts to adaptation studies is constantly undermined by its unwillingness to engage its predecessors in a field of which it is largely ignorant, it does not follow that the challenge is worthless, or that commentators both inside and outside the disciplinary network should not be working on better versions of it and better responses to it. This is a lesson for which adaptation studies, of all disciplines, should be grateful.

Thomas Leitch teaches English and directs the Film Studies programme at the University of Delaware.

---

[50]   Jameson: Afterword, p. 218.
[51]   Jameson: Afterword, p. 222.

Graham Allen

Adaptation, Intertextuality, Interpretation: Reading *A Clockwork Orange*

Adaptation Study and the Slippery Slope

Throughout its emergence as a discipline, adaptation study has struggled to clarify its relationship with intertextuality. Julia Sanders calls adaptation and appropriation sub-sections "of the over-arching practice of intertextuality."[1] However, the fact of the matter is that there are a host of different theories and practices associated with the concept of intertextuality, many of them incompatible with one another.[2] The overtly poststructuralist articulations of intertextuality can seem alarming to those wishing to establish some kind of methodological grounding for the study of adaptation. Christine Geraghty writes of a Bahktinian intertextuality in which "all texts depend on an interplay of cultural references and sources," an interplay which is limitless and thus unmanageable.[3] Similarly Thomas Leitch, in his essay for the inaugural issue of the journal *Adaptation*, has written about adaptation theory's liberation from two dead-ends: "the fidelity discourse universally attacked by theorists [...] [and] Bakhtinian intertextuality – with each text, avowed adaptation or not, afloat upon a sea of countless, earlier texts from which it could not help borrowing."[4] The obvious move would appear to be towards the more circumscribed versions of intertextual theory and practice found, for example, in the work of Gérard Genette, who has indeed proved a frequent reference point.

Adaptation as a phenomenon, however, involves its students and scholars in just as protean an array of forms and styles as does intertextuality. Linda Hutcheon opens her influential study of the subject with the assertion "[a]daptation has run amok."[5] This has led, in many cases, to an argument that adaptation study should focus on the processes of adaptation itself, rather than the attempt to fix an unfixable relation between text and source text, a relationship which inevitably falls back into versions of an outmoded evaluation of fidelity anyway. As Thomas Leitch puts it:

---

[1]   Julia Sanders: Adaptation and Appropriation. London: Routledge, 2006, p. 17.
[2]   See Graham Allen: Intertextuality. 2nd edn. London: Routledge, 2011.
[3]   Christine Geraghty: Foregrounding the Media. *Atonement* (2007) as an Adaptation. In: Adaptation 2/2 (2009), p. 91-209, here p. 94.
[4]   Thomas Leitch: Adaptation Studies at the Crossroads. In: Adaptation 1/1 (2008), p. 63-77, here p. 63. The point about the practical difficulties of utilizing poststructuralist versions of intertextuality was made in very similar fashion in Jonathan Culler: Presupposition and Intertextuality. In: J. Culler: The Pursuit of Signs. Semiotics, Literature, Deconstruction. London: Routledge and Kegan Paul, 1981, p. 100-18.
[5]   Linda Hutcheon: A Theory of Adaptation. London: Routledge, 2006, p. xi.

"Whenever students of adaptation gather, a call invariably arises for an alternative to a remarkably persistent model of adaptation studies: the one-to-one case study that takes a single novel or play or story as a privileged context for its film adaptation." Against this Leitch argues for "a different model based on a different context by defining adaptation as a genre with its own rules, procedures, and textual markers that are just as powerful as any single ostensible source text in determining the shape a given adaptation takes."[6] Instead of getting lost in what Roland Barthes called a "multi-dimensional space in which a variety of writings, none of them original, blend and clash,"[7] Leitch and others argue for a concentration on the critical enumeration and analysis of kinds of adaptative practice. In this essay Leitch comes up with four main markers of the genre of adaptation: custom; music; obsession with authors, books and words; explanatory intertitles. The attempts at categorization may well remind readers of the five codes by which Barthes follows the signifiers of Balzac's short story *Sarrasine* in *S/Z*.[8] But while Barthes offers his five codes as just one way of arbitrarily marking a text which can never be stabilized in terms of its meaning, the motivations for Leitch's generic markers seem to hover more ambiguously between a recognition of play, adaptation's on-going contribution to the rewriting of all narratives and all texts, and a desire for established norms and thus fixed types by which adaptation can differentiate itself from the general ocean of intertextual transposition.

This ambiguity within Leitch's work, which is itself metonymic of the same ambiguity within adaptation study generally, can best be seen by attending to a core chapter in his recent *Adaptation and Its Discontents*, "Between Adaptation and Allusion."[9] Leitch begins this chapter by summarizing various attempts to categorize and enumerate types of adaptation. Geoffrey Wagner presents three types (transposition, commentary, analogy), Dudley Andrew offers an alternative three types (borrowing, intersecting, transforming), Kamilla Elliot raises the stakes with six offerings, whilst Genette "defines five modes of possible relations between one text and another."[10] As these alternative lists of types and modes of adaptation multiply, we might agree with Deborah Cartmell, who, summarizing the same lists from Wagner and Andrew, concludes: "the more we study adaptations, the more it becomes apparent that the categories are limitless."[11] Leitch appears to agree and offers a rationale: "The problem with Genette's painstaking taxonomy, like that of

---

6   Thomas Leitch: Adaptation, the Genre. In: Adaptation 1/2 (2008), p. 106-20, here p. 106.
7   Roland Barthes: Image-Music-Text. Trans. Stephen Heath. London: Fontana, 1977, p. 146.
8   Roland Barthes: S/Z. An Essay. Trans. Richard Miller. New York: Hill and Wang, 1974.
9   Thomas Leitch: Adaptation and Its Discontents. From *Gone with the Wind* to *The Passion of the Christ*. Baltimore, MD: Johns Hopkins University Press, 2007, p. 93-126.
10   Leitch: Adaptation and Its Discontents, p. 94.
11   Deborah Cartmell: Introduction. In: Deborah Cartmell and Imelda Whelehan (eds.): Adaptations. From Text to Screen, Screen to Text. London: Routledge, 1999, p. 23-28, here p. 24.

other distinctions among modes and types of adaptation, is that it does not adequately demarcate the frontiers of adaptation, the places where it shades off into allusion."[12] The reason for this, he continues, is that "most categorical discussions of adaptation ignore these problems [of allusive rather than adaptive relations] entirely by privileging a small number of intertextual relations as exemplary of all adaptation and passing over the others in silence."[13]

As usual the major problems within the theory and practice of adaptation studies stem from a recalcitrant fidelity model of book to film or at least intertext to adaptative text.[14] What that model avoids are all the other modes of adaptation which take us closer to that dangerous amorphous ocean of intertextual relations. Referring back to Genette's distinction between "intertextual relations like quotation and allusion and hypertextual relations like adaptation," Leitch, perhaps displaying the ambiguity mentioned earlier, decides, in the light of the wider array of adaptive relations, to "propound a grammar of hypertextual relations as they shade off to the intertextual."[15] It would appear that the scholar of adaptation studies must rigorously police the border between the manageable hypertextual relations suitable for study and the lawless and limitless domain of threatening intertextuality. Or, on the contrary, is Leitch not in fact courageously leading those fearful students of the novel into film variety toward the awful precipice of infinite intertextual connection and reconnection? The latter is what the last sentence of this chapter would appear to suggest, Leitch concluding:

> There is no normative model for adaptation. Both adaptation and allusion are clearly intelligible only within a broader study of intertextuality that will not begin until students of adaptation abandon their fondness for huddling on the near end of the slippery slope between adaptation and allusion, where categorical distinctions still seem seductively plausible.[16]

This is a fascinating final position in an essay the bulk of which has elaborated precisely an expanded list of ten kinds of adaptive relationships, each one of them containing a number of sub-divisions. It is worth citing more of Leitch's paragraph in order to capture the fact that what he is presenting is a failed attempt at categorization, and, as I would read it, a fully self-conscious statement about adaptation study's paradoxical compulsion towards a mode of metacritical commentary it knows is ultimately unavailable:

> It seems clear that the categories I have proposed in this chapter for bridging the gap between adaptation and allusion, however useful they may be in

---

[12] Leitch: Adaptation and Its Discontents, p. 94.
[13] Leitch: Adaptation and Its Discontents, p. 95.
[14] An "adaptative text" is used here to mean a text that is an adaptation of a previous text.
[15] Leitch: Adaptation and Its Discontents, p. 95.
[16] Leitch: Adaptation and Its Discontents, p. 126.

distinguishing particular strategies, are unable to separate particular adaptations into categories because even apparently straightforward adaptations typically make use of many different intertextual strategies. The slippery slope between adaptation and allusion cannot be divided into discrete stages because it really is slippery. The moral to draw from this chapter's failed exercise in demarcation is that intertextuality takes myriad forms that resist reduction to even so comprehensive a grammar as Bakhtin's or Genette's.[17]

The rather large question remains, however, what is to be done? Is adaptation study doomed to invent ever more baroque and nuanced lists of categories, knowing that they can never adequately control and police the border between transpositional relations which are structured and in some way intentional and those which are simply part of the background noise of the intertextual? Leitch's work is always scrupulously provocative, and the ending he provides for what is perhaps the most important chapter in his book is certainly that, since it leaves us with a set of questions we have ourselves to articulate before we can begin to answer them. One clear question, in this author's ears at least, concerns adaptation study's tendency to strive towards a mode of metacommentary which is in many respects analogous to the forms of structuralist analysis concepts such as intertextuality were designed to disrupt and deconstruct. By getting a little closer to Leitch's ten kinds of adaptive relations, I want briefly to demonstrate how this tendency towards metacommentary, even in such a brilliant exponent as Leitch himself, produces certain blind spots. I will concentrate on one key blind spot in Leitch's work, which will tell us something about the inevitable instability and non-totalizing nature of metacommentary. This will then provide a platform to explore one practical example in the concluding part of this essay.

The Intertext is an Intertext

It is beyond the powers of this essay to investigate all ten of Leitch's categories in detail: celebrations; adjustment; neoclassical imitation; revision; colonization; deconstruction or (meta)commentary; analogy; parody and pastiche; secondary, tertiary, and quaternary imitation; allusion. Each one of them is involved in a series of sub-categories, the distinctions between categories and sub-categories becoming increasingly difficult to maintain. One thing becomes clear as these categories are presented and discussed, however: they are all concerned with how adaptative texts respond to what are still frequently called "original texts" or "sources" or "literary sources" or "progenitor texts" or "classic texts" or "models." As has already been seen, I wish to call these "intertexts." The point at hand is that in Leitch's wide-ranging survey of different kinds of adaptive relation the phenomenon being studied

---

[17]   Leitch: Adaptation and Its Discontents, p. 126.

(adaptation as a definable genre) occurs exclusively in the adaptative text or texts. The intertext (not necessarily in the singular) remains a source, an original, a stable ground from which modes of adaptative play, revision and transposition are created.

Leitch structures his summative chapter on adaptation and allusion by restricting his examples to adaptations of Shakespeare, Jane Austen and monster stories. Different approaches to adapting Shakespeare are analysed, but the fact that Shakespeare's plays were themselves almost exclusively adaptations is not at issue. Holinshed, Plutarch, and Geoffrey of Monmorth do not appear in the index of Leitch's book. The tradition of adapting Mary Shelley's *Frankenstein* is explored from various angles, but the fact that it was stitched together from various literary sources, including the Jacobin novels of her father, William Godwin, does not arise. When discussing Spike Jonze's *Adaptation* under the category of "deconstruction or (meta)commentary," Leitch writes that *"Adaptation* achieves its comic effect by showing that anything like a faithful adaptation of [Susan] Orlean's book, and by extension of any literary text, is a contradiction in terms."[18] He mentions Laurence Sterne's *Tristram Shandy*, along with texts by Diderot, Sartre, Robbe-Grillet, John Barth and André Gide in order to cite a tradition of texts which deconstruct the very idea of telling their own or anyone else's story. What is not included as part of that tradition of impossible narration, however, is the fact that each of these cited texts is in itself an intertext, which is to say that each one is a text the existence of which is dependent upon acts of adaptation, allusion, transposition and intertextual collage. *Tristram Shandy*, for example, derives so much of its meaning and comic effect from its relation to the philosophy of John Locke, in particular *An Essay Concerning Human Understanding* (1690), that there is little sense, as it demonstrates so thoroughly, in calling it a "source text."

When dealing with the category of the "analogue," Leitch's use of the film adaptations of Helen Fielding's *Bridget Jones's Diary* can show the intertextual nature of Fielding's novel. However Austen's novels, the intertext for Fielding's work, remain steadfastly "sources," rather than the intertextual combination of discourses and codes they "originally" were. Similarly when dealing with pastiche and with the film adaptation of Valerie Martin's novel *Mary Reilly*, the adaptative novel is viewed as intertextual, whilst Robert Louis Stevenson's *The Strange Case of Dr. Jekyll and Mr. Hyde* is not. The discussion, in other words, is not of the novel by Stevenson, but of its adaptation into film and novel. As far as Stevenson's novel is concerned, Leitch's approach is unremittingly metacritical, treating it as a signifying unit rather than a successful adaptation of the Gothic novel tradition. In these multi-intertext examples, it becomes even clearer that for adaptation study, as practiced by someone like Leitch, there has to be an anchor text (a "source" text) upon which all the adaptational activity is founded. The fearful prospect intertextual

---

[18]   Leitch: Adaptation and Its Discontents, p. 112. Jonze's film concerns the unsuccessful efforts of a character called Charlie Kaufman (also the name of the film's screenwriter) to adapt to screen Susan Orlean's non-fictional text *The Orchid Thief.*

theory offers is of the loss of all such anchoring points, a textual universe without origins and without originals.

Leitch's work, seminal as it undoubtedly is and will be, constantly demonstrates a blindness to the intertextual nature of what I wish to call "the intertext," that is a text (and there are usually an indefinite number) to which a later text refers in some signifying way. It would appear that the radical danger posited in the poststructuralist ("Bakhtinian") concept of intertextuality finds one of its key expressions in the idea of the "source text" as itself an "intertext." Leitch's approach, to concentrate on the processes of adaptation, is an obvious and a productive one. At the end of his opening chapter he writes: "I hope my focus is consistent: the status of adaptations as examples of rewriting that can inspire storytellers and analysts alike to their own productive and inevitable rewriting of everything they need not and cannot simply read. The text is dead; long live the text."[19] The statement is partly inspired by a Barthesian notion of the writerly as opposed to the readerly text. Leitch discusses that distinction directly in his opening chapter, championing the open, productive writerly text which promotes rereading and rewriting rather the traditional idea of a closed, final, definitive, irreversible reading of the consumable text. From this Barthesian distinction Leitch declares:

> For half a century and more adaptation study has drastically limited its horizons by its insistence on treating source texts as canonical authoritative discourse or readerly works rather than internally persuasive discourse or writerly texts, refusing in consequence to learn what one might have expected to be the primary lesson of film adaptation: that texts remain alive only to the extent that they can be rewritten and that to experience a text in all its power requires each reader to rewrite it. The whole process of film adaptation offers an obvious practical demonstration of the necessity of rewriting that many commentators have ignored because of their devotion to literature.[20]

One can agree wholeheartedly with the championing of the writerly and the unending process of rewriting here, while at the same time registering that even here the "source" texts that are being constantly rewritten are not viewed themselves as productions of the processes of rewriting they inspire. Those "texts remain alive" but only in some ghostly static state somehow immune from the very world of activity they help to produce.

Leitch's work is important, not only because it is one of the most self-critical and theoretically informed articulations of adaptation study we have, but also because within it can be seen the most conspicuous lacunae and aporias for that discipline. The desire to liberate adaptation studies from a former "devotion to literature," in which the literary text remained the arbiter of value and meaning, paradoxically means that the literary text remains untouched by the liberatory force of the writerly

---

[19]   Leitch: Adaptation and Its Discontents, p. 21.
[20]   Leitch: Adaptation and Its Discontents, p. 12-13.

championed by Leitch. His approach seems unable to allow the intertext (usually literary) into the purview of analysis, because to do so would disrupt the specified field of study (generic processes of adaptation) leaving no border between adaptative texts and "source" texts. Without that firm border, everything becomes a form of adaptation and adaptation itself slips back down into an amorphous unmanageable intertextuality. As Leitch writes, at the very end of his book, "the slippery slope way from adaptation studies to intertextual studies seems dangerous indeed."[21]

How are we to negotiate that slope? In his concluding paragraph Leitch reiterates that this negotiation has to be through a redirection of our attention "away from films that present themselves as based on a single identifiable literary source [...] and toward the process of adaptation." He then concludes:

> Instead of distinguishing sharply between original texts and intertexts, future students of adaptation will need to focus less on texts and more on textualizing (the processes by which some intertexts become sanctified as texts while others do not) and textuality (the institutional characteristics that mark some texts, but not others, as texts). The study of adaptation offers a matchless opportunity to treat every text, whether or not it is canonical, true, or even physically extant, as the work-in-progress of institutional practices of rewriting. Instead of viewing literature from afar and from below as a collection of canonized works, it offers a foundational invitation to scholars in textual studies to place at the center of their investigations the theory and practice in allegedly original texts, in their rereading through adaptation, in our own work, and the work of our students, of still further rereading and rewriting – of literacy.[22]

Much of this last statement, a kind of future vision for adaptation studies, is indisputable. What is also evident, given what his essay has concentrated on so far, however, is a desire to retain a meta-role for adaptation study, now on the level of canonization and institutionalization, on the level of an analysis of industry and academy, along with a persistent but unresolved problematic regarding the relation to "allegedly original texts," and hence to the discipline of literary studies from which adaptation studies has still, apparently, to extricate itself fully. As he states in his opening chapter: "until quite recently, adaptation study has stood apart from the main currents in film theory. The field traces its descent more directly from literary studies."[23] It is unclear what Leitch means, in the concluding paragraph cited above, by his assertion that the study of adaptation "offers a foundational invitation to scholars in textual studies to place at the center of their investigations the theory and practice in allegedly original texts." What I take from that enigmatic clause is the need to explore the consequences of a mode of analysis which liberates itself from

---

21 Leitch: Adaptation and Its Discontents, p. 302.
22 Leitch: Adaptation and Its Discontents, p. 302-03.
23 Leitch: Adaptation and Its Discontents, p. 2-3.

the novel to film traditional dyad not by simply moving to metalevels of summative commentary but by exploding that dyad in ways more akin to poststructuralist understandings of text and intertextuality. In particular, I take from that clause the need for adaptation studies to give up the notion of an original source for adaptation and to recognize the consequences such a liberation has for the analysis and the analyst.

I would suggest that one of the consequences of reviving our perception of the intertextual nature of the intertext is that the analyst him- or herself is plunged back into the realm of interpretation, a realm precisely "of still further rereading and rewriting – of literacy." This repositioning of the analyst, from metacommentor on generic kinds of adaptational practice to interpreter of a shifting, unstable intertext, redraws the relationship between analyst and adaptative text, both of them (analysis and adaptative text) now on an interpretive level with the "source text," which we can no longer see as anything more than an intertext, and which itself exists in an interpretive relation to other intertexts. This interpretive relationship is thus a triadic rather than a dyadic one, with each of its three points engaged in an act of rereading, rewriting and adaptation.[24] This is not to eschew rhetorically the kind of metatextual investigations in which many of those practicing adaptation study have recently engaged. Such perspectives are critical. But they cannot be the end of the story, because if they are then adaptation study will always struggle to develop an adequate and productive interpretive practice, even while it continues to call out for one. The kind of triadic interpretive practice I am alluding to here cannot establish itself as a stable method, since in its triadic nature it treats each encounter with adaptative text and intertext in its own terms. What it does do each time is to build an interpretation of the intertext which it then compares and contrasts with an interpretation of the adaptative text understood itself as an interpretation of the intertext. Analyst and adaptative text are both involved in interpreting the form of interpretation, adaptation and transposition which generated the intertext. Two interpretations face a third interpretive act and the question is how these interpretations can be made to speak to each other. The point, I stress, of such a triadic practice is not to finalize a reading but to improve and enhance understanding by allowing different interpretations of the same interpretive act (the intertext) to form a dialogue.[25] I want to use a classic example of adaptation as example, Stanley Kubrick's adaptation of Anthony Burgess's *A Clockwork Orange*.

---

[24]   To call the relation triadic is to embody the point, since in that concept I cannot help but adapt Harold Bloom's adaptation of Charles Sanders Pierce's notion of Thirdness. What I am adapting in particular is Bloom's move from a dyadic understanding of the relation between text and intertext to a triadic one, see Harold Bloom: Kabbalah and Criticism. New York: Continuum, 1975, p. 56-57. For an example of a dyadic reading of "adaptive text" and "source text" see Greg Jenkins: Stanley Kubrick and the Art of Adaptation. Three Novels, Three Films. Jefferson, NC: McFarland, 1997.

[25]   It will not escape readers, I am sure, that the notion of an interpretive triadic relationship has already been compromised by examples from Leitch, such as the *Dr. Jekyll and Mr.*

Burgess/Kubrick/Beethoven/Shelley

A good example of the kind of triadic approach I am outlining here comes in Peter J. Rabinowitz's "'A Bird of Like Rarest Spun Heavenmetal': Music in *A Clockwork Orange.*"[26] What makes possible Rabinowitz's provocative reading is the manner in which he treats Burgess's use of Beethoven, and the German musical tradition more generally, as part of a discernable intertextual network. Rabinowitz states: "*A Clockwork Orange* participates in [...] a [...] specific, critical tradition that probes the tie between the classical German tradition and masculine violence."[27] Reading Burgess's novel in this manner allows Rabinowitz to draw his interpretation of the novel to a pseudo-Nietzschean conclusion. In this reading Alex slowly learns the necessity of combining the violent Dionysian forces associated with German symphonic music with the more controlled Apollonian approach to music signified in his move, in the last chapter, to the tradition of German Lieder.[28] Making much of the imaginary music Burgess includes in his novel (Geoffrey Plautus, Friedrich Gitterfenster), Rabinowitz's reading of *A Clockwork Orange* allows him to establish an intertextually informed interpretation which he can then compare and contrast to Kubrick's own interpretation and adaptation of music in the film.

On this comparative basis Kubrick does not do very well. He famously follows the U.S. edition of the novel and leaves out the last chapter, thus leaving Alexander de Large "an unreconstructed Dionysiac poised for a return to a life of violence."[29] Worse than this, however, he fails, according to Rabinowitz, to understand Burgess's cultural argument about German symphonic music and its association with masculine violence. Kubrick uses Beethoven, Rossini, Rimsky-Korsakov and Elgar because they are, Rabinowitz argues, already culturally signified as "classical"

Hyde (novel) – *Mary Reilly (*novel) – *Mary Reilly* (film) example. These examples demonstrate that what I am calling a triadic relationship has more than three points of intertextual relation. I will also immediately go on to complicate the triadic relation in another way in the next section, when I use an alternative interpretation of Kubrick's adaptation of Burgess's novel, thus providing a "fourth" point of interpretation. It is rare, after all, for analyses of adaptive texts and intertexts to occur in an interpretive vacuum. Clearly the point in describing the interpretive scene as triadic is not to fix on a kind of triangulation between intertext, adaptative text and analysis but rather to emphasize the fact that each point in the adaptive-interpretive process (however many there are) is active, in the sense of being itself the product of acts of adaptation, transposition and interpretation and also being itself productive of further examples of adaptation, transposition and interpretation.

[26] Peter J. Rabinowitz: "A Bird of Like Rarest Spun Heavenmetal." Music in *A Clockwork Orange.* In: Stuart Y. McDougal (ed.): Stanley Kubrick's *A Clockwork Orange.* Cambridge: Cambridge University Press, 2003, p. 109-30.

[27] Rabinowitz: Music in *A Clockwork Orange*, p. 119-20.

[28] The Nietzschean focus is taken from Burgess's description of the last chapter of his novel, see Anthony Burgess: A Clockwork Orange. A Play with Music Based on His Novella of the Same Name. London: Hutchinson, 1987, p. x.

[29] Rabinowitz: Music in *A Clockwork Orange*, p. 121.

art. Juxtaposed with the popular music which Kubrick's Alex, unlike Burgess's, seems happy also to consume, and at times popularly "treated" in Walter (Wendy) Carlos's Moog-based adaptations, Kubrick's "classical music" is emptied of the national and thus political connotations it possesses in the novel. Rabinowitz writes:

> Beethoven, in Kubrick's film, stands in for 'good music' in the most general sense; he is not a central figure, as he appears to be for Burgess, in a *national* tradition that often defined itself in opposition to the music, say, from France or Rossini's Italy [...]. It is undeniable that the film's eclectic array of music blurs the lines separating the cultural-historical categories so important to Burgess [...]. [T]here is little doubt that Kubrick's extensive use of Rossini (a composer for whom the Germanophilic Alex would probably have only contempt) provides a substantively different mapping of musical terrain from the one we find in the original novel.[30]

Rabinowitz's ultimate critique of Kubrick then follows from this, in that while Burgess forces us to question our cultural assumptions about music (such as Beethoven's status), Kubrick's use of music to soften the violence and alienation of the film relies on the audience's pre-existent cultural assumptions regarding that music. Kubrick's film, in other words, is devoid of the argument about music and nationalism subtly implied within Burgess's sonata-like novel. As Rabinowitz wittily concludes:

> [W]e can understand why, in Burgess's own 1986 dramatic adaptation of the novel, Kubrick appears at the very end, performing "in exquisite counterpoint, 'Singin' in the Rain' on a trumpet" – only to be "kicked off the stage."[31]

The very characteristic of intertextuality that sometimes appears to alarm theorists of adaptation studies kicks in again here, inasmuch as this is not, nor ever could be, the end of the story. Rabinowitz, of course, builds up a whole reading of the adaptation of *A Clockwork Orange* (meant in all the senses of that phrase) by focusing in depth on one main intertextual thread (music). That other intertextual threads, within the novel and potentially within the film, would pull in other directions, even loosening the reading Rabinowitz has knitted together, is inevitable. This is, I would suggest, not a matter of despair. Intertextual density is, I would argue, an aesthetic feature of texts (of whatever media) which inevitably provides them with cultural value, in that this density means that we tend to return again and again to such texts for more interpretive acts. The texts we tend to canonize are usually the most elaborately, intertextually woven.

---

[30]   Rabinowitz: Music in *A Clockwork Orange*, p. 123.
[31]   Rabinowitz: Music in *A Clockwork Orange*, p. 127. See Anthony Burgess: A Clockwork Orange (1962). London: Penguin, 1996, p. 48.

Having briefly explored one intertextual reading of *A Clockwork Orange* concentrating on music, I would like to offer another such reading focused this time on literary intertexts. This reading will help us to answer and revise some of the conclusions in Rabinowitz's essay. The reading is an example of how intertextuality, from sometimes very minor textual details, can produce significant changes in our general understanding of texts. It is an intertext which once again appears lost on Kubrick, who changed the specificities of Alex's and his droog's masks into generic "horrorshow" uniform disguises:

> We put our maskies on – new jobs these were, real horrorshow, wonderfully done really; they were like faces of historical personalities (they gave you the names when you bought) and I had Disraeli, Pete had Elvis Presley, George had Henry VIII and poor Dim had a poet veck called Peebee Shelley[...].[32]

I am sure that each one of these "maskies" would deliver a fascinating set of connotative meanings if critically pursued. Disraeli seems a very provocative disguise for Alex. I will simply argue in what follows that the reference to P.B. Shelley is peculiarly complex and rewarding of investigation.

That Burgess meant us to make the intertextual connection with P.B. Shelley's poetry and prose is clear from the manner in which he sets it up: "So poor old Dim, masked like Peebee Shelley, had a good loud smeck at that, roaring like some animal."[33] Just in case we had not noticed the reference, Burgess repeats it two pages later near the end of what was to become the "Singing in the Rain" scene in Kubrick's film version: "Then after me it was right old Dim should have his turn, which he did in a beasty snorty howly sort of a way with his Peebee Shelley maskie taking no notice, while I held on to her."[34] The idea of Dim partaking in a gang rape wearing a mask of a poet so associated with Republican democratic politics and with an Enlightenment belief in the essentially rational and socially generous nature of human nature is grotesque in itself. That Burgess subtly emphasizes this grotesque irony by describing the "maskie" as "taking no notice" while Dim rapes the woman is in itself worth noting. Do Shelley and Enlightenment thinkers like him *take no notice* of the violence inherently embedded in the human creature, explaining it away in terms of social conditioning? Does Shelley here come to stand for an Enlightenment, liberal understanding of humanity which is radically challenged and undermined by the facts of teenage, institutional and ultimately international violence? Or is it that the very Enlightenment that a poet like Shelley represents and embodies conceals in its rational and perfectibilist façade a violence and irrationality it would encourage us to ignore? We are left with a question: is the Shelley intertext meant to provide a positive or negative, an optimistic or pessimistic reminder of the

---

[32]   Burgess: A Clockwork Orange, p. 9.
[33]   Burgess: A Clockwork Orange, p. 18.
[34]   Burgess: A Clockwork Orange, p. 20.

Enlightenment?[35] The answer would feed into the debates about nihilism and the social responsibility and influence of art works which the novel and then the film generated and in which they were so massively caught up.[36] One form of adaptation that I cannot analyse here is the "copy cat" film to street variety (in the form of real acts of violence and liberal critiques of the influence of certain forms of art) which has caused both texts so much controversy over the past fifty years.

This reading of the intertext begins by sticking closely to the actualities of its delivery, that is to say the droog's masks. We might note, for example, that it is not simply contingent that Dim wears a Shelley mask. For Shelley, as W.B. Yeats well knew, the figure of the mask is a figure for ideological misfiguration. In Shelley's unfinished last poem, masks (alternatively described as shadows and phantoms) hover around the humans caught up in the progress of the Chariot of Life. The figure of the mask here is precisely one in which human beings are doomed to wear false identities, ideologically skewed personas.[37]

In *Prometheus Unbound*, as the Spirit of the Earth describes the post-apocalyptic state of the human realm, we get a reverse image in which these distorting masks leave human faces, humanity returning to its authentic, pre-ideological state:

[...]. and soon
Those ugly human shapes and visages
Of which I spoke as having wrought me pain,
Passed floating through the air, and fading still
Into the winds that scattered them; and those
From whom they passed seemed mild and lovely forms
After some foul disguise had fallen; and all
Were somewhat changed [...].[38]

Burgess's Shelley references raise the question of this Enlightenment notion of an authentic humanity, "mild and lovely" before it is distorted by the corruptions of society which are transcended in *Prometheus Unbound* and yet seem to be inescapable in *The Triumph of Life*. The fact that Shelley could write such apparently opposed poems on this theme, one poem positive and one poem negative

---

[35]   We could notice, of course, that the intertextual referent itself, P.B. Shelley and, beyond him, the Romanticism he is most directly associated with, was in itself divided between what we can call Enlightenment and Counter-Enlightenment trends. This point might then appear to chime well with Rabinowitz's thesis.

[36]   For a summary see Janet Staiger: Cultural Productions of *A Clockwork Orange*. In: McDougal (ed.): Stanley Kubrick's *A Clockwork Orange*, p. 37-60. See also James Howard: Stanley Kubrick Companion. London: B.T. Batsford, 1999, p. 117-32.

[37]   See Donald H. Reiman and Sharon B. Powers (eds.): Shelley's Poetry and Prose. New York: W.W. Norton, 1977, p. 469-70.

[38]   The Poems of Shelley. Ed. by Kelvin Everest and Geoffrey Matthews. Vol. II: 1817-1819. London: Longman, 2000, p. 600-01.

about the prospects of a return to that authentic human form, does not for a moment disrupt his clear belief in it.

At the very end of the book, in the last chapter in which Alex finally begins to grow up and as a consequence grow bored of the old ultraviolence, the positive note this appears to be introducing into the novel seems greatly tempered, even destroyed, by Alex's vision of his son and his son's son engaging in an unstoppable repetition of his own antisocial story.[39] The manner in which this dark repetition of the same is expressed is worth dwelling upon:

> My son, my son. When I had a son I would explain all that to him when he was starry enough to like understand. But then I knew he would not understand or would not want to understand at all and would do all the vesches I had done, yes perhaps even killing some poor starry forella surrounded with mewing kots and koshkas, and I would not be able to really stop him. And nor would he be able to stop his own son, brother. And so it would itty on to like the end of the world, round and round and round, like some bolshy gigantic like chelloveck, like old Bog Himself (by courtesy of Korova Milk-bar) turning and turning and turning a vonny grahzny orange in his gigantic rookers.[40]

The image of God is undermined immediately by imagining it as an illusion created by the milk plus available at the Korova Milk-bar. It is also clear that we are in part left with an image of society in which the young and the adult, if we can use those apparently neutral terms, are in a perpetual conflict with each other. But there is also, of course, an image of historical determinism which undermines any more positive effect created by Alex's own personal maturation. Whether it is an act of God or what Shelley, after William Godwin, called Necessity, is neither here nor there. The question raised here is: what is the effect and the meaning of this perpetual repetition of the same violence and the same generational conflict? What image of history are we left with?

---

[39] Interestingly, when Burgess came to rewrite this ending in the musical version, he made changes which emphasize that Alex's story is one of maturation from violent teenager to mature adult. See Burgess: A Clockwork Orange. A Play with Music, p. 47. I see these changes as Burgess's attempt to eliminate the possibility of the reading I am making here of the original novel.

[40] Burgess: A Clockwork Orange, p. 140-41. In the musical version the image of "old Bog Himself" is significantly altered: "I am not young, not no longer, ah no. Alex like groweth up, ah yes. Tomorrow is all like sweet flowers and the turning vonny earth, like a juicy orange in the gigantic rookers of Bog." Burgess: A Clockwork Orange. A Play with Music, p. 48. The effect is to present an image of a deity controlling the whole of nature, now figured as the clockwork orange, rather than directly playing with human beings, originally figured as clockwork oranges, and is intended to support the story's theological allegory of human, individual and collective, maturation. Burgess wrote: "What I had tried to write was, as well as a novella, a sort of allegory of Christian free will" (p. vii). Burgess's revision naturalizes the clockwork orange, and in doing so naturalizes Alex's Dionysian violence.

The negative view of history I have read in Burgess's original ending serves to place us in a position in some ways equivalent to that of the young offender Alex, strapped to a chair, his eyelids clipped and "pulled up and up and up," being shown an apparently unending series of violent scenes and images from the archives of recent human history.[41] Just as Alex is presented with an unendurable series of "horrorshow film[s]" of human ultraviolence, so the reader, despite Burgess's intentions, ends the film having to contemplate the fact that, to utilize James Joyce's famous phrase, human history is a nightmare of ultraviolence from which it is not possible to imagine how we are ever to awaken.

It is just this vision of human history as a Hegelian slaughter-bench which provides the key torture of Shelley's hero-god Prometheus in the verse-drama of his and humanity's ultimate liberation. Refusing to inform Jupiter of the term of his reign, Prometheus is tortured by avenging Furies, and their method of torture is to display to Prometheus how hopeless in their resistance to tyranny and violence all human revolutions have proven to be. The scene is a torture scene disguised as a scene of teaching, which is precisely how we can describe Alex's Reclamation treatment. Despite the fact that the forces of irrational tyranny torture/educate Prometheus, and the forces of science and reason torture/educate Alex, the similarity in situation and in subject is so deep as to suggest that this indeed is the deeper intertextual connection and structural parallel hinted at in Burgess's apparently throwaway joke regarding Dim's mask.

Alex's education/torture is an upgrading of the visionary education/torture afflicted upon Prometheus tied to a rocky precipice in the Indian Caucasus. Kubrick's film comes to supply on a material level what Shelley can only provide on a mythological and poetically figurative level.[42] Prometheus's response, importantly, makes little distinction between the images he is shown and those who inflict them upon him. Torture and torturers are ultimately all part of the same devastating lesson about the unavoidability of violence. Prometheus states:

He whom some dreadful voice invokes is here,
Prometheus, the chained Titan. Horrible forms,
What and who are ye? Never yet there came
Phantasms so foul through monster-teeming Hell
From the all-miscreative brain of Jove;
Whilst I behold such execrable shapes
Methinks I grow like what I contemplate,
And laugh and stare in loathsome sympathy.[43]

[41] Burgess: A Clockwork Orange, p. 76
[42] In this context, Alexander Walker's discussion of the mythological quality of Alex's suffering in the Ludovico Treatment seems extremely pertinent. See Alexander Walker: Stanley Kubrick Directs. London: Abacus, 1973, p. 292-93.
[43] Poems of Shelley, vol. II, p. 504.

The penultimate line sums up Shelley's understanding of the nature of ideological conditioning and the possibilities philosophy and poetry have to resist and finally transcend it. What one looks at for long enough one eventually becomes. So that the greatest challenge and torture for a Prometheus who has long since given up on violent resistance and has embraced an ethics and a politics of love, is to "viddy" a sustained atrocity exhibition in which every attempt in the human sphere for enlightenment and social transformation ends in a return of violence, tyranny and power. The climax of this tortuous history lesson is famously summed up in the following way:

In each human heart terror survives
The ravin it has gorged: the loftiest fear
All that they would disdain to think were true:
Hypocrisy and custom make their minds
The fanes of many a worship, now outworn.
They dare not devise good for man's estate,
And yet they know not that they do not dare.
The good want power, but to weep barren tears.
The powerful goodness want: worse need for them.
The wise want love, and those who love want wisdom;
And all best things are thus confused to ill.
Many are strong and rich, and would be just,
But live among their suffering fellow men
As if none felt: they know not what they do.[44]

This is the nightmare vision of perpetual violence and misrule which for Shelley, if accepted, would spell the end of any faith in the Enlightenment. That history is a nightmare is indisputable. Shelley returns to the idea in *The Triumph of Life*, as the Poet figure contemplates, interestingly for us, the shade of Napoleon:

[...] I felt my cheek
Alter to see the great form pass away
Whose grasp had left the giant world so weak

That every pigmy kicked it as it lay.
And much I grieved to think how power and will
In opposition rule our mortal day,

And why God made irreconcilable
Good and the means of good; and for despair
I half disdained mine eye's desire to fill

---

[44]   Poems of Shelley, vol. II, p. 514-15

With the spent vision of the times that were
And scarce have ceased to be [...].[45]

It would be enough to make you want to look away. The lesson of human history, a slaughter-bench of war and tyranny, would turn any viewer into just another victim of Life, just another enslaved subject, unless that viewer could avert his or her eyes. In *Prometheus Unbound*, as first Prometheus and then, in Act II, Asia undergo their education/torture by history, the possibility emerges of looking not backwards towards the nightmares of the past but forwards towards the future, or in other words to what it is still possible for rational and imaginative human beings to contemplate becoming. The liberation of Prometheus and the Earth begins the moment Asia learns to stop asking Demogorgon questions about power and blame, mastery and slavery, cause and effect, and starts asking questions about the future:

Asia: "[...] Prometheus shall arise
Henceforth the Sun of this rejoicing world:
When shall the destined hour arrive?"
Demogorgon: "Behold!"[46]

As soon as Asia asks her question about when rather than why, as soon as she looks away from history for an answer and begins to look towards the future, the future arrives and history begins to be transcended. To awaken from history, Shelley makes clear in *Prometheus Unbound*, we must stop looking at it. At least we must stop looking at it for an answer and for any form of liberation and enlightenment. The lesson of human history in *Prometheus Unbound* is that we need to become something more than it.

Burgess's scenario in some respects seems the reverse. A prisoner still committed to the pleasures of violence is shown "[a] real show of horrors," including Nazi and Japanese World War Two atrocities. Alex could be said to be revising for the cinematic age Shelley's statement about contemplation when he states: "It's funny how the colours of the like real world only seem really real when you viddy them on the screen."[47] The purpose of the treatment is to cure Alex not to punish him. The intertextual connection might appear to deliver a sardonic parody on Shelley's Enlightenment epic, presenting mechanical inhuman cure (Alex turned into a clockwork orange) rather than heroic human resistance and final liberation. The fact remains, however, that a "real" vision (display, exhibition, "sinny") of history is abhorrent to both characters. The individual who is subjected to that vision needs to escape it.

Burgess's scenario in some respects seems the reverse. The problem for Alex, of course, is that his Reclamation Treatment is designed not to offer a release from the historical repetition of violence (it is meant to offer

---

45   Reiman and Powers: Shelley's Poetry and Prose, p. 461.
46   Poems of Shelley, vol. II, p. 565.
47   Burgess: A Clockwork Orange, p. 77.

society that) but a release from self. Alex, as the Prison Chaplain and later F. Alexander argue, has no choice. As Dr Brodsky states:

> Our subject is, you see, impelled towards the good by, paradoxically, being impelled towards evil. The intention to act violently is accompanied by strong feelings of physical distress. To counter these, the subject has to switch to a diametrically opposed attitude.[48]

Alex can no longer match his desires with his actions, and the nauseating effect upon his body and mind of the music he still loves is testament to the forced loss of his subjecthood, something which makes him suicidal:

> [B]ut what I'd forgotten was something I shouldn't have forgotten and now made me want to snuff it. It was that these doctor bratchnies had so fixed things that any music that was like for the emotions would make me sick just like viddying or wanting to do violence. It was because all those violence films had music with them.[49]

The novel is clearly designed to tap into an interminable public debate about free will versus social conditioning and public order that, after the events of the summer of 2011 in London, can be said to be alive and well. But what about Rabinowitz's argument and the distinctions he makes between Burgess and Kubrick?

In the torture by history scene in Act One of *Prometheus Unbound*, the Furies concentrate on showing two critical moments in human history in which revolutionary force was betrayed into further bouts of violence and despotism. The latter event is the French Revolution, which collapsed into the Terror; the first event is the revolutionary promise offered by Christ and its betrayal in and by the Christian church. Christ in this scenario, unwitting instigator of a despotic religion, is left "Wailing for the faith he kindled."[50] The ideals of liberty, equality and fraternity turn into the rule of Madame Guillotine. The meaning is clear, the imaginative desire and capacity (fire) Prometheus gifted to humanity has left human beings constantly trying to effect a liberation they can imagine but are doomed never to be able to achieve. Christ's message of love and the French Revolution are two central examples of this failure to unite "good and the means of good," a failure at the very centre of the Enlightenment project which Shelley presents to his mythical hero and heroine and to his readers and, of course, to himself as an ultimate challenge.

The scene in which Alex, back in his home bedroom, "slooshying" (listening) to Beethoven's Ninth as he masturbates to his own inner "sinny" of violent images, juxtaposes images of the four dancing camp Jesuses, Alex's pet snake Basil

---

[48] Burgess: A Clockwork Orange, p. 94.
[49] Burgess: A Clockwork Orange, p. 104.
[50] Poems of Shelley, vol. II, p. 511.

exploring a poster woman in a sexualized pose, and a window blind embossed with a portrait of Beethoven.[51] It is as if Alex were the embodiment of precisely the juxtaposition of civilization and barbarity that apparently controls human history in the tortuous vision presented to Prometheus. The last scene of the film, in which Alex's pornographic sexual encounter with the kind of "devotchka" he had previously been compelled to resist is juxtaposed with Victorian propriety, and in which he announces "I was cured alright," clearly references this earlier scene, a point which is enforced by the further use of Beethoven's Ninth. The use of the image of Beethoven in the earlier scene, accompanied by the four dancing Jesuses, need not be solely associated with German symphonic musical tradition and could as plausibly be associated with the French Revolution and the Napoleonic period. Kubrick's film *Napoleon*, if it had ever been made, would surely have included the music of Beethoven, so associated as he was with that most Romantic of all historical figures.[52]

For Burgess, as Rabinowitz suggests, Alex must leave his violent teenage years, filled and fuelled by the Dionysian spirit, and find a mature balance of reason and passion. In that theological allegory, Alex, until the last chapter, represents just one stage in each human being's spiritual development. For Kubrick, however, Alex represents the entire state of the human *qua human*, and does so in ways which could be termed secular, historical and evolutionary, and which link his adaptation back to his most famous and immediately prior film, *2001: A Space Odyssey*. The Shelley intertext we have been analysing comes back into focus here and connects with the Beethoven-Napoleon context of the French Revolution and its challenge to the Enlightenment ideals which spawned it.

In a central speech in the screenplay for *Napoleon*, Kubrick has his protagonist sum up the central mistake of the Enlightenment project:

Napoleon: The revolution failed because the foundation of its political philosophy was in error. Its central dogma was the transference of original sin from man to society. It had the rosy vision that by nature man is good, and that

---

[51]   See Tom Ingham: *A Clockwork Orange*. Kubrick's Practice Explained. Cambridge: Kaplan, 2002, p. 23-24 and Mario Falsetto: Stanley Kubrick. A Narrative and Stylistic Analysis. New expanded edn. Westport, CT: Praeger, 2001, p. 56

[52]   Kubrick had been forced, temporarily he thought, to put aside his plans to make his film *Napoleon* when Terry Southern's idea of adapting *A Clockwork Orange* was resurrected. See John Baxter: Stanley Kubrick. A Biography. London: HarperCollins, 1997, p. 240. The famous scene in which Beethoven crosses out the dedication of his Third Symphony to Napoleon upon hearing news of the proclamation of the Empire is, according to Alison Castle, one of the "key events that Kubrick found particularly compelling in his quest to flesh out the character of Napoleon." Alison Castle (ed.): Stanley Kubrick's "Napoleon." The Greatest Film Never Made. Cologne: Taschen, 2011, p. 16. As Castle notes: "Beethoven had been a great admirer of Napoleon, as were many German intellectuals and artists, including Goethe, who all supported the original liberal ideals of the French Revolution" (p. 17; see also p. 191).

he is only corrupted by an incorrectly organized society. Destroy the offending social institutions, tinker with the machine a bit, and you have Utopia – presto! – natural man back in all his goodness.

Laughter at the table.

Napoleon: It's a very attractive idea but it simply isn't true. They had the whole thing backwards. Society is corrupt because man is corrupt – because he is weak, selfish, hypocritical and greedy. And he is not made this way by society, he is born this way – you can see it even in the youngest children. It's no good trying to build a better society on false assumptions – authority's main job is to keep man from being at his worst and, thus, make life tolerable, for the greater number of people.

Monsieur Trillaud: Your Majesty, you certainly have a very pessimistic view of human nature.

Napoleon: My dear Monsieur Trillaud, I am not paid for finding it better.

The exchange might seem to confirm the frequent accusation of pessimism against Kubrick himself, and might even offer up a reading of *A Clockwork Orange* in which the Minister of the Interior rather than the Prison Chaplain is the spokesperson for the work's central message.[53] That Napoleon's words were paraphrased as Kubrick's own in an interview with Michael Ciment would seem to confirm that charge of pessimism.[54] However, Kubrick immediately goes on in the same interview to rule out the alternative reading we have just countenanced. For Kubrick, society inevitably finds itself "groping for the right balance" and relying on "a certain amount of luck."[55]

In a number of interviews, when questioned directly about the apparent attractiveness of Alex, Kubrick describes him as a manifestation of the unconscious.[56] As he puts it: "the unconscious has no conscience – and the perception of this makes some people very anxious and angry."[57] Answering similar questions from Philip Strick and Penelope Houston, Kubrick states: "you can regard Alex as a creature of the id. He is within us all."[58] The play between violence and

---

[53] Both Kubrick and Burgess make it clear that the Prison Chaplain's speeches concerning the necessity of free choice are the work's core ethical message. See Burgess: A Clockwork Orange: A Play with Music, p. vii. See also Gene D. Phillips (ed.): Stanley Kubrick Interviews. Jackson, MS: University Press of Mississippi, 2001, p. 122.

[54] Michael Ciment: Kubrick. The Definitive Edition. New York: Faber and Faber, 2001, p. 163.

[55] Ciment: Kubrick, p. 163.

[56] Phillips: Stanley Kubrick Interviews, p. 122-23.

[57] Phillips: Stanley Kubrick Interviews, p. 123.

[58] Phillips: Stanley Kubrick Interviews, p. 29.

enlightenment in key scenes in *2001* has been well documented and discussed. In Kubrick's interview with Joseph Gemlis, he makes it clear that the film is meant to portray a real possibility of future evolution for a species which at the present moment is still burdened with a violent nature that was, as the "Descent of Man" section of *2001* demonstrates, an evolutionary advantage once upon a time.[59] In this context, it becomes more understandable why Kubrick distinguishes between the level of *A Clockwork Orange* which functions as a social satire, and that deeper level he describes as "closer to a dream than anything else."[60] He goes on:

> In this daydream, if you like, one can explore ideas and situations which one is not able to do in reality. One could obviously not enjoy the activities of Richard III if one were actually involved with them, but we *do* enjoy Richard III – and so with Alex.[61]

Caught between the eyes of the evolved human "star child" of *2001* and the Dionysian violence of Alex's eyes at the start of *A Clockwork Orange*, Kubrick's audience is offered a dialectical prospect of transcendence through a psychological liberation of the normally repressed id.[62] By seeing ourselves in Alex, we begin the journey beyond him. By looking at the worst we are impelled to seek out the good that might still arrive. This dialectical vision seems far closer to the Shelleyan intertext we have located within Burgess's novel. The novel may possess the intertext but the film more radically reiterates its meaning, allusion slips into intertextuality.

Professor Graham Allen works in the School of English, University College Cork.

---

[59]   Phillips: Stanley Kubrick Interviews, p. 80-104.
[60]   Phillips: Stanley Kubrick Interviews, p. 110.
[61]   Phillips: Stanley Kubrick Interviews, 110.
[62]   See Thomas Allen Nelson: Kubrick. Inside a Film Artist's Maze. Bloomington, IN: Indiana University Press, 2000, p. 136-65.

Siobhán Donovan

Berg's Opera *Wozzeck* on Stage and Screen in Frankfurt: Multiple Adaptation and Intertextuality

As *Irish Times* music critic Michael Dervan observed in March 2012: "The death of opera has been not just predicted but declared again and again. And again and again the art form simply refuses to go away."[1] This is perhaps because, of all the art forms practised and enjoyed today, opera must surely hold the record for hybridity, interdisciplinarity, intermediality, and proclivity to adaptation. Of course, *imitatio* or *mimesis* – always also implying variation and creativity – has existed as long as art itself, spinning a web of citations and intertextual relations,[2] while intertexuality (both implicit and explicit) is now generally recognized as "perhaps the defining principle of any adaptation."[3] The new media and technologies have arguably made it easier than ever to adapt existing works and simultaneously effect an experience of them *as* reproduced art. The digital revolution, the conduit for reproduced art *par excellence*, is rekindling long-standing debates about intellectual property, ownership, originality, authority and purity – issues of critical importance to adaptation studies. At the same time, it is ensuring the survival of 'sources,' their afterlife, as it were, in remediated guises.[4]

"Survival" naturally implies the threat of extinction, and in the arts and cultural studies in particular one is used to grim warnings of "the death of x."[5] One means of promoting the survival and expansion of opera – an art form beset, despite its resilience, in Ireland particularly, by funding cuts and reproaches of elitism – is the popular live screening from the New York Metropolitan Opera, "Live in H[igh]

---

[1]   Michael Dervan: Opera's Refusal to Die on Stage. In: The Irish Times, 27.03.2012. http://www.irishtimes.com/newspaper/features/2012/0327/1224313941065.html (last accessed 23.05.2012).

[2]   Linda Hutcheon: A Theory of Adaptation. London: Routledge, 2006, p. 20.

[3]   Deborah Cartmell: Introduction. In: Deborah Cartmell and Imelda Whelehan (eds): Adaptations. From Text to Screen, Screen to Text. London: Routledge, 1999, p. 23-28, here p. 27.

[4]   See Walter Benjamin's essays "Die Aufgabe des Übersetzers" (1923) and "Das Kunstwerk im Zeitalter seiner technischen Reproduzierbarkeit" (1936).

[5]   The most obvious example, perhaps, is Barthes's famous "The Death of the Author" (1967). Also pertinent is the debate in the 1990s on "The death of the book." On this, see Simone Murray: 'Remix my Lit.' Towards an Open Access Literary Culture. In: Convergence. The International Journal of Research into New Media Technologies 16/1 (2010), p. 23-38, and Andrew Gallix: In Theory: The Death of Literature. In: The Guardian, 10.01.2012. http://www.guardian.co.uk/books/2012/jan/10/in-theory-death-of-literature (last accessed 23.05.2012).

D[efinition]," launched in December 2006.[6] Other lifelines include, of course, the proliferation of opera productions on DVD and the myriad of clips available via YouTube and on the websites of the larger opera houses. By bringing opera to different and younger audiences, these media unite and blend what are often termed 'high' and 'popular' art forms.[7] The resulting experiences of reproduced opera, whether viewed on the big screen in a public space or on a much smaller screen in the relative solitude of the domestic sphere, obviously differ unavoidably and fundamentally from the experience of live opera in the theatre.

One opera that, so far, has been conspicuous by its absence from the list of Met HD transmissions, despite its firm place in the operatic repertoire, is Alban Berg's *Wozzeck* (1925), the ground-breaking operatic adaptation of Büchner's dramatic fragment *Woyzeck* (genesis 1836/37, posthumous publication 1879, first performance 1913).[8] As a *Literaturoper* (i.e. an opera that, as faithfully *as possible* – and the possibilities here are the salient point – sets to music a pre-existing, self-contained and usually well-known literary work), Berg's expressionist masterpiece (of which he was both librettist and composer) is a particularly interesting case for adaptation studies, given the composer's reverence for his literary source, the pronounced intertextuality of that source (which itself is an adaptation of a documented true story, rich in literary allusions and stock literary topoi),[9] and the resulting palimpsestic nature of the libretto. And if we conceive of performance as an "inherently adaptive art,"[10] an especially intriguing instantiation in the context of film adaptation is the neo-expressionist, visually arresting, erotically charged and highly stylized production of *Wozzeck* from the Frankfurt Opera (premièred in 1993) under the baton of Sylvain Cambreling and the direction of Peter Mussbach, and recorded and adapted for television in 1996 using digital technology.[11] While

---

[6]   http://www.metoperafamily.org/metopera/broadcast/hd_pastseasons.aspx?id=8626#stoz
      (last accessed 23.05.2012).

[7]   See the evaluation of the Met's general manager, Peter Gelb, in The Guardian,
      08.12.2011. http://www.guardian.co.uk/music/2011/dec/08/opera-big-screen-peter-gelb
      (last accessed 26.05.2012).

[8]   Despite the forthcoming bicentenary of Büchner's death in 2013, *Wozzeck* does not
      feature in the Met's 2012-13 season:
      http://www.metoperafamily.org/metopera/liveinhd/liveinhd1213.aspx   (last   accessed
      23.05.2012).

[9]   For an overview of the sources, see Kenneth Segar: Georg Büchner's *Woyzeck*. An
      Interpretation. In: Nicholas John (ed.): *Wozzeck*. Alban Berg (= English National Opera
      Guide 42). London: John Calder and New York: Riverrun Press, 1990, p. 15-22. On
      stock topoi, see Gary Schmidgall: Literature as Opera. New York: Oxford University
      Press, 1977, p. 302 ("images of abyss, darkness, and vacuum").

[10] Julie Sanders: Adaptation and Appropriation. London: Routledge, 2006, p. 48. "[E]ach
      staging," Sanders continues, should be viewed as "a collaborative interpretation."

[11] Frankfurter Museumsorchester, choir and children's choir of the Frankfurter Oper,
      conductor Silvain Cambreling, stage design and direction Peter Mussbach, ZDF
      production (in association with RM Arts and Tevel Israel International Communication),

incontestably an interpretation that owes more to experimental and often-controversial *Regietheater* than *Werktreue* [faithfulness], its neo-expressionist concept and staging correspond to the period of the opera's composition and the original expressionist set-design (by Panos Aravantinos) of the explosive première.[12]

Writing detailed stage directions into the libretto, pronouncing in 1928 that one of the tasks of the composer is to take on the duties of an "ideal stage director,"[13] and providing extra notes in 1930 on the staging of his opera,[14] Berg seems to have subscribed to ideas of intellectual property and authorial ownership, putting himself in a somewhat proprietorial position vis-à-vis the text, despite the fact that he was himself an adapter. His requirement that the director have "precise knowledge of the Büchner drama"[15] is certainly in evidence in the emphatically intertextual Frankfurt production, which however, somewhat ironically, is both true to the original while simultaneously a pronounced adaptation inasmuch as it is obliged to "fill in" various "lacunae" in that unfinished literary source.[16]

The staging of Berg's *Wozzeck* thus presents opportunities and challenges aplenty. According to Douglas Jarman, the opera "makes particular and unusual demands on the production team, for few operas (and perhaps no other opera apart from Berg's own *Lulu*) offer less scope for 'creative' directorial additions."[17] While the "'creative' directorial additions" of the Frankfurt production may initially seem

---

1996 (produced by Rolf Herrmann, directed by Peter Mussbach), Arthaus Musik DVD Video, 2006.

[12] Ernst Hilmar: Von der Texteinrichtung bis zur Uraufführung der Oper *Wozzeck*. In: Attila Csampai and Dietmar Holland (eds.): Alban Berg. *Wozzeck*. Texte, Materialien, Kommentare. Reinbek bei Hamburg: Rowohlt, 1985, p. 105-47, here p. 145. This work also contains the libretto on p. 39-76, and subsequent references to it in this edition will be given in parentheses in the flowing text.

[13] The operatic adaptation of a dramatic source text, Berg wrote in his 1928 essay "Das Opernproblem," was an undertaking that demanded "vom Komponisten alle wesentlichen Aufgaben eines idealen Regisseurs." In: Neue Musik-Zeitung 49/9 (1928), p. 285-86. Reprint in Csampai and Holland (eds.): Alban Berg. *Wozzeck*, p. 153-56, here p. 154. A frequently-cited English translation of the second part of the essay was published in Modern Music 5/1 (November-December 1928) under the title "A Word about *Wozzeck*." Reprint in Douglas Jarman: Alban Berg. *Wozzeck*. Cambridge: Cambridge University Press, 1989, p. 152-53. The English version of this sentence is somewhat ambiguous: "The function of a composer is to solve the problems of an ideal stage director" (p. 152).

[14] Alban Berg: The Preparation and Staging of *Wozzeck* (original German: Praktische Anweisungen zur Einstudierung des *Wozzeck*, 1930); this 1968 English translation is reprinted in Appendix I of George Perle: The Operas of Alban Berg. Vol. I: *Wozzeck*. Berkeley: University of California Press, 1980, p. 203-06.

[15] Berg: The Preparation and Staging of *Wozzeck*, p. 205.

[16] Robert Stam: Introduction. In: Robert Stam and Alessandra Raengo (eds.): Literature and Film. A Guide to the Theory and Practice of Film Adaptation. Oxford: Blackwell, 2005, p. 1-52, here p. 10.

[17] Jarman: Alban Berg. *Wozzeck*, p. 89.

to be in conflict with Berg's own demands, they illustrate what Robert Stam, borrowing Bakhtinian terminology, has called "intertextual dialogism."[18] According to Stam, such intertextuality can help us "transcend the aporias of 'fidelity'" that have hitherto dominated or haunted adaptation studies.[19]

Having briefly sketched the symbiotic relationship between opera and film, this article will go on to adumbrate the aesthetic links between expressionism and opera, before turning to Berg's own adaptive process and Mussbach's production of *Wozzeck* for the Frankfurt Opera.

Opera and Screen

While opera and cinema may at first glance seem to be competitors, they have a long history of mutual influence, and, as Marcia Citron points out, share many "social and aesthetic characteristics."[20] Theatre, cinema and opera are communal and public performance rituals, and, Citron continues, many large motion pictures are, like opera, "grand affairs."[21] Long before cinema, opera (like spoken theatre) provided an outlet for social critique. And, with its heightened gestures, mannered acting style and love of excess and exaggeration, opera – especially nineteenth-century opera[22] – may be seen as a precursor to silent cinema, influencing both its soundtracks and its plots. But the process of influence was by no means one-way: The introduction of sound to film allowed the emergence of the "strange mixed form"[23] that was the screen opera or opera film, and also enabled live telecast broadcasts.[24] Dissatisfaction with the static camera used for live broadcast led to the production of ever more opera films (particularly in Europe) up to the mid-eighties, when television started to compete with cinema in this sphere,[25] and recorded productions became available commercially. Operas written exclusively for the medium of television – and often based on literary classics – were another means of bridging the perceived gap between 'high' and 'popular' culture. And advances in camera

---

[18]   Robert Stam: Beyond Fidelity. The Dialogics of Adaptation. In: James Naremore (ed.): Film Adaptation. New Brunswick, NJ: Rutgers University Press, 2000, p. 54-76, here p. 64. Simone Murray refers to the "shibboleth" of "fidelity critique" prior to the new wave of adaptation studies that emerged in the first decade of the twenty-first century. Simone Murray: The Adaptation Industry. The Cultural Economy of Contemporary Literary Adaptation. London: Routledge, 2011, p. 7.

[19]   Stam: Beyond Fidelity, p. 64.

[20]   Marcia Citron: Opera on Screen. New Haven, CT: Yale University Press, 2000, p. 42.

[21]   Citron: Opera on Screen, p. 60.

[22]   Citron: Opera on Screen, p. 24.

[23]   Hutcheon: A Theory of Adaptation, p. 49.

[24]   Live radio broadcasts existed much earlier: Humperdinck's *Hänsel und Gretel* broadcast from the New York Met on Christmas Day 1931 was the first.
       See: www.metoperafamily.org/metopera/about/ourstory.aspx (last accessed 26.05.2012).

[25]   Citron: Opera on Screen, p. 62.

technology facilitated a comeback of the relay or live opera broadcast on both the small and large screens.[26]

The different media involved make for completely different operatic experiences, each manipulating interpretations and viewers in its own way.[27] Cinema and, to a greater extent television, are faster-moving and more action-dependent, while the slow pace of opera and its many static moments arguably render it quite "unfilmic," by today's criteria at least.[28] The camera's potential for dynamism (especially close-ups and zooms) can strengthen the visual impact, thereby creating a more "intimate relationship with characters and singers,"[29] affording the music a more subsidiary role and bringing the narrative especially to the fore.[30]

Similarly, film has influenced opera (compositions and productions) in no small way,[31] and Berg and his contemporaries were writing in response to what was then a fast-growing new medium.[32] Not long before his death, Berg had high filmic hopes for *Wozzeck* (provided the actors and singers were hand-picked), claiming that "a film would be able to realize certain details to perfection by means of close-ups and long shots [...] – details that never emerged with the desired clarity in the theatre."[33] Perhaps inevitably (given its contemporaneity and inclination to stylization), the expressionist ethos impacted on the burgeoning film industry, and the cinematographic potential of Berg's literary source as well as of his operatic adaptation of it has not gone unnoticed.[34]

---

[26]   Jennifer Barnes: Television Opera. The Fall of Opera Commissioned for Television. Woodbridge, Suffolk: Boydell Press, 2003, p. vii.

[27]   Citron: Opera on Screen, p. 1.

[28]   Jeremy Tambling: Opera, Ideology and Film. Manchester: Manchester University Press, 1987, p. 6.

[29]   Citron: Opera on Screen, p. 7. Conversely, live opera with its "bodily realities" can create a greater sense of greater eroticism and immediacy. See Linda Hutcheon and Michael Hutcheon: Bodily Charm: Living Opera. Lincoln: University of Nebraska Press, 2000, p. xiii.

[30]   Film can "make the musical-dramatic text show itself as it cannot in the opera house." Tambling: Opera, Ideology and Film, p. 6. Of course, the (optional) screen subtitles within the visual frame further strengthen the narrative impact.

[31]   See Tambling: Opera, Ideology and Film, p. 68-90. Berg's other opera *Lulu* (1937), an adaptation of Wedekind's plays *Erdgeist* (1895) and *Die Büchse der Pandora* (1902), contains a silent film sequence in act two.

[32]   See Tambling: Opera, Ideology and Film, p. 68-86.

[33]   Reich's summary of a conversation with Berg in August 1935. Willi Reich: The Life and Work of Alban Berg. Trans. Cornelius Cardew. London: Thames and Hudson, 1965, p. 102.

[34]   For example Mark DeVoto: *Wozzeck* in Context. In: John: *Wozzeck*, p. 7-14, here p. 8; Citron: Opera on Screen, p. 23; Schmidgall: Literature as Opera, p. 312; Tambling: Opera, Ideology and Film, p. 84, where he instances Berg's music and its "mechanical precision [as] in a way analogous to film." Kerman says the disconnect between the vocal and instrumental music is reminiscent of a film soundtrack. See Joseph Kerman:

Opera and Expressionism

Expressionist art strives to express intense, extreme and often violent moods and emotions (both conscious and subconscious) subjectively, by means of exaggeration, black and white contrasts, distortions and – in literature – an exclamatory, abrupt style. It thereby rejects convention, rational thinking, logical motivation and any mimetic or naturalistic depiction of external reality.[35] As such, and as Schmidgall observes, expressionism has much in common with the aesthetic of opera: "The genre is inevitably possessed of what the Expressionists called a *Steigerungstendenz*, an inclination towards enhancement."[36] A rhetorical (in the sense of grandiloquent), non-mimetic art, opera seeks to arouse passions, appeal to the senses and emotions, and for this reason melodramatic[37] worlds offer particularly attractive subject matter.

Büchner's *Woyzeck*, with its wilful and contrasting characters, numerous short and disconnected scenes, staccato-style, declamatory language and extremes of emotion, certainly earns the epithet "proto-Expressionist,"[38] something that possibly accounts for the fact that its belated première took place in 1913 at the dawn of German expressionism. In addition to markedly expressionist elements, it also has many characteristically operatic moments, featuring the stock operatic themes of love, lust, infidelity, jealousy, murder, revenge, madness etc., a prayer scene, and crowd scenes with the possibilities they offer for operatic choruses.[39] And with its many songs for Marie and Andres – although just one for its eponymous protagonist in the second tavern scene – it seems clear that Büchner conceived of the work as a melodrama in the historical sense of the word: a spoken piece containing short pieces of music.

Arnold Schönberg and his pupils Alban Berg and Anton Webern, the three principal representatives of musical expressionism in German-speaking culture, sought to establish a new language and means of expression – in particular of the subconscious – by both playing with and renouncing established musical traditions and forms. They favoured dissonance, melodic distortion, a broad dynamic range, extremes of sound, angular leaps, greater rhythmic freedom and a declamatory style of singing that gave greater emphasis to the words. Expressionist compositions may sound arbitrary to ears attuned to the European classical tradition: the effect is intentionally unsettling, disturbing and jarring due to its systematic rejection of

---

Opera as Drama. New and revised edn. Berkeley, CA: University of California Press, 1988, p. 182.

[35] See Ulrich Weisstein: Expressionism as an International Literary Phenomenon. Paris: Didier and Budapest: Akadémiai Kiadó, 1973, p. 15-28.

[36] Schmidgall: Literature as Opera, p. 11, p. 385 n. 4; see also p. 316-17.

[37] "Melodramatic" in its secondary sense of exaggerated or sensational. See Hutcheon: A Theory of Adaptation, p. 15.

[38] Schmidgall: Literature as Opera, p. 297.

[39] Herbert Lindenberger: Opera. The Extravagant Art. Ithaca, NY: Cornell University Press, 1984, esp. p. 31-41.

traditional harmony and key systems in favour of atonality and complex and highly organized original structures. In this sense, the creative process of the three composers of the so-called Second Viennese School may be deemed adaptive, referring as it does, albeit *ex negativo*, to the established musical tradition.

Opera and Adaptation: Berg on Adaptation

Adapting a literary source for a libretto usually involves radical compression (especially of lengthy discursive passages), restructuring, simplification of the characters in order to allow space for musical characterization, and generally ensuring that the libretto is singable. Shifts in emphasis are thus *de rigueur* in a changed medium with different logistical requirements. Whereas earlier scholarship tended to focus more on the purely narratological and issues of fidelity, almost overlooking the fact that, as a paratext, an opera needs music to make it complete and bring it to life, current approaches in librettology have re-evaluated the libretto, emphasizing opera's unique dramaturgical principles and looking at issues of intermediality and intertextuality.[40] New musicology is more interested in opera as performance, furthering our understanding of the genre by exploring how productions challenge and unsettle us,[41] as well as looking at the complex relationship between the composition and the performance.

The explicitly palimpsestic genesis and nature of Berg's opera recalls Genette's fourth and all-important type of transtextual relations, hypertextuality: "the relation uniting a text B (which I shall call the hypertext) to an earlier text A (I shall, of course, call it the hypotext), upon which it is grafted in a manner that is not that of a commentary."[42] Berg's many sketches for *Wozzeck* (which were effectively grafted onto the literary source) constitute, according to Patricia Hall, "a cumulative creative record equivalent to Büchner's handwritten fragment," thus "present[ing] similar challenges for study."[43] This idea of equivalence is intriguing in the context of

---

[40] See Albert Gier: Das Libretto. Theorie und Geschichte einer musikoliterarischen Gattung. 2nd edn. Frankfurt: Insel, 2000; also Dieter Borchmeyer: Libretto. In: L. Finscher (ed.): Die Musik in Geschichte und Gegenwart. Allgemeine Enzyklopädie der Musik, begründet von Friedrich Blume. Vol. VIII. 2nd revised edn. Kassel: Bärenreiter, 1994-2008, p. 1116-23. Recent publications draw on adaptation theory and librettology, e.g. Forum for Modern Languages, 48/2 (2012), issue on "Opera and the Novel"; David Francis Urrows (ed.): Essays on Word/Music Adaptation and on Surveying the Field (= Word and Music Studies, vol. 9). Amsterdam: Rodopi, 2008.

[41] See David J. Levin: Unsettling Opera. Staging Mozart, Verdi, Wagner, and Zemlinsky. Chicago: University of Chicago Press, 2007, p. 1.

[42] Jean Genette: Palimpsests. Literature in the Second Degree. Trans. Channa Newman and Claude Doubinsky. Lincoln: University of Nebraska Press, 1997, p. 5.

[43] Patricia Hall: Berg's *Wozzeck* (= Studies in Musical Genesis, Structure, and Interpretation). New York: Oxford University Press, 2011, p. 3. Digital images of the

Berg's adaptive processes that involve extensions to or grafts onto a source text (although the similarity to which Hall draws our attention is, it should be noted, not between Berg's opera and the source, but between Berg's sketches relating to *Wozzeck*, which provide an incomplete record of the adaptive process, and Büchner's similarly fragmentary 'original'). Nevertheless, as we shall see, how equivalence or fidelity is pursued across two different media with two different sets of demands is what is at stake here.

Berg's acquaintance with Büchner's play was made at its Viennese première on 5 May 1915. Some years later he wrote about the deep and defining impression this performance left on him: "Ich habe den Wozzeck [...] aufgeführt gesehn und einen so ungeheuren Eindruck gehabt, daß ich sofort (auch nach einem 2ten Anhören) den Entschluß faßte, ihn in Musik zu setzen."[44] Using all the editions available to him, but especially the one prepared by Paul Landau in 1909 (which was effectively a re-ordering of Franzos's edition of 1879) and re-issued by Insel Verlag in 1913,[45] which he annotated in detail, he clearly viewed his writing of the libretto as an extensive rewriting or adaptation ("weitgehende Bearbeitung").[46] It was only in November 1919 that he learned to his dismay that the edition he believed to be accurate or original was actually severely flawed and contained many passages embellished by Franzos. In short, the version he had been working with amounted more to an adaptation than an edition, but Berg's composition was by this stage so advanced that he could only make small changes based on the Witkowski edition of 1920 (particularly in the first tavern scene, act two, scene four).[47] Military service during the First World War had interrupted his work on the composition, but, crucially, had also provided him with personal experiences and motifs that he wove

---

manuscripts referred to are available online at www.oup.com/us/bergswozzeck using the username and password provided in the volume.

[44] Letter of 19.08.1918 to Anton Webern, cited in Hilmar's essay in Csampai and Holland (eds.): Alban Berg. *Wozzeck*, p. 119. See also Paul Elbogen: Firsthand Reminiscence of a Historic Night. In: San Francisco Chronicle, 27.10.1981, p. 40. Cited in Jarman: Alban Berg. *Wozzeck*, p. 1.

[45] Georg Büchner: Woyzeck-Lenz. Zwei Fragmente. Ed. by Wilhelm Hausenstein. Leipzig: Insel, 1913. This was also most likely the version used for the Viennese performance Berg attended. On Berg's printed sources and the influence of the Viennese performance, see Peter Petersen: Alban Berg. *Wozzeck*. Eine semantische Analyse unter Einbeziehung der Skizzen und Dokumente aus dem Nachlaß Bergs. Munich: Text + Kritik, 1985, p. 12-40; also Hall (who identifies a tenth source from 1923): Berg's *Wozzeck*, p. 82.

[46] Letter to E. Hertzka, 29.4.1922, cited in Csampai and Holland (eds.): Alban Berg. *Wozzeck*, p. 117. For a comparison between the libretto and its source, see Jarman: Alban Berg. *Wozzeck*, p. 7-15. For a tabular overview of the scene selection, see Petersen: Alban Berg. *Wozzeck*, p. 52.

[47] On the extent of Franzos's interpretative changes, see Petersen: Alban Berg. *Wozzeck*, p. 41-53 (with a chart of the chronology of scenes in Franzos, Landau and Berg on p. 52). On Berg's use of Witkowski for act two, scene four, see Petersen: Alban Berg. *Wozzeck*, p. 34-38; also Perle: The Operas of Alban Berg: *Wozzeck*, p. 72-73.

into both libretto and score.[48] Above all, he identified closely with Büchner's protagonist: "Steckt doch auch ein Stück von mir in seiner [Wozzecks] Figur, seit ich ebenso abhängig von verhaßten Menschen, gebunden, kränklich, unfrei, resigniert, ja gedemütigt, diese Kriegsjahre verbringe."[49]

As Schmidgall notes, composers attracted to literary works as sources must feel some "equivalence of sensibilities or form."[50] In "A Word about *Wozzeck*" Berg expressed his reverence for Büchner's drama, stating his intentions towards the text, which he couched, interestingly, both in terms of duty and serving, as well as in terms of the developments and translations that the specificities of the musical idiom required:[51]

> I simply wanted to compose good music; to develop musically the contents of Georg Büchner's immortal drama; to translate his poetic language into music. Other than that, when I decided to write an opera, my only intention, as related to the technique of composition, was to give to the theatre what belongs to the theatre. The music was to be so formed that at each moment it would fulfil its duty of serving the action.[52]

Put like this, it is clear that Berg saw his opera as paying tribute to Büchner's text, a work he referred to as having "vast social implications [...] which by far transcend the personal destiny of Wozzeck."[53] His esteem for Büchner's message and language, content and form, led him to alter very little of the Büchner-Franzos text, thereby giving the work the stamp of a *Literaturoper*. Presumably because the pre-eminent role afforded to the text threatens to render the music subservient, the genre of the *Literaturoper*[54] has met with less acceptance in musicology than in reception

---

[48]   See Jarman: Alban Berg. *Wozzeck*, p. 66-68.

[49]   Letter from Berg to his wife, 07.08.1918, cited in Petersen: Alban Berg. *Wozzeck*, p. 54.

[50]   Schmidgall: Literature as Opera, p. 6.

[51]   On the issue of "intentionality in adaptations," see Hutcheon: A Theory of Adaptation, p. 105-11.

[52]   Cited in Jarman: Alban Berg. *Wozzeck*, p. 152-53, here p. 152. For the German original, see the essay "Das Opernproblem" cited in Csampai and Holland (eds.): Alban Berg. *Wozzeck*, p. 153-56, here p. 154.

[53]   Cited in Jarman: Alban Berg. *Wozzeck*, p. 153.

[54]   Joseph Kerman employs the less frequently used English term "sung play." Kerman: Opera as Drama, p. 140-57, and with reference to *Wozzeck*, p. 180-90. On Literaturoper in general, see Peter Petersen and Hans-Gerd Winter: Die Büchner-Opern im Überblick. Zugleich ein Diskussionsbeitrag zur Literaturoper. In: Petersen and Winter (eds.): Büchner-Opern. Georg Büchner in der Musik des 20. Jahrhunderts. Frankfurt a.M.: Lang, 1997, p. 7-31; also Sigrid Wiesmann (ed.): Für und Wider die Literaturoper. Zur Situation nach 1945. Laaber: Laaber Verlag, 1982, especially Carl Dahlhaus's essays "Zur Dramaturgie der Literaturoper," p. 147-63 (discussion of the genre as a contradiction in terms: the close alignment to the literary text weakening the argument for genre-specific dramaturgies); and "'Am Text entlang komponiert.' Bemerkungen zu einem Schlagwort," p. 185-95.

and adaptation studies. Dahlhaus contends that the score of a *Literaturoper* can amount to little more than a series of effects akin to a film soundtrack.[55] Structural modifications of the literary text are customary in such an opera,[56] and Berg's are particularly intriguing (especially given his general fidelity to the hypotext), and his reasons for them well documented.

Ironically, the way in which Berg imposed dramatic unity on his selection (and contraction) of scenes, regrouping them into three symmetrical acts of five scenes each, suggests the traditional dramatic form rejected by expressionist dramatists.[57] While the acts of *Wozzeck* correspond to the analytical structure of exposition, development or dénouement and catastrophe or epilogue, and are labelled accordingly,[58] this was, however, done for musical rather than dramaturgical reasons. The problem, as Berg saw it, was "more musical than literary, and had to be solved by the laws of musical structure rather than by the rules of dramaturgy."[59] The first act consists of five "character pieces" (each scene corresponding to an older musical form), the second is a symphony comprising five movements, and the third a series of musical "inventions" (exercises, usually for keyboard instruments).[60] Orchestral interludes link many of the scenes, and while a pause is signalled after each act, it is usual to perform the opera without a break, thus intensifying the sense of oppression and creating a musical claustrophobia. Given that the older musical forms adapted by Berg are traditional ones, thus triggering associations with earlier (instrumental) works, the resulting score is an intricate musical palimpsest, a veritable "network of esoteric allusions."[61] And yet, this structure would, according to Berg, only be evident to the musically initiated studying it in detail, but is not the main focus and should go unnoticed by the majority of listeners.[62]

---

55 Dahlhaus: 'Am Text entlang komponiert,' p. 186.
56 Thomas Koebner: Vom Arbeitsverhältnis zwischen Drama, Musik und Szene. In: Wiesmann: Für und Wider die Literaturoper, p. 65-81, here p. 65.
57 Reich claims that Berg felt in 1935 that the "formal arrangement" of the libretto "corresponded almost exactly to the technique of film." Reich: The Life and Work of Alban Berg, p. 101-02.
58 A chart showing the formal design was drawn up by one of Berg's pupils and sent to critics along with the 1923 vocal score. See Jarman: Alban Berg. *Wozzeck*, p. 41-42.
59 Berg: A Word about *Wozzeck*, p. 153.
60 Jarman: Alban Berg. *Wozzeck*, p. 42. See also Berg: A Lecture on *Wozzeck*, cited in Jarman: Alban Berg. *Wozzeck*, p. 154-70, here p. 154.
61 Hirsbrunner: Musical Form and Dramatic Expression in Alban Berg's *Wozzeck*. In: John: *Wozzeck*. Alban Berg, p. 25-36, here p. 26.
62 "No one in the audience […] pays any attention to the various fugues, inventions, suites, sonata movements, variations, and passacaglias about which so much has been written." Berg: A Word about *Wozzeck*, p. 153.

Mussbach's Stage and Screen Adaptation of *Wozzeck*

Mussbach's colourful production of Berg's *Wozzeck* recorded in 1996 "under studio conditions from the stage of the Frankfurter Oper"[63] is interesting for its dramaturgical concept and adaptation to the small-screen medium using digital engineering. A technical hybrid, the concept is equally heterogeneous, marrying a psychoanalytical interpretation[64] with in-depth knowledge of, and fidelity to, both Berg's libretto and its hypotext,[65] the servant of two masters, as it were. While Berg's "unconditional requirement" of 1930 that the director have detailed knowledge of the source is fulfilled by this production, his "demand for the greatest possible realism" (instancing details like the water in the drowning scene) most certainly is not in what is a symbolic, abstract, minimalist and neo-expressionist staging. The three scenes Berg singled out as granting "much greater leeway" to the "fantasy of the producer," and where "liberties may be taken," are scenes that particularly stand out in Mussbach's production for their imaginative staging and intertextual nature: These are the scene between Wozzeck and the Doktor in the latter's study (I/4), and the two tavern scenes. But even here Berg has suggestions to make about the kind of liberties to be taken, saying that "the seemingly harmless fun of the first (II/4) and the uncanny, almost daemonic exuberance of the second (III/3) should be well differentiated," and adding that the second tavern scene "may be given an immaterial, ghostly effect, for which it would suffice to have a mere suggestion of the place."[66] We will return to these scenes again in the discussion below.

"Der Mensch ist ein Abgrund, es schwindelt Einem, wenn man hinunterschaut ... mich schwindelt ..." (II/3, p. 63).[67] Wozzeck's words of despair, uttered at the close of the central scene of the opera in which Marie rejects his accusations of having committed the "Todsünde" (II/3, p. 62) of infidelity, seem to be the guiding principle behind Mussbach's concept. This is the only scene that is played out at the front edge of the stage before the dropped curtain, which – on this occasion only – is coloured purple and later contains an ominous stain in a lighter shade, symbolizing Marie's transgression and anticipating her later penitence.

---

[63]   As cited on the back cover of the DVD booklet. See note 11 above.
[64]   A reviewer in *Opernwelt* described it as a "fast psychoanalytische, doch niemals besserwisserische Studie." Manuel Brug: *Wozzeck* als Sendebote einer neuen Ära. Spielzeiteröffnungen mit Berg in Frankfurt und Nürnberg. In: Opernwelt (December 1993), p. 27-29, here p. 28.
[65]   Graham Allen observes that Genette's hypertextuality emphasizes intentional and "self-conscious relations." Allen: Intertextuality. London: Routledge, 2000, p. 108.
[66]   Berg: The Preparation and Staging of *Wozzeck*, p. 205-06.
[67]   The corresponding scene in the Landau-Franzos edition of *Woyzeck* is practically identical. The edition is reprinted as Appendix II in Perle: The Operas of Alban Berg: *Wozzeck*, p. 207-21, here p. 215.

In general, voids, chasms and dizziness are suggested by a staging that plays with space and movement within a box-like set, creating an intensely claustrophobic milieu that amplifies the claustrophobia present in the score. Blue neon lighting around the proscenium arch is visible at the opening and closing of the colourfully lit scenes that contrast with the surrounding black void in which the box stage appears almost suspended. This framed stage is reminiscent of the television set or computer screen, and provides the viewer with a window-like perspective onto Wozzeck's psyche. The individual sets subsequently present the action from his perspective, thus denoting his subjective response to reality rather than an objective production of it, and lending visual weight to Kerman's view that the opera "takes place not in any dream world, but in the real world seen through abnormal eyes," where the eyes are "Wozzeck's, and the abnormality is evidently paranoia."[68] The emphasis is on distortions, with cross-sections of yellow slopes (particularly for the outdoor scenes), slanting floor surfaces, sharp angles and sheer sides, moving partitions, podiums and props. The characters are both literally and metaphorically teetering on the edge of an abyss. In the screen rendition, this is further accentuated by the digital graphics that accompany the instrumental interludes between the individual scenes: here computer-generated images of large breeze-blocks rotate and free-fall in what is clearly meant to be the cosmos, gradually filling the screen. The last interlude, following the drowning scene, and resulting in what Kerman terms an "Aristotelian catharsis,"[69] shows one of these breeze-blocks getting smaller and then disappearing against a backdrop of splinters of light, illustrating the sense of resolution suggested by the music. The final scene in this production is even more "epilogue"-like and symbolic:[70] the changed perspective is achieved by breaking the dramatic illusion and seemingly shifting the action backstage, in front of several of the sets used during the production (some of them side-ways on). Groups of children, all of them sedentary and still, wearing white masks, vests and trousers, flank a main frame (containing Wozzeck and Marie's child and others) that is now no longer edged with neon lighting.

As the reviewer in *Opernwelt* noted, the final scene is redolent of an altarpiece in the style of a tryptich.[71] This is just one of several ways in which the production intensifies the religious symbolism grafted onto the Büchner source by Franzos (who attributed prayers and remorse to Woyzeck),[72] and retained by Berg. Equally, the fatalism dominating both play and libretto, as evinced by leitmotivic references and colour symbolism, is rendered more pronounced in Mussbach's production: the omnipotence of fate within a mechanistic universe is suggested by stylized acting, mechanical movements, the animation of material things, and various symbolic representations of death.

---

[68] Kerman: Opera as Drama, p. 186.
[69] Kerman: Opera as Drama, p. 188.
[70] Kerman refers to it as an epilogue. Kerman: Opera as Drama, p. 181.
[71] Brug: *Wozzeck* als Sendebote einer neuen Ära, p. 28.
[72] Petersen: Alban Berg. *Wozzeck*, p. 44-45.

The visit to the Doktor's study in act one, scene four, clinically played out in a sloping white set with low walls cut off halfway, illustrates the overarching concept of this production: the individual as puppet and innocent victim (wearing only white boxer shorts rather than his dirty and loose-fitting white trousers and jacket) controlled by malevolent forces in both the microcosm and macrocosm. In this case, the Doktor is the ashen-faced, sinister puppeteer in black tails, his eyes hidden behind black sunglasses, controlling the object of his experiment from the corner of the scene with his cane.[73] His behaviour clearly references those scenes omitted from the libretto: the two fairground scenes with the performing animals (which were also cut from the Viennese première)[74] and the second scene with the Doktor where the performing Wozzeck has to catch the cat and then move his ears for the student audience.[75] Mussbach's hairy-chested Wozzeck crawls and moves around the scene just like the animals in the excised scenes. However, the rigid, stiff movements of the Doktor suggest that he is not the autonomous individual that he asserts man to be either: "In dem Menschen verklärt sich die Individualität zur Freiheit" (I/4, p. 51). He is also just a puppet at the mercy of fate.

The first tavern scene develops this theme further using puppets (which resemble effigies) to stage the beginning of the provocative dance between the Tambourmajor and Marie, which also serves to demonstrate the purely physical nature of their relationship. Controlled by mysterious figures in black, this takes place in front of a symbolic red curtain. The podium on which they dance is in a constant side-ways motion, as too are the bright pink artificial carnations (a deliberate reference to the second apprentice's drunk vision: "Die ganze Welt ist rosarot!" II/4, p. 64). This podium, home also to the costumed onstage band, is just one of many sets or props in constant motion, reminiscent of the image of the world rotating on its axis that so terrifies the Hauptmann (I/1, p. 44), and reflects the many other circular images, palindromes, and images of motion in both text and music.[76] Other moving parts are Wozzeck's bunk in the barracks scene (II/5): a glass coffin-like box that he shares with other soldiers (Andres sitting on top, in a position of power), which hangs on wires and rocks gently. No less ominously suspended on a wire are the player-less instruments in the military tattoo (I/3), and the beer bottles in the first tavern scene.

The "daemonic" and "ghostly"[77] atmosphere that Berg stipulated for the second tavern scene is expressed in the Frankfurt production by Wozzeck's precarious balancing on a ledge bridging the sloped sets of the murder and pond scenes, physically detached and emotionally alienated from the tavern below him (not dancing with Margret as indicated in the stage directions), his puppet-like position and contortions enacting a solitary and anticipatory *Totentanz*.

---

[73] In the libretto the cane is only specified for the later street scene between the Doktor and the Hauptmann in II/2.

[74] Petersen: Alban Berg. *Wozzeck*, p. 25.

[75] Landau-Franzos edition, cited in Perle: The Operas of Alban Berg: *Wozzeck*, p. 211-13.

[76] See Jarman: Alban Berg. *Wozzeck*, p. 60-66.

[77] Berg: The Preparation and Staging of *Wozzeck*, p. 206, 205.

As Petersen has pointed out, Berg's opera is more focused on the murder than Büchner's drama – by his own doing (the elimination of distracting scenes), but also as a direct result of Franzos's imbuing the protagonist with a greater self-awareness and sense of guilt.[78] In a production where the inevitable looms large, death is omnipresent.

The production opens with the close-up of a knife – a dagger rather than a shaving knife – ominously held upright by a hand (Wozzeck's) against the head and neck of the Hauptmann whom Wozzeck is shaving. The inevitability of death is thus evoked from the outset. In addition to its presence in subsequent scenes, the image of the vertical knife is recalled in the street scene where the Hauptmann and Doktor taunt Wozzeck about Marie's infidelity, calling him an "offenes Rasiermesser" (II/2, p. 59). Jutting out centre-stage in the white-box set used for the Doktor's study is an elongated, slanting, phallic structure that goes to a knife-point, and which is symbolically mounted by the three characters at different stages during the scene. The parting shot of Wozzeck shows him clutching on to the pyramid for dear life singing "Gott im Himmel! Man könnte Lust bekommen, sich aufzuhängen!" (II/2, p. 61). The omitted "Kloben" of the play[79] is arguably still there in the production, alluded to by the threatening edifice, which, taken together with Wozzeck's intercession to God, gives an expressionist slant to the crucifixion imagery.[80]

Other overt references to death in this staging include the skull in the first tavern scene, cradled by the fool who prophetically smells blood (another of Franzos's additions). The inclusion of Andres in this scene to function as minstrel and conductor is entirely Berg's, but Mussbach's decision to have Andres brandishing one of the large sticks from act one, scene two in the manner of a rifle (accompanying the chorus's song about hunting) gives him an even more active role as accuser and persecutor. A fiery and energetic red-head dressed in black with a tail, the Andres of this production is a much more complex operatic and psychological creation, combining devilish, bestial as well as clownish attributes. While mocking Wozzeck, he also demonstrates tenderness and sensitivity, unlike Büchner-Franzos's purely passive Andres.

Wozzeck's obsessive persecution of Marie for her affair with the Tambourmajor culminates in her brutal murder, which, in this production is more expressly presented as a love scene by means of softer yellow lighting. Wozzeck's drowning is portrayed by his rolling into the water (i.e. down the yellow slope) while embracing and pulling Marie with him – suggesting a 'Liebestod.'

---

[78]   The cries of "Mörder, Mörder" at the end of the murder scene and in the drowning scene are Franzos's additions. Landau-Franzos edition, cited in Perle: The Operas of Alban Berg: *Wozzeck*, p. 220. On the tighter focus and *Wozzeck*'s self-reflection, see Petersen: Alban Berg. *Wozzeck*, p. 42-46, p. 65.

[79]   "Gott im Himmel! Man könnt' Lust bekommen, einen Kloben hineinzuschlagen und sich dran aufzuhängen." Landau-Franzos edition, cited in Perle: The Operas of Alban Berg: *Wozzeck*, p. 214.

[80]   See Petersen: Alban Berg. *Wozzeck*, p. 45.

The product of their relationship is, of course, their child, whose role is enlarged by Berg and again by Mussbach. At the end of act two, scene one, the scene in which Wozzeck confronts Marie over the earrings, Marie's desperate cry in the hypotext: "Geht doch alles zum Teufel, Mann und Weib!"[81] is extended by Berg to include the child: "Mann und Weib und Kind!" (II/1, p. 57). Their son is frequently seen in the Mussbach production on his own either in close-up or long shot. Even in the final scene there is none of the interaction and movement requested by the stage directions. Hidden, like the other children, behind an oversized mask with a cut-out smile, he is arguably more a plaything for Marie, whose maternal role is secondary to her sexualized nature. Her caressing of the child can border on the erotic, while at other times he is left to his own devices or is comforting her. Clothed in white trousers like Wozzeck, he apparently performs the roles of lover and comforter that Marie aches for in Wozzeck.

The stark colour symbolism present in both hypotext and libretto is exaggerated and given expressionist contours in this production. The black/white contrast in certain sets and costumes is a case in point, as are the scenes containing explicit references to blood, murder and sexual behaviour which are often bathed in red light or involve red props, costumes, make-up or accessories (such as the gaudy red earrings given to Marie by the Tambourmajor). Those scenes that take place inside or in front of Marie's house usually feature the slope – upright or inverted – and contain the outline of a small red house that becomes larger as Marie becomes more aroused. At times of sexual abandonment (for example, the seduction scene, I/5), a close-up of the characters is set against a completely flooded red background.

The markedly (auto-)erotic undercurrent of the production is farcically depicted in the cross-dressing of the bloated, "aufgedunsen" Hauptmann (II/2, p. 58). Wearing an oversized red and pink pantomime costume, striped ballet-tights, high-heeled shoes, his lips painted red, he is a distorted projection of his own lewd fantasies, verbalized in the hypotext, but excised from the libretto.[82] The contrast to the macabre dissipation of the Doktor could hardly be more striking, and yet both are equally grotesque and freakish, sadistic and insane. A duo already in the libretto (emphasized by their reappearance just after Wozzeck's drowning, rather than the two anonymous passers-by of the hypotext), their double-act is heightened and even camped up in this production.

---

[81] Landau-Franzos edition, cited in Perle: The Operas of Alban Berg: *Wozzeck*, p. 213.

[82] Hauptmann: "Wenn ich am Fenster lieg', wenn's geregnet hat, und den weißen Strümpfen so nachseh', wie sie über die Gasse springen – verdammt! *Wozzeck*, da kommt mir die Liebe! Ich hab' auch Fleisch und Blut!" Landau-Franzos edition, cited in Perle: The Operas of Alban Berg: *Wozzeck*, p. 208.

Conclusion

It is perhaps the postmodern approach, the audacious mix of pantomime, playfulness, colour and camp in this eclectic production that caused the reviewer in *Opernwelt* to remark there had seldom been a *Wozzeck*-ambience that was "so farbig, so antiexpressionistisch, so untrist."[83] Overbrimming with intentional incongruities, extremes and distortions, and aiming to provoke, challenge and unsettle, the colourful production – and especially its screen rendition / recording – is expressionistic, nihilistic and *triste* to its very core.

Two scenes in particular stand out for their varied camera montage in a production that generally uses quite simple transitions between scenes: the first tavern scene (II/4) and the scene in which Marie reads from the Bible (III/1). With its onstage band and provocative dance between Marie and the Tambourmajor, the tavern scene is clearly self-reflexive, a performance within a performance. The fades effecting transitions – unique to this scene – suggest the passage of time, and effectively put the spectator in the uncomfortable role of voyeur. In the Bible scene where, according to the libretto, Marie is alone with her child (the fool is also absent from the Landau-Franzos edition), the production draws on video engineering to spotlight Marie's anguish and remorse. Her internal dialogue with God and asides to her son become a dialogue with her alter ego. The frame is a sea of darkness, containing Marie in miniature, suspended near the middle of the frame and often doubled, although not identically but rather shot from slightly different angles. Her son is spatially separated from her and captured in another miniature spot at the bottom right-hand corner, unable to console her or be consoled by her as indicated in the stage directions. The gilded Bible that she presses to her breast during her anguished prayer affords her some solace, but also recalls her embraces with the Tambourmajor, and so heightens her guilt and shame.

Visually arresting and cinematographically varied, with the unseen pit orchestra almost functioning as a soundtrack, the Frankfurt production as recorded for television certainly displays features of the opera film. The expressionist concept and psychoanalytical perspective in combination with close (inter)textual awareness demonstrate that *Regietheater* and *Werktreue* are not necessarily mutually exclusive. Relatively conventional readings of the two main characters go hand in hand with daring interpretations that expand on figures already redrawn by the libretto.

"Individual-Studie" was the headline of a review of the Frankfurt première.[84] Given the expressionist interpretation that presents events on stage as the projections of the insane anti-hero, one can readily imagine how the stage rendition seemed performatively to embody the study of an individual and his destiny. The technology involved in capturing and reproducing the live stage performance for the new medium of the small screen, although ostensibly only engaged in a simple process of

---

[83]   Brug: *Wozzeck* als Sendebote einer neuen Ära, p. 28.
[84]   Brug: *Wozzeck* als Sendebote einer neuen Ära, p. 27.

recording, necessitated interpretive decisions which themselves engendered shifts in emphasis and focus. Put simply, the viewer has much less control and is drawn much more into the action, the camera dictating where the emphasis lies. In this particular production, the range of shots employed, including close-ups of all the characters – not just Wozzeck – at salient moments, heighten the claustrophobic atmosphere while also delineating other more secondary characters more fully. The visual accompaniment to the interludes has the effect of intensifying Wozzeck's individual sense of alienation but also of giving this specific existential crisis a universal dimension. In this respect the production arguably successfully stages Berg's own belief that "the vast social implications of the work [...] by far transcend the personal destiny of Wozzeck."[85] The adaptive processes involved in performing Berg's opera on stage and small screen involve creatively alterations in the means by which fidelity and equivalence – hallmarks of a *Literaturoper* – are achieved.

Siobhán Donovan teaches German language and literature in the School of Languages and Literatures at University College Dublin.

---

[85]   Berg: A Word about *Wozzeck*, p. 153.

Stefanie Orphal

Die vergessene Gattung: Lyrikverfilmung als Impuls für die Adaptionsforschung

Einleitung

Wenn Thomas Leitch in seinem Aufsatz *Adaptation Studies at a Crossroads*[1] die Literaturbezogenheit der meisten Adaptionsstudien beklagt und eine Erweiterung der Forschung auf andere Fragen und auf intermediale Phänomene überhaupt einfordert, dann bezieht er sich in erster Linie auf den Roman und auf dramatische Texte, nicht aber auf die dritte traditionelle Gattung: die Lyrik. Damit schließt Leitch an eine lange Tradition der Kritik an, welche es ablehnt, das Kino an den Maßstäben der Literatur zu messen, dabei aber hauptsächlich die erzählende Literatur und das Drama im Blick hat. So nimmt etwa Germaine Dulac als Vertreterin des *cinéma pur* die Lyrik (*poésie*) explizit von dem Verdikt eines negativen Einflusses der Literatur auf den Film in seiner Entwicklung als eigenständige Kunst aus:

> Jusqu'à ce jour le cinématographe s'est contenté d'être anecdotique et narratif, se rattachant ainsi à la littérature. Il n'a été qu'une suite d'images animées captant le mouvement de la vie, il a pu s'élever jusqu'à la description d'états d'âmes, atteignant une forme psychologique ou poétique, mais sans se dégager jamais [...] de l'intrigue qui le confine dans le cercle du théâtre et du roman.[2]

Ist die „dead hand of literature",[3] die Leitch zufolge die Adaptionsforschung heimsucht, also vielleicht eher die tote Hand der Handlung, welche aus Roman oder Drama abstrahiert und zum einzigen Vergleichspunkt zwischen Literatur und Verfilmung gemacht wird? Offensichtlich ist Lyrik, ausgesprochen oder unausgesprochen, meist nicht mitgemeint, wenn von der Herrschaft der Literatur geschrieben wird. Nun ist die Verfilmung von Gedichten – in der Filmgeschichte und der Geschichte audiovisueller Medien im weiteren Sinne – tatsächlich eine Randerscheinung. Allerdings ist sie das nicht in dem Maße, dass es das geringe bisherige wissenschaftliche Interesse rechtfertigen würde. Anne Bohnenkamp, die in ihrer Einführung zu einem einschlägigen Sammelband das Verhältnis von Adaption und Gattung diskutiert, gehört zu den Wenigen, die die Frage konkret aufwerfen: „Und woran liegt es eigentlich, dass die dritte große literarische Gattung, die Lyrik,

---

[1] Thomas Leitch: Adaptation Studies at a Crossroads. In: Adaptation 1/1 (2008), S. 63-77.
[2] Germaine Dulac: Quelques réflexions sur le 'cinéma pur', [1926]. In: Dulac: Ecrits sur le cinéma. 1919–1937. Hg. Prosper Hillairet. Paris: Editions Paris expérimental, 1994, S. 73-74, hier S. 73.
[3] Leitch: Adaptation Studies at a Crossroads, S. 65.

in der Verfilmung seit jeher lediglich eine marginale Rolle spielt […]?"[4]

Der Filmkritiker Scott MacDonald widmet sich in einem längeren Aufsatz der Adaption lyrischer Texte und nennt drei Beispiele für Gedichtverfilmungen,[5] die er in unterschiedlicher Ausführlichkeit bespricht. Dabei entwickelt er eine neue Perspektive auf den Prozess der Adaption, die sich von den bestehenden Taxonomien der Adaptionsforschung[6] in einem wichtigen Punkt unterscheidet. Für MacDonald stellt sich die Praxis der audiovisuellen Realisierung von Gedichten als eine Form der Edition dar, die der schriftlichen Veröffentlichung weder unter- noch nachgeordnet sein muss:

> First, each makes available to an audience a previously published poem or set of poems in a new, cinematic form, and second, each makes the presentation of the poems, which are included in their entirety, the foreground of the film experience. That is, these films do not adapt the poems (revising them for use in a new context), they deliver the original words in their original senses, as pre-cisely as possible, to new audiences through a different medium. They are, in other words, closer to new editions than to adaptations.[7]

Auch wenn MacDonald nicht berücksichtigt, dass es einen ‚orignial sense' nicht geben kann, da Bedeutung durch *jede* Lektüre mitkonstituiert und daher verändert wird, ist seinen Bemerkungen doch insofern zuzustimmen, dass sich mit der ‚präzisen' und unveränderten Wiedergabe der Worte, die keiner Einbindung in ein Narrativ unterliegen, der Fokus der Adaption verschiebt. Trotz aller Emphase für das Original zeigen MacDonalds Ausführungen, dass dem Phänomen Gedichtverfilmung mit dem Maßstab der Werktreue nicht mehr beizukommen ist, da Treue im Sinne einer Nähe zum Text kein sinnvolles Bescheibungskriterium sein kann, wenn das Gedicht in seiner Gänze in den Film integriert wird. Vielmehr ist zu fragen, wie das Gedicht mit den hinzutretenden audiovisuellen Mitteln interagiert. Ich möchte anders als MacDonald allerdings dafür plädieren, den Begriff der Adaption für die audiovisuelle Umsetzung von Gedichten vorerst noch nicht aufzugeben, denn ich glaube, dass sich an diesem Phänomen Eigenschaften beobachten lassen, die zu einem erweiterten Blick auf Adaptionen beitragen und sich daher auch für die Untersuchung von Literaturverfilmungen im traditionellen Sinn als produktiv erweisen könnten.

---

[4] Anne Bohnenkamp: Literaturverfilmungen. Stuttgart: Reclam, 2005, hier S. 29.

[5] *Waterworx (A Clear Day and No Memories)* (Kanada, 1982, 6 min); *Nebel* (D, 2000, 12 min); *Trains of Winnipeg – 14 Film Poems* (Kanada, 2004, 88 min).

[6] Leitch: Adaptation Studies at a Crossroads, S. 64.

[7] Scott MacDonald: Poetry and Avant-Garde Film: Three Recent Contributions, In: Poetics Today 28/1 (2007), S. 1-41, hier S. 14-15.

Spezifika von Lyrikadaptionen

Die Beschäftigung mit der Adaption von Gedichten kann an verschiedenen Punkten ansetzen. Sie kann sich beispielsweise an den Ergebnissen der Adaptionsforschung zu ‚schwer verfilmbaren‘ oder als unverfilmbar deklarierten Texten orientieren,[8] nicht nur, weil Gedichte von diesem Diktum direkt betroffen sind,[9] sondern weil die Erforschung der Problematik medienspezifischer und besonders ‚sprachspezifischer‘ Phänomene in der Adaption zu einer Eigenschaft hinführt, die für Lyrik charakteristisch ist. Lyrik ist „Repräsentation von Sprache als generisches Display sprachlicher Medialität"[10] und macht sprachliche Sinnbildungsprozesse und sprachliche Materialität evident. Es gilt als Merkmal von Lyrik, dass sie eine Rezeption befördert, die nicht allein auf die Ebene des Inhalts bzw. der Information der sprachlichen Darstellung ausgerichtet ist, sondern die Aufmerksamkeit auf die Ebene der sprachlichen Zeichen selbst lenkt.[11] Daher bereiten Gedichtadaptionen Schwierigkeiten, wenn es um die Frage geht, was es denn eigentlich sei, was adaptiert wird. Den Theorien, die davon ausgehen, dass der Kern der Adaption eine Fabel ist, die in verschiedenen Zeichensystemen ausgedrückt werden kann, liegt ja die Überlegung zugrunde, dass sich Form (*expression*) und Inhalt (*idea*) grundsätzlich voneinander trennen lassen.[12] Während dies auf theoretische Überlegungen und produktionsästhetische Prozesse durchaus zutreffen mag, ist dieser Punkt für die lyrische Gattung komplizierter, da Lyrik ihre Wirkung gerade aus der engen Verknüpfung von Inhalt und Form, genauer gesagt Information und Faktur, zieht.[13] Eine Adaption kann auf unterschiedliche Weise auf die Herausforderung der sprachlichen Spezifik von Lyrik eingehen. Sie kann das Gedicht in die audiovisuelle Botschaft integrieren und ihm dabei in seiner sprachlichen Gestalt einen besonderen Platz einräumen. Sie kann audiovisuelle Analogien bzw. Äquivalente für poetische Verfahren suchen[14] und dabei dem

---

[8] Vgl. Irmela Schneider: Der verwandelte Text. Wege zu einer Theorie der Literaturverfilmung. Tübingen: Niemeyer, 1981, S. 158. Als Beispiele außerhalb der Lyrik ließen sich Texte wie Uwe Johnsons Roman-Zyklus *Jahrestage* nennen.

[9] Alfred Estermann: Die Verfilmung literarischer Werke. Bonn: Bouvier, 1965, S. 326.

[10] Rüdiger Zymner: Lyrik. Umriss und Begriff. Paderborn: mentis-Verlag, 2009, S. 96. (Eine neuere Definition, die an die poetische Funktion Roman Jakobsons erinnert, aber über sie hinausgeht).

[11] In semiotischer Begrifflichkeit lässt sich Literarizität als eine „spezifische Signifikantenpraxis" bestimmen, der eine bestimmte Rezeption adäquat ist, die sich eben vor allem auf die Ebene der Signifikanten konzentriert und in deren Verlauf es zu einem „Zusammenspiel von Signifikanten-Anordnung und signifikater Ebene" kommt. Bezeichnenderweise gilt die moderne Lyrik als Extrembeispiel dieser Rezeptionsweise (Schneider: Der verwandelte Text, 120-21).

[12] Linda Hutcheon: A Theory of Adaptation. New York: Routledge, 2006, S. 10.

[13] Zymner: Lyrik. Umriss und Begriff, S. 57.

[14] Zur Problematik des Äquivalents: Robert Stam: Introduction. In: Robert Stam und Alessandra Raengo (Hg.): Literature and Film. A Guide to the Theory and Practice of

Gedicht neue Dimensionen hinzufügen oder Verfahren der Entautomatisierung und Verfremdung auf die eigene Medialität übertragen und die eigenen ästhetischen Mittel einer solchen Lyrisierung unterwerfen.

Ein weiterer Anknüpfungspunkt ergibt sich aus der traditionellen Gegenüberstellung von literarischem Text und filmischem Bild, welche durch Lyrikadaptionen besonders effektvoll unterlaufen wird, eine traditionsreiche Dichotomie, die auch Kamilla Elliot im Zusammenhang mit dem illustrierten Roman kritisiert:

> Novels have been illustrated: nineteenth century novels in particular are brimful of pictorial initials, vignettes, full-page plates, frontispieces, and endpieces. Films abound in dialogue, intertitles, subtitles, voice-over narration, credits, and graphic words on sets and props. Yet scholars continue to designate the novel 'words' and the film 'images' and to define them according to Lessing's categorizations of poetry and painting.[15]

Hinzu kommt, dass lyrische Dichtung nicht gleichbedeutend ist mit (schriftlich niedergelegter) Literatur.[16] Gedichte sind keineswegs an eine Rezeption in der stillen Lektüre gebunden, sondern verwirklichen einige ihrer zentralen Eigenschaften erst im mündlichen Vortrag, in der Rezitation. Weit davon entfernt, reiner Text zu sein, der sich als abstrakt sprachliche Bedeutungsvermittlung dem sinnlich erfahrbaren Bild entgegengesetzt, zeichnet sich das Gedicht selbst bereits durch ikonische, klangliche und rhythmische Dimensionen aus, die im stimmlichen Vortrag zur Entfaltung kommen.[17] Mag diese Performance-Dimension in der Adaption von Lyrik auch in einer Beziehung der Spannung zur filmischen Medialität stehen, so muss doch festgestellt werden, dass von einer Dichotomie Buch/Film oder Text/Bild zu sprechen, wie es in der Adaptionsforschung lange üblich war, in diesem Zusammenhang keinen Sinn mehr hat. Zum einen besteht Dichtung nicht nur aus Sprache, sondern äußert sich als Schriftbild oder Klang und lässt sich sowohl visuell als auch akustisch rezipieren und zum anderen ist Film kein rein ‚visuelles Medium',[18] sondern ein komplexes, polyphones Gebilde aus Musik, Sprache,

---

Film Adaptation. Malden, MA: Blackwell, 2005, S. 1-52. Ich beziehe mich hier auf Irmela Schneiders Konzept von Analogien im Zeichengebrauch. (Schneider: Der verwandelte Text, S. 161)

[15]   Kamilla Elliott: Rethinking the Novel/Film Debate. Cambridge: Cambridge University Press, 2003, S. 12–13.

[16]   Reinhart Meyer-Kalkus: Stimme, Performanz und Sprechkunst. In: Thomas Anz (Hg.): Handbuch Literaturwissenschaft. [Gegenstände – Konzepte – Institutionen]. Stuttgart: Metzler, 2007, S. 213-23, hier S. 213.

[17]   Sybille Krämer: Sagen und Zeigen. Sechs Perspektiven, in denen das Diskursive und das Ikonische in der Sprache konvergieren. In: Zeitschrift für Germanistik 3 (2003), S. 509-19.

[18]   W.J.T. Mitchell: There Are No Visual Media. In: Oliver Grau (Hg.): MediaArtHistories. Cambridge, MA.: Leonardo, 2007, S. 395-406, hier S. 396.

Montagerhythmus *und* bewegten Bildern.[19]

Dichtung besitzt selbst eine performative, nicht texthafte Dimension, ebenso wie Film aus zahlreichen nicht-bildlichen Elementen besteht. Eine Lyrikadaption lässt sich also nicht als Übertragung eines Textes in ein visuelles Medium beschreiben, zumal, wenn das Gedicht in gesprochener oder geschriebener Form vollständig anwesend, les- oder hörbar bleibt. Letzteres trifft sogar auf den Großteil aller ausgewiesenen Lyrikverfilmungen zu, die ich daher, auch um sie von anderen Formen abzugrenzen, *Gedichtfilme* nennen möchte. Das Gedicht wechselt zwar in einen anderen medialen – das heißt technischen, ökonomischen, rechtlichen und kulturellen – Kontext, bleibt jedoch als sprach- oder sprechkünstlerisches Werk, als Dichtung erfahrbar. Daher passt hier die Metaphorik der Übersetzung nicht. Meine Überlegungen gehen in diesem Punkt über MacDonald hinaus, der an drei Filmbeispielen überzeugend nachweist, dass die Gedichte von den Filmemachern nicht als Rohmaterial sondern „as finished works, each with its own integrity" behandelt werden, und der ganz richtig hervorhebt, dass die *Präsentation* der Gedichte dabei in den Vordergrund rückt.[20] Sein Begriff der Lyrikadaption als Edition bleibt jedoch dem gedruckten Wort verpflichtet und ist zu sehr auf rein sprachliche Aspekte konzentriert. Die Gedichte werden in audiovisuellen Adaptionen eben nicht nur als Text veröffentlicht, sondern erfahren eine Aufführung, eine Performance. Das hat zur Folge, dass der Fokus der Untersuchung, indem er über die Wort-Bild-Differenz hinausgeht, auf die Performance und Realisierung des Gedichtes selbst ausgeweitet werden muss.

Text-Bild-Beziehungen

In den meisten Gedichtfilmen werden Wörter nicht durch Bilder ersetzt, sondern es findet eine Kombination von Wort und Bild in Gestalt von „Wort-Bild-Formen" statt,[21] in denen die Verse des Gedichts gesprochen oder geschrieben mit filmischen Bilder konfrontiert werden. Im Reden über Lyrikadaptionen ist die Angst vor den Bildern, welche die Literatur-Film-Debatte lange bestimmt hat, noch spürbar.[22] Besonders in journalistischen Kritiken von Lyrikadaptionen trifft man auf eine gewisse Empfindlichkeit gegenüber dem Bild, die sich häufig im Vorwurf der

---

[19]   Stam: Introduction, S. 21.

[20]   MacDonald: Poetry and Avant-Garde Film, S. 14.

[21]   Gottfried Willems: Theorie der Wort-Bild-Beziehungen. In: Wolfgang Harms (Hg.): Text und Bild, Bild und Text. Stuttgart: Metzler, 1990, S. 414-29, hier S. 415.

[22]   Stam: Introduction, S. 5. Jene Ikonophobie lässt sich bis zu den jüdischen, islamischen und protestantischen Bilderverboten zurückverfolgen, kommt aber auch in der platonischen und neoplatonischen Ablehnung der Bilder aufgrund ihres illusionären und abgeleiteten Charakters zum Tragen (Stam, S. 5).

Redundanz bzw. der Illustration oder Bebilderung äußert.[23] Wiederholt die visuelle Ebene lediglich Motive des Gedichts und beraubt es damit seiner poetischen Vieldeutigkeit? Oder ist die Macht der Bilder zu groß und erstickt den „assoziativen Zauber" des poetischen Textes? Traditionell wird der Lyrik eine erhöhte sprachliche Bildlichkeit zugeschrieben, die sich unter anderem in einer prononcierten Verwendung von Metaphern und anderen Tropen äußert.[24] Wenn es heißt, dass „mit sprachlichen Mitteln Bilder" erzeugt werden, so ist damit eine gesteigerte Anschaulichkeit gemeint, die entweder punktuell erreicht wird (durch Metapher, Metonymie und Synekdoche) oder den ganzen Text als Bild erscheinen lässt.[25] Angesichts einer so verstandenen Bildhaftigkeit lyrischer Texte herrscht Skepsis, ob Verfilmungen notwendigerweise eine semantische Reduktion erzeugen. Statt die Problematik, die sich aus der Begegnung (z.B. metaphorischer) sprachlicher Bilder mit tatsächlichen, also visuellen, medialen Bildern ergibt, tatsächlich aufzugreifen, wird generalisierend von einem „sinnlichen overkill" gesprochen, der die angemessene Rezeption des Textes beeinträchtige.[26] Die Frage, in welches Verhältnis sich Wort und Bild unter den besonderen Bedingungen der Lyrikverfilmung begeben, wird dabei meist nicht eingehend untersucht.

Eines der wichtigsten Bücher zum Thema Adaption, Linda Hutcheons *A Theory of Adaptation,* gibt zumindest erste Hinweise. Hutcheon erwähnt den ‚Transfer von poetischen Texten auf den Bildschirm' im Zusammenhang mit der Bewegung der Adaption aus dem Modus des *telling* zum Modus des *showing,* um zu zeigen, dass viele der dabei auftretenden Verluste nicht an eine technische Medienspezifik gebunden sind, sondern an die Konventionen des linearen, naturalistischen Films. Der Avantgardefilm dagegen verfüge über ein breites Spektrum an Gestaltungsmitteln, das besonders bei der Adaption von Gedichten ausgeschöpft werde: „the texts are read or sung and their story elements and even their metaphoric language are translated into evocative visual images".[27] Diese ‚Übersetzung' metaphorischer Sprache in konkrete visuelle Bildlichkeit verdient etwas näher betrachtet zu werden. Wie könnte eine Metapher als sprachliches Bild, das durch die „Verknüpfung von Bildspender und Bildempfänger"[28] gebildet wird, in ein reales,

---

[23] Evelyn Finger: Wo die Verse laufen lernen. In: Die Zeit 2002/29 (11.07.2002) und Norbert Kron: Poetry in Motion. In: Die Welt, 13.7.2002.

[24] Bei der Rede von der Lyrik als bildliche Gattung handelt es sich um eine Verkürzung. Rüdiger Zymner beschreibt die Metaphorik als *ein* Verfahren der lyriktypischen „stilistischen Konzision der Faktur" (Zymner: Lyrik. Umriss und Begriff, S. 85) bei gleichzeitiger Ausweitung des Assoziationsraumes auf Ebene der Information. Zum anderen kommt in allen Gattungen und auch in außerliterarischen Textsorten bildliche Rede zum Einsatz.

[25] Dieter Burdorf: Einführung in die Gedichtanalyse. 2., überarbeitete u. aktualisierte Aufl., [Nachdr.]. Stuttgart: Metzler, 2007, S. 143.

[26] Martin Jankowski: Filmlyrische Hybridkultur. Warum Poetry Clips nichts Besonderes sind. In: Neue Deutsche Literatur 2 (2003), hier S. 184.

[27] Hutcheon: A Theory of Adaptation, S. 44.

[28] Burdorf: Einführung in die Gedichtanalyse, S. 152.

filmisches Bild übertragen werden?

Um solche Fragestellungen genau untersuchen zu können, soll zunächst nach dem Modell von Gottfried Willems zwischen den verschiedenen Ebenen der Wort-Bild-Beziehungen unterschieden werden: der Wort-Bild-Form, dem Austausch von Stoffen und Formen sowie den inneren Wort-Bild-Beziehungen (bildliche Rede und redende Bilder).[29] Für die Analyse der Lyrikadaption als Wort-Bild-Form empfiehlt es sich, „die Frage in den Mittelpunkt zu rücken, auf welche Weise und mit welchen Ergebnissen Wort und Bild in ihr zusammenwirken, heißt mithin, nach der Integration von Wort und Bild zu fragen".[30] Dabei lässt sich wiederum zwischen drei Ebenen der Integration (der äußeren Faktur, des Inhalts und der inneren Faktur) unterscheiden, die allerdings eng miteinander zusammenhängen.[31] Auf der Ebene der äußeren Faktur ist die Anordnung von gesprochenen oder geschriebenen Gedichten im Rahmen des audiovisuellen Mediums zu beschreiben. Das Gedicht kann als Voice-Over oder *on screen* gesprochen werden, auf Zwischentiteln eingeblendet werden oder auf einer abgefilmten Handschrift erscheinen. Auf der zweiten Ebene ist zu fragen, ob und wie „Inhalte aus dem selben stofflichen Zusammenhang" gestaltet werden,[32] wobei sich ein Feld von Möglichkeiten zwischen den Polen Verdopplung und Ergänzung aufspannt. So könnte etwa in einer Adaption von Jandls Gedicht *der winter* die Zeile „das ganze land ist tief verschneit"[33] mit guten Gründen von Bildern einer verschneiten Ebene begleitet werden, die das Gesagte verdoppeln. Genauso aber könnten die Worte durch andere Motive ergänzt werden, die nicht im Text genannt sind. In einem solchen Fall der Aufteilung des Stoffes „fällt demgegenüber vor allem die äußere Faktur als Ebene der Integration ins Auge".[34] Auf der dritten Ebene lokalisiert Willems die innere Faktur: „Damit ist die Gestaltung des Bilds mit Rücksicht auf das benachbarte Wort und die des Worts mit Rücksicht auf das benachbarte Bild gemeint."[35]

Wird das Wort angesichts der Möglichkeit einer bildlichen Visualisierung von der Funktion der Anschaulichkeit entlastet? Von noch größerer Bedeutung ist im Falle der Lyrikadaption die von Willems nicht thematisierte Frage, wie die innere Bildlichkeit eines Gedichts mit dem realen Bild interagiert, etwa wenn eine sprachliche Metapher mit medialen Bildern kombiniert wird. In dieses Feld gehören auch die viel diskutierten filmischen Analogiebildungen oder Äquivalenzen zu sprachkünstlerischen Verfahren. Die visuelle Wiederholung einer sprachlichen Information ist zum Beispiel bei weitem nicht die einzige Möglichkeit, ein sprachliches Bild filmisch auszudrücken. Statt die sprachliche Information (den Bildspender) zu visualisieren, kann der Film beispielsweise selbst eine Metapher

---

[29] Willems: Theorie der Wort-Bild-Beziehungen, S. 414-15.
[30] Willems: Theorie der Wort-Bild-Beziehungen, S. 419.
[31] Willems: Theorie der Wort-Bild-Beziehungen, S. 419.
[32] Willems: Theorie der Wort-Bild-Beziehungen, S. 419.
[33] Ernst Jandl: der gelbe hund. gedichte. Darmstadt: Luchterhand, 1980, S. 14.
[34] Willems: Theorie der Wort-Bild-Beziehungen, S. 420.
[35] Willems: Theorie der Wort-Bild-Beziehungen, S. 420.

bilden, etwa indem er in einer Montage verschiedene visuelle Elemente vergleichend nebeneinander stellt und damit auf ein nicht sichtbares Drittes verweist.[36]

Wie die bisher zusammengetragenen Aspekte – audiovisuelle Präsentation des Gedichtes als Performance, Verhältnis von Information und Faktur, Zusammenspiel von Wort und Bild – für die Analyse von Lyrikadaptionen nutzbar gemacht werden können, soll im folgenden Abschnitt am Beispiel vom Matthias Müllers Film *Nebel* gezeigt werden.

Eine Adaption von Jandls *gedichten an die kindheit*

Matthias Müllers Film *Nebel*[37] gehört als audiovisuelles Werk, in dem Gedichte in mündlicher Form realisiert werden, zur oben erwähnten Gruppe der Gedichtfilme. Er beruht auf fünfzehn Gedichten aus Ernst Jandls Zyklus *gedichte an die kindheit*, welcher Anmerkungen des Dichters zufolge im Jahr 1977 entstand und damit in zeitlicher und inhaltlicher Nähe zu jenen Arbeiten steht, die sich der „heruntergekommenen Sprache", dem gebrochenen, unvollständig erlernten, fremden Deutsch, widmen:

> aus der thematik des zyklus und einer aufhellung der seelenverfassung des autors bot sich, zum vorerst einmaligen gebrauch, eine ‚verkindlichte sprache' an. sie enthält fehlerhaftes, widersprüchliches und banales, wird aber im gegensatz zur ‚heruntergekommenen' abart deutlich gesteuert durch eine der andauernden sprachschulung ausgesetzte intelligenz.[38]

Diese Intelligenz wird in den Operationen des Ordnens und Bezeichnens erkennbar, welche die einzelnen Gedichte sprachlich durchführen. In einem Verfahren des vergleichenden In-Beziehung-Setzens werden die Dinge der Welt an ihren Platz gestellt: „das dorf ist kleiner als die stadt, / aber nicht so klein wie das haus. / es besteht aus mehreren von ihnen" (S. 13). Das lyrische Subjekt ist allerdings nicht selbst ein Kind, sondern entpuppt sich als alternder Mann, der auf seine Kindheit zurückkommt. Dieses Zurückgehen in die Vergangenheit zeigt sich in einer fortschreitenden Verkindlichung des Sprachstils und der Themen, die sich von Gedicht zu Gedicht von zunächst abstrakten Gegenständen wie Einsamkeit, Vergänglichkeit und Dankbarkeit immer mehr der konkreten, kindlichen Vorstellungswelt annähern, die mit Weihnachtsmann und Christkind, dem Kanni-

---

[36]   Hanno Möbius: Montage und Collage. Literatur, bildende Künste, Film, Fotografie, Musik, Theater bis 1933. München: Fink, 2000, 375.

[37]   Nebel. Nach Ernst Jandls ‚Gedichte an die Kindheit', 35 mm, Deutschland 2000, 12 min, Regie: Matthias Müller.

[38]   Ernst Jandl: der gelbe hund. gedichte. Darmstadt: Luchterhand, 1980, S. 16. Die Seitenzahlen in Klammern beziehen sich im Weiteren auf diese Ausgabe, die auch den Gedichtzyklus *gedichte an die kindheit* enthält.

balen und dem lieben Gott beschäftigt ist.

Die Bewegung des Zurück, welche die *gedichte an die kindheit* durchzieht, bestimmt auch Matthias Müllers filmische Bearbeitung. Sie beginnt mit einem Rauschen und einem kratzenden Geräusch, das an das Zurückspulen von Tonband- oder Filmspulen erinnert. Noch bevor das erste Wort gesprochen worden ist, wird so die materielle Beschaffenheit des Films, sein Status als Aufzeichnung markiert. Mit der Entscheidung, vorgefundenes Filmmaterial (*found footage*) aus Archiven und dem Besitz des Regisseurs in den Film zu integrieren, wird die filmische Materialität für die ästhetische Wirkung des Films funktionalisiert.

Das Bild zeigt einen alten Mann, auf seinen Stock gestützt gehend, und kurz darauf Kinder, wobei die Bilder schadhaft und verrauscht wirken. Sie sind vom zeitlichen Verfall gezeichnet und als Erinnerungen an ein längst Vergangenes stets von der Auslöschung bedroht. Den gesamten Film hindurch erfolgt diese Betonung der Materialität des filmischen Mediums, das ausgebleicht, zerkratzt, löchrig wirkt. Die Einwirkung der Zeit lässt die aufgezeichneten Bilder bis zur Ununterscheidbarkeit verblassen – ein Vergessen, welches die Bewegungen einstmaligen Lebens zu immer schwächeren Schatten werden lässt.

Um die mediale Verfasstheit von Erinnerungen geht es auch Jandl. Die *gedichte an die kindheit* thematisieren das Gedächtnis in einer Metapher der Schriftlichkeit: „die spuren, die ich hinterlasse, / sind in mancher schrift / geschrieben und gedruckt" (S. 11). Als Spuren werden sie von der „luftbewegung der zeit" (S. 11) verwischt. Im Auslöschen der Schrift als Spur erscheint der Tod, der sich von Anfang an in den Gedichten ankündigt. Das Motiv erfährt seine Variation im Gedicht *winter*, in dem vom Schnee die Rede ist, der die Welt mit seiner Weiße überzieht. Das Weiße ist das Nichts, ist das, was nach dem Auswischen der Schrift auf den Seiten verbleibt, dieses Weiße ist es auch, was den Sprecher aus jedem gewöhnlichen Ding her blendet und als Nichts nun in allem ist: „das wird das ganze zimmer / in das ich eingesperrt bin / groß und weiß und / blendend wunderbar" (S. 13).

Die fünfzehn kurzen Gedichte (das längste umfasst achtundzwanzig Verse) werden von einer Stimme aus dem Off rezitiert, welche die Bilder begleitet. Der Sprechende selbst ist von der Welt, die in den Bildern gezeigt wird, getrennt. Er spricht aus einer zeitlichen oder räumlichen Distanz, während die Geräusche (Meeresrauschen, Dschungelgeschrei, Eisenbahn) zumindest in stilisierter Form auf die Bildräume Bezug nehmen. Auch wenn wiederkehrende Motive und rhythmische Makrostrukturen lose Verbindungen herstellen, lässt sich von einer zusammenhängenden kohärenten filmischen Diegese nicht sprechen. Vielmehr setzt sich der Film aus separaten, durch Schwarzblenden markierten Abschnitten zusammen, die der Reihenfolge der Gedichte folgen. Die lyrische Sprecherposition besteht nicht in einer organisierenden, kontrollierten, distanzierten Retrospektion, sondern nähert sich immer mehr einem kindlichen Zustand: „das möchte manchmal jeder, / zu werden noch ein kind. / ich möchte es immer mehr, / je älter ich werde" (S. 10-11). Diese Rückwärtsbewegung kann kein Erinnern im Sinne eines Wiedergewinnens des Vergangenen sein, denn der „nebel", den Müller zum Titel wählt, liegt dicht über den entfernten Dingen und der Versuch, das Leben vom Ende her zu betrachten, konfrontiert mit dem Vergessen. Der Autor der Gedichte dagegen bedient sich der bereits erwähnten „verkindlichten Sprache" (S. 16), mit eingestreuten einfachen Reimen, häufigen Wiederholungen und redundanten Satzstrukturen. Kindlich gibt sich auch das Verhältnis zur Sprache selbst, die in einer fast magischen Weise Worte und Dinge in Eins setzen will: „der nebel ist das leben, / wenn man es von hinten beginnt" (S. 10). In dieser umkehrbaren Umkehrung, welche durch das Palindrom in Gang gebracht wird, verdichtet sich die Bewegung des gesamten Zyklus, der von dem Bestreben durchdrungen ist, wieder Kind zu werden und das Leben vor sich zu haben.[39]

Gedicht 1, *der seelenhirte* (S. 10), wird vor dem klanglichen Hintergrund eines Meeresrauschens rezitiert, während ein Volleyballspiel am Strand zu sehen ist. Die Spieler sind nur schemenhaft im Gegenlicht zu erkennen, während das Steigen und Fallen des Balls einen gleichmäßigen Rhythmus vorgibt, der mit der durch ein Meeresrauschen evozierten Brandung korreliert. Mit dem Auf und Ab des Balles wird zugleich eine Pendelbewegung aufgenommen, die vom Gedicht als Hinein- und Zurückschnappen der Seele aus dem Körper der einzelnen Menschen beschrieben wird. Im Zusammenspiel von Text und Bild erscheint so der fallende Ball als rückkehrender, die ihn immer wieder auffangende und freigebende Gruppe von Spielern am unteren Bildrand gleicht dem „einzigen großen seelenleib" (S. 10), aus dem er aufsteigt und in den er wieder eingeht.

Die Art und Weise, wie Matthias Müllers Film das Motiv vom Ballspiel als Metapher einsetzt, erinnert an einen anderen Dichter dessen Name in Jandls Werk mehrfach genannt wird.[40] In Rilkes Gedicht *Der Ball* wird die Bewegung des Balls zwischen Werfen und Fangen, im Moment der Umkehr, zu einer umfassenden Metonymie stilisiert.[41] Wie das Steigen und Fallen der Fontäne dient Rilke der Moment,

---

[39] „das möchte manchmal jeder, / zu werden noch ein kind." (S. 11); „ich will zurück / bis in das alter von drei jahren" (S. 14); „lieber gott, / mach mich neu / daß ich mich wieder freu" (S. 15).

[40] Ein gewisser „rilke" tritt im Gedichtzyklus *der gewöhnliche rilke* auf, wo er in der Verrichtung von alltäglichen Handlungen beschrieben wird. Der Zyklus entstand 1975 und eröffnet den Gedichtband *die bearbeitung der mütze* von 1978, welcher dem *gelben hund* vorausgeht. Nähere Analysen des Rilke-Bezuges finden sich bei Helmut Neundlinger: Beruf: rilke, Zustand: labil. Innen- und Außenperspektiven einer Krise der Subjektivität. In: Bernhard Fetz und Hannes Schweiger (Hg.): Ernst Jandl. Musik, Rhythmus, radikale Dichtung. Wien: Zsolnay, 2005, S. 80-90; und Heinz F. Schafroth: Jandl live, oder: Wie schreit man? In: Wendelin Schmidt-Dengler (Hg.): Ernst Jandl, Materialienbuch. Darmstadt: Luchterhand, 1982, 364, 57-75.

[41] „ […] du zwischen Fall und Flug / noch Unentschlossener: der, wenn er steigt, / als hätte er ihn mit hinaufgehoben, / den Wurf entführt und freilässt –, und sich neigt / und einhält und den Spielenden von oben / auf einmal eine neue Stelle zeigt, / sie ordnend wie zu einer Tanzfigur […]." Rainer Maria Rilke: Der Ball. In: Rilke: Gedichte. 8. Auflage. Frankfurt a.M.: Insel, 1996, S. 585.

in dem der Ball sich wieder der Erde zuwendet, dazu, das epiphanische Erlebnis eines Umschlags oder Übergangs zur Anschauung zu bringen.[42] In der „reinen Bewegung",[43] welche in Ballwurf und Fontäne symbolisch zum Ausdruck gelangt, ist jedoch auch das Prinzip einer versöhnlichen Vergänglichkeit enthalten, welche einen Bogen zu Jandls *seelenhirten* schlägt: „Aber Verfall: ist er trauriger, als der Fontäne / Rückkehr zum Spiegel, den sie mit Schimmer bestäubt?"[44] Der Vergleich mit Rilke veranschaulicht, wie poetische und filmische Bilder ineinander greifen. Mit den Mitteln des Films kann die Metapher des Ballwurfs in den Film eingebracht werden, wobei die Bewegung nicht nur evoziert, sondern als Bewegung wahrnehmbar und erlebbar wird. Sie steht zu den gesprochenen Versen nicht in einem Bezug der Redundanz oder des Kontrastes, sondern bietet assoziative Anknüpfungspunkte, die im Zusammenspiel ein Drittes ergeben.

Das zweite Gedicht, *nebel*, wird von einer zunehmenden Unschärfe des Bildes begleitet, welche den im Text angesprochenen „schleier / über die nahen dinge" (S. 10) legt und sie verschwommen erscheinen lässt. Mit dem filmtechnischen Kniff einer abweichenden Fokussierung antwortet der Film auf die im Gedicht aufgeworfene Verunsicherung der Erkennbarkeit der Dinge. Die Metapher des Schleiers wird dabei also nicht einfach abgebildet, sondern mit filmischen Mitteln evoziert. Auch die folgenden Einstellungen, welche ein Observatorium oder einen Aussichtpunkt mit Fernrohren zeigen, nehmen die Problematik des Sehens und Beobachtens auf, wodurch die Filmrezeption eine selbst-reflexive Entautomatisierung erfährt.

Mit dem Einsetzen des dritten Gedichtes kehrt der Film zum Motiv des Ballspiels zurück. Auf den ersten Blick ist ein Kind im Spiel mit der Mutter zu sehen, doch erweist sich die Pendelbewegung des Balles bei genauerem Hinsehen als eine Bewegung, die allein durch den abwechselnden Vor- und Rücklauf der Filmbilder erzeugt wird, der auch auf der Tonebene deutlich zu hören ist.[45] Der steigende und fallende Ball in Müllers filmischer Umsetzung ist also ein filmisches Palindrom, in welchem das Element der Bewegung in ähnlicher Weise metaphorisiert wird wie es bei Jandl mit der Reihenfolge der Buchstaben geschieht. Auch im Gedicht erzeugt das Palindrom „Nebel", das sich rückwärts als „Leben" lesen lässt, durch eine rein formale Rückwärtsbewegung einen inhaltlichen Effekt. Damit gelingt Müller tatsächlich ein audiovisuelles Äquivalent zu Jandls rhetorischer Figur. Mit den letzten Zeilen des Gedichtes wird eine Veränderung eingeführt, die das Motiv des ewigen Ballspiels auf drastische Weise variiert. Ein weiteres Mal ist das Steigen und Fallen des Balls zu sehen, der sich vor einem blauen Himmel abhebt, dann landet er im Schlamm und rollt in eine Pfütze. Dieser abrupte Abbruch des Spiels markiert

---

[42] Vgl. Wolfgang G. Müller: Neue Gedichte / Der neuen Gedichte anderer Teil. In: Manfred Engel (Hg.): Rilke-Handbuch. Leben – Werk – Wirkung. Lizenzausg. Darmstadt, 2004, S. 296-317, S. 304.

[43] Müller: Neue Gedichte / Der neuen Gedichte anderer Teil, S. 307.

[44] Vgl. das Gedicht *Vergänglichkeit* (Rilke: Gedichte. 8. Auflage. Frankfurt a.M.: Insel, 1996, S. 945)

[45] MacDonald: Poetry and Avant-Garde Film, S. 26.

schmerzlich die unbesetzte Stelle der Mutter und enttäuscht zugleich die Hoffnung auf die Wiederkehr in den „seelenleib" (S. 10) im Sinne einer bergenden Transzendenz, welche sich zuvor im Ballspiel verbildlicht hatte. Der Aufprall des Balls auf dem schlammigen Boden trifft mit den Schlussversen des Gedichtes zusammen, in welchen durch eine leichte Verschiebung zwischen übertragener und buchstäblicher Bedeutung, zwischen „mutter erde" und „mutter in der erde" (S. 11), der Tod auf ein materielles Ende reduziert wird.

Am Ende des Films wird mit dem letzten Gedicht *die bitte* (S. 15) das Ballmotiv nochmals aufgenommen. Die Worte „lieber gott, / mach mich neu / daß ich mich wieder freu" (S. 15) wirken wie ein Kindergebet, doch ein betendes Kind ist nur für wenige Momente im Bild. Kurz darauf ist der alte Mann vom Beginn des Filmes zu sehen und erscheint als der wahrscheinlichere Sprecher der Bitte, in der es vor allem darum geht, dem Tod zu entgehen: „nur nicht zu alt / mach mich halt / bitte" (S. 15). In seiner letzten Einstellung erfüllt der Film diese Bitte, indem das rückwärts ablaufende Filmbild den Ball aus der Pfütze herausspringen lässt, deren Oberfläche sich glättet und den Blick auf die darin spiegelnden Wolken freigibt. *Nebel* entstand kurz nach Jandls Tod im Jahr 2000, und nachdem tatsächlich zunächst vorgesehen war, dass der Dichter selbst als begnadeter Performer seiner Werke die Gedichte einspricht, hat schließlich der Schauspieler und Hörspielsprecher Ernst-August Schepmann die Rezitation übernommen.[46] Anders als bei einem schriftlich präsentierten Text richtet sich die Aufmerksamkeit zunächst auf die Physiognomie der Stimme, welche bereits einen entscheidenden Anteil an der Sinnbildung des Filmes hat. Es handelt sich um eine recht tiefe Stimme mit einem warmen Timbre, das eine mittelstarke Rauheit aufweist und fast zu einem Knarren wird. Im Kontext der *gedichte an die kindheit* ist natürlich entscheidend, dass hier keine Kinderstimme zu hören ist, sondern dass sich im Sprechen durchaus der Eindruck einer etwas gealterten Stimme vermittelt, in die sich die Spuren des gelebten Lebens eingezeichnet haben, ohne dass es sich jedoch um die Stimme eines Greises handeln würde. Schepmann spricht die Gedichte bedächtig und in einem langsamen Grundtempo, das nur an wenigen Stellen akzentuierend leicht angehoben wird. Auch Tonhöhenverlauf und Lautstärke (Dynamik) bewegen sich auf einer begrenzten Skala und werden nicht durch auffällige Wechsel dramatisiert, so dass insgesamt der Eindruck einer gesetzten, ruhigen Sprechweise entsteht. Hier kommt nicht zuletzt der Umstand zum Tragen, dass unter den Bedingungen der Mikrophonaufzeichnungen viele traditionelle sprechkünstlerische Mittel obsolet geworden sind. Die technische Verstärkung der Stimme suggeriert eine Situation der Nähe und befördert damit eine intime Sprechweise, die jedoch nicht gleichbedeutend mit einem Verzicht an Pathosformeln ist.[47] So akzentuiert Schepmann vor allem durch eine sorgfältige Pausensetzung sowie Vokaldehnung und deutungsbezogene

---

[46] MacDonald: Poetry and Avant-Garde Film, S. 23.
[47] Reinhart Meyer-Kalkus: Stimme und Sprechkünste im 20. Jahrhundert. Berlin: Akademie-Verlag, 2001, S. 262.

Wortakzente. Sein Vortrag, der die Versgrenzen durch kurze Pausen markiert und damit die gesprochenen Worte als Gedichte ausweist, beweist generell ein Gespür für den Rhythmus des Textes. Die Zeilen „groß und weiß und / blendend wunderbar" (S. 14) werden durch Pausensetzung und Dehnung der Vokale rhythmisiert. Mit dem Beginn des Gedichtes *die dankbarkeit* (S. 12), das an sechster Stelle steht, und noch deutlicher in *der kannibale* (S. 13) ändert sich die globale Tonhöhe der Rezitation, mit anderen Worten: Schepmann intoniert deutlich höher und dehnt einzelne Silben stärker aus. Auch auf der Ebene der Rezitation äußert sich also, wie in der einfacher werdenden Sprache, die fortschreitende Verkindlichung, welche das lyrische Subjekt durchläuft.

Wie stark Rezitation, Gedicht und audiovisuelle Medialität zueinander in Beziehung treten können, lässt sich anhand des Abschnitts zu den Gedichten 12 (*ein großer wunsch*) und 13 (ohne Titel) verdeutlichen. Die ersten Einstellungen zeigen ein Kleinkind, das offenbar soeben laufen lernt und auf wackeligen Beinen auf eine Frau zustolpert, die es mit offenen Armen erwartet, sich jedoch rückwärts entfernt, worin sich erneut die Thematik von der Rückkehr zur Mutter andeutet. Damit wird zunächst eine Information der gleichzeitig gesprochenen Verse („das alter von drei jahren" [S. 14]) visualisiert, während eine weitere Information, das „zurück" der Rückschau bzw. des Erinnerns, auf der Tonebene aufgegriffen wird. Man vermeint, das Geräusch eines Filmprojektors im Verbund mit einer wie rückwärts abgespielten Musik zu hören. Die Markierung des filmischen Mediums übernimmt hier selbst die Funktion einer Metapher für die Erinnerung. Als das Kind plötzlich nach hinten umkippt, endet die Retrospektion abrupt: Die Bewegung des Zurück scheitert im Filmriss, die Bilder setzen aus und lassen das Filmmaterial sichtbar werden, auf dem Markierungen, Buchstaben und Zahlen erscheinen. Mit der einsetzenden Rezitation des Gedichtes Nummer 13, das sich der Schreibweise des Dichters widmet, wendet sich auch der Film der Medialität der Erinnerung zu:

13
er hat zu jeder alterszeit
die art und weise, wie
   er schreibt.
jetzt ist er alt genug
zu schreiben wie ein kind.
jedes gedicht ist jetzt ein
   brief an das christkind. (S. 15)

Die Verse werden in bemerkenswerter Weise mechanisch, leiernd und gedehnt intoniert und erinnern darin an die Sprechweise eines Menschen, der das Lesen gerade erlernt oder der beim Schreiben spricht. Sowohl die wiederkehrende Thematik des Schreibens als auch die kindliche Sprache („zu schreiben wie ein kind") werden also in der Performance des Gedichts evoziert. Nicht nur wird lyrisches Schreiben inhaltlich verhandelt, sondern das Gedicht wird selbst als

Geschriebenes markiert. Erinnerung wird zunächst als Bild, dann als durch oder besser in der Sprache (re-)konstruiert vorgeführt, ohne dass dabei jedoch eins als dem anderen überlegen ausgewiesen würde. Visuell-bildliche und akustisch-sprachliche Elemente sind wechselseitig aufeinander bezogen und erweitern sich zu einem gemeinsamen Bedeutungsraum.

Impulse für die Adaptionsforschung

Viele Theorien der Adaption sind auf die Dimension des Narrativen beschränkt. So gilt selbst Linda Hutcheons theoretisches Interesse trotz ihrer stark erweiterten Perspektive, die unterschiedliche Medien und Genres von Oper bis Videospiel einschließt, weiter der Adaption von Geschichten: „[…] some media and genre are used to *tell* stories (for example, novels, short stories); others *show* them (for instance, all performance media); and still others allow us to interact physically and kinesthetically with them (as in videogames or theme park rides)."[48] Lyrikadaptionen können dazu inspirieren, die erprobten handlungsorientierten und narratologischen Methoden der Adaptionsforschung zu ergänzen und sie um Analysekategorien für Tongestaltung und sprechkünstlerische Aspekte in ihrer audiovisuellen Einbettung, das Studium rhythmischer Strukturen sowie einen erweiterten Begriff von Wort-Bild-Beziehungen zu bereichern. Dies wird durch die Auflösung der binären Opposition von Text und Bild ermöglicht, welche die Adaptionsforschung noch immer prägt. Die von Robert Stam als Ausdruck dichotomischen Denkens monierte Gegenüberstellung von Wort und Bild, Text und Film wird obsolet. Sie ist zudem an eine Reihe von Vorurteilen gekoppelt, welche von einer Theorie der Lyrikadaption ebenfalls überwunden werden kann.

Hinter der von Robert Stam beobachteten Einstellung der Anti-Körperlichkeit („anti-corporeality") beispielsweise, verbirgt sich nicht nur eine Abwertung des Films, sondern auch eine Ignoranz gegenüber den sinnlich erfahrbaren, nicht-diskursiven und vor allem akustisch erlebbaren Dimensionen der Literatur. Infolgedessen wird Filmen ein „Engagement with bodies" zugeschrieben, da sie die Sinne stärker affizieren und in ihnen die Körperlichkeit der Darsteller, sowie Dinge und Landschaften sichtbar und hörbar werden.[49] Dabei wird ausgeblendet, dass auch Literatur bei weitem keine körperlose Kunst ist, sondern, nicht nur in Form lyrischer Dichtung, auf Rhythmus und Klang beruht. Das Modell des Gedichtfilms lehrt, Adaption nicht nur als Recodierung von Bedeutung sondern auch als Aufführung eines Textes zu verstehen: Wie werden jene sinnlich erfahrbaren Dimensionen von Literatur im audiovisuellen Medium realisiert? Wie wird das Ereignis Sprache inszeniert? Wie wirken sich Physiognomien und Sprechweisen von Stimmen aus und wie werden sie im filmischen Raum verortet?

---

[48] Hutcheon: Theory of Adaptation, S. XIV.
[49] Stam: Introduction, S. 6-7.

Auch die mit der Text-Bild-Dichotomie in Zusammenhang stehende Ikonophobie[50] wird in Frage gestellt, denn bei der Adaption von Lyrik im audiovisuellen Medium kommt es nicht zwangsläufig zu einer Ersetzung des Wortes durch das Bild, sondern zu interessanten Verklammerungen beider Bereiche, die durch die technische Trennung von Ton- und Bildebene im Film ermöglicht werden. Insbesondere durch Voice-Over entstehen ungewohnte Text-Bild-Bezüge, die die Bilder keineswegs auf eine Abbildung des Gesagten festlegen. Hier gilt es, jenseits einer vermeintlichen Feindschaft der Zeichensysteme das Zusammenspiel von Wort und Bild, aber auch von Wort und Geräusch bzw. Wort und Musik zu untersuchen. Wie die Analyse von *Nebel* gezeigt hat, bilden sich zwischen den Ebenen Verbindungen heraus, die neue Bedeutungen erzeugen. Insofern zeigt die Untersuchung von Gedichtfilmen auch, wie nötig es ist, die Klangdimension des Films, die durch die Übermittlung von gesprochener Sprache, Geräuschen und Musik jede filmische Adaption mit konstituiert, stärker zu berücksichtigen. Auch die Adaptionsforschung allgemein darf nicht auf das Bild fixiert bleiben, sondern gewinnt viel, wenn sie Film als *audio*visuelles Medium begreift und ihr Analyseinstrumentarium entsprechend anpasst.

Gedichtfilme verdeutlichen paradigmatisch die Polyphonie des Films und, vielleicht mehr noch, der neueren audiovisuellen Medien, auf die bereits Robert Stam mit Nachdruck hinweist.[51] Sie stellen darüber hinaus eine Vielzahl von Beispielen bereit, die davor warnen, Phänomene als Medienspezifika zu verbuchen, die eigentlich in der Dominanz des Erzählkinos begründet sind, denn Lyrikadaptionen wie *Nebel* brechen mit zahlreichen Konventionen des narrativen Films und erinnern dadurch an die Potentiale des Audiovisuellen: „A culturally polyrhythmic, heterochronic, multiple-velocity and contrapuntal cinema becomes a real possibility."[52] Ich hoffe gezeigt zu haben, dass die Verwirklichung dieser Möglichkeit nicht eine Absage an die Literatur erfordert, sondern einfach eine Erweiterung des Blicks auf sie. Adaptionen von Lyrik zeigen sich als komplexe Interaktion von Klang, Text, Bild und Montagerhythmus. Auf diese Weise durchkreuzen ‚Gedichtverfilmungen' viele der binären Oppositionen (Original/ Kopie, Sprache/Bild, Medialität/Performativität, Bildebene/Tonspur), die die Untersuchung von Literaturverfilmungen bisher bestimmt haben.

Stefanie Orphal is a doctoral candidate at the Friedrich Schlegel Graduate School of Literary Studies at the Freie Universität Berlin

---

[50] Stam: Introducion, S. 5.
[51] Stam: Introduction, S. 21.
[52] Stam: Introduction, S. 21.

Christiane Schönfeld

Erfolg und Misserfolg von Verfilmungen:
Manfred Gregors *Die Brücke* und die Nahaufnahmen des Krieges
in Kino und Fernsehen

Der autobiographische Roman *Die Brücke,* den der junge Journalist Gregor
Dorfmeister 1958 unter dem Pseudonym Manfred Gregor veröffentlichte, gelangte
durch Bernhard Wickis gleichnamige Kinoverfilmung im darauf folgenden Jahr zu
nationalem Ruhm und internationaler Bekanntheit. Wickis Film, der nicht nur mit
einer Reihe deutscher Filmpreise ausgezeichnet wurde, sondern 1960 auch den
Golden Globe in der Kategorie *Best Foreign Language Film* und andere
internationale Preise gewann, zählt bis heute zu den besten Antikriegsfilmen aller
Zeiten. Die Ausdrucksstärke und Überzeugungskraft, die dieser ersten Verfilmung
von Gregor Dorfmeisters Roman immer wieder bestätigt wurden,[1] fehlten, so die
Reaktionen der Presse, der zweiten Verfilmung von 2008 unter der Regie von
Wolfgang Panzer gänzlich. Die ProSieben-Fernsehproduktion wurde von Kritikern
als „erbärmlich" bezeichnet,[2] als Film, der es nicht verdient, „in Erinnerung zu
bleiben", wie es Dieter Bartetzko im Feuilleton der *FAZ* formulierte.[3] Warum eine
Verfilmung überzeugt und sich für immer in die Erinnerung eingräbt und eine
andere verärgert und schnell wieder vergessen wird, ist die Frage, die sich dieser
Aufsatz stellt. Es soll hier nicht darum gehen, gute mit schlechter Regie oder
schauspielerische Fähigkeiten zu vergleichen, sondern den Prozess der Verfilmung
eines autobiographischen Romans im Kontext des Antikriegsfilm-Genre
aufzuzeigen und die Ursachen für die wahrgenommene Effektivität sowie den
Affekt der Verfilmung zu untersuchen. Die Gründe, die die eine Adaption bis heute
zum „ehrlichste[n] und erschütterndste[n] deutsche[n] Film über den zweiten
Weltkrieg"[4] machen und der anderen einen Platz auf der „Liste der scheußlichsten

[1] Die Bedeutung von Bernhard Wickis Film wird im Band zum Kriegsfilm, der bei Reclam
     in der Filmgenres-Reihe erschienen ist, zusammengefasst. Siehe Norbert Grob und
     Thomas Klein: Die Brücke. In: Thomas Klein, Marcus Stiglegger und Bodo Traber
     (Hg.): Filmgenres – Kriegsfilm. Stuttgart: Reclam, 2006, S. 154-59. Zur weiterführenden
     Bibliographie siehe S. 159.
[2] Christian Buß: Und dann hat es ‚Bumm‘ gemacht. In: Spiegel Online, 29.09.2008.
     www.spiegel.de/kultur/gesellschaft/0,1518,581092,00.html (konsultiert am 19.07.2012).
[3] Dieter Bartetzko: ‘Die Brücke’ neuverfilmt – An das Spektakel verschenkt. In:
     Frankfurter Allgemeine Zeitung, 29.08.2008.
     http://www.faz.net/aktuell/feuilleton/medien/die-bruecke-neuverfilmt-an-das-spektakel-
     verschenkt-1695530.html (konsultiert am 19.07.2012).
[4] Aus der Filmbesprechung im Weser Kurier vom 09.12.1959. Siehe auch die Kritik in der
     Süddeutschen Zeitung vom 25.10.1959. Robert C. und Carol J. Reimer beschreiben

TV-Momente 2008"[5] bescheren, sind zwar vielschichtig, aber im Wesentlichen auf die Darstellung der unmittelbaren Wirkung von Krieg auf das Individuum im Einzelnen zurückzuführen.

Gregor Dorfmeisters Roman stellt den Schrecken, Schmerz und Wahnsinn des Krieges am Schicksal von sieben Jugendlichen dar und ermöglicht vor allem durch Rückblenden eine effektive Gegenüberstellung der Jungen als lebensfrohe Kinder oder Heranwachsende einerseits und todgeweihte Soldaten im schon längst verlorenen 2. Weltkrieg andererseits. Dorfmeisters Text beginnt mit einleitenden Worten des Ich-Erzählers, die den Roman als autobiographisch, als ein Buch der Erinnerung und des Bekenntnisses bezeichnen.[6] Es ist die Geschichte von sieben 15- bis 16-jährigen Klassenkameraden, die in den letzten Kriegstagen eingezogen werden und den Befehl erhalten, eine Brücke in ihrer Heimatstadt zu verteidigen. Nur einer der Jungen überlebt die Ereignisse auf der Brücke. Die mit Heldengeschichten, Indianerspiel und Nazi-Ideologie groß gewordenen Kinder werden durch den allzu frühen Tod des Jüngsten unter ihnen an diesem strategisch unbedeutenden Ort zu einer unentrinnbaren Schicksalsgemeinschaft zusammen geschlossen. Sie geben trotz mehrmaliger Warnungen der Erwachsenen die Brücke nicht auf und verteidigen sie, als ob sie durch ihr eigenes Handeln, im Sinne von Blut-und-Boden-Ideologie und Indianerspiel den Tod Siegis im Nachhinein noch bedeutungsvoll werden lassen könnten. Die sieben Jungen kämpfen buchstäblich bis zum letzten Mann und für den einzig Überlebenden wird die letzte Bitte seines sterbenden besten Freundes zum Diktat: „Nicht vergessen – nicht vergessen – nicht…".[7]

Wie könnte man etwas vergessen, das man nicht verstehen kann, fragt sich zehn Jahre später der Ich-Erzähler, der „Albert Mutz" des Romans. Zu Beginn des Romans steht nicht die Erinnerung an die schrecklichen Kriegserlebnisse im Vordergrund, sondern die Schönheit der Brücke, auf der zu stehen ein „Erlebnis"

Wickis *Die Brücke* in ihrem Buch *Nazi Retro Film* als „one of the most hard-hitting, relentless, bitterest antiwar films that ever was projected on the screen". Robert C. und Carol J. Reimer: Nazi Retro Film. New York: Twayne, 1992, S. 64.

[5]   Buß: Und dann hat es ‚Bumm‘ gemacht.

[6]   In einem Interview schildert Gregor Dorfmeister, wie ihm und zwei weiteren Hitler-Jungen der Befehl gegeben wurde, die Brücke in Bad Tölz gegen die amerikanischen Truppen zu verteidigen „komme da was wolle". Als die Feldgendarmen verschwanden, war dies für Gregor Dorfmeister das Signal, dass auch die Jungen sich in Sicherheit bringen sollten. Einer der Jungen kam von der Napola, ein „Körndlg'fudderter", d.h. ein Fanatiker, und er erinnerte Dorfmeister und seinen Freund Knut daran, dass sie einem Befehl zu folgen hatten. Dorfmeister machte sich allerdings trotzdem auf den Weg nach Hause, legte zwischendurch Karabiner und Stahlhelm ab, und wurde von seinen erleichterten Eltern zu Hause freudig in Empfang genommen. „Bis auf ein paar Schrammen hatte ich nichts abbekommen", erzählt er im Interview. Siehe: Die Brücke (2008) DVD, Bonusmaterial.

[7]   Manfred Gregor: Die Brücke. München: DVA, 2005, S. 204. Im Weiteren erfolgt die Seitenangabe direkt im Anschluss an das jeweilige Zitat in Klammern.

und „Vergnügen" ist. Auf dem Kiesgrund liegt allerdings, noch immer sichtbar, ein Gewehr: „Es war ein Sturmgewehr. Herstellungsjahr 1944. Das Magazin war leer" (S. 7). Der Ich-Erzähler lenkt unseren Blick auf den im Wasser liegenden Gegenstand und erklärt:

> Die Waffe fiel einem deutschen Soldaten am 2. Mai 1945, abends um 17.20 Uhr aus der Hand, rutschte zwischen Brückenkante und Geländer durch, blieb mit dem Magazin an der Kante hängen und pendelte hin und her. Ungefähr eine Sekunde lang. Dann sackte der Soldat in sich zusammen und stieß im Fallen das Gewehr endgültig in die Tiefe. Der Soldat hatte genau einen Monat früher seinen sechzehnten Geburtstag gefeiert, und als er in sich zusammensackte, bewegten sich seine Lippen, als wollten sie die Worte eines Gebetes formen. Ich wußte, daß ich ihn und die anderen nicht vergessen würde. (S. 8)

Der Akt der Erinnerung lässt Einzelheiten ins Bewusstsein des Ich-Erzählers gleiten; kleine Gesten und scheinbar unwichtige Details werden zu Platzhaltern für den Wahnsinn dieses Krieges, dessen grausame Konsequenz für alle Kriege gilt.

Die Altersangabe des oben erwähnten Soldaten schafft schon in den einleitenden Seiten die auf Gegensätze angelegte Dynamik, die den Roman bestimmt. Es ist die Spannung zwischen Kind und Erwachsenen, Indianerspiel und Soldatenwerk, Naivität und Erfahrung, Frieden und Krieg, und es sind die dramatischen Veränderungen, die die sieben Jungen im Mai 1945 auf der Brücke in dieser deutschen Kleinstadt durchleben müssen. Der schon wenige Jahre nach Ende des 2. Weltkriegs geschriebene Roman thematisiert die ethische Komplexität der im Nationalsozialismus sozialisierten und indoktrinierten Kinder kaum. Dorfmeister stellt Jugendliche dar und seine antizipierte Leserschaft war sich im Klaren darüber, dass diese Jungs seit ihrem dritten oder vierten Lebensjahr dem Propaganda-Apparat des NS-Regimes ausgesetzt waren, oft schon ab dem zehnten Lebensjahr als Pimpfe, bzw. Jungvolk in die Hitlerjugend integriert wurden und die Ideale des „Tausendjährigen Reiches" wie Wehrhaftigkeit und Opferbereitschaft nicht in Frage stellen.

Der Einberufungsbefehl zum Volkssturm, den die Jungs erhalten, wird von ihnen zunächst in freudiger Aufregung als Eintritt in die Männerwelt wahrgenommen, ist jedoch ein *rite de passage*,[8] der nicht den Übergang vom Kind zum Mann einleitet, sondern Siegi Bernhard, Jürgen Borchart, Karl Horber, Klaus Hager, Walter Forst

---

[8] Der Begriff des *rite de passage* wurde 1908 von dem Ethnographen Arnold van Gennep eingeführt (Arnold van Gennep: The Rites of Passage. Chicago: Chicago University Press, 1960). Eine detailliertere Analyse der Übergangsriten in Manfred Gregors *Die Brücke* und Bernhard Wickis gleichnamigen Film findet sich hier: Christiane Schönfeld: Representing Pain in Literature and Film: Reflections on *Die Brücke* (*The Bridge*) by Manfred Gregor and Bernhard Wicki. In: Comunicação & Cultura 5 (2008), S. 45-62. Siehe auch Victor Turner: From Ritual to Theatre: The Human Seriousness of Play. New York: PAJ Books, 1982.

und Ernst Scholten vom Leben zum Tod befördert und nur Albert Mutz als Einzigen von ihnen leben, jedoch vom Unschuldigen zu einem Mörder, also Schuldigen, werden lässt. Jedes der toten Kinder wird innerhalb der erinnerten Binnenerzählung, die sich von Blödeleien im Kasernenwaschraum bis zur Rückkehr des Überlebenden zieht, in einer weiteren Rückblende eingeführt und als froher, witziger oder schüchtern ringender, Dummheiten machender und anderen Streiche spielender Heranwachsender dargestellt. Jede eingeschobene und oft unterhaltsame Rückblende endet beim Wiedereintritt in die Erzählung auf der Brücke Anfang Mai 1945 mit dem Tod des Jugendlichen. Die Leichtigkeit der Vergangenheit wird der Schwere und Unwiderrufbarkeit des Krieges und Todes gegenübergestellt.

Ernst Scholten, der von seinen Eltern aus der oft Bombardierungen ausgesetzten Großstadt auf einen Bauernhof in der Nähe der Kleinstadt geschickt wurde, spielt gern Indianer und „liebte das Leben" (S. 85). Er hat als Einziger die Vorahnung, dass er nicht zurückkehren wird und eröffnet als Erster das Feuer auf die anrückenden amerikanischen Truppen. Der Jüngste unter ihnen, der 15-jährige Siegi Bernhard, ist zu diesem Zeitpunkt schon tot. Müde und verängstigt hatte Siegi auf der Brücke begonnen zu weinen und von seinen Kameraden Spott und Verachtung geerntet. Er war immer der Kleine in der Gruppe gewesen, und nun wollte er zeigen, dass auch er ein Held wie die von ihm geliebten Buchgestalten sein konnte. Beim nächsten Angriff feindlicher Flieger wirft er sich nicht, wie die anderen, auf den Boden, sondern bleibt verkrampft stehen und erleidet eine tödliche Kopfverletzung:

> Leg dich hin, du Idiot! hämmerte sein Gehirn. Leg dich endlich hin! Siegi Bernhard aber hörte nicht auf sein Gehirn. Vor seinen Augen stand wie ein Bild die Erdspalte und der Ritter Curtius. ‚Er war ein Held', hörte er sich selbst sagen, ‚ein Held...ein Held...!' [...] Nach dem Angriff der *Lightnings* also fehlte Siegi Bernhard. (S. 54-55)

Gregor Dorfmeister betont wiederholt die Verhaltensmuster, die die Kinder aus Heldengeschichten und Abenteuerromanen kennen und auf Indianerspiel, und nun – mit fatalen Konsequenzen – auf den Kriegsschauplatz übertragen. Die Brücke wird zum „Indianerhinterhalt" und obgleich den Jugendlichen zunächst „eine vollendete Überraschung gelang [...], weil sie ihre Stellungen und Positionen in so haarsträubendem Gegensatz zu jeder militärischen Überlegung gewählt hatten [und/...] die Brücke so völlig wider jede gebräuchliche Strategie verteidigt wurde", sind Indianerspiel und eine „vierzehntägige militärische Ausbildung", die sich „im Geländedienst und der flüchtigen Erklärung der Waffen" erschöpfte (S. 86), nicht ausreichend, um die Leben der Kinder zu schützen.

Nachdem sich die amerikanischen Truppen kurzzeitig zurückgezogen haben, erscheinen deutsche Soldaten, die die Brücke sprengen sollen. Doch Albert Mutz und Ernst Scholten, die einzig noch lebenden der sieben Jungs weigern sich, die Brücke aufzugeben, als ob die Sprengung den Tod ihrer Freunde noch sinnloser werden ließe. Sie bestehen darauf, dem Befehl des Generals Folge leistend die

Brücke zu halten und eröffnen das Feuer auf die deutschen Soldaten. Albert Mutz erschießt einen Leutnant, um seinen Freund zu schützen, und hört seine Mutter sagen: „Du sollst nicht töten, du sollst keinen Menschen und kein Tier quälen, du sollst keine Schmerzen bereiten. So will es Gott. Und jetzt war er ein Mörder geworden" (S. 198).

Für Ernst Scholten werden nicht christliche Moralvorstellungen manifest, sondern wiederum wird das Indianerspiel in diesem für das Kind jeglichen Sinn entleerten Raum scheinbar sinngebend.

> Er hörte einen Schrei und bissige Freude stieg in ihm hoch. Er war kein Soldat mehr, er war wieder beim Indianerspielen. Er war Winnetou, der große Häuptling. Von da drüben hatte ihn einer an der linken Schulter erwischt; er würde das Bleichgesicht töten.
> Ernst Scholten wurde müde und schläfrig, er hatte immer noch den Finger am Abzug, aber das Gewehr war längst verstummt, das Magazin war leer.
> Wo sind die Feiglinge, dachte Ernst Scholten, sie sollen kommen, damit ich sie skalpieren kann, alle. Dann hörte er den Motor des Lastwagens, aber er wußte nicht mehr, was das bedeutete.
> Und er dachte: Wie kommt ein Lastwagen mitten in die Prärie? (S. 201-02)

In seinen letzten Momenten dankt Ernst Scholten noch flüsternd in wahrer Indianermanier seinem „weißen Bruder, er hat mir das Leben gerettet" (S. 202). Weder die dem Jungen zur Verfügung stehende Vorstellungs- und Erfahrungswelt, die seine Sprachwahl bestimmt und durch die gewählte Form dem sinnlosen Ereignis Bedeutung verschaffen soll, noch die Tatsache, dass sein Leben gerettet wurde, entspricht der Realität. Das Konzept des Krieges ist für den Jugendlichen unverständlich, da die nun erfahrene Realität und die von Nazi-Ideologie vermittelte Vorstellungswelt sich nicht überschneiden, sondern im Gegenteil weit auseinanderklaffen.[9] Als er in den Armen von Albert Mutz sterbend zusammensackt, stößt sein Fuß gegen das Sturmgewehr, das – wie zu Beginn des Romans beschrieben – in den Fluss fällt und in seinem Kiesbett liegen bleibt.

In Gregor Dorfmeisters Roman, in dem die Repräsentanten der Erwachsenenwelt ein breites Spektrum abdecken, die Mütter voller Angst oder erzwungener Beherrschung sind, die Väter abwesend, verständnisvoll oder auch feige und brutal, und es unter den Nazis abstoßende Fanatiker, zweifelnde Idealisten und gute Deutsche gibt, soll den toten Jungen ein Denkmal gesetzt werden, da sie als allzu junge Soldaten und naive Kinder zum Opfer geworden sind. In den Augen des Autors trifft sie keine Schuld und er schreibt am Ende des Romans: „Die Jugend ist nicht gut und nicht schlecht. Sie ist wie die Zeit, in der sie lebt" (S. 210). Die Ereignisse sind tragisch,

---

[9]   Man könnte für eine weiterführende Analyse das viel diskutierte semiotische Dreieck heranziehen, das von Ogden und Richards 1923 erstmals formuliert wurde. C.K. Ogden and I.A. Richards: The Meaning of Meaning. A Study of the Influence of Language upon Thought and of the Science of Symbolism. London: Kegan Paul, 1923.

darin besteht kein Zweifel, und das Kindhafte der jungen Soldaten wird immer wieder, vor allem in den Rückblenden, betont. Die Jungs interessieren sich für Bücherhelden, wie Siegi Bernhard, oder für die Offizierslaufbahn, Leibesübungen und die junge Turnlehrerin, wie Jürgen Borchart, der seinen Vater als Oberst im Krieg bereits verloren hat. Karl Horber ist ein Lausbub, der eigentlich ängstlich ist, aber alles daran setzt, vor seinen Klassenkameraden nicht als Feigling dazustehen. Klaus Hager, behütet aufgewachsen und äußerst empfindsam, erlebt kurz vor seinem Tod noch die erste Liebe mit der neuen Klassenkameradin Franziska Feller, und der höfliche Walter Forst hasst seinen sadistischen Vater, den Standartenführer, der ihn dafür, dass er mit neun Jahren trotz seines Verbotes weiter mit einem jüdischen Freund spielte, brutal zusammengeschlagen hatte.[10] Die Rückblenden sowie die Einblicke, die Gregor Dorfmeister durch die präzisen Beschreibungen der letzten Momente des jeweilig sterbenden oder schon toten Kindes ermöglicht, verlangsamen die Erzählung und nähern die Lesenden mit großer emotiver Wirkung an das tragische Geschehen an. Dieser Affekt, der das Sterben der Kinder so bedeutsam werden lässt, wird in der ersten Verfilmung des Romans durch Bernhard Wicki vor allem durch die Kamera und speziell durch den gekonnten Einsatz von Nah-, Groß- und Detailaufnahmen erzeugt. Selbstverständlich tragen auch das Drehbuch,[11] die Dialoge und sowie der Ton im Allgemeinen, der Filmschnitt wie die Montage, die Maske und Kostüme, sogar die Beleuchtung zum Erfolg dieser Verfilmung bei. Die Entscheidung des Regisseurs, bei der Gestaltung der emotiven Wirkung des Antikriegsfilms vor allem auf *close-ups* zu setzen, um dadurch, wie in Dorfmeisters Text angedeutet, innezuhalten und das Hinsehen der Zuschauer zu erzwingen, gerade in den Augenblicken, in denen sie lieber die Augen verschließen oder den Kopf abwenden würden, lässt diese Verfilmung nicht nur als Umsetzung eines vorhandenen literarischen Stoffes sondern als Kunstwerk bestehen.

Es ist hier keine detaillierte vergleichende Studie zwischen dem Roman und seinen Verfilmungen angestrebt und inhaltliche Abweichungen sollen nur da diskutiert werden, wo die Veränderungen zur Wirkung des Films beitragen. Die binäre Beziehung zwischen dem verbalen System des Romans und dem verbalen, wie visuellen System der Verfilmung beeinflusst natürlich viele Entscheidungen, die im Zuge der Übertragung des autobiographisch-literarischen Textes auf die Kinoleinwand, bzw. den Fernsehbildschirm getroffen werden. Beide hier zu behandelnden Filme haben ihren Ausgangspunkt in der von Gregor Dorfmeister erinnerten und erzählten Geschichte, und doch geht es nicht nur um die Unterschiede zwischen den beiden Medien, denn auch Filme erzählen eine Geschichte und sind zumindest in diesem Sinne, wie T. Jefferson Kline betont,

---

[10]   Gregor: Die Brücke, S. 127-39, S. 146-64.

[11]   Das Drehbuch schrieb Bernhard Wicki zusammen mit Michael Mansfeld und Heinrich Pauck (der unter seinem Pseudonym Karl-Wilhelm Vivier genannt wird). Bernhard Wickis Beitrag zum Drehbuch blieb unerwähnt.

literarisch.[12] Wickis Verfilmung orientiert sich in zahlreichen Punkten eng an der literarischen Vorlage, sie fungiert aber gleichzeitig als Kommentar, der weit über die Romanvorlage hinausgeht.[13] Eigentlich wollte Bernhard Wicki *Die Brücke* gar nicht verfilmen, „denn der Roman von Gregor Dorfmeister ist ja ein hohes Lied auf deutsche Tapferkeit. Er hat die Geschichte von der Brücke selber erlebt und er setzt in dem Roman seinen Freunden, die damals gefallen sind, ein Denkmal".[14] Gerade die Anlehnung an Werte des NS-Regimes wollte Wicki unter allen Umständen vermeiden – im Gegensatz zur Verfilmung durch Wolfgang Panzer, die Werte wie Tapferkeit und Durchhaltevermögen durchaus unterstreicht. Bernhard Wicki hingegen veränderte, von seiner kritischen Haltung gegenüber Dorfmeisters Roman motiviert, die Struktur des Erzählten, um die Gewalt, die den Kindern angetan wird und die sie selbst, als Produkte ihrer Zeit, erzeugen und multiplizieren, mimetisch wiederzugeben. Erst durch die Verfilmung von 1959 wird so die Erzählung in einem eindeutig kritischen Antikriegskontext verankert.

Schon in der literarischen Vorlage wird allerdings die Gewalt des Krieges im Moment der Unmittelbarkeit als außerhalb der Vorstellungs- und Erfahrungswelt, und so der Verständnismöglichkeiten der Jungen angesiedelt und, als unsinnig wahrgenommen, stellt sie implizit auch die Rechtsordnung der Zeit in Frage, die es ermöglicht, Kinder zu Kriegshandlungen zu missbrauchen. Als etwa Karl Horber tödlich verletzt wird, sieht sein Freund Klaus Hager „die Verletzung an der Stirn Horbers" zwar, „aber irgendwie war nicht in sein Bewußtsein gedrungen, was das häßliche, klaffende Loch zwischen Horbers Augen bedeutete" (S. 118).

Die Herausforderung bei jeder Darstellung von Gewalt ist die von zahlreichen Schriftstellern und Philosophen beschriebene, unausweichliche Fragmentierung und

---

[12] Jefferson T. Kline: Screening the Text: Intertextuality in New Wave French Cinema. Baltimore, MD: Johns Hopkins Press, 1992, S. 2. Ebenfalls relevant in diesem Kontext ist Robert Scholes: Semiotics and Interpretation. New Haven, CT: Yale University Press, 1982, S. 57-72; Robert Stam: Introduction: The Theory and Practice of Adaptation. In: Robert Stam und Alessandra Raengo (Hg.): Literature and Film: A Guide to the Theory and Practice of Film Adaptation. London: Blackwell, 2005, S. 1-52; Dudley Andrew: The Impact of the Novel on French Cinema of the 30's. In: L'Esprit Créateur 30.2 (1990), S. 3-13; sowie meine Einführung in Processes of Transposition: German Literature and Film. Amsterdam: Rodopi, 2007, S. 11-26.

[13] Verfilmungen werden meist in drei Kategorien aufgeteilt: eng an der Vorlage orientierte und dadurch oft recht langweilige Verfilmungen, Kommentare und freie, durch den literarischen Text inspirierte Übertragungen. Siehe v.a. Geoffrey Wagner: The Novel and the Cinema. Rutherford, NJ: Dickinson University Press, 1975, S. 222-31; Dudley Andrew: Concepts in Film Theory. Oxford: Oxford University Press, 1984, S. 98-104; Robert Giddings, Keith Selby und Chris Wensley: Screening the Novel: The Theory and Practice of Literary Dramatization. Houndmills: Macmillan, 1990, S. 11-12.

[14] Bernhard Wicki in: Produktionsnotizen: Bernhard Wicki über *Die Brücke*. Filmbegleitheft zum Film *Die Brücke* (veröffentlicht vom Bernhard Wicki Gedächtnisfonds), S. 54. Erhältlich auch über die Website des Gedächtnisfonds: http//www.bernhardwickigedaechtnisfonds.de/filmbegleithefte/bruecke.pdf (konsultiert am 19.07.2012).

Distanzierung vom eigentlichen Akt der Gewalt durch ihre Repräsentation. Eine Darstellung, die zum Zeugnis werden soll, kann dies immer nur unvollständig und vereinzelt leisten,[15] und doch wird sie bei Bernhard Wicki gerade durch eine Fragmentierung, nämlich gezielt eingesetzte Nah-, Groß- und Detailaufnahmen vermittelbar. Die Annäherung an das Gesicht von Klaus (gespielt von Volker Lechtenbrink) etwa, das vor Schock und Angst verzerrt ist und in Großaufnahme die Kinoleinwand ausfüllt, zeigt, dass diese Gewalt, die soeben das Leben seines Freundes beendete, weder angemessen noch gerechtfertigt ist. Obwohl die Kinder in einem System aufgewachsen sind, das Gewalt monopolisiert und den Heldentod auf dem Schlachtfeld idealisiert, wird in einer dem Film geradezu entgegengesetzten Bewegung sowohl die Unrechtmässigkeit der Gewalt wie des kriegsversessenen und größenwahnsinnigen Staates deutlich.[16] Im Moment größter Anspannung und hektischer Panik hält der Film inne und Wicki lässt die Kamera auf dem verzerrt schreienden, schmutzigen und von Tränen verschmierten Gesicht des Jungen ruhen.[17] Die Distanz zwischen dem Geschehen auf der Kinoleinwand und dem Zuschauer wird auf ein Minimum reduziert und der Betrachter mit dem jungen Protagonisten verknüpft. Der Regisseur vertraut hier auf den gängigen Effekt der Einstellungsgröße, die gerade im Zusammenhang mit einer Verlangsamung des Filmgeschehens die Gefühle eines Protagonisten klar zum Ausdruck bringen und so Emotionen bei den Zuschauern auslösen kann und soll. Eine Identifizierung mit den Jugendlichen, die im Film ihren Tod finden, wird durch die Großaufnahmen ihrer schmerzverzerrten oder leblosen Gesichter möglich und die Botschaft des Antikriegsfilms umso überzeugender.

---

[15]   Auf diesen Umstand hat etwa der Holocaust-Überlebende Elie Wiesel wiederholt hingewiesen. Siehe z.B. Elie Wiesel: From the Kingdom of Memory. New York: Schocken, 1990. Siehe auch Maurice Blanchot: The Writing of Disaster. Übers. a. d. Franz. v. Ann Smock. Lincoln: University of Nebraska Press, 1986; Andreas Huyssen: Denkmal und Erinnerung im Zeitalter der Postmoderne. In: James E. Young (Hg.): Mahnmale des Holocaust: Motive, Rituale und Stätten des Gedenkens. München: Prestel, 1994, S. 9-17.

[16]   Interessant in diesem Kontext ist auch Walter Benjamins Aufsatz „Kritik der Gewalt" (1921). Walter Benjamin: Zur Kritik der Gewalt und andere Aufsätze. Frankfurt a.M.: Suhrkamp, 1965, S. 29-65.

[17]   Auch die Uraufführungsplakate, die den Film in BRD und DDR ankündigten, zeigten beide das Gesicht eines Jugendlichen in Großaufnahme. Die Zeichnung in der BRD Version zeigt das Gesicht eines Jungen, dessen nach oben gerichteter Blick in die Ferne schweift. In einer Überblendung ist die Brücke, an deren Mauer im Vordergrund ein Gewehr mit einem Stahlhelm lehnt und im Hintergrund der Schauplatz des tödlichen Gefechts erscheint, über das Kindergesicht gelegt. Das Erstaufführungsplakat der DDR ist direkter in seiner politischen Aussage und zeigt nur das Gesicht von Volker Lechtenbrink unter dem gemalten Stahlhelm, das ein über das Foto in Mischtechnik gemaltes, verlaufenes und blutig rotes Hakenkreuz trägt, das dem Jungen über sein linkes Auge und Teile seines Gesichts fließt.
Siehe http://www.filmportal.de/node/3067/material/684370 (konsultiert am 19.07.2012).

Der vielschichtige Text des menschlichen Gesichts,[18] das in Nah- und Großaufnahme von Gilles Deleuze in seinem ersten Kinobuch *Cinema 1: L'Image-Mouvement* nicht als einzig mögliches, aber als ideales Vehikel des Affektbildes, ja als Affektbild selbst begriffen wird,[19] ist in den nahen Aufnahmen kurzzeitig losgelöst von Zeit und Raum. Ohne den momentan ablenkenden Kontext ist die emotive Wirkung des Bildes umso stärker. Das Gesicht wird so zum filmischen Zeichen, das in der Atempause zwischen Aktion und Reaktion nur die Angst und den Schmerz des Kindes vermittelt.[20] Wickis Verfilmung beginnt nicht, wie der Roman, mit der Erinnerung an ein im Rückblick erzähltes, nie vergessenes und traumatisierendes Kriegserlebnis, sondern mit friedlich dahinfließendem Wasser unterhalb einer Brücke, in das plötzlich, nach einer knappen halben Minute eine Bombe fällt und explodiert, womit die Ereignisse, die sich 1945 in der Kleinstadt zugetragen haben, ihren Lauf nehmen. Wickis Film erzählt die Geschichte der sieben Jungen nicht wie Gregor Dorfmeister unter Verwendung von Rückblicken, sondern bettet das Geschehen und den Alltag der Jungen in das sich anbahnende Kriegsgeschehen über nur drei Tage und zwei Nächte ein. Für wenige Minuten wird der Ort des Geschehens eingeführt – eine idyllische, scheinbar friedliche bayrische Kleinstadt –, bis auch dieses Bild gestört wird, diesmal aural durch den Fliegeralarm, der ertönt und die Kamera auf sich lenkt, bis sie einem Kesselwagen folgt, der durch eine der engen Straßen fährt. Die Bilder, die für ein paar Sekunden friedliche Idylle suggerieren, werden durch die visuellen und auralen Konjunktionen gestört und der Betrachter erkennt schnell, dass der Ort der Erzählung ein liminaler und gefährdeter ist, fragil und im Umbruch begriffen. Die hier lebenden Menschen können sich nicht in Sicherheit wiegen, denn dieser Ort befindet sich nach zwölf Jahren Hitler-Diktatur und fast sechs Jahren Krieg, der schon lange verloren ist und doch nicht enden darf, in einem Schwellenzustand.[21] Die Hauptdarsteller in diesem Film verkörpern gleichfalls diesen Zustand der Liminalität, da sie nicht mehr ganz Kind sind, aber eben auch noch nicht erwachsen. Als pubertierende Jugendliche, die wir im ersten Teil des Films [0:01:06 - 0:41:55][22] kennen lernen, sind sie

---

[18]   Vgl. z.B. Susan Stewart: On Longing: Narratives of the Miniature, the Gigantic, the Souvenir, the Collection. Baltimore, MD: Johns Hopkins University Press, 1984, S. 127f.

[19]   Gilles Deleuze: Cinema 1: L'Image-Mouvement. Paris: Minuit, 1983. Siehe die deutsche Übersetzung von Ulrike Bokelmann und Ulrich Christians: Das Bewegungs-Bild: Kino 1. Frankfurt a.M.: Suhrkamp, 1996. Das Gesicht, das dem „affection image" gleichbedeutend wird, ist in der englischen Ausgabe vor allem ab S. 89 beschrieben. Siehe Gilles Deleuze: Cinema 1. The Movement Image. London: Continuum, 2005, S. 89-104.

[20]   Siehe auch Mary Ann Doane: The Close-Up. Scale and Detail in the Cinema. In: differences 14.3 (2003), S. 89-111.

[21]   Siehe Victor Turner: Betwixt and Between. The Liminal Period in Rites de Passage. In: Melford Spiro (Hg.): Symposium on New Approaches to the Study of Religion. Seattle: American Ethnological Society, 1964, S. 3-19; and: Liminalität und Communitas. In: Ritualtheorien. Opladen: Westdeutscher Verlag, 1998, S. 251-64.

[22]   Die Brücke/ Film-Sequenzen 1.1 bis 10.2. Vgl. das Sequenzprotokoll im Filmbegleitheft:

verletzlich,[23] und die militärischen Entscheidungen einer fanatischen Führerriege gefährden nun zusätzlich die Jungen. Die ersten Worte, die in Wickis Film gesprochen werden, sind von Frau Bernhard (gespielt von Edith Schultze-Westrum), die sich um ihren Sohn Sigi [sic] (gespielt von Günther Hoffmann) sorgt: „Meinen Jungen haben sie nämlich auch noch gemustert" sagt die Mutter zu ihrem Arbeitgeber, dessen Wäsche sie soeben in einem kleinen Leiterwagen zum Waschen und Stopfen abholt. Die Antwort des Doktors beruhigt weder Frau Bernhard noch die Zuschauer: „Den Sigi? Aber den können sie doch nicht mehr holen."

Das Kindhafte der schon bald zu Soldaten werdenden Jungen wird in dieser ersten Handlungsphase des Films beständig wiederholt. Als Sigi von einem Polizisten dabei erwischt wird, wie er eine Eierlikörflasche aus dem von den Kindern am Fluss gefundenen Vorrat holt, sieht dieser zwar von einer Strafanzeige ab, als er von der Einberufung hört, bringt Sigi – der vor Schreck in den Fluss fiel – aber zum „Trockenlegen" zu seiner Mutter. Frau Bernhard sitzt währenddessen mit sorgenvollem Blick in ihrer Küche und sagt verzweifelt zum Schutzmann, als dieser mit dem triefenden Sigi hereinkommt: „Der kann doch nicht zu den Soldaten, der ist doch noch ein Kind!"

Bernhard Wicki lässt in dieser ersten, langen Handlungsphase keine Gelegenheit aus, die Schüler als pubertierende Jugendliche darzustellen, die in ihrer Kindhaftigkeit allesamt sympathisch werden. In über vierzig Minuten führt Wicki die Hauptdarsteller ein, jeder der sieben Jungen wird individuell charakterisiert und der soziale, vor allem familiäre Hintergrund eingeführt. Die dramaturgische Entscheidung dieser langen und auf die einzelnen Jungen bezogenen ersten Handlungsphase beeinflusst in den folgenden Handlungsphasen die Wirkung der affektiven Bilder maßgeblich. Die Kamera rückt im Verlauf des Filmes immer näher, wie die amerikanischen Truppen und damit der Krieg, der das Leben der Kinder gefährdet.

Im ersten Teil des Films tauchen kaum Nahaufnahmen auf, nur wenige Momente, die von großer Intensität sind, werden in Nah- und Großaufnahmen gezeigt – wie Sigis Mutter, die um ihren einzigen Sohn bangt, Klaus Hager, der Franziska (gespielt von Cordula Trantow) liebt und sie gegen Karl Horbers (Karl Michael Balzer) Anklage, dass „alle Frauen Schlampen" seien, mit einem Faustschlag verteidigt. Wir sehen Karls Gesicht mit blutender Nase als erste Großaufnahme in Wickis Film, in der das Gesicht des Jugendlichen den Bildrahmen beinahe ausfüllt. Das verletzte, leidende und verzweifelt wirkende Kindergesicht leitet den zweiten Hauptteil des Films ein. Kurz danach beginnt die zweite Handlungsphase, als die Jungen die Nachricht der Einberufung erreicht. Die Jugendlichen nehmen die Nachricht begeistert auf, lachen wie in Erwartung eines

---

http://www.bernhardwickigedaechtnisfonds.de/filmbegleithefte/bruecke.pdf (konsultiert am 19.07.2012)

[23] Siehe z.B. Bruno Bettelheim: Symbolic Wounds. Glencoe, Ill.: Free Press, 1954.

unterhaltsamen Abenteuers, und nur ihr Lehrer, Studienrat Stern (gespielt von Wolfgang Stumpf) verlässt mit ernstem, sorgenvollem Blick den Bildausschnitt. Die negativen Erwartungsaffekte[24] wie Sorge und Angst mancher Erwachsener treffen hier noch auf die positiven Erwartungsaffekte der Jungen, die die Einberufung freudig wie eine Einladung zum Schulausflug wahrnehmen – auch im Roman wird auf die anfängliche „Schulausflugsstimmung" hingewiesen (S. 37) – und vereinnahmen so die Zuschauer. Mit zunehmender emotionaler Intensität nehmen auch die Nahaufnahmen im Film zu. Als Karl kurz danach zu Hause von seinem Vater (Klaus Hellmold) den Einberufungsbefehl erhält, verliert der Junge die Fassung, als er Barbara (Edeltraud Elsner) sieht, die mit seinem Vater eine Beziehung eingegangen ist und die Karl liebt. Sein in Nahaufnahme gezeigtes und verzerrtes Gesicht schreit Barbara an: „Raus, gehen Sie, ich will Sie nicht mehr sehen! Raus, gehen Sie!" und zum Vater: „Ihr seid ja froh, dass ich weg muss dann seid ihr allein ihr beiden." Karls Vater quittiert den Ausbruch für Karl hörbar zu Barbara, während Karl schon das Haus verlässt: „Solche Kinder wollen Sie in den Krieg schicken! So was gehört nicht in die Kaserne, sondern in den Kindergarten!" [Sequenz 7.3; 0:29:42].

Nahaufnahmen dienen jedoch in diesem Teil des Films nicht nur dazu, für die Zuschauer wütende Auseinandersetzungen wie zwischen Karl und Klaus oder Karl und seinem Vater visuell zu intensivieren, sondern werden auch eingesetzt, um Intimität und das Gefühl der Vertrautheit und der mütterlichen Sorge zu vermitteln, wie in der Abschiedsszene zwischen Alberts Mutter (gespielt von Ruth Hausmeister) und dem bei ihr einquartierten Hans Scholten (Folker Bohnet),[25] oder in der Abschiedsszene zwischen den Verliebten Klaus und Franziska, die ihren letzten Abend im Postamt verbringen, wo Klaus auf ein Telefongespräch mit seinen Eltern in Bremen wartet.

Karl ist der erste, der sich in der Kaserne meldet, in den kurzen Hosen eines Schuljungen, ein „Rotzjunge", wie der ebenfalls kurze Hosen tragende Walter Forst (Michael Hinz) noch am selben Abend von seinem Vater, dem Ortsgruppenleiter Forst (gespielt von Hans Elwenspoeck) genannt wird. Wicki leitet hier durch eine Überblendung vom Zivil- zum Soldatenleben der Jungen, indem er in einem *match-cut* Walter erst in ziviler Kleidung weinend an die verschlossene Tür in seinem Elternhaus mit dem Rücken zum Betrachter gelehnt zeigt und ihn dann mit dem am Boden liegenden Jungen in Uniform überblendet. Wie scharf der Kontrast zwischen den Schuljungen in kurzen Hosen und den Soldaten in Uniform ist, wird verbal von Unteroffizier Heilmann (Günter Pfitzmann) unterstrichen, der den die jungen

---

24   Ernst Bloch: Das Prinzip Hoffnung. Bd 1. Frankfurt a.M.: Suhrkamp, 1985, S. 121-26. Siehe auch z.B. Lothar Mikos, der in seinem einführenden UTB Werk zur Filmanalyse auf das Film- und Fernseherleben eingeht. Vgl. Kapitel 1.2 in Lothar Mikos: Film- und Fernsehanalyse. Konstanz: Universitätsverlag Konstanz, 2008, S. 30-37.

25   Es ist unklar, warum Bernhard Wicki den Ernst Scholten des Romans in seinem Film Hans nennt.

Rekruten trainierenden Offizier fragt: „Willst du aus den Hosenscheißern etwa noch Soldaten machen?"

Eine Folge von Nahaufnahmen schließt diese Handlungssequenz ab. In der Nacht, Sekunden bevor die Jungen vom Alarm aufgeschreckt werden, ruht die Kamera auf ihren schlafenden, entspannten Gesichtern. Die Kamera zoomt zuerst auf den im unteren Stockbett liegenden Sigi, der als erstes auf der Brücke sterben wird, verweilt für einige Sekunden auf seinem friedlichen Gesicht, bis ein harter Schnitt zur nächsten Nahaufnahme überleitet, diesmal von Hans (dem Ernst Scholten des Romans), der das letzte Opfer auf der Brücke wird. Abgelöst wird diese Nahaufnahme von anderen *close-ups* auf die noch schlafenden und einige Stunden später schon toten Kindern. Als Mittel filmischen Erzählens dienen Nahaufnahme, Großaufnahme und Detailaufnahme hier wiederum nicht nur dazu, die Psychologie der jeweiligen Figur zu beleuchten und bildliche wie inhaltliche Akzente zu setzen, sondern auch dazu, die affektive Wirkung eines Bildes zu verstärken. In Wickis Film nehmen die nahen Kameraeinstellungen zu, je bedrohter die Jugendlichen sind und je aussichtsloser ihre Situation sich gestaltet.[26] Erst als Kugeln und Granaten die Körper der Jugendlichen treffen, ist die Kamera ganz nah auf die Kindergesichter gerichtet und lässt den Zuschauer so jegliche verbleibende Distanz zum Kriegsgeschehen und der komplett sinnentleerten Gewalt verlieren. Das erschütternde Weinen der Jungen, die gerade noch Männer sein wollten, ihr verzweifeltes Schreien kommuniziert das Unbeschreibliche des Krieges, seine rohe Grausamkeit, wie Absurdität und den unwiederbringlichen Verlust junger Leben. Die Nahaufnahmen nehmen im selben Maße zu, wie zuerst ihr Mut und dann die Leben der Kinder abnehmen. Wicki und Kameramann Gerd von Bonin verzichten meist auf den Zoom, eine Annäherung bei laufender und stationärer Kamera; stattdessen wählen sie in erster Linie harte Schnitte, um in derart strukturierten Montagen das Unausweichliche der Situation, in der diese jungen Menschen gefangen sind, zu unterstreichen.

Auch bildliche und verbale Wiederholungen und Zitate stellen den Widerspruch der in Uniformen steckenden Schülern dar und kritisieren die Befehlshaber und ihren Bellizismus, dem die entsprechend indoktrinierten Kinder meist widerspruchs-los und unhinterfragt folgen. Kurz bevor die Soldaten ausrücken und die sieben Jungen zur Verteidigung der Brücke abgestellt werden, hält Hauptmann Fröhlich noch eine klärende Rede:

Soldaten! Die Amerikaner sind gestern nachmittag auf breiter Front zum Angriff angetreten. [...] Jeder Quadratmeter, den wir jetzt verteidigen, ist ein Stück vom

---

[26] Mit Nahen werden Aufnahmen von Kopf und Schultern bezeichnet; eine Großaufnahme zeigt den Kopf des Protagonisten, dessen Stahlhelm aber z.B. nur zum Teil sichtbar wird, wie auch die Schultern, die oft abgeschnitten wirken. Der Ausdruck des Gesichts steht hier durch das Ausblenden jeglicher weiterer Kontexte im Vordergrund; die Detailaufnahme zeigt nur einen Gesichtsausschnitt, wie etwa nur die Augen oder einen schreienden Mund.

Herzen unserer Heimat. Und wer auch nur einen Quadratmeter deutschen Boden bis zum Letzten verteidigt, der verteidigt Deutschland. Wir sind uns darüber klar, dass die Lage verdammt ernst ist. Aber – wir sind Soldaten! Ob wir leben oder sterben, wir müssen vor der Geschichte verantworten, ob wir unsere Pflicht erfüllt haben. Die jungen Soldaten, die ihrem ersten Einsatz entgegensehen, sollen wissen, dass unser Bataillon nur ein Vorwärts kennt, niemals ein Zurück. Unser Bataillon kennt nur Kampf, Sieg oder Tod. Ich erwarte, dass sich das Vaterland in dieser ernsten Stunde auf euch verlassen kann! Auch für den kommenden Einsatz gilt die Parole: Vorwärts für Führer, Volk und Vaterland! [00:51:18 – 00:52:40]

Als kurz danach unter den Jungen Zweifel an der strategischen Bedeutung ihres Auftrags laut werden, erinnert der kleine Sigi, indem er den Hauptmann zitiert, die anderen an den Sinn des Befehls, der scheinbar weit über die Ufer des Flusses hinausragt: „Aber, wer nur einen Quadratmeter deutschen Boden verteidigt, der verteidigt Deutschland!" [01:13:00-01:13:55]

Die Struktur der eingesetzten Nah-, Groß- und Detailaufnahmen unterstützt die von Wicki dargestellte Handlung sowie die Haltung des Films semiotisch, da die Annäherung der Kamera an das Geschehen die interne Logik des zu Vermittelnden unterstreicht. Vor allem die Gesichter der Kinder, die in Großaufnahmen erscheinen und durch ihre Mimik ihren jeweiligen Gefühlszustand wie auch die Subjektivität der Jungen ausdrücken, laden zur Reflektion ein. Das Gesicht ist in der Großaufnahme vom Körper des jeweiligen Jugendlichen losgelöst und erscheint demnach als Fragment, wird aber so, wie Mary Ann Doane betont,[27] für den Betrachter zur Aufforderung, jedes vergrößerte Detail genau und als autonom wahrzunehmen, und so Einblick zu gewinnen in das Unbewusste des Kindes und Eigentliche des Dargestellten.

Vor allem in zwei Szenen werden Großaufnahmen und sogar eine Detailaufnahme gekonnt eingesetzt, um die Haltung des Films zu verdeutlichen. Die Kinder, die die Zuschauer im langen ersten Teil individuell kennen gelernt haben, sehen sie nun als ‚Soldaten' sterben. Das erste Opfer ist, wie schon erwähnt, der jüngste und kleinste unter ihnen, Sigi Bernhard. Wickis Verfilmung dieser Szene orientiert sich eng an der oben erwähnten Vorlage Gregor Dorfmeisters, in der Siegi sich vornimmt „nun endlich etwas zu tun, das den anderen zeigen würde: Ich bin kein Waschlappen, ich bin kein Schlappschwanz – schaut her, was ich mache!" (S. 139)

Bei Bernhard Wicki unterscheidet sich das Hohngelächter, das der „Kleine" erntet, weil er sich verfrüht in Erwartung eines Angriffs auf den Boden wirft [00:48:00], nicht von anderen Sticheleien seiner Freunde, und seine Reaktion,

---

[27] „Any viewer is invited to examine its gigantic detail, its contingencies, its idiosyncrasies. The close-up is always, at some level, an autonomous entity, a fragment, a 'for-itself'". Doane: The Close-Up, S. 90. Mary Ann Doane bezieht sich hier auf Jean Epstein's „Bonjour Cinema" Aufsatz (1921).

nämlich beim nächsten Anflug des Tieffliegers stehen zu bleiben, ist ebenfalls als beinahe spielerischer Mutbeweis gedacht. Die so geschaffene verbale und visuelle Rekurrenz[28] betont das Unvorbereitetsein der Kinder auf den Krieg und die Unverhältnismäßigkeit ihrer Reaktionen auf Gefechtssituationen. Das Kindergesicht Sigis unter dem Stahlhelm, das in seinen letzten verzweifelten Momenten in Großaufnahme auf der Leinwand erscheint, ist losgelöst von dem Ort des Geschehens. Raum und Zeit, die dargestellte Welt wird auf das Bild des jungen Gesichts reduziert und als stark affektives Bild wirft es den Betrachter auf sich selbst zurück,[29] da er erkennen muss, dass dieser junge Mensch mit falschen Idealen und Irrationalität fehlgeleitet wurde und nun zum Opfer wird. Ganz nah blicken wir in Sigis Gesicht mit den weit aufgerissenen Augen und werden scheinbar zu Zeugen der letzten Momente seines Lebens. Die cinematographische Repräsentation des Todes eines Schuljungen ist in gerade dieser Kameraeinstellung von einer affektiven Überzeugungskraft, die über die Dramatisierung einer zwar von tatsächlichen Erlebnissen inspirierten, aber dennoch fiktiven Erzählung hinwegtäuscht. In diesem Moment, wenn die Kamera innehält, der Film den Atem anzuhalten scheint und nichts als das ungläubig staunende Gesicht des sterbenden Sigi zeigt, wird die Darstellung von Gewalt durch die emotive Bindung an die Betrachter möglich. Für ein paar Sekunden losgelöst vom Geschehen auf der Brücke verhilft der dokumentarische Charakter der Einstellung dem Film zu einer hybriden Form, die den Spielfilm noch überzeugender werden lässt. Erst als Sigi tot auf der Brücke liegt, distanziert sich die Kamera wieder und betont so den Gegensatz zwischen Leben und Tod zusätzlich. Der letzte Blick auf das ungläubig starrende Kindergesicht markiert eine Wende im Film, die das Spiel der Jungen zu einem Kampf um Leben und Tod werden lässt. In dieser dritten Handlungsphase setzt der Tod Sigis demnach „den *point of no return*. Ab diesem Zeitpunkt ist es den Jungen kognitiv und emotional nicht mehr möglich, ihren Einsatzort aufzugeben und nach Hause zu gehen".[30]

In der zweiten Szenenfolge, die genauer betrachtet werden soll, ist die Kamera nah auf Karl und Klaus gerichtet, die nebeneinander in einem Graben kauern und mit einem Maschinengewehr auf die Amerikaner schießen, die sich im Haus gegenüber verschanzt haben. Die Kampfhandlungen kommen plötzlich zum Still-stand und ein Soldat der U.S. Army tritt hinter einem brennenden Panzer hervor, um die Kinder davon zu überzeugen, dass sie nach Hause gehen sollen. „Hey, stop shooting! Come on, give up! We don't fight kids! Go home... or go to ... kindergarden! [...] Wir nix schießen auf kindergarden!" [Sequenz 21.1; 1:28:35] ruft er, und erinnert Karl an den Streit mit seinem Vater am Vorabend. In Großaufnahme wird die Reaktion Karls auf das Wort „kindergarden" gezeigt und kurz danach schießt er wütend auf den GI, der, sich den getroffenen, aufklaffenden und stark

---

[28]   Eine Liste weiterer Rekurrenzen findet sich im Begleitheft zum Film auf S. 50.
[29]   Siehe Deleuze: Cinema 1, S. 95f., und Doane: The Close-Up, S. 91.
[30]   Begleitheft zum Film, S. 30.

blutenden Magen haltend, auf die Kamera zutorkelt, bis er zusammenbricht. Sein verzerrtes Gesicht wird ebenfalls nach einem harten Schnitt in Nahaufnahme gezeigt. Klaus, merklich erschüttert von dem Anblick, erträgt den Todeskampf des vor Schmerzen schreienden amerikanischen Soldaten nicht und ruft mehrmals: „Karl, schieß doch, Karl!" um dem Leiden und Schreien ein Ende zu bereiten. Erst als er seinen Freund am Kragen packt und schüttelt, fällt dessen Helm vom Kopf und sein erstarrender Blick wird in der Montage mit dem Sterben des GI gleichgesetzt. Nach einem Moment der Lähmung, der die Dynamik dieser Szenenfolge zu einem plötzlichen Ende bringt, zoomt die Kamera auf das staubige, fassungslose Gesicht von Klaus zu, dessen Zusammensinken von Maschinengewehrsalven begleitet wird. Der harte Schnitt zum Gesicht von Karl, dessen Nase blutet, löst bei Klaus in Erinnerung an die Auseinandersetzung auf dem Schulhof Schuldgefühle aus – die Nahaufnahme von Karls Gesicht mit blutender Nase weist große Ähnlichkeit mit der eine gute Stunde zuvor im Film gezeigten Einstellung auf – und er fühlt sich verantwortlich für den Tod seines Freundes. Zum ersten und einzigen Mal in Wickis Film wird in einer Detailaufnahme nur ein Ausschnitt von Klaus Gesicht gezeigt: die weit aufgerissenen Augen und die Nase. Wir hören seine Rufe – „Karl, ich wollte dich doch nicht schlagen!" – sehen aber seinen Mund nicht. Nach einem kurzen, nahen Blick auf Karl, der mit verdrehten Augen und blutiger Nase an der Grabenwand liegt, distanziert sich die Kamera bis zur Nahaufnahme von Klaus, der Karl versichert: „Es war doch nur wegen Franziska, Karl" und seinen toten Freund anfleht: „Schlag mich doch wieder, Karl! Ich wollt' dich nicht schlagen, bestimmt nicht, Karl! -- Hilfe! Hilfe!" Und zu Hans, der helfend zu ihm eilt: „Ich hab' ihn umgebracht! Ich hab' ihn totgeschlagen!" Karl lässt sich nicht festhalten, bedroht Hans in seiner Verzweiflung sogar mit dem Messer, klettert aus dem Graben und rennt in die Salve der amerikanischen Maschinengewehre. Er ist sofort tot.

Sigis Kindergesicht in Großaufnahme und die Detailaufnahme von Klaus' Augen sind die Bilder, die den Zuschauern bei Aufführungen von Wickis *Die Brücke* noch lange in Erinnerung bleiben. Wenn der Ausschnitt von Klaus' Gesicht die Kinoleinwand ausfüllt, vermittelt Wicki affektiv und äußerst effektiv einerseits die Totalität der subjektiven Erfahrungen dieser so früh zum Opfer des Nationalsozialismus gewordenen Kinder und andererseits den Schrecken des Krieges. Wie Mary Ann Doane erklärt: „the close-up performs the inextricability of these two seemingly opposed formulations, simultaneously posing as both microcosm and macrocosm, detail and whole".[31] Diese Gleichzeitigkeit, die Doane betont, verstärkt die Wirkung der Detailaufnahme. Nur dieses einzige Mal wird in Wickis Film eine Detailaufnahme verwendet und so die Szene, in der Klaus die Gewalt des Krieges nicht länger ertragen kann und Selbstmord begeht, symbolisch für das Verbrecherische eines Regimes, das Kinder mit Nazi-Ideologie,

---

[31] Doane: The Close-Up, S. 93.

Heldengeschichten und Tod fürs Vaterland-Gedichten füttert, [32] in Uniformen steckt und an der Heimatfront sterben lässt. Wicki und von Bonin verwenden hier eine heute so genannte italienische Einstellung, die in Schuss-Gegenschuss-Sequenzen oft in Duell-Szenen im Western Genre auftaucht und besonders im Spaghetti-Western der 1960er Jahre populär wurde. [33] Doch Klaus blickt nicht in die Augen seines Gegners, sondern erst auf seinen toten Freund und dann in die Leere. Er sieht nicht die Möglichkeit von Sieg und Ruhm, die Nationalsozialismus und Heldengeschichten immer wieder versprochen haben, sondern nur ein grauenvolles Nichts. Diese Einstellung ist als Affektbild äußerst wirksam, und unterstreicht Bernhard Wickis Abneigung gegen „Heldenstories"[34] und sein Bedürfnis, hier einen pazifistischen Film zu drehen, in dem sich dieses „humanitäre Anliegen"[35] manifestiert. In Wickis Film sterben die Jungen nicht, weil sie tapfer dem Befehl eines Generals folgen, wie im Roman, sondern „sie sterben, weil sie einfach so erzogen worden sind. Sie verteidigen diese Brücke, weil es auch ihr Kinderspielplatz ist."[36] Und obwohl Wicki die wesentlichen Teile der Handlung des Romans übernimmt und nur die narrative Struktur grundlegend verändert, gelingt es ihm gerade durch den gezielten Einsatz von Nah-, Groß- und Detailaufnahmen die Haltung der Geschichte grundlegend zu verändern und einen Antikriegsfilm zu drehen, wie es sein Ziel war.

Im Gegensatz zu Wickis Film, in dem die Kampfhandlungen nur etwa ein Drittel des Films ausmachen und viel Zeit auf die Charakterisierung der Jugendlichen verwendet wird, liegt Siegi in Wolfgang Panzers Verfilmung von 2008 schon nach einer halben Stunde tot auf der Brücke und erst in den letzten Minuten des Films hören wir die Namen der gefallenen jungen Soldaten, die nie individuell charakterisiert werden – bis auf Albert, der zumindest als Klavier spielender, sensibler junger Mann in den Vordergrund tritt. Die Verfilmung, die für ProSieben als „TV Event Movie" produziert wurde,[37] sowie das Drehbuch von Wolfgang Kirchner, weichen an zahlreichen Stellen von der literarischen Vorlage ab und auch

---

[32]   Ich verweise hier auf die Szene [10.2 im Szenenprotokoll] zwischen Studienrat Stern und Hauptmann Fröhlich, in der Hauptmann Fröhlich den Lehrer daran erinnert, dass Hölderlins Gedichte, wie etwa die *Ode an die Unsterblichkeit* und *Der Tod fürs Vaterland,* die er im Unterricht mit seinen Schülern bespricht, die im 3. Reich groß werdenden Kinder den Tod auf dem Schlachtfeld idealisieren und so froh in die Schlacht ziehen lässt [0:42:53].

[33]   Siehe z.B. das Duell zwischen Henry Fonda and Charles Bronson in Sergio Leones *C'era una volt ail West,* der international, aber auch gerade in Deutschland unter dem Titel *Spiel mir das Lied vom Tod* (1968) große Erfolge erzielte.

[34]   Richard Blank: Jenseits der Brücke: Berhard Wicki. Ein Leben für den Film. München: Econ, 1999, S. 102.

[35]   Produktionsnotizen, zitiert im Begleitheft zum Film, S. 52.

[36]   Siehe Produktionsnotizen im Begleitheft, S. 52.

[37]   Der TV-Event-Movie für ProSieben kostete 3.4 Millionen Euro und wurde in 30 Drehtagen (Sept/Okt 2007) in Lettland gedreht. Siehe Audio-Kommentar von Wolfgang Panzer und dem Produzent Marian Redmann.

von den tatsächlichen Ereignissen, die Gregor Dorfmeister in seinem Interview beschreibt.[38] Zwar ist Albert auch in Panzers Verfilmung der einzig Überlebende, aber als Bombenflüchtling ein Außenseiter; Walter Forst ist das letzte Opfer und stirbt in den Armen seiner Lehrerin (gespielt von Franke Potente), die zugleich seine Geliebte ist. Die sieben Jungen, die zum Teil eher wie ausgewachsene Männer aussehen (und zum Zeitpunkt der Dreharbeiten schon um die 20 sind), interessieren sich für Sex, begehen Diebstahl, und werden insgesamt mit Ausnahme vom Außenseiter Albert in aller Oberflächlichkeit eher negativ gezeichnet. Untersucht man den Film in Hinblick auf die Verwendung von Nahaufnahmen, wird deutlich, dass Nahen und Großaufnahmen von der Anfangssequenz an als den Film vermeintlich bewegende Elemente eingesetzt werden. Durch ihre Undifferenziertheit und Beliebigkeit verpufft die potentielle Zeichensetzung der Aufnahme jedoch im Moment ihres Erscheinens und markiert so die nahe Einstellung nicht als bedeutungsvoll sondern als Kitsch.

Albert Mutz (gespielt von François Goeske) sitzt zu Beginn des Films ordentlich in HJ-Uniform gekleidet in einem ‚Kraft durch Freude' Lastwagen, der ihn in die Kleinstadt bringt, und blickt durch ein Loch in der Plane. Er erscheint wiederholt in halbnahen Einstellungen und auch Großaufnahmen, unterbrochen von Blicken in die vorbeiziehende Landschaft, einem Schwenk vorbei an den weiteren Fahrgästen und der ersten von zahlreichen Detailaufnahmen dieses Films: die Uhr des Jungen – die Zeiger stehen auf 5 vor 12 [0:01:17]. Kurz danach der harte Schnitt zur Brücke [0:01:27] und in die melodisch-phrasenhafte Musik von Filippo Trecca, die eben noch nach einer kitschigen Rosamunde Pilcher Verfilmung für das deutsche Fernsehen klang, mischen sich Marschklänge und dunklere Töne. Die Brücke wird als Ort der Bedrohung gekennzeichnet und die Zeit auf der Uhr verweist zumindest umgangssprachlich auf gebotene Eile. Wofür, bleibt unklar. Der Lastwagen fährt in die Kleinstadt und bringt „wieder eine Ladung Bombenflüchtlinge" [0:02:10], wie eine seufzende Anwohnerin feststellt. Albert Mutz ist in dieser Verfilmung zusammen mit seiner Mutter unter den Flüchtlingen und wird bei Familie Fink untergebracht. Die Tochter der Familie Paula Fink (gespielt von Paula Schramm) wird nicht nur seine Klassenkameradin sondern auch Alberts Freundin. Im Gegensatz zu Wickis Verfilmung endet Wolfgang Panzers Film mit der Wiedervereinigung der Liebenden, die sich nach überlebtem Kampf glücklich und erschöpft in die Arme sinken. Bei Gregor Dorfmeister läuft Albert allein nach Hause, denkt an jeden seiner toten Freunde, an Selbstmord, aber auch an seine Mutter und – hier klingt die Panzer Verfilmung an – an „das Mädchen Traudl und fühlte eine tiefe Zärtlichkeit. Sie würden sich ihr Leben gestalten, wenn das alles einmal vorbei wäre" (S. 209).

Die Nah-, Groß-, und sogar Detailaufnahmen in Panzers Film sind kaum motiviert und die Kamera differenziert nicht zwischen einem Jungen, der in die Landschaft blickt, und einem, der sich vor Schmerzen und Angst windet oder im

---

[38] Die Brücke (2008) DVD, Bonusmaterial.

Sterben liegt. Allein in den ersten zehn Minuten des Films richtet sich die Kamera neunzehnmal nah auf das Gesicht eines der Protagonisten. Albert wird als zentrale Gestalt auch visuell betont, aber die Sexszenen zwischen Walter Forst (gespielt vom 22-jährigen Lars Steinhöfel) und seiner Lehrerin Elfie Bauer (Franka Potente) sind im Kontext der Nah- und Großaufnahmen der Gesichter gleichwertig.

Schon nach fünfzehn Filmminuten kommt Standartenführer Forst in die Klasse und ruft die sieben Jungs dazu auf, „den Führer und das Vaterland zu verteidigen" und sich am nächsten Morgen bei der Kommandozentrale der deutschen Wehrmacht zu melden. Außer Albert, der als Flüchtling den Krieg schon kennen gelernt hat, und Walter, der seinen Vater wie in Roman und Erstverfilmung hasst, sind alle begeistert. Nach einer kurzen Ausbildung durch Ernst Scholten, hier ein Napola-Ausgebildeter,[39] stehen die Jungen allein nachts auf der dunklen Brücke. Am nächsten Morgen fällt eine Bombe in den Fluss – eine Hommage an die Anfangssequenz bei Bernhard Wicki –, doch wird hier schon Siegi in einer sonst eng an dem Roman und Wickis Verfilmung orientierten Szene durch einen Splitter dieser Bombe tödlich verletzt. Zwar wird Siegis Gesicht in Nahaufnahme gezeigt, als er seinen Kopf nach dem Fehlalarm wieder hebt und seine Kameraden ihn verspotten [0:36:40], doch als er blutend auf dem Boden liegt, bleibt die Kamera im Vergleich distanziert. Denn in dieser Verfilmung geht es weniger um die Sinnlosigkeit und Zerstörungskraft des Krieges als um den Mut und Kampfeswillen dieser Jugendlichen.

Bei aller Beliebigkeit, die in der Wahl der Kameraeinstellungen wiederholt deutlich wird, lässt sich feststellen, dass im Kontext der Kampfszenen der Einsatz von Großaufnahmen die Wirkung des Einsatzwillens dieser deutschen Jungen auf beunruhigende Weise hervorhebt. Entgegen Wickis Erstverfilmung und Dorfmeisters Roman werden die Vorbereitungen auf der Brücke von einem Abstecher des verliebten Alberts zu seiner Paula [0:48:38] und von Verhören wegen der Verführung Minderjähriger, die die Lehrerin nach einer Anzeige über sich ergehen lassen muss, sowie ihren Versuchen die Jugendlichen zu retten, unterbrochen. In der mittlerweile dritten Nacht – die jungen deutschen Soldaten scheinen nun beinahe konstant unter Beschuss, haben aber noch immer keine weiteren Toten zu beklagen – verweist Panzer wiederholt auf ihr Durchhaltevermögen, wobei die floskelhafte Filmmusik stets die Spannung und das auf deutscher Seite implizierte Heldentum unterstützt. Letzteres gilt aber nur für die Hitlerjugend, nicht für die Befehlshaber, die entweder im Eigeninteresse die Jugend opfern oder betrunken dem Kriegsende entgegensehen. Nur die Jungen sind wirklich entschlossen, ihren Auftrag für den Führer zu erfüllen.

Eine zentrale Szene, die dem Regisseur nach eigener Aussage besonders am Herzen lag, stellt den Kampf zwischen Walter und einem amerikanischen GI dar. Im Schuss-Gegenschuss-Verfahren werden die beiden geschickt verknüpft, und als

---

[39]   Eine Referenz auf die tatsächlichen, von Gregor Dorfmeister im Interview beschriebenen Ereignisse. Siehe Fußnote 6.

Walter den Zweikampf gewinnt und das Gewehr auf den vor ihm liegenden GI richtet, sehen sich in zwei Nahaufnahmen ähnlich junge Gesichter an. Walter verschont den amerikanischen Soldaten, der sich zur Seite dreht und weint [1:10:32]. Walter wird hier in einer halbnahen Einstellung von unten gefilmt, das mit Brandwunden übersäte Gesicht wirkt gefestigt und nicht unsensibel und gleicht in schockierend unkritischer Weise dem Bild eines jungen deutschen Helden. In dem der DVD-Version angehängten Interview weist Wolfgang Panzer darauf hin, wie wichtig ihm gerade diese Szene war und die Tatsache, dass der deutsche Soldat, den amerikanischen GI nicht einfach „absticht": Obgleich er „sich nachher als Feigling [fühlt], [...] ist doch das durchgekommen, was richtig war in ihm". Wir haben es also mit einem guten Deutschen zu tun, betont der Regisseur. Nach dem Kampf robbt Walter zurück zum Gefechtsstand, scheint getroffen, seine Kameraden sind erschüttert und einer der Jungs beginnt in Nahaufnahme zu weinen. Doch da zeigt Wolfgang Panzer uns schon den auf der Straße liegenden Walter, der verschmitzt in die Kamera blickt und seinen Kameraden die ‚thumbs up' gibt [1:13:14] – so leicht ist dieser ‚deutsche Held' natürlich nicht umzubringen. Mit heroischer Musikuntermalung springt er auf und rennt über die Straße, das Gesicht eines seiner Kameraden geht in Großaufnahme von Trauer zu Begeisterung über, die anderen geben ihm Deckung, und wir sehen das ratternde Maschinengewehr in einer Detailaufnahme.[40] Ganz im Gegensatz zu dem Roman und der Erstverfilmung wird hier ein Team gezeigt, das gut organisiert ist und militärisch effektiv handelt. Walter kann sich erfolgreich in Sicherheit bringen [1:13:32], schreit vor Begeisterung und trommelt sich wie Tarzan auf die Brust. Nur Albert äußert Kritik in Anbetracht des halsbrecherischen Manövers, doch Walter antwortet: „Jetzt sei mal nicht so zimperlich. Es hat Spaß gemacht!" [1:13:45]

Als Paula die Amerikaner darüber informiert, dass es sich in dem Gefechtsstand um „Kinder" handelt,[41] und – in Anlehnung an Bernhard Wickis Verfilmung – das Feuer eingestellt wird und ein amerikanischer Soldat versucht, die Kinder zur Aufgabe zu bewegen, will nur Albert kapitulieren. Wir sehen Ernst, der als Scharfschütze im Baum Stellung bezogen hat, in Großaufnahme. Erst nimmt er konzentriert die Muttergottes-Statue im Haus gegenüber ins Visier und bald schon schießt er auf den unbewaffneten Amerikaner [1:18:15]. Den schreiend am Boden liegenden GI sehen die Zuschauer bei Bernhard Wicki in Großaufnahme, sekundenlang ruht die Kamera auf dem schmerzverzerrten Gesicht. Wolfgang Panzer vermeidet eine affektive Kameraeinstellung und zeigt den schreienden Amerikaner nur aus der Entfernung, bis er von einem Sanitäter aus dem Bildausschnitt gezerrt wird. Sein Gesicht bleibt unsichtbar und auch jede weitere dramatische Bildverknüpfung mit dem deutschen Schützen und seinem Opfer wird

---

[40] Detailaufnahmen der Waffen, vor allem des MG Abzugs tauchen an mehreren Stellen im Film auf.

[41] „They are kids, they are children, they are my friends!" [1:14:45]

vermieden. Auf diese Weise wird die Verantwortung des Jungen für seine Tat zumindest cinematographisch für unerheblich erklärt.

Am dritten Morgen [1:25:00] erwacht Walter, dessen Gesicht und Oberkörper wir in Nahaufnahme sehen, voller Angst: „Wir haben kein funktionierendes MG mehr, keine Munition, jetzt kommen sie und machen uns kalt" [1:25:52]. Diese Szene wird wiederum untermalt von tragischer Musik und die affektive Wirkung in Verbindung mit dem von Brandwunden gezeichneten, erschöpften jungen Mann ist Mitleid, der Held wird nun zum Opfer. Doch zum Glück haben sich die amerikanischen Truppen zurückgezogen. Napola-Ernst will noch eine Panzerfaust holen und explodiert, sein toter Körper landet vor der Kamera, ein Arm ist abgerissen und die Schulter blutet in die Pfütze, auch hier mit tragisch-pathetischer Filmmusik untermalt. Erst auf der Brücke, die Walter „unser bestes Stück" nennt, fragt Albert: „War's das wert?" und zählt zum ersten Mal die Namen der Opfer auf: Siegi, Jürgen, Klaus, Karl, Ernst. Doch für Walter zählt nur die Brücke und es überrascht nicht, dass es mit dem Sprengkommando – wie bei Dorfmeister und Wicki – zur letzten Auseinandersetzung kommt. Als Walter mit Bauchschuss auf dem Gehsteig liegt [1:31:20], kommt seine Lehrerin angelaufen,. Die Nahaufnahme, in der man sie zuerst nur bis zum Knie sieht, wirkt deplaziert, denn zu diesem Zeitpunkt liegt der Fokus sicherlich nicht auf ihrer Körperlichkeit oder sexuellen Anziehungskraft. Auf Walters „Ich hab's geschafft" antwortet sie bestätigend „Ja, das hast du" [1:33:06] und unterstreicht so noch einmal die Sinnhaftigkeit dieses sinnlosen Unternehmens. Traurige Lamentationen begleiten musikalisch die Großaufnahmen der beiden Gesichter, als Walter stirbt. Die Amerikaner marschieren langsam über die Brücke, die Kamera schwenkt an den Gesichtern der Soldaten vorbei; Albert geht in die entgegengesetzte Richtung, vorbei am Gefechtsstand, wo ihm Paula barfuß entgegenläuft, vor der er weinend zusammenbricht. Der Film endet mit dem weinenden Gesicht Alberts in Großaufnahme [1:36:00]. Die vom Regisseur gewählte Verbindung aus stereotypischem *close-up* und musikalischer Untermalung, die den Zuschauern Trauer über den Tod der Helden suggeriert und ihn gleichzeitig problemlos konsumierbar gestaltet, erreicht in der tröstenden Vereinigung der Liebenden in der Schlusssequenz ihren kitschigen Höhepunkt.

Im Gegensatz zu dieser letzten Einstellung, die junge Liebe und zukünftige Idylle suggeriert, erzählt Gregor Dorfmeister im Interview von seiner tatsächlichen Rückkehr auf die Brücke am 2. Mai 1945, nachdem er sich zu Hause ausreichend ausgeschlafen hatte. Auf der Brücke findet er die Leichen seines Freundes Knut und des Napola-Ausgebildeten. Zu seiner Erschütterung spuckt eine schwarz gekleidete Frau, die über die Brücke geht, die Leichen an, und Gregor Dorfmeister erklärt, dass diese „Geste der Verachtung" den ursprünglichen Auslöser für den Roman *Die Brücke* gegeben hat. Die Frage, die sich ihm zu dieser Zeit stellte, war: „Warum versteht uns keiner?" Jahre später war der Roman zu einem Denkmal für die so jung gefallenen, tapferen Soldaten geworden und eine implizite Kritik an dem Regime, das diese Opfer zu verantworten hatte. Wolfgang Panzers Film scheint der Versuch, die verachtende Geste der alten Frau auszulöschen, indem die sieben Vertreter der Hitlerjugend hier zu letztlich unschuldigen Helden gemacht werden. Das Resultat, das den „Geist der Vorlage erhalten" wollte, wie der Produzent Marian Redmann im Kommentar erklärt, ist ein schlechter, desorientierter Film, dessen unkritische Haltung gegenüber der Hitlerjugend und Heldenideologie des NS-Regimes beunruhigt.

Bernhard Wicki, der immer von der emotionalen und suggestiven Kraft von Film überzeugt war, sagte einmal: „Film kann die Welt nicht verändern oder verbessern, er kann aber Stimmung schaffen."[42] Er zeigt uns in seinem Antikriegsfilm vor Angst und Schmerz verzerrte und tote Kindergesichter und lässt durch Großaufnahmen die Gesichter seiner Protagonisten zu Zeichen werden.[43] Als epistemologische Wegweiser lassen sie die Haltung des Films stets durchschimmern. Und obgleich sich Gregor Dorfmeisters Geschichte in ihrer Haltung von Bernhard Wickis Verfilmung unterscheidet, lebt sie im Benjaminschen Sinne gerade durch diese Verfilmung ‚fort'.[44]

In der zweiten Verfilmung von Dorfmeisters Roman unter der Regie von Wolfgang Panzer, die in ihrer Oberflächlichkeit und Beliebigkeit sowohl den Sinn des Romans als auch der Wicki Verfilmung verfälscht, schlagen sich „entwertet[e] Formen und Floskeln" nieder, die trotz ihrer Plakativität manipulativ auf die Zuschauer einwirken sollen, ganz gemäß Theodor W. Adornos Definition von Kitsch.[45]

Wickis Verfilmung hingegen, die uns in wenigen, präzise bestimmten Augenblicken ganz nah an die Kriegserfahrung dieser jungen Menschen heranrückt und uns die Wirkung von Krieg auf das Individuum begreifen lässt, hat die Geschichte erneuert und im Antikriegsfilmgenre ihr ‚Fortleben' gesichert. Wie eine Übersetzung – um nochmals auf Walter Benjamin zu verweisen –, die das Original in neuer und veränderter Form weiterträgt, ist der autobiographische Roman Gregor Dorfmeisters durch Bernhard Wickis Verfilmung im Sinne André Bazins „multipliziert" worden.[46] In diesem spezifischen Fall könnte man sogar sagen, dass

---

[42] Bernhard Wicki, zitiert in: Die Brücke Begleitheft, S. 2.

[43] Mary Ann Doane verweist auf Sergei Eisensteins Auseinandersetzung mit Film und vor allem der Nahaufnahme als Vehikel der Wahrnehmung; siehe Sergei Eisenstein: Film Form: Essays in Film Theory. Hg. und übers. Jay Leyda. San Diego: Harcourt, 1949.

[44] Siehe Walter Benjamin: „Denn in seinem Fortleben, das so nicht heißen dürfte, wenn es nicht Wandlung und Erneuerung des Lebendigen wäre, ändert sich das Original." Walter Benjamin: Die Aufgabe des Übersetzers. In: Benjamin: Illuminationen. Frankfurt a.M.: Suhrkamp, 1977, S. 50-67, hier S. 53.

[45] Theodor W. Adorno: Kitsch. In: Adorno: Gesammelte Schriften. Hg. Rolf Tiedemann. Bd. 18. Darmstadt: Wissenschaftliche Buchgesellschaft, 1998, S. 791-94, hier S. 791.

[46] André Bazin setzt sich in zwei Aufsätzen, die Anfang der 1950er Jahre in den *Cahiers du Cinema* erschienen, mit Verfilmung, bzw. deren Erfolg als Kunstwerk auseinander. Vor allem in „Journal d'un cure de campagne", in dem er die Dialektik zwischen Literatur und Film anhand von Robert Bressons gleichnamiger Verfilmung von 1951 des 1937 erschienenen Romans von Georges Bernanos untersucht, aber auch in „Pour un cinéma

der Roman erst durch die Verfilmung Bernhard Wickis zum Kunstwerk wurde und in die Filmgeschichte einging. Ein Platz, der Wolfgang Panzers kitschiger Verfilmung sicherlich verwehrt bleiben wird.

Christiane Schönfeld is Head of German Studies at Mary Immaculate College, University of Limerick.

impur: defense de l'adaption" verteidigt er Verfilmungen als das Kino potentiell bereichernde Kunstform. Siehe auch André Bazin: Qu'est-ce que le cinema? Paris: Cerf, 1975. Bazin wird u.a. zitiert in Robert Giddings: Screening the Novel, S. 13. Siehe auch Christiane Schönfeld: Introduction. In: Christiane Schönfeld (Hg.): Processes of Transposition: German Literature and Film. Amsterdam and New York: Rodopi, 2007, S. 11-26, hier S. 25f.

Ates Gürpinar

Das Kapital adaptieren?

Als Beispiele für Grenzfälle einer Adaption können die Überlegungen in Sergej Eisensteins Notizen zur Verfilmung von Karl Marx' *Das Kapital* wie auch Alexander Kluges 9,5-stündiger Film *Nachrichten aus der ideologischen Antike: Marx – Eisenstein – Das Kapital* gelten. Wenn auch die Frage naheliegen mag, ob Kluges Film eine Adaption darstellt, zeigt sich gerade aufgrund der nicht gänzlich passenden Begriffe *Adaption* und *Film*, welche eben nicht das gesamte Projekt umfassen, eine andere Sicht auf das Prinzip der Adaption. Die Analyse eines bisher unbeachteten Grenzfalls ermöglicht für gewöhnlich eine Bewusstwerdung bzw. eine Hinterfragung einer Definition und erfordert eine neue Distinktion: Entweder dieser Grenzfall wird aktiv ein- oder eindeutig ausgeschlossen; auch wenn der Grenzfall als ein solcher bestehen bleibt, wird neu reflektiert, welche Veränderung der Definition diesen Grenzfall dann aus- oder eben einschließen würde. In den folgenden Seiten soll jedoch nicht in erster Linie ein ‚Begriffskampf' geführt werden. Vielmehr wird versucht, anhand des konkreten Beispiels bei Kluge und der Reflexion zu den Überlegungen einer Adaption des *Kapitals* durch Sergej Eisenstein die Idee der Transformierung und Adaptierung innerhalb verschiedener Medien und Gattungen[1] zu analysieren und zu verstehen. Eine eventuell vorzuschlagende Neudefinierung wird an dieser Stelle nicht angestrebt und wäre ein nächster Schritt.

Als These kann festgehalten werden, dass die Anpassung an ein neues Medium eine ähnliche Form in diesem Medium benötigt. Damit wird der üblichen Umschreibung, dass eine Adaption eine Übertragung eines bestimmten Stoffes oder Themas ist, nicht entsprochen, da der Stoff eben nur über das Medium und die Gattung erst fasslich werden kann oder weitergehend der Stoff bzw. das Thema ohne bestimmte ähnliche Gattungen gar nicht zu denken ist.

Als zweite These lässt sich eine doppelte Bedeutung einer Anpassung ausmachen: Adaptionen sind Anpassungen an das neue Medium, die ansonsten übliche Form in dem neuen Medium benötigt jedoch eine Anpassung an die Form des ursprünglichen Mediums.

---

[1] Aufgrund des interdisziplinären Charakters der Arbeit wäre eine Klärung der genauen Begriffe zwar wünschenswert, kann aber in diesem Rahmen nicht geleistet werden. Insbesondere der Charakter der *Gattung* in Unterscheidung beispielsweise zum *Format* oder zum *Genre* wäre näher zu analysieren. Ich werde mich hier im Bezug auf den Text auf den Begriff ‚Gattung' beschränken und mit dem Begriff ‚Genre' ausschließlich auf das Medium Film Bezug nehmen.

Der Adaptionsversuch Sergej Eisensteins

Eisensteins Filmüberlegungen zum *Kapital* sind von Relevanz, weil sie einen nicht durchgeführten ersten Adaptionsversuch darstellen und Arbeitsüberlegungen Eisensteins wiedergeben, die teilweise dann bei Kluge reflektiert und berücksichtigt werden. Die auch in Kluges Werk wiederholt aufgegriffenen Zitate Eisensteins beschreiben eigentlich eine größere Bindung seines Werks an das *Kapital* als die eines Originals an seine Adaption. Eisenstein beschreibt in seinen Notizen, dass der Entschluss feststehe, „das ‚Kapital' nach dem Szenarium von K. Marx zu verfilmen",[2] und begreift sein zukünftiges Werk als eine Arbeit „nach dem Libretto von Karl Marx".[3] Die Begriffe „Szenarium" und „Libretto" lassen aufhorchen, da Eisenstein damit einerseits die gewöhnliche normative Wertung der defizitären Adaption umdreht und sein geplantes Werk sogar als ein Vollständigeres begreift,[4] andererseits aber ein intermediales Konzept insofern voraussetzt, als dass bei beiden Begriffen, anders als bei der Adaption, eine Bindung an bzw. ein Bezug zur medialen Transformation besteht. Szenarien wie Libretti liegen in anderen Medien und Gattungen vor als das endgültige Werk. Es existiert also jeweils eine Vorlage, eine mediale Ordnung, die in einem anderen Medium eine andere Ordnung verlangt, deren Übertragung aber möglich ist, ohne dass die konkrete Form sich verliert. Zumindest das Libretto, aber auch das Szenarium scheint wieder in seine ursprüngliche mediale Form rückübertragbar zu sein.

Da Eisenstein seine Idee nicht verwirklicht hat, fehlt die analysierbare Adaption. Auch wenn den wenigen Aufzeichnungen, Notizen und Ideen Eisensteins zur Verfilmung des *Kapitals* zwar sicherlich aufgrund ihres Themas ein zu hoher Stellenwert zugesprochen wird,[5] lassen sie Überlegungen hinsichtlich der Spezifizität und Schwierigkeit dieses Adaptionsversuchs zu. Hieran und an weiteren Überlegungen Eisensteins zur Filmsprache lässt sich feststellen, wo einerseits die Möglichkeiten und Grenzen einer Adaption bestehen, wie andererseits jedoch die Anpassung eines solchen Werks funktionieren kann.

Eisenstein geht davon aus, dass „[a]us dem ‚Kapital' [...] endlos Themen kinofiziert werden [können] (‚Mehrwert', ‚Preis', ‚Profit'). Wir wollen das Thema

---

[2] Vgl. Sergej M. Eisenstein: Notate zu einer Verfilmung des Marxschen ‚Kapital'. In: Eisenstein: Schriften. Hg. Hans-Joachim Schlegel. Band III: Oktober. Mit den Notaten zur Verfilmung von Marx ‚Kapital'. München: Hanser 1975, S. 289-315, hier S. 289.

[3] Eisenstein: Notate, S. 290.

[4] Im Vergleich zum Original wird die Adaption häufig geringer und nach der Nähe zum Original bewertet, was sicherlich seinen Ursprung bei Platon hat. Im Gegensatz dazu können in den meisten Diskursen sowohl Libretti als auch Szenarien zwar ‚gut' sein, ihnen fehlt aber etwas zur wirklichen Komplettierung. Allerdings hat das Szenarium für gewöhnlich einen noch technischeren Charakter, während dem Libretto als solchem schon ein poetischer Charakter und damit eine ästhetische Form zugesprochen wird.

[5] Die Aufzeichnungen, die auf *Das Kapital* hindeuten, sind im Vergleich zum sonstigen Werk Eisensteins rein quantitativ eher dürftig und erhalten ihre Relevanz sicherlich vor allem aufgrund der Prominenz der Personen Marx und Eisenstein in der Sowjetunion.

der *Marxschen Methode* kinofizieren".[6] Insbesondere der letzte Satz deutet aber schon durch den Begriff der „Methode" über die reine Behandlung von Marx' Thema in einem Film hinaus darauf hin, eine filmische Form finden zu wollen, die einer wie auch immer zu beschreibenden Marx'schen Methode entspricht. Die Entwicklung einer neuen Filmsprache, welche ich als Form – innerhalb des Mediums Film – begreifen möchte, ist dann auch eines seiner erklärten Ziele. Allerdings ist in diesem Punkt ein Problem festzustellen, dass Eisenstein zu übersehen scheint oder nicht klärt. Dieses besteht darin, dass Eisenstein nach einer neuen Filmsprache bzw. vielmehr auf einer semiotischen Ebene Neues sucht, während die so bezeichnete Marx'sche Methode keine in der Form neue, sondern eine typisch wissenschaftliche ist. Es finden sich bei Marx sowohl auf Zeichenebene wie auch auf Gattungsebene keine ‚neuen' Formen, sondern, dies stellt auch Stollmann in der Verfilmung Kluges heraus, wissenschaftliche Arbeitsweisen im Geist der Zeit, ein Text, der der wissenschaftlichen Gattung zugeordnet werden kann.[7]

Insbesondere ist das dialektische Montageprinzip zu berücksichtigen, das Eisenstein zu etablieren sucht und welches zumindest der Sprache nach eine Übertragung einer bestimmten Methode in den Film bedeutete. Ob diese Dialektik dem wissenschaftlichen, ebenfalls schwer als Methode zu begreifenden dialektischen Gestus entspricht, soll hier nicht weiter analysiert werden. Mir erscheint ein anderes Merkmal wichtiger, da Eisenstein abgesehen von der dialektischen Methode keine spezifisch Marx'sche, sondern eine wissenschaftliche Methode bzw. Sprache für den Film etablieren möchte. Seine Überlegungen für eine Wissenschaftssprache im Film zeigen sich hier als charakteristisch für mediale Vermittlung generell, indem sie einem typischen Wunsch in der Medienentwicklung folgen, dem Streben nach der Auflösung von *langue* und *parole*, welches Hartmut

---

[6] Eisenstein: Notate, S. 307.
[7] Die Bezeichnung ‚wissenschaftlich' bedürfte einer genaueren Erläuterung, selbstverständlich unterscheidet sich der Anspruch an Wissenschaftlichkeit von der heutigen typisch wissenschaftlichen Veröffentlichung. Stollmann beschreibt die Anlehnung an naturwissenschaftliche Arbeiten (vgl. Alexander Kluge: DVD III: Paradoxe der Tauschgesellschaft. In: Kluge: Nachrichten aus der ideologischen Antike. Marx – Eisenstein – Das Kapital. Frankfurt a.M.: Filmedition Suhrkamp 2008). Auch wenn man die Hegel'sche Dialektik als Methode begreifen möchte, die Marx allerdings nicht durchgängig übernimmt, wäre diese nicht neu. Die Debatte um die Methode und den Stil von Marx kann hier allerdings nicht wiedergegeben werden (vgl. hierzu Ingo Elbe, Tobias Reichardt und Dieter Wolf: Gesellschaftliche Praxis und ihre wissenschaftliche Darstellung. Beiträge zur Kapital-Diskussion. Berlin: Argument 2008). Häufig werden Marx rhetorische Mittel unterstellt, die für gewöhnlich nicht mit Wissenschaftlichkeit in Verbindung gebracht werden (vgl. Francis Wheen: Karl Marx. München: Wilhelm Goldmann 2002, S. 349-74 und auch Stollmann erwähnt neben der Wissenschaftlichkeit noch andere Formen).

Winkler beschreibt.[8] Winkler geht von der Annahme aus, „daß die Dynamik der Medienentwicklung in bestimmten Wunschstrukturen ihre Ursache hat und daß die Mediengeschichte beschreibbare Sets impliziter Utopien verfolgt".[9] Diese Suche nach einer *Eindeutigkeit*, welche ich zwar nicht als allgemeinen Antrieb der Mediengeschichte beschreiben würde,[10] die sich aber sicherlich häufig bei der Entwicklung der Wissenschaftssprache nachweisen lässt, wird bei Eisenstein insbesondere in den Beschreibungen der intellektuellen Montage deutlich. Bestimmte Montagen und Rhythmen, dies vermittelt Eisenstein des Öfteren, sollten eindeutig sein. Dies bestätigt auch Schmitz, wenn er schreibt, dass Eisenstein die

> Wahrnehmung [des Zuschauers] möglichst eindeutig [...] zu organisieren trachtet, z.B. bei der präzisen Kalkulation der Einstellungsdauer, wenn nämlich der zeitliche Abstand zwischen den Schnitten immer von der Vermittlung des sachlichen Gehalts oder eines klaren emotionalen Werts bestimmt wird.[11]

Nach ihm gehe es um eine „Vereindeutigung zur Steigerung der Effizienz der Publikumswahrnehmung [...]. Aus dem szientistischen Anspruch des Konstruktivisten folgert also für die filmische Form eine Tendenz zur Vereinfachung als Vereindeutigung".[12]

Das deckt sich mit dem von Eisenstein häufig genannten Streben, eine Synthese von Wissenschaft und Kunst zu versuchen.[13] Die ständige Kommentierung bzw. Benennung der Bedeutung in Beiwerken verweist jedoch gerade darauf, dass diese eben nicht selbsterklärend und eindeutig sind. Eisenstein bespricht viele einzelne Szenen und Montagen in Sekundärtexten, die eine eindeutige Rezeptionshaltung aufzeigen sollen, aber erst durch seine ,Nachlieferung' des Sinns eindeutig werden, einfach dadurch, dass sie schon gedeutet sind.[14] Diese Kommentierung seiner eigenen Werke verweist auf die eigentlich selbstverständliche Notwendigkeit, eine neue Sprache erst einmal übersetzen zu müssen, bevor man sie benutzen kann. Obgleich er seiner Filmsprache eine Natürlichkeit zuspricht und damit nahelegt,

---

[8]   Vgl. Hartmut Winkler: Docuverse. Zur Medientheorie der Computer. München: Boers 1997, S. 49. Dass die bei Winkler besondere Verwendung dieser Begriffe hinterfragt werden müsste, soll hier nicht diskutiert werden.

[9]   Winkler: Docuverse, S. 17.

[10] Winkler stellt seine Überlegungen bezüglich einer gesamten Mediengeschichte an, denen ich kritisch begegne. Vgl. Ates Gürpinar: Von Kittler zu Latour. Beziehung von Mensch und Technik in Theorien der Medienwissenschaft. Siegen: universi 2012, S. 61-63.

[11] Norbert M. Schmitz: Das Historienbild lebt weiter. Historizität und Medialität in interdisziplinärer Perspektive. In: Fabio Crivellari et al. (Hg.): Die Medien der Geschichte. Konstanz: Universitätsverlag Konstanz 2004, S. 297–316, hier S. 306.

[12] Schmitz: Historienbild, S. 306.

[13] Sergej M. Eisenstein: Dramaturgie der Film-Form. Der dialektische Zugang zur Film-Form. In: Franz Josef Albersmeier: Texte zur Theorie des Films. 5., durchgesehene und erweiterte Auflage. Stuttgart: Reclam, S. 275-304, hier S. 301.

[14] Vgl. Eisenstein: Dramaturgie, S. 289-301.

dass sein Werk ,von sich aus' verständlich sei, muss er seine Filme mit vielerlei Interpretationen, Kommentaren und Erklärungen verschalten, um dieses Werk erst zugänglich und diese neue Sprache verstehbar zu machen. Diese liegen alle als Schrift vor, nicht als Film. Er übersetzt diese Filme, deren Sprache er als organischer behauptet, mühevoll zurück in Schriftsprache, um sie dem Zuschauer verständlich zu machen. Für das neue, eigentlich Bezeichnende, muss er eine andere, bekannte Sprache finden, um dieses Neue verstehbar zu machen. Damit wird das, was eigentlich Bezeichnendes sein soll, aber automatisch Bezeichnetes. Dahingehend liegt Siegfried Kracauer richtig, wenn er davon ausgeht, dass der Zuschauer die Bedeutung der verschiedenen Bildaneinanderreihungen in Eisensteins Filmen nicht verstehen wird, und Eisenstein mit einem eigentlich altbekannten Prinzip sprachlicher Zeichen kritisiert: der Arbitrarität: „Eisenstein überschätzt die Symbolkraft von Bildern und setzt daher alles daran, das von ihnen Gemeinte willkürlich mit Bedeutungen seiner eigenen Wahl zu überlagern."[15] Diese Propagierung einer eindeutigen Lesbarkeit in Kombination mit einer ständigen Kommentierung bestätigt auch Ian Christie, der Eisenstein selbst als den „first and most persuasive expert on ,Eisenstein'" bezeichnet.[16] Gewissermaßen übersetzt er seine Filme, um sie eindeutig lesbar zu machen. Eisenstein lädt also in seinen schriftlichen Texten die Symbole, semiotisch verstanden eben auf Konventionen beruhende arbiträre Zeichen, mit Bedeutung auf und benennt diese Bedeutung in seinen schriftlichen Texten, also bekannten Formen, einfach selbst, welche dem Rezipienten immer nur zum Teil schlüssig erscheinen. Gleichzeitig sucht er aber nach einer Form für einen rein intellektuellen Film, „der – befreit von traditioneller Bedingtheit – ohne jede Transition und Umschreibung direkte Formen für Gedanken, Systeme und Begriffe erzielen wird".[17]

Aber Eisensteins Versuch einer neuen Filmsprache, die eine Eindeutigkeit aufweisen soll, geht einher mit dem allgemeinen Gedanken wissenschaftlicher Gattungen, Eindeutigkeit und Stringenz zu erzeugen. Hiermit ist ihm interessanterweise in gewisser Hinsicht auch Erfolg beschieden: Der Vergleich der Texte Eisensteins mit anderen Autoren, die seine Filme analysierten, zeigt, dass vieles von Eisensteins eigener Filmanalyse als Basis übernommen wurde.[18]

Auf Inhaltsebene eher anschaulichen Charakter haben die simplen Geschichten, die Eisenstein sich als Grundlage überlegt, die eben durch ihre Narration eine

---

[15] Siegfried Kracauer: Theorie des Films. Die Errettung der äußeren Wirklichkeit. Frankfurt a.M.: Suhrkamp 1985, S. 278.

[16] Ian Christie: Introduction. Rediscovering Eisenstein. In: Ian Christie und Richard Taylor (Hg.): Eisenstein Rediscovered. London: Routledge 1993, S. 1-30, hier S. 3.

[17] Eisenstein: Dramaturgie, S. 301.

[18] Ob dies dem von de Saussure postulierten Gedanken widerspricht, der nicht an eine Einflussmöglichkeit von Individuen auf Sprache glaubt (vgl. Ferdinand de Saussure: Grundfragen der allgemeinen Sprachwissenschaft. 2. Auflage. De Gruyter: Berlin 1967, S. 87; 90), sei dahingestellt, weil sich dennoch das Montageprinzip von Eisenstein nur bedingt durchgesetzt hat.

Bedeutung innehaben und einen Bezug herstellen zu manchen Themen des *Kapitals*, die er schlicht und einfach wiederum selbst benennt: Eisenstein kritisiert z.b. die Linderung von ‚sozialer' Aufgebrachtheit, indem er eine Geschichte erzählt, in der eine Frau für ihren arbeitenden Mann Suppe bereitet. Mit der Befriedigung durch die Mahlzeit lasse die für die Revolution notwendige Wut nach.[19] Hier wird jedoch auch deutlich, worauf später bei Kluge noch einzugehen sein wird, dass die Erzählung nicht nur als Veranschaulichung von Marx gelten kann, sondern dass das marxistische Denken als bekannt vorausgesetzt wird und die Erzählung selbst eher das Prinzip eines Beispiels verfolgt: Dem Zuschauer würde allein durch das Beispiel nicht bewusst, dass die warme Suppe nicht förderlich ist, wenn er die grundlegenden Prinzipien marxistischen Denkens nicht schon verstanden hätte.

Den Eisenstein'schen Diskurs an dieser Stelle abschließend, zeigt sich, dass seine Sprache sich einerseits an Veranschaulichungen und narrativ erzählten Beispielen orientiert, also Altbekanntes aufgreift, und andererseits seine neue Sprache, die er gleichzeitig einem alten Natürlichkeitsdiskurs entsprechend als die eigentlich natürliche betrachtet, übersetzt in eine bekannte Sprache: den schriftlich verfassten Text. Die Nichtrealisierung könnte aber genau hier ihre Ursache haben, da der Versuch der Wissenschaftlichkeit scheitert, die Eisenstein sucht, weil die Filmsprache eben nicht an sich eindeutig ist, sondern kommentiert werden muss. Auf der anderen Seite wird aber auch im Hinblick auf Kluge schon deutlich, dass es bei einer Adaption nicht ausschließlich um die Übertragung eines gleichen Stoffes gehen kann, sondern dass Eisenstein einen Großteil seiner Arbeit auf die Etablierung einer neuen Sprache verwendet und eine Anpassung an die wissenschaftliche Sprache versucht. Seine Überlegungen zielen damit vielmehr auf der Gattungsebene auf eine Anpassung. Hierbei zeigt sich, dass weniger nur ein Thema bzw. ein Stoff, sondern vielmehr bestimmte Gattungsprinzipien übertragen werden, was bei gewöhnlichen Adaptionen, die erzählende Werke transformieren, nicht auffällt, da ähnliche Prinzipien wie Narrativität sowohl bei Film als auch bei der Literatur schon vorhanden sind.

Das Projekt Alexander Kluges

Im Folgenden soll nun dargestellt werden, welche Aspekte einer typischen wissenschaftlichen Gattung Kluge in seinem Werk übernimmt, die er schon in Ansätzen in den von ihm genutzten Medien vorfindet. Allerdings zeigt sich ein deutlicher Unterschied zu Eisenstein, weil hier die Behauptung, das Werk sei eine Adaption, schwierig zu halten ist. Eisenstein betont den Aspekt der Medienumformung, während Kluge schon einen anderen Bezug in seinem Titel wählt. Erstens sind mehrere Werke – eben von Marx und Eisenstein – verbunden, zweitens werden beide zeitlich in Differenz zu seinem eigenen Projekt betrachtet.

---

[19]   Vgl. Eisenstein: Notate, S. 304.

Drittens wird in dem Anspruch an das Projekt, Eisenstein ein Denkmal zu setzen, deutlich, dass dies keinesfalls eine reine Adaption darstellt, sondern vielmehr ein Kommentar, eine Würdigung beabsichtigt ist. Allerdings lassen sich bei Kluges Werk verschiedene typisch wissenschaftliche Charakteristika erkennen, die einer wissenschaftlichen Gattung entsprechen. Das Werk zeigt sich als Adaption insofern, als es Überlegungen und Gedanken, solches, was sowohl bei Marx als auch bei Eisenstein als ‚Wesentliches', als ‚Inhalt' verstanden wird, neu anpasst, indem es Gattungsaspekte des Originals übernimmt. Meines Erachtens bietet Kluges Werk drei typisch wissenschaftliche Gattungsaspekte. Erstens ist dies eine nach bestimmtem wissenschaftsähnlichem Schema montierte Zugangsmöglichkeit, die eine solche Sammlung ähnlich einem Aufsatzband nach wissenschaftlichem Schema präsentiert. Zweitens finden sich zahlreiche Elemente, die einen exemplarischen Charakter einnehmen bzw. Gedankenexperimente darstellen. Diese sind zwar in sich stark narrativ, von Assoziationen durchsetzt und dadurch nicht typisch wissenschaftlich, funktionieren also nicht nach kausalen Regeln, gleichen jedoch in ihrem exemplarischen Charakter einer typisch wissenschaftlichen Arbeitsweise,[20] indem ein Satz oder eine Regel durch den konkreten Fall eine Bestätigung erfährt.[20] Als letzter Punkt, der, wie oben schon erwähnt, eigentlich gerade einer üblichen Adaption widerspricht, sei das Aufgreifen eines Diskurses erwähnt, eine implizite bzw. explizite Reflexion der zeitlichen Differenz. Dies, so die Behauptung, findet sich eben auch bei Adaptionen.[21]

Um den ersten Aspekt des Wissenschaftlichen zu verstehen, bedarf es zunächst der Wiederaufnahme des eingangs schon in Frage gestellten Ansatzes Kluges Projekt als Film einzustufen. Das Projekt *Nachrichten aus der ideologischen Antike* umfasst eine Vielzahl verschiedener Gattungen auch nicht-filmischer Art, deren Beziehung zueinander einen meines Erachtens wesentlichen Teil des Werks ausmacht. Nach dem Beiheft konzentrieren sich zwar „[d]ie *Nachrichten aus der ideologischen Antike* [...] auf drei DVDs",[22] neben diesen Speichermedien existiert aber ein Booklet, welches außer zu erwartenden inhaltlichen Beschreibungen einen Essay von Kluge, Zitate aus Eisensteins Notizen zu seinem eigenen Verfilmungsversuch und *Geschichten für Marx-Interessierte*, entnommen aus anderen Werken von Alexander Kluge, beinhaltet. Darüber hinaus enthalten alle DVDs neben dem Film weitere *Geschichten für Marx-Interessierte* im nicht über

---

[20]   Interessanterweise stellt Siegbert Salomon Prawer eine ähnliche Funktion der Nutzung von Literatur als Belege bei Marx selbst fest, die er zur Bestätigung seiner Sichtweisen genutzt habe (vgl. Siegbert Salomon Prawer: Karl Marx and World Literature. Oxford: Oxford University Press, 1978, S. 399).

[21]   Ein wissenschaftlicher bzw. pseudo-wissenschaftlicher Aufbau und die schwierig zu unterscheidende Vermischung von Fiktionalität und Faktualität zeigen sich auch schon in anderen eigentlich nicht wissenschaftlichen Werken bei Kluge, z.B. bei der *Schlachtbeschreibung* (vgl. Alexander Kluge: Schlachtbeschreibung. Olten: Walter, 1964).

[22]   Kluge: Nachrichten, S. 6. [Hervorhebung im Text.]

das DVD-Menü zugänglichen PDF-Format.[23]Auch das Filmmaterial ist in vielerlei
Hinsicht nicht ‚filmüblich‘, da die einzelnen DVDs jeweils durch ein übergeordnetes
Thema gegliedert sind, welches wiederum im Booklet beschrieben wird. Des
Weiteren bestehen neben dem Film davon unabhängig in DVD II einsehbare
Extras,[24] insbesondere Kurzfilme und Interviews.

Reichmann vergleicht Kluges Werke im Allgemeinen mit Arachne bzw. einem
Weber, der „zwischen fremden Texten, Dokumenten, zwischen Bildern und anderen
eingesammelten Fundstücken und seinen eigenen Geschichten einen inter- und
intratextuellen Zusammenhang herstellt".[25] Dadurch werde der Zuschauer bzw.
Leser zu einer selbstständigen Entdeckungsreise eingeladen. Hier orientiert sich
Reichmann auch am Booklet, in dem Kluge mit Eisenstein ein lineares Erzählprinzip
zugunsten eines so bezeichneten kugelförmigen aufgibt.[26] Ich möchte diese
Überlegung aufgreifen, dies aber vor dem Hintergrund der eigentlichen Idee der
Umformung des Marx'schen *Kapital*, also eines wissenschaftlichen Werks, gerade
nicht in erster Linie als eine reine Sammlung verstehen, da das Projekt einen
filmunüblichen systematischen Zugang bereitstellt, der insbesondere durch das
Booklet und die DVD ermöglicht wird. Im Booklet werden verschiedene
Zugangsmöglichkeiten zum Werk geliefert, die der wissenschaftlichen Gattung
gleichen. So funktionieren *Vorwort*, Kapitel I: *Drei DVDs in der filmedition
suhrkamp*, Kapitel IV: *Kommentare zu den drei DVDs* und *Übersicht über die drei
DVDs* nicht nur in ihrer Form, sondern auch im Aufbau als Einleitung, letzteres
sogar als Gliederung. Alle kommentieren die Kapitel und das Zusatzmaterial.
Insbesondere Kapitel IV und die *Übersicht über die drei DVDs* offenbaren Aufbau
und die Einteilung der verschiedenen DVDs, beschreiben die verschiedenen
Verweismöglichkeiten untereinander und gliedern die Teile. Diese Herangehens-
weise erinnert stark an typisch wissenschaftliche Arbeitsweisen. Die Inhalts-
wiedergaben in Kapitel IV verweisen, einer Einleitung in einem Aufsatzband gleich,
auf den Inhalt der einzelnen Abschnitte, die *Übersicht* liefert eine Untergliederung,
teilweise bis zur dritten Ebene. Damit verschafft sie einen wissenschaftsähnlichen
Überblick, indem sie einer linearen Arbeit,[27] die dennoch nicht linear gelesen wird,

---

[23]   Diese Geschichten sind anderen Texten Kluges entnommen und sind wiederum – bis auf
       eine Ausnahme – andere als die des DVD-Booklets.

[24]   Diese Extras haben jedoch nicht den Status ‚unverwendeter Szenen‘ wie bei einer
       üblichen Film-DVD, auch wenn sie augenscheinlich dem eigentlichen Film
       nachgeordnet sind, vgl. Alexander Kluge: DVD II. Alle Dinge sind verzauberte
       Menschen. In: Alexander Kluge: Nachrichten aus der ideologischen Antike. Marx –
       Eisenstein – Das Kapital. Frankfurt a.M.: Filmedition Suhrkamp 2008.

[25]   Wolfgang Reichmann: Der Chronist Alexander Kluge. Poetik und Erzählstrategien.
       Bielefeld: Aisthesis 2009, S. 122.

[26]   Vgl. Kluge: Notate, S. 15; Reichmann: Der Chronist, S. 123, FN 472.

[27]   Vgl. dazu die abweichend scheinende Meinung Kluges; er behauptet, dass das, „was auf
       den drei DVDs erzählt wird, [...] nicht systematisch, sondern filmisch geordnet" sei
       (Kluge: Nachrichten, S. 39). Mir leuchtet aber zum einen der Gegensatz zwischen

mit dem Booklet eine Untergliederung gewissermaßen voranstellt und dem Rezipienten eine Strukturerfassung ermöglicht.[28] Das Projekt der DVD nimmt also einen wissenschaftlichen Charakter insofern an, als dass zum Großteil zwar eine lineare Ordnung existiert, diese jedoch nicht befolgt werden muss. Wie ein wissenschaftliches Werk zwar eine Linearität vorgibt, dieser jedoch – wie mit Sicherheit auch bei Marx – nur selten wirklich Folge leistet, ist auch Kluges ‚Film' zwar innerfilmisch linear, muss aber– durch die Unterstützung von Gliederungen und Einleitung – nicht gänzlich linear gelesen werden: Die Titelüberschriften, Gliederungen und Kommentare ermöglichen einen nicht-linearen Zugang.[29] Indem Kluge einige wissenschaftliche Formen übernimmt, die eigentlich genau die Unterscheidung zum Typus Film ausmachen, indem hier mit den Inhaltsbeschreibungen, Überschriften und Kommentierungen etwas eingeführt wird, was das Medium Film zunächst nicht aufweist und erst durch die DVD ermöglicht wird, adaptiert er wissenschaftliche Gattungsspezifika. *Nachrichten aus der ideologischen Antike* übernimmt auf Gattungsebene Teile des heutigen wissenschaftlichen Konsens und überträgt diese: Hier ist Kluges Werk eine Adaption, gerade weil es kein typischer Film ist.

Auf einer anderen formalen Ebene arbeitet Kluge jedoch in einem zweiten Punkt wissenschaftlich. Dies ist seine Arbeit in verschiedenen Bereichen mit Beispielen bzw. Experimenten, was in Ansätzen ebenfalls einer ‚wissenschaftlichen' Arbeitsweise entspricht.[30] Für gewöhnlich werden die verschiedenen Gattungen, die bei Kluge auftauchen, nicht als wissenschaftlich empfunden. Nebeneinander stehen schriftliche Essays, Interviews, Spielfilme, Kabarett, Theateraufzeichnungen und Lesungen. Durch die Gattungen und Genres, die auch nicht auf einer Ebene anzuordnen sind, ergeben sich verschiedenste Bezüge zueinander.

---

systematisch und *filmisch* nicht ein, zum anderen ist es ja gerade ein Text und kein Film, der die Systematik herstellt.

[28] Hier ist der Unterschied zu wissenschaftlichen Büchern wie zu Filmen offensichtlich, da die Inhaltswiedergabe nicht wie in einem tatsächlich linear aufgebauten Werk vorangestellt, sondern im Booklet mitgeliefert wird. Filme wiederum werden für gewöhnlich nicht mit einer Szenenbeschreibung bedacht und der Geschichte folgend mit höherer Wahrscheinlichkeit linear angeschaut.

[29] Diese ‚wissenschaftliche' Schreibweise zeigt sich aber nur bedingt als allgemeingültig und lässt sich bezüglich Marx' eigenem Werk nicht vollständig anwenden. Denn dort finden sich nur die Überschriften und Gliederungen, die einen nicht-linearen Zugang erlauben, weitere, heute wissenschaftlich übliche Merkmale wie Einleitung und Schluss sind bei Marx in der Form nicht berücksichtigt; *Das Kapital* wird aber mit Sicherheit dennoch nur selten linear und direkt gelesen, sondern vielmehr über Kommentare und vermittelnde Einleitungen, Nachträge etc. Somit ist davon auszugehen, dass Marx' Werk, obwohl es einen anderen wissenschaftlichen Zugang beinhaltet als heute üblich, ähnlich gelesen wird wie heutige wissenschaftliche Werke.

[30] Das Problem des Beispiels als Instrument zur Unterlegung wissenschaftlicher Untersuchungen ist seit der Antike bekannt, eine Zusammenfassung hierfür findet sich in Jens Ruchatz, Stefan Willer und Nicolas Pethes (Hg.): Das Beispiel. Epistemologie des Exemplarischen. Berlin. Kadmos 2007.

Ich möchte dem jedoch das Prinzip des Gedankenexperiments voranstellen, bei dem es nicht entscheidend ist, ob etwas stattgefunden hat, ob es fiktionalen oder faktualen Charakter hat, sondern vielmehr, ob es vorstellbar bzw. möglich ist. Wenn diesem Experiment gefolgt werden kann und es für schlüssig empfunden wird, dient es als Beispiel für bestimmte Thesen und stützt diese. Wenn dem so ist, wird jedoch wiederum ein wissenschaftliches Prinzip befolgt. Zunächst ist hierzu festzuhalten, dass die Bereiche Fiktionalität und Faktualität nicht auf einfache Weise distinkt voneinander unterscheidbar sind, so auch in diesem Film nicht, sondern ineinander übergehen bzw. faktuale Elemente in fiktionalen Szenen angenommen werden oder Teile davon bilden. Hierfür sind gleich zwei Beispiele paradigmatisch: Erstens die verschiedenen schriftlichen *Geschichten für Marx-Interessierte*, die, wie anfangs erwähnt, sowohl im Booklet als auch auf jeder der DVDs sind und teilweise offensichtlich, teilweise verdeckt fiktional sind, teilweise aber auch als faktuale Texte verstanden werden können. Hier zeigt sich die bewusste Bedienung des Grenzfalls der Geschichtsschreibung, welche im konkret vorliegenden Fall schon durch die Pluralform als *Geschichten* zwischen Faktualität und Fiktionalität changiert und eher fiktionale Gestalt annimmt, dennoch durch die Setzung mancher Fakten innerhalb der Geschichten nur bei genauerem Hinsehen als fiktional auszumachen ist.

Noch deutlicher wird dies an einem Filmbeispiel, das auch als Beleg meiner These gelten soll. Wim Wenders' *Der Mensch im Ding*, der von Kluge selbst als Filmessay bezeichnet wird,[31] leitet die zweite DVD ein. Hier ist zwar nicht eindeutig auszumachen, aber sehr wahrscheinlich, dass die Szenerie einer sich in Eile befindlichen weiblichen Person eine fingierte Situation darstellt, welche dann eher dem fiktionalen Bereich zuzuordnen wäre.[32] Diese Frage ist aber für den Essayfilm gänzlich unwesentlich. Im Film werden die in dem Bildkader ersichtlichen Dinge in ihren historischen Kontext gesetzt und eine Geschichte der Dinge im Zusammenhang mit einer typischen Berliner Szene erzählt, wie sie sein *könnte*, nämlich die Szene auf einer Nebenstraße mit einer Person, die sich in Eile befindet und die sie umgebenden Dinge dadurch nicht wahrnimmt. Der Film endet mit einem Zitat aus dem *Kapital* und könnte so als Ausführung dieses Zitats gelten, als Belegbeispiel für den Satz von Marx: „Eine Ware scheint auf den ersten Blick ein selbstverständliches, triviales Ding. Ihre Analyse ergibt, daß sie ein sehr vertracktes Ding ist, voll metaphysischer Spitzfindigkeiten und theologischer Mucken."[33]

Dieses gilt nun schon als erstes Beispiel für die Beziehung zwischen manchen Teilen innerhalb Kluges Werk. Auch die *Geschichten für Marx-Interessierte* lassen sich hier einordnen. Damit wird das Fiktionale jedoch in einen bestimmten Kontext

---

[31] Vgl. Kluge: Nachrichten, S. 34.
[32] Es ist anzunehmen, dass sie nur Eile vortäuscht und insgesamt die Situation nur nachgeahmt wird, was dann eher fiktionalen Charakter hätte.
[33] Karl Marx und Friedrich Engels: Gesamtausgabe. Band 23 [MEGA]. Das Kapital. Band I. Dietz: Berlin 1962, S. 85. Während das Booklet dies auch so zitiert, fügt Wenders am Ende des ersten Satzes ein „zu sein" ein, vgl. Kluge: Notate, S. 35; Kluge: DVD II.

gesetzt und bekommt eine konkrete Aufgabe im Werk Kluges; es besitzt einen eher wissenschaftlichen Status und nimmt – vorausgesetzt, dass dem Gedankenexperiment gefolgt werden kann – beispielhaften, kausalen Charakter an. Wenn man der innerfilmischen Darstellung folgen kann, das nicht tatsächliche Experiment also stimmig ist, liegt Marx mit seiner Aussage, welche den Film abschließt, richtig.

So verhalten sich jedoch auch weitere Szenen und Kapitel, die fiktionale Elemente einbeziehen, zu bestimmten Aussagen. Am interessantesten hierfür scheinen mir die verschiedenen Interviews mit unterschiedlichen, von Helge Schneider gespielten Figuren, davon am deutlichsten *Der Gesamtarbeiter vor Verdun*. Hier interviewt Kluge einen deutschen Tunnelarbeiter bzw. Sprengmeister. Diese Situation beschreibt ein (Gedanken-)Experiment, in dem die beiden Interviewpartner eine Szenerie durchspielen, die anschaulich macht, wie die Arbeit im Krieg getätigt wird, und damit mehrere politisch linke Thesen oder Sätze zu bestätigen sucht.

Selbstverständlich sind die Interviews nicht als solche ernstzunehmen. Aber dieser *Unernst* ist für gewöhnlich weniger als lustig, sondern eher als ein Spiel zu verstehen. Dies spiegelt m.E. das Interesse Kluges am Kontrafaktischen, Nicht-Tatsächlichen wieder und steht in Zusammenhang mit dem sehr alten Diskurs um das Ästhetische, welcher die Möglichkeit des Spiels beschreibt, um zur Erkenntnis zu gelangen.[34] Bei Kluge steht dies immer in einem Bezug zu Marx oder anderen politisch linken Ideen und Theorien. Diese Sätze werden durch verschiedene Beispiele teils faktischer, teils kontrafaktischer Natur belegt.

Als letzten Punkt, der die Grenzen dieser Adaption deutlich macht, aber gleichzeitig ein weiteres Charakteristikum von Adaptionen berücksichtigt, sei der Einbezug der zeitlichen Differenz zum eigentlichen Werk deutlich gemacht. Kluge bezieht sich nicht nur auf Marx' Werk, sondern außer auf Eisenstein auch auf bestehende und vergangene Diskurse, welche nicht mit dem *Kapital*, sondern nur mit Marx und teilweise nur über den Bezug zum *Realsozialismus* zusammenhängen, so z.B. in *Der große Kopf von Chemnitz*.[35] Hiermit zeigt sich der Begriff der Adaption einerseits als irreführend, insbesondere weil eben *Das Kapital* oder der wie auch immer herauszuarbeitende Stoff gar nicht auftauchen. Andererseits lässt sich wiederum aufzeigen, worin eventuell Ähnlichkeiten zu üblichen Adaptionen, allerdings insbesondere auch zur wissenschaftlichen Gattung bestehen: die Aufnahme des gegenwärtigen Diskurses in das Werk oder die implizite oder explizite Betonung des zeitlichen Transfers. Die Adaption üblicher Werke transformiert das Werk nicht nur in eine andere Gattung oder ein anderes Medium, sondern zeigt für gewöhnlich gleichzeitig eine zeitliche Transformierung auf, die bei einer wissenschaftlichen Gattung wiederum zu einer korrekten Arbeit dazugehört.

---

[34] Zu diesem Diskurs, der auch Kant und Schiller aufgreift, vgl. Marcus Düwell: Ästhetische Erfahrung und Moral. Zur Bedeutung des Ästhetischen für die Handlungsspielräume des Menschen. Freiburg: Alber Thesen 1999.

[35] Vgl. Kluge: DVD III.

Hierbei ist selbstverständlich nicht gemeint, dass der Stoff notwendigerweise in eine andere Zeit auf der fiktionalen Ebene ‚versetzt' wird. Es findet aber eine Reflexion des zeitlichen Kontextes der Adaption allein dadurch statt, dass befragt wird, warum und wie ein Stoff neu aufgegriffen wird.

Es wird also deutlich, dass sich auf Gattungsebene bei Kluge ein wissenschaftlicher Charakter feststellen lässt; dies wurde mit den drei wissenschaftsähnlichen Aspekten, dem nicht-linearen Zugang, der Arbeit mit Beispielen und Experimenten sowie dem Rekurs auf die zeitliche Transformation deutlich. Diese Aspekte könnten weitergeführt werden, so z.B. in der Nutzung der Sprache, die sowohl in Schrift als auch in Ton intensiv eingesetzt wird und der gegenüber das Bild, dessen Nutzung im wissenschaftlichen Kontext im Vergleich zur Sprache marginal ist, auch bei Kluges Werk häufig eine untergeordnete Rolle zu spielen scheint. Diese These bedürfte aber einer weiteren Auseinandersetzung.

Die Grenzfälle einer Adaption als Überlegung über das Prinzip der Adaption

Die vorangegangenen Überlegungen haben deutlich werden lassen, dass eine Adaption weniger als eine Übertragung reiner Inhalte, Themen oder Stoffe zu verstehen ist. Vielmehr ermöglicht die Übertragung gewisser Formprinzipien erst die Adaption, damit diese in einer Ähnlichkeitsbeziehung zum Originalwerk stehen kann, welche trotz des Gattungs- bzw. des medialen Transfers Bestand hat. Diese Ähnlichkeitsbeziehung, so glaube ich, besteht also nicht in erster Linie darin, dass – wie sonst typisch – bestimmte, nicht näher eingrenzbare Inhalte von einem Medium in ein anderes übertragen werden. Dies wurde in den vorangegangenen Beispielen insofern ersichtlich, als dass Eisenstein eine neue Formsprache erfinden wollte, in der er wie in der wissenschaftlichen Gattung das Prinzip der Eindeutigkeit zu übernehmen suchte. Auch zu nennen sind hier weitere, nur angedeutete Aspekte wie der Versuch der Etablierung einer Dialektik in der Filmsprache. Zwar kann also das Medium wechseln, aber es müssen auf anderer Ebene Anpassungen an das ursprüngliche Medium bzw. an die eigentliche Gattung vorgenommen werden.

Während Eisenstein versuchte, das Prinzip der Dialektik und Eindeutigkeit zu transformieren und eine Filmsprache – also eine Form – zu entwickeln, um eine Adaption zu ermöglichen, verwendet Kluge verschiedene andere wissenschaftliche Prinzipien, die teilweise durch Medien wie die DVD erst ermöglicht werden, um eine wissenschaftsähnliche Gattung im Film zu etablieren. Herausgestellt wurden hierbei die Gliederung und die Kommentierung des Werks, das Verfahren mit Beispielen und Gedankenexperimenten sowie der Einbezug der zeitlichen Differenz durch Aufnahme des Diskurses.

Auch ist hervorzuheben, dass hier kein Plädoyer dafür erfolgen sollte, Kluges Werk als übliche Adaption zu Marx' *Kapital* zu verstehen. In mancher Hinsicht ist aber durchaus festzustellen, dass hier zu vielen Teilen eine mediale Transformation wie bei einer Adaption erkennbar ist. Eine Adaption benötigt ähnliche Prinzipen zur

Vorlage, wobei es jedoch nicht um den gleichen ‚Inhalt' oder den Stoff geht. Da Inhalt an Form und Medium gebunden ist, müssen mehrere Aspekte auf den verschiedenen Ebenen gleich bleiben, um die generelle Anpassung gewährleisten und ein Werk als Adaption bezeichnen zu können. Dies fällt erst bei einem solchen Grenzfall auf, weil bei gewöhnlichen Literaturverfilmungen ähnliche Prinzipien übernommen werden, so beispielsweise das narratologische Element. Eine Adaption bedarf also auch auf Gattungsebene einer Übertragung bzw. einer Anpassung. Sollte der Adaptionsbegriff allerdings auf narrative Gattungen eingeschränkt werden, wäre zu überprüfen, inwiefern Kunstwerke aus dem Bereich der Bildenden Kunst, die für gewöhnlich nicht als narrativ begriffen werden, Quell- oder Zielmedium einer Adaption werden könnten.

Solange aber ist festzuhalten, dass Eisenstein einen Adaptionsversuch startete, indem er eine Wissenschaftlichkeit im Film etablieren wollte. Gleichzeitig schien dies notwendige Bedingung, um eine Adaption allererst zu ermöglichen, wie an dem Wunsch nach Eindeutigkeit der Filmsprache deutlich wurde. Kluge hat andere in der Wissenschaft vorhandene Phänomene genutzt, um ein adaptionsähnliches Werk zu schaffen.

Ates Gürpinar is a Ph.D. candidate in Media Studies at the Institute for Theatre and Media Studies at the University of Erlangen.

Andreas Musolff

The Popular Image of Genocide: Adaptation and Blending of Hitler's *Annihilation* Prophecy and the *Parasite* Metaphor in *Der Ewige Jude*

Introduction

On 30 January 1939, Adolf Hitler, Chancellor of the German Reich, which in the preceding year had annexed Austria and the "Sudeten" territories of Czechoslovakia, gave an address to the Reichstag on the occasion of the sixth anniversary of his accession to power, taking more than two hours to list his supposedly triumphant achievements. For the future, he promised more of the same, even if it meant that Germany would be "dragged" into a war:

> Ich bin in meinem Leben sehr oft Prophet gewesen und wurde meistens ausgelacht. In der Zeit meines Kampfes um die Macht war es in erster Linie das jüdische Volk, das nur mit Gelächter meine Prophezeiungen hinnahm, ich würde einmal in Deutschland die Führung des Staates und damit des ganzen Volkes übernehmen und dann unter vielen anderen auch das jüdische Problem zur Lösung bringen. Ich glaube, daß dieses damalige schallende Gelächter dem Judentum in Deutschland unterdes wohl schon in der Kehle erstickt ist. Ich will heute wieder ein Prophet sein: Wenn es dem internationalen Finanzjudentum in und außerhalb Europas gelingen sollte, die Völker noch einmal in einen Weltkrieg zu stürzen, dann wird das Ergebnis nicht die Bolschewisierung der Erde und damit der Sieg des Judentums sein, sondern die Vernichtung der jüdischen Rasse in Europa.[1]

This 'prophetic' threat has often been cited by historians as an explicit proclamation of Hitler's murderous intentions towards the European Jews.[2] It came at the climax of an extended passage in Hitler's speech that dealt almost exclusively with the

---

[1] Max Domarus: Hitler. Reden und Proklamationen 1932-1945. Kommentiert von einem deutschen Zeitgenossen. Vol. II. Munich: Süddeutscher Verlag, 1965, p. 1058.

[2] See, for example, Saul Friedländer: Nazi Germany and the Jews. Vol. I: The Years of Persecution, 1933-1939. London: Phoenix, 1998, p. 310; Ian Kershaw: Hitler, 1936-1945. Nemesis. London: Allen Lane, 2000, p. 152-53; Michael Burleigh: The Third Reich. A New History. London: Pan, 2001, p. 340; Peter Longerich: The Unwritten Order. Hitler's Role in the Final Solution. Stroud: Tempus, 2003, p. 70-71; Richard J. Evans: The Third Reich in Power, 1933-1939. London: Allen Lane, 2005, p. 604-05; Jeffrey Herf: The Jewish Enemy. Cambridge, MA: Harvard University Press, 2006, p. 5-6, 52-53.

Jews. Having alluded sarcastically to the failure of international agreements concerning the admission of Jewish-German refugees into the "Demokratien,"[3] Hitler portrayed Germany as a country that had over the centuries allowed the Jews to infiltrate and sponge off the nation "obwohl sie außer ansteckenden politischen und sanitären Krankheiten nichts besaßen," until they had turned the Germans into beggars in their own country.[4] Facetiously, he considered the possibility that the earth might have "Siedlungsraum" for all, but insisted that the precondition to any constructive solution to the Jewish question had to be the end of the misconception that "das jüdische Volk vom lieben Gott eben dazu bestimmt [sei], in einem gewissen Prozentsatz Nutznießer am Körper und an der produktiven Arbeit anderer Völker zu sein;" otherwise Jewry would suffer a crisis "von unvorstellbarem Ausmaße."[5] This already threatening prediction was followed by the "prophecy" cited above which was reiterated once more with minor variations: if another war broke out, the world would experience the same "Aufklärung" about the Jews' evil plans that Germany had already witnessed under Hitler's leadership, an insight which would inevitably lead within a few short years to Jewry's complete demise.[6]

With historical hindsight, it is almost impossible not to read Hitler's prophecy of 1939 as a weird précis of things to come, blaming his victims in advance, as it were, for bringing upon themselves what he intended to do to them later. The prophecy was based on Hitler's ideological core metaphor of 'the Jew' as a *parasite* feeding on the German *body politic*, and, at a universal level, *as a parasite on all peoples*, an idea which had since the 1920s been used to 'justify' Nazi plans to *eliminate* Jews from Germany.[7]

More than a year later, the metaphor and associated prophecy resurfaced in a unique blend in one of the central propaganda artefacts produced by the Nazis to popularize their brand of "redemptive anti-Semitism":[8] the film *Der Ewige Jude* [*The Eternal Jew*] in the version shown to the German public.[9] Together with *Jud*

---

[3]   Domarus: Hitler. Reden und Proklamationen, p. 1056.
[4]   Domarus: Hitler. Reden und Proklamationen, p. 1056-1057.
[5]   Domarus: Hitler. Reden und Proklamationen, p. 1057.
[6]   Domarus: Hitler. Reden und Proklamationen, p. 1058.
[7]   See Alexander Bein: Der jüdische Parasit. In: Vierteljahreshefte für Zeitgeschichte 13 (1965), p. 121-49; Paul Chilton: Manipulation, Memes and Metaphors. The Case of Mein Kampf. In: Louis de Saussure and Peter Schulz (eds.): Manipulation and Ideologies in the Twentieth Century. Amsterdam: Benjamins, 2005, p. 15-43; Felicity Rash: The Language of Violence. Adolf Hitler's Mein Kampf. New York: Lang, 2006: p. 172-81; Andreas Musolff: Metaphor, Nation, and the Holocaust. The Concept of the Body Politic. London: Routledge, 2010, p. 23-42.
[8]   Saul Friedländer: Nazi Germany and the Jews. Vol. I. New York: HarperCollins, 1998, p. 87.
[9]   In later versions of *Der Ewige Jude* intended for international audiences, parts of Hitler's speech were omitted along with scenes relating to the Weimar Republic. See Susan Tegel: Nazis and the Cinema. London: Continuum, 2007, p. 153. On its release and impact in occupied Europe, see Joseph Wulf: Theater und Film im Dritten Reich. Frankfurt a.M., Vienna and Berlin: Ullstein, 1966, p. 458-59; Daniel Rafaelić: The

Süss, which focused on the biography of the eponymous antihero, Joseph Süss-Oppenheimer, and *Die Rothschilds,* which provided a historical sketch of the banking family's rise to alleged world domination, *Der Ewige Jude* formed part of an infamous mini-series of films specifically designed to foster anti-Semitism.[10] All three films appeared in 1940 during what was a transition period between the "onslaught"[11] against the Jews in the pogroms of November 1938, and the start of systematic genocide in 1941. The remainder of this paper concentrates on the question of how Hitler's "prophecy" of Jewish annihilation and the *parasite-illness* metaphor in the film *Der Ewige Jude* worked together to lead audiences to the intended conclusion that the murder of all Jewish people in Europe was a necessity.[12]

The Eternal Jew and Its Political Context

When *Der Ewige Jude* appeared in cinemas in late autumn 1940, "ordinary" Germans had just experienced an extraordinary year.[13] The country had been at war since September 1939, and had witnessed a series of *Blitzkrieg*-triumphs that were

---

Influence of German Cinema and Newly Established Croatian Cinematography, 1941-45. In: Roel Vande Winkel and David Welch (eds.): Cinema and the Swastika. The International Expansion of Third Reich Cinema. Basingstoke: Palgrave Macmillan, 2007, p. 99-111, here p. 108; Ingo Schieweck: Dutch-German Film Relations under German Pressure and Nazi Occupation, 1933-45. In: Vande Winkel and Welch (eds.): Cinema and the Swastika, 207-19, here p. 219.

[10] The three films constitute something of an exception to general film production in the Third Reich, the vast majority of which was devoted to the glorification of German/Aryan heroism, comradeship and leadership on the one hand, and escapist entertainment on the other. See David Welch: Propaganda and the German Cinema, 1933-1945. Revised edn. London: Tauris, 2007, p. 266-67.

[11] Friedländer: Nazi Germany and the Jews.

[12] All quotations from and descriptions of passages from *Der ewige Jude* relate to the film copy at the Imperial War Museum, London (see www.iwmcollections.org.uk/).

[13] The term "ordinary Germans" (alluding as it does to Christopher Browning: Ordinary Men. Reserve Battalion 101 and the Final Solution in Poland. New York: HarperCollins, 1992), is used here to indicate that part of the population that was neither regarded by the Nazis as completely loyal nor saw themselves as thoroughgoing supporters of National Socialism and its specific murderous form of anti-Semitism. On the fragmentation of German society under Nazism see Ian Kershaw: Popular Opinion and Political Dissent in the Third Reich. Bavaria 1933-1945. Oxford: Oxford University Press, 1983, and Hitler, the Germans and the Final Solution. Jerusalem: Yad Vashem and New Haven, CT: Yale University Press, 2008; David Bankier: The Germans and the Final Solution. Public Opinion under Nazism. Oxford: Blackwell, 1992; Robert Gellately: The Gestapo and German Society. Enforcing Racial Policy, 1933-1945. Oxford: Oxford University Press, 1990; Backing Hitler. Consent and Coercion in Nazi Germany. Oxford: Oxford University Press, 2001; Peter Longerich: "Davon haben wir nichts gewusst!" Die Deutschen und die Judenverfolgung 1933-1945. Munich: Siedler, 2006.

without precedent and had put most of continental Europe from the Atlantic to the borders of Soviet Russia under German control. The only significant enemy force that was left was the army of the British Empire but, according to Nazi propaganda at least, it was isolated and certain to surrender at some point. The USA was still a neutral state, and relations with the USSR were officially amicable (their Commissar for Foreign Affairs, Molotov, visited Berlin in November). Of course, the Nazi leadership was all the while laying plans for an invasion of the USSR, but these were naturally not publicized.[14] In terms of the strategic situation, then, the Reich seemed almost unassailable at this point.

As far as the Jewish population was concerned, the *Altreich* territories had seen the mass deportations of Jews from Pomerania to the Lublin ghetto in occupied Poland in February 1940, and from Baden and the Palatinate to occupied France in October,[15] as well as a never-ending series of anti-Jewish laws and administrative regulations designed to achieve the systematic isolation of Jews from the non-Jewish population. These policies included the compulsory use of the "Jewish" names "Israel" and "Sara" on identification papers and compulsory re-homing in so-called *Judenhäuser*.[16] While in reality Jewish people were forced to retreat and disappear from actual public life, completely anathematized and disempowered, a supposedly dangerous collective identity was all the while being invented for them. Anti-Semitic films played a crucial role in this public re-invention of Jews as a deadly, parasitic enemy. Their production had been ordered by Goebbels after the start of the war, with massive resources allocated to them, huge attention paid to their planning, and detailed input from Goebbels and Hitler himself.[17] The films constituted a concerted attempt to convince as many Germans as possible of the necessity of the "annihilation of the Jewish race in Europe" which Hitler had so prophetically 'foreseen' in January 1939. It was an idea he was to reiterate on several occasions, for example in the anniversary speeches of 30 January 1941 and 1942, and again in September 1942, each time, however, with a very telling mistake: he consistently misdated the original prophecy to 1 September 1939, in other words to the day of the attack on Poland which marked the outbreak of the Second World

---

[14]   See Richard J. Evans: The Third Reich at War, 1939-1945. London: Allen Lane, 2008, p. 161.

[15]   See Christopher Browning: The Path to Genocide. Cambridge: Cambridge University Press, 1992, p. 1-27; Otto Dov Kulka and Eberhard Jäckel (eds.): Die Juden in den geheimen NS-Stimmungsberichten 1933-1945. Düsseldorf: Droste, 2004, p. 634-36.

[16]   See Kulka and Jäckel: Die Juden in den geheimen NS-Stimmungsberichten, p. 626-32; Friedländer: Nazi Germany and the Jews, p. 53-127.

[17]   See Welch: Propaganda and the German Cinema 1933-1945, p. 222-29, 239-57; Tegel: Nazis and the Cinema, 2007, p. 151-53; also Fritz Hippler: Die Verstrickung. Einstellungen und Rückblenden von Fritz Hippler, ehem. Reichsfilmintendant unter Josef Goebbels. Düsseldorf: Verlag Mehr Wissen, 1981, p. 207. However, Hippler, the film's official director and Chief of Film Production from 1939-1943, clearly had a vested interest in downplaying his own involvement and in making as much as possible of Hitler and Goebbels' input into the film.

War.[18] Early military triumphs may have made it seem opportune to the Nazi-leadership to "re-date" Hitler's prediction, moving it from January to September, thereby giving the impression that the *Führer* had explicitly linked the outbreak of the war to the start of the "annihilation of the Jewish race in Europe" at the precise moment that that chain of events was triggered.

In *Der Ewige Jude*, a recording of the 1939 prophecy provides the climax of the whole film, a film which purported in its subtitle to be a "Filmbeitrag zum Problem des Weltjudentums" and to reveal the true identity of "the Jew", which allegedly had previously remained hidden under the civilized cultural camouflage of Western and Central European Jewry. This revelation of what the film claimed to be the true Jewish racial character had only been made possible, it declared, by the German occupation of Poland in 1939: only now, the voice-over claimed, could the Jews be shown in their 'nesting site' in the ghettos, and in what it asserted was their "natural" condition, a site, of course, by then well under the control of the German occupation forces.[19]

From the start, the film portrays Jews as the "Pestherd der Menschheit." This idea is visualized in images of Jewish living quarters that are "schmutzig und verwahrlost," as the speaker states in supposedly 'simple honest German' ("auf Deutsch gesagt"). Then Jews are systematically categorized as a "Volk von Parasiten," followed by the explanation (attributed to Richard Wagner) that "immer dort wo sich am Volkskörper eine Wunde zeigt, setzen sie sich fest und ziehen aus dem verfallenden Organismus ihre Nahrung." Having established the idea that Jews infiltrate wounds on the body of the nation, the film goes on to play with motifs of parasitism, sponging, decay, decomposition and illness, while the myth of the "Wandernder Jude" (Ahasverus), referenced in the film's title, is, strangely, not dwelt on in any detail. Nevertheless, the theme of Jewish geographic migration forms a central concern of the film. It is established and conceptually reinforced at three different levels:

a) Migration is presented as the original *modus vivendi* of the Jewish "race," practiced by them for the past four millennia. Starting from Mesopotamia, they moved via Egypt, Canaan and, later, the Greek and Roman Empires into all of Europe, and, then, after reconsolidation in Eastern Europe (following anti-Jewish pogroms in medieval Western Europe, which are construed as a kind of European "self-defence"), spread across the world.

---

[18]   See Domarus: Hitler. Reden und Proklamationen, p. 1163, 1829, 1920. For detailed interpretations see Ian Kershaw: Hitler, 1889-1936. Hubris. London: Allen Lane, 1999, p. 152-53, 487, 494; Friedländer: Nazi Germany and the Jews, p. 132, 331-33; Longerich: "Davon haben wir nichts gewusst!" p. 201-04; Herf: The Jewish Enemy, p. 144-45, 166-67.

[19]   The magazine *Film-Kurier* of 20 January 1941, for instance, praised the film's foresight at having recorded "a true picture of that stinking quagmire which fed the never-ending flow of World Jewry." Quoted in: Wulf: Theater und Film im Dritten Reich, p. 458.

b) An "exemplary" case is provided by the Rothschild family, whose banking empire is shown to have spread from a single banking house in Frankfurt, first extending across Europe and then across the globe; this family is used a kind of prototype, supposedly exemplifying global Jewish financial influence, the catastrophic consequences of which are, it is suggested, amply and dreadfully demonstrated by the banking crises of the 1920s.

c) Running parallel to these claims of inexorable and cataclysmic financial spread, and supported by inter-cutting techniques and various assertions in the commentary, Jewish migration patterns are also identified with the migration patterns of parasitic vermin, specifically rats, which spread diseases such as plague, leprosy, typhoid, cholera, and dysentery.

The analogy drawn between Jews-as-race/nation/clan/class and disease-spreading rats forms the most concentrated filmic visualization of the *illness-therapy* metaphor. The only possible inference that this is designed to allow is that the therapeutic-hygienic practices used to combat contagious vermin, namely extermination, have equally and logically also to be applied to these, their human counterparts. While this image of rats may have been exceeded in terms of sheer goriness by later scenes showing ritual cattle slaughter,[20] it was the idea of the illness-spreading migration of pests that formed the crucial conceptual basis for the characterization of Jewry as a mortal danger, neatly linking ideas of "des ewigen Schmarotzertums" (parasitism) to that of "des ewigen Juden."

The end of the film, in the words of the contemporary review magazine *Der deutsche Film*, provided the audience with "a return to the light." "German people and German life surround us once more. It is as if we have travelled to distant parts and we feel the difference that separates us from the Jew with a horrifying shudder."[21] Various measures introduced by the *Führer* to deal with these 'racial parasites' are recalled and praised: the prohibition of ritual slaughter practices and the Nuremberg laws of 1935; and, providing a kind of climax, this is followed by the recording of the 1939 "prophecy" that announced the annihilation of Jews in Europe. After that, the film wallows in pictures of Aryan boys and girls, banners, and marching troops taking the German viewers back to the present of autumn 1940.

The Film's Impact

Was *Der Ewige Jude* just a filmic version, then, of other well-known statements by Hitler, or did it make a more significant contribution to the propaganda that paved

---

[20]   These slaughter scenes were also omitted in special versions shown to youths and sensitive spectators. See Tegel: Nazis and the Cinema, 2007, p. 153.

[21]   Der Deutsche Film, 06.12.1940. Cited in Welch: Propaganda and the German Cinema 1933-1945, p. 252.

the way to the Holocaust? In order to model its cognitive impact, we need to define more precisely how and what the audiences 'understood' as its message. For this purpose, "Conceptual Blending Theory," a version of cognitive metaphor theory developed by Gilles Fauconnier and Mark Turner, provides a useful theoretical basis.[22] It views concepts as "mental spaces" which function as input into various types of "conceptual integration" networks, and examines the integration of several, often incongruous, input spaces within metaphors (as well as in counterfactual conditional statements), giving rise to what it calls "double-scope" or "multiple-scope" networks that not only include the conceptual structure of all input spaces in a "generic space," but whose "blended space" contains a new "emergent structure of its own."[23] Viewed from this perspective, *Der ewige Jude* is not at all what it purports to be. In other words, it is not an "informative" documentary, or a reprise of various older strands of propaganda, but rather a highly artificial blending of various inputs to create a new argumentative and conceptual whole: in this case, an endorsement of the annihilation of *Jews-as-parasite* as a necessary action and as prophesied by the *Führer*, adding a crucial ideological message to the anti-Semitic propaganda the Nazis had developed up until 1939/40.

To appreciate the new, emergent conceptual structure, we must first briefly recall what was *not* new about it. For anyone in Germany who had been exposed to Nazi propaganda from 1933 onwards, the 'Jew-as-parasite' metaphor would have come as no surprise. Even the scenes from Polish ghettos had already been shown in many a *Wochenschau* reel as well as in the popular campaign "documentary" *Feldzug in Polen* (which was also made by Fritz Hippler, director of *Der Ewige Jude,*).[24] The equation of Jews and illness-carrying parasites had, in fact, been part and parcel of anti-Semitic racism since the second half of the nineteenth century.[25] In this sense, the film presented no new 'facts,' or opinions about the "Jewish problem" as defined by the Nazis. In terms of conceptual integration theory, the amalgamation of political, socio-biological and eschatological concepts found here represent a complex blend, but by 1940 film makers could assume that this was already a familiar cognitive "input space" for any cinema goer. Apart from reiterating and disseminating the standard Nazi view, the film's 'innovative' contribution lay in its linking of the core parasite metaphor to Hitler's extermination prophecy. This link had already been implicit in his January 1939 speech, but back then, Hitler's prophecy still only referred to a (potential) future state of affairs. Even an astute critical observer like Victor Klemperer attached no particularly ominous significance

---

22 See Gilles Fauconnier and Mark Turner: The Way We Think. Conceptual Blending and the Mind's Hidden Complexities. New York: Basic Books, 2002.

23 Fauconnier and Turner: The Way We Think, p. 131; see also p. 299-303.

24 See Welch: Propaganda and the German Cinema 1933-1945, p. 166, 173.

25 See Jacob Katz: From Prejudice to Destruction. Anti-Semitism, 1700-1933. Cambridge, MA: Harvard University Press, 1980; Brigitte Hamann: Hitlers Wien. Lehrjahre eines Diktators. Munich: Piper, 1996; Walter Laqueur: Gesichter des Antisemitismus. Von den Anfängen bis heute. Berlin: Propyläen, 2008.

to it when he read it for the first time, noting the speech in his diary as merely an instance of Hitler's trick of making "all his enemies into Jews."[26]

Had the 'parasite-annihilation-in-case-of-war' policy been announced on 1 September 1939, as Hitler later claimed it had, it would arguably have attracted more attention and alarm. However, this 'timing error' was irrelevant to the 1940 film. Crucial here was the sequential ordering of scenes that first 'demonstrated' the Jewish *parasite* problem, then introduced Hitler's prophecy, and finally showed Germany's recent war triumphs, thereby providing a new and dangerous blended space for the parasite metaphor: it was placed in a coherent narrative framework in which the war had now started (and was progressing victoriously). This recontextualization engendered in the audience the intended inference that the time for the "annihilation of the Jewish race in Europe" had finally come. The victory in Poland had first of all 'exposed' the 'parasite race' in all its supposed evil and ugliness and in its very 'nesting site'; secondly, the war condition stipulated by the *Führer* as the trigger for annihilation was now operative. The two main conditions for his prophecy were therefore fulfilled; all that was left for Germans was to draw the practical conclusion from it and make the *Führer's* prediction come true.

The film opened on 28 November 1940 in thirty-six cinemas in Berlin alone,[27] and on the same day in film theatres all over Germany, accompanied by a massive propaganda campaign of posters, advertising and newspaper reviews. Building on *Die Rothschilds* (released in July) and *Jud Süß* (released in September), it was intended to put the finishing touches to the anti-Semitic indoctrination of the general public. However, despite the concerted marketing campaign, spectator numbers lagged far behind expectations, for which several reasons have been given: *Der Ewige Jude* was released into an already rather saturated market niche, it was dry, and included high levels of abstract propaganda that demanded sustained attention on the part of the audience. It compared unfavourably with *Jud Süß'* engrossing plot and the vivid, engaging performances by popular actors of the Nazi period such as Ferdinand Marian, Werner Krauss and Kristina Söderbaum. The result was that audiences for *Der Ewige Jude* were from the beginning smaller than those for *Jud Süß*, and fell away further after the initial performances.[28]

However, as Saul Friedländer, has pointed out, "the commercial success of *Jud Süß* and the limited commercial appeal of *Der Ewige Jude* should not be viewed as contrary results in terms of Goebbels' intentions: [...] both films can be considered two different facets of an endlessly renewed stream of anti-Jewish horror stories, images, and arguments."[29] Where *Jud Süß* told an engaging story, *Der Ewige Jude* purported to be 'informative.' It could not be expected, therefore, to become a

---

[26] Victor Klemperer: Ich will Zeugnis ablegen bis zum letzten. Tagebücher 1933-1945. Vol. I. Berlin: Aufbau-Verlag, 1995, p. 461.

[27] See Tegel: Nazis and the Cinema, 2007, p. 167.

[28] Welch: Propaganda and the German Cinema 1933-1945, p. 252-53; Tegel: Nazis and the Cinema, p. 166-67; Evans: The Third Reich at War, 1939-1945, p. 571-72.

[29] Friedländer: Nazi Germany and the Jews, p.102.

blockbuster, but it did turn out to be the perfect manifestation of genocidal propaganda in an age of mechanical reproduction, to quote Benjamin: although not a run-away success as a film maybe, its images reappeared and proliferated in posters, pamphlets, and cartoons. The film was shown to the *Wehrmacht* and police units directly involved in the mass murders of Jewish civilians, and found its way into the training journals and manuals of the genocide's killers:

> The word [sic; = prophecy] of the Führer that a new war, instigated by Jewry, will not bring about the destruction of anti-Semitic Germany but rather the end of Jewry is now being carried out. The gigantic spaces of the east, which Germany and Europe have now at their disposition for colonization, also facilitate the definitive solution of the Jewish problem in the near future. This means not only removing the race of parasites from power, but its elimination from the family of European peoples.[30]

For the perpetrators, then, the combination of the 'parasite'-metaphor and the *Führer*-prophecy was a succinct affirmation of the work they were engaged in, namely the mass killing of all Jewish people they could get hold of. However, we must also ask what ordinary "bystanders," to use Raul Hilberg's term,[31] or – in the special case of cinema audiences – 'ordinary spectators,' made of the film version of the annihilation scenario. Reports on popular opinion compiled by the SS *Sicherheitsdienst* as well as by police divisions and local or regional Nazi Party organizations give us a detailed, although, it should be noted, not necessarily objective or comprehensive, picture.

In January 1941, the *Reichssicherheitshauptamt* drew some initial conclusions from reports on the film that had come in from all over the Reich. Aspects singled out for particular praise included the film's demonstration that Eastern and Western Jews were the same race 'deep down,' despite any superficial differences in outward appearance, and that verminous and Jewish migration patterns were similar. The section containing Hitler's prophetic announcement of the problem's solution was claimed to have elicited "befreit[en] und begeistert[en])" applause.[32] On the other hand, the report conceded that the film had attracted mainly the already 'politically

---

[30]   See Mitteilungsblätter für die weltanschauliche Schulung der Ordnungspolizei, issue 27, 1 December 1941, quoted in translation in Jürgen Matthäus: Operation Barbarossa and the Onset of the Holocaust, June-December 1941. In: Christopher Browning: The Origins of the Final Solution. The Evolution of Nazi Jewish Policy, September 1939 - March 1942. With Contributions by Jürgen Matthäus. London: William Heinemann, 2004, p. 244-308; here p. 300. See also Browning: Ordinary Men, p. 179.

[31]   See Raul Hilberg: Perpetrators, Victors, Bystanders. The Jewish Catastrophe 1933-1945. New York: HarperCollins, 1992.

[32]   See Kulka and Jäckel: Die Juden in den geheimen NS-Stimmungsberichten, p. 440; Heinz Boberach (ed.): Meldungen aus dem Reich, 1938-1945. Die geheimen Lageberichte des Sicherheitsdienstes der SS. No. 155: 20.01.1941. Herrsching: Pawlak, 1984, p. 1917-1919.

active' part of the population, whereas the typical cinema goer who had enjoyed *Jud Süss* did not attend in great numbers, no doubt scared off by rumours about the disturbing animal slaughter scenes – allegedly, women and younger men had fainted. The portrayal of "diesen jüdischen Dreck" was deemed to be slightly excessive,[33] although a local report from rural Westphalia, where animal slaughter scenes would have been part and parcel of the farming every-day life, noted "[d]as Dargestellte sei alles gut und richtig, aber in der gebrachten Form etwas langweilig."[34]

What is conspicuous by its absence is, despite various adverse reactions to scenes of ritual animal slaughter, any hint of dissent, let alone criticism. Of course, it is debatable whether such criticism would have found its way into SD reports anyway.[35] Moreover, serious dissidents would have been unlikely to attend a film of this kind in the first place, and, had they done so, would have been guarded about voicing their true feelings to anyone outside a small circle of friends given the general atmosphere of surveillance and denunciation. Nevertheless, SD reports, designed after all covertly to take the pulse of the population, did on other occasions contain details of popular dissent and even unrest, for example during the November 1938 pogroms, and also later on in the war when Goebbels' attempts to denounce the Allied bombing campaign or to exploit Soviet war atrocities as evidence of Jewish-Bolshevik cruelty not only met with scepticism but even with damning comparisons of these crimes to the German treatment of Jews as well as of Polish and Russian civilians.[36] If there had been massive un- or sub-official protest or dissent on the part of film audiences of *Der Ewige Jude*, we may therefore presume that these could, in principle at least, have found their way into SD reports.

Although it is notoriously difficult to draw conclusions from negative evidence, the absence of any known dissenting voices among the film's audience of 1940/41 can be interpreted at the very least as evidence that *Der Ewige Jude's* blended message of the 'Jew-as-parasite' and the prophecy of annihilation-in-war (this wartime now having come) was understood as something not to be questioned. The shock effect of the vermin and slaughter scenes may even have been 'functional' in this respect: anyone who did not have the nerve to watch these scenes would have to shut their eyes – both to the film and to its implications. These Germans (whom the chief of the SS, Heinrich Himmler, would scornfully deride as 'humanitarian

---

[33] See Kulka and Jäckel: Die Juden in den geheimen NS-Stimmungsberichten, p. 441.

[34] SD Außenstelle Höxter, 07.02.1941, quoted in Kulka and Jäckel: Die Juden in den geheimen NS-Stimmungsberichten, p. 441.

[35] On the reliability of SD-reports regarding the Jewish question see Kulka and Jäckel: Die Juden in den geheimen NS-Stimmungsberichten, p. 15-21, and Longerich, "Davon haben wir nichts gewusst!" p. 218-22.

[36] See, for example, the reports in Kulka and Jäckel: Die Juden in den geheimen NS-Stimmungsberichten, p. 516-20, 525, 546.

weaklings' in his infamous Posen speech of October 1943),[37] could then pretend (and did pretend after 1945) that they had understood Hitler's prophecy as nothing more than hyperbolic figurative rhetoric. Fervent Nazis, on the other hand, would feel encouraged to redouble their efforts, joining with greater enthusiasm in anti-Semitic actions. Moderate supporters could feel reassured that the *Führer* had found and was implementing a definitive 'solution' to the 'Jewish question': the blend of 'parasite'-imagery and *Führer*-'prophecy' was sufficiently unambiguous to make it abundantly clear that the 'treatment' of the 'parasitic' Jews was now underway. Sceptics and doubters were implicitly warned by the same film to leave this nonnegotiable aspect of Nazi policy well alone. Finally, anyone who contemplated opposing the Nazi regime's core project, and thereby thwarting the fulfilment of the *Führer's* prophecy, was left in no doubt about the risk of being caught up in the annihilation process as another of its victim.

Conclusion

Through its historical recontextualization and its blending of the 'parasite' metaphor with the annihilation prophecy, *Der Ewige Jude* catered to a variety of audiences in Nazi Germany, offering a message that could be understood on several levels at the same time. Its propagandistic success lay less in winning more people over to active support of the regime's murders than in its triumphant advertising of the impending fulfilment of the *Führer's* prophecy. It portrayed the "taboo"[38] of the mass murder of all European Jews, presenting it as a 'natural' solution and as the coming-into-being of the *Führer's* prediction without spelling it out literally. The audience had to make the inferential leap from the metaphor-prophecy blend to its impending implementation in genocide for itself. The film left no doubt about what the Nazis were planning for the Jews, but the responsibility for "accepting" this knowledge was left to the spectators. Rather than merely reasserting the Nazis' well-known anti-Semitic clichés, the film announced in this unique way that an officially non-existent policy was now being put into practice, and thus made a crucial contribution to the National Socialist's regime's plan to turn the German populace into their willing accomplices.

Andreas Musolff teaches Intercultural Linguistics at the University of East Anglia.

---

[37]   Heinrich Himmler: Geheimreden 1933 bis 1945 und andere Ansprachen von Heinrich Himmler. Ed. by Bradley F. Smith and Agnes F. Peterson. Berlin: Propyläen Verlag, 1974, p. 169; Friedländer: Nazi Germany and the Jews, p. 542-544.

[38]   See Marion A. Kaplan: Between Dignity and Despair. Jewish Life in Nazi Germany. New York: Oxford University Press, 1998, p. 44.

Claudia Buffagni

Romanadaptation als sprachliches Wagnis: Versuch einer soziolinguistischen Untersuchung von Kurt Maetzigs *Das Kaninchen bin ich* (1965)

> „Charmingly independent, the attractive Maria *fends off* the customers at the cafe *with knowing remarks*. Only the school and prison officials are *incapable of understanding a joke*; they seem duty-bound to disapprove of any and all natural human behaviors."[1]

> „[It] was in part because of her [Maria's] honesty – in voiceover she offers *her saucy commentary laced with biting Berlin humor* on the glaring hypocrisies around her – that led to the film's banishment."[2]

Einleitung

Der vorliegende Aufsatz beschäftigt sich mit der filmischen Adaptation von Manfred Bielers Roman *Maria Morzeck oder Das Kaninchen bin ich*, der, 1963 verfasst, in der DDR verboten wurde. Das Romanmanuskript fand im legendären DEFA-Mitbegründer-Regisseur Kurt Maetzig einen aufmerksamen Leser, der daraus mit Bieler ein Drehbuch verfasste und 1965 den Film drehte. Dieser erfuhr ein ähnliches Schicksal wie der Roman: Er kam zwar in die Kinosäle, wurde aber schnell verboten und zurückgezogen, um erst 1990 wieder gezeigt zu werden.

Hier soll die These vertreten werden, dass die Gründe für das Roman- und Filmverbot nicht nur in dem heiklen Thema (Justizfrage), sondern in großem Maße auch in dem von den Figuren an den Tag gelegten Sprachgebrauch[3] zu suchen sind, der implizit eine noch schärfere Kritik an der damaligen Verwaltung der Justiz und im weiteren Sinne an den Machtverhältnissen in der DDR überhaupt darstellt.

Der Beitrag geht zuerst auf einige Merkmale der Sprachvarietäten ein, die im Roman vorkommen und konzentriert sich dann auf die genauere Analyse einiger Sprachvarietäten in der filmischen Fassung. Im Mittelpunkt des Interesses steht die

---

[1]   Glenn Erickson: The Rabbit is Me (Rezension).
     http://www.dvdtalk.com/dvdsavant/s2541rabb.html (konsultiert am 02.04.12).

[2]   Betheny Moore Roberts: The Rabbit is Me and the Banned Films of 1965/66. Essay, DVD-Extras.

[3]   Heinrich Löffler: Germanistische Soziolinguistik. 4. Aufl. Berlin: Erich Schmidt Verlag, 2010, S. 79-112. Vgl. dazu auch Jörn Albrecht: Übersetzung und Varietätenlinguistik: Soziostilistische Probleme der Übersetzung. In: Jörn Albrecht: Übersetzung und Linguistik. Tübingen: Narr, 2005, S. 230-50.

gesprochene Sprache, die aus soziolinguistischer Perspektive untersucht wird.[4] Es wird gezeigt, wie die Figuren durch ihren Sprachgebrauch eine soziale Identität manifestieren,[5] die nicht unbedingt regimekonform ist.

Manfred Bielers Roman: Handlung und Sprache

Manfred Bielers Roman *Maria Morzeck oder Das Kaninchen bin ich* wurde 1963 verfasst, in der DDR verboten, 1969 in der BRD veröffentlicht und erst 1989 DDR-Lesern zugänglich gemacht. Der Autor, der zahlreiche Stücke und Drehbücher sowie weitere erfolgreiche Erzählwerke verfasst hat,[6] war zwar überzeugter Sozialist, hatte aber öffentlich Kritik am damaligen Regime geübt. Ferner hatte er auf die anschließend gegen ihn gerichteten Maßnahmen reagiert, indem er noch im selben Jahr (1963) die DDR verließ und sich mit seiner tschechischen Frau in Prag niederließ, um später in der BRD ansässig zu werden.

Im Mittelpunkt des Romans steht die Geschichte der neunzehnjährigen Maria Morzeck, die „nicht zu den ‚vom Leben bevorzugten Glückskindern' [gehört]".[7] Sie hat mit neun Jahren den Vater und mit siebzehn die Mutter verloren, wohnt mit einer kindlich-naiven Tante, einer eitel-dämlichen jüngeren Schwester (Antje) und einem älteren, zu Gewalt und schlechter Gesellschaft neigenden Bruder (Dieter) zusammen. Letzterer wird wegen Staatshetze zu vier Jahren Gefängnis verurteilt, ohne dass Maria und ihre Tante erfahren können, was für ein Verbrechen der Junge eigentlich begangen hat. Maria darf aus diesem Grund – trotz ihrer guten Noten – nicht Slawistik studieren, um später Dolmetscherin zu werden. Als sie aus Not als Kellnerin in einem Berliner Lokal arbeitet, lernt sie zufälligerweise den Richter Paul Deister kennen, der ihren Bruder verurteilt hat, und beginnt – anfangs noch mit

---

[4] Jannis Androutsopoulos: Intermediale Varietätendynamik. Ein explorativer Blick auf die Inszenierung und Aushandlung von ‚Dialekt' auf YouTube. In: Sociolinguistica 26 (2012).   http://jannisandroutsopoulos.files.wordpress.com/2012/02/2012-intermediale-varietacc88tendynamik-sociolinguistica26_v3_fin.pdf (14 S.) (konsultiert am 24.03.2012).

[5] Ulla Fix: Identität durch Sprache? Eine nachträgliche Konstruktion. In: Nina Janich, Christiane Thim-Mabrey und Abrecht Greule (Hg.): Sprachidentität – Identität durch Sprache. Tübingen: Narr 2003, S. 107-24. Vgl. auch Hans-Werner Eroms: Identität durch Sprache in der neueren deutschen Literatur. In: Janich et al. (Hg.): Sprachidentität – Identität durch Sprache, S. 137-52; sowie Albrecht: Übersetzung und Linguistik, S. 151ff.

[6] Z.B. die Romane *Der Mädchenkrieg* (1975), *Der Kanal* (1978), *Der Bär* (1983) und *Still wie die Nacht* (1989).

[7] Kurt Maetzig: Konzeption für die Entwicklung des Spielfilms nach einem Romanmanuskript von Manfred Bieler. In: Christiane Mückenberger (Hg.): Prädikat: besonders schädlich. Das Kaninchen bin ich. Denk bloß nicht, ich heule. Berlin: Hentschel Verlag, 1990, S. 307-11, hier S. 308. Im Folgenden als *Prädikat: Besonders schädlich* abgekürzt.

dem Hintergedanken, dadurch Dieter helfen zu können – eine Affäre mit ihm. Sie verliebt sich allmählich wirklich in Paul, kommt allerdings ihrem ursprünglichen Ziel, dem Bruder zu helfen, gar nicht näher, da sie ihn ihrem Freund gegenüber nicht einmal erwähnen darf. Erst durch ihre Freundin Edith erfährt sie, was Dieter tatsächlich begangen hat, nämlich etwas, was sich letztlich als ein harmlos-unbeholfener Jugendstreich erweist und unverhältnismäßig hoch bestraft wurde. An ihrer eigenen Haut muss sie also erfahren, dass die Justiz zuweilen nicht funktioniert. Schließlich verfasst sie gegen den Rat ihres Geliebten, von dem sie sich kurze Zeit später trennt, ein Gnadengesuch. Inzwischen wird ihr Bruder freigelassen und schlägt sie brutal, als er von ihrem Verhältnis mit Paul erfährt. Maria, die immer noch Dolmetscherin werden will, leidet an Schlafstörungen und fängt an, ihre Geschichte in der Hoffnung niederzuschreiben, dadurch ihre Gesundheit wiederherzustellen. Das bildet die durchwegs aus der Ich-Perspektive erfolgende Rahmenerzählung.

Sprachlich zeichnet sich der Roman durch die Lebendigkeit der Dialoge aus, die meist Berlinisch gefärbt sind und sich je nach geschildertem sozialem Milieu differenzieren: So kommen Schülersprache, Lokaljargon, Untergrundjargon, Ganovensprache, FDJ-Jargon und juristische Sprache vor.

Marias Sprechweise signalisiert eine große Schlagfertigkeit. Wenn sie allein ist, denkt sie zwar mit Sehnsucht an die verstorbene Mutter, sonst legt sie aber als Schutz eine aus berlinischer Altklugheit bestehende Maske an, die ihr soziales Image als selbstbewusstes Mädchen konstituiert:

> Ich hatte schwarze Ringe um die Augen, aber das war zu der Zeit noch nicht modern, das kam von meinen Nachtwachen [wegen Antjes schwerer Krankheit]. Einer von den Jungs fragte mich, wie lange ich so im Durchschnitt auf'n Freier warten muß, am Oranienburger Tor. „Ich schaffe zehne in der Stunde", antwortete ich, „bei mir macht's die Menge, nicht die Qualität!"[8]

Dass es sich dabei um eine bewusst aufgelegte, schützende Maske handelt, ergibt sich aus dem direkt darauf folgenden Kommentar der Ich-Erzählerin, die einen Dialog mit dem Leser fingiert und auf dessen erwartbare Reaktion antwortet („Hätte ich [...]? Nee."):

> Er wurde rot und drehte ab, aber ich hab mir das gemerkt. Auf die Weise wird man die Brüder am besten los: wenn man sie übertrumpft. Hätte ich sagen sollen: Ich muß die ganze Nacht bei meiner kleinen Schwester sitzen, damit sie meiner Mutter nicht Gesellschaft leistet...? Nee. Er hätte meine Mutter und meine Schwester auch noch *in 'n Dreck gezogen*. Gleich Saures und *eins übers Maul* und fertig. *Penner*.[9]

---

8   Manfred Bieler: Maria Morzeck oder das Kaninchen bin ich. Berlin: Ullstein, 1998, S.24.
9   Bieler: Maria Morzeck, S.24. [Die Kursivierung hier und in weiteren Zitaten dient der Hervorhebung der besprochenen Merkmale und stammt jeweils von der Verfasserin.]

Durch die letzte kommentierende Bemerkung (die *Penner* als umgangssprachliche Bezeichnung für einen unangenehmen Menschen verwendet) und zwei Phraseologismen (*jdn. in den Dreck ziehen, ein[e]s übers Maul [hauen]*) lässt sie erkennen, wie peinlich ihr im Grunde diese Kommunikationsart ist, was durch den folgenden Satz bestätigt wird („Gott sei Dank sind nicht alle so. Ulli, zum Beispiel, war anders").

Die Erzählerstimme berichtet aus der Perspektive einer nun einundzwanzigjährigen Frau über Geschehnisse der vergangenen vier Jahre. Das führt dazu, dass der Erzählduktus die meisten Züge mit Marias Figurenrede gemeinsam hat. Die Erzählerstimme weist dabei Merkmale einer – fingierten[10] – gesprochenen Alltagssprache auf, die berlinisch gefärbt ist:

a. Syntaktische Ebene:
    - häufige Parataxe („Jetzt habe ich einen Bogen in die Schreibmaschine gespannt und schreibe. Mal sehn. Vielleicht hilft's. Vielleicht wird's besser davon. [...] Bei so was blättere ich immer gleich weiter, denn Himmel und Sterne lassen mich verhältnismäßig kalt.")
    - Pausen und Wiederholungen
b. Lexikalische Ebene:
    - umgangssprachliche Lexik (*Textilbude, saust, Bums, transusig*)[11]
    - viele Abtönungspartikel („Aber so geht's *ja* nicht weiter, nicht ewig", „weil's *ja doch* nichts weiter ist [...]", „ich will *mal* sagen")[12]
c. Phonetische Ebene:
    - phonetische Sprecherleichterungen und Verschleifungen (*sehn, kuckt, fuffzig*)[13] und die gesprochene Sprache kennzeichnende Auslassungen (*'ne* Antenne, mir's)[14]
    - viele Abtönungen
    - dazu kommen vereinzelt dialektale Züge (phonetisch und vor allem lexikalisch, vgl.: „Wenn meine Mutter [...] einen kleinen *getütert* hatte [...]")[15]
d. Textebene:
    - die Behandlung des Themas wirkt sprunghaft, nicht linear

Als idiolektaler Zug lässt sich – auf der lexikalischen Ebene – ferner eine Vorliebe für bestimmte Phraseologismen erkennen („Das ist nicht mein Bier", „wer weiß

---

[10] Vgl. dazu auch Eroms: Identität durch Sprache in der neueren deutschen Literatur, S. 137-52; Heinz-Helmut Lüger: Höflichkeit und Textstil. In: Zofia Bilut-Homplewicz et al. (Hg.): Text und Stil. Frankfurt a.M.: Peter Lang, 2010, S. 261-77.

[11]. Bieler: Maria Morzeck, S. 6, S. 189.

[12]. Bieler: Maria Morzeck, S. 5.

[13] Bieler: Maria Morzeck S. 5, S. 7, S.9.

[14] Bieler: Maria Morzeck, S. 5. Vgl. Löffler: Germanistische Soziolinguistik, S. 85f.

[15] Bieler: Maria Morzeck, S. 7.

Käse", „Dieter sah aus wie Braunbier mit Spucke", „'na Mahlzeit").[16] Außerdem sind einige gruppenspezifische, die Jugendsprache kennzeichnende, gezielt eingeführte Fremdwörter zu verzeichnen, insbesondere Anglizismen.[17]
Das Berlinische gibt sich u.a. durch folgende lautliche Besonderheiten zu erkennen:

1. Spirantisierung von /g/ zu [j] (*gehabt –> jehabt*)
2. Ersatz des palatalen Frikativs /ç/ (Ich-Lautes) durch stimmlosen velaren Verschlusslaut [k] (z.B. Personalpronomen ich –> *ick* oder *icke*][18]
3. Ersatz des alveolaren Frikativs /s/ durch stimmlosen dentalen Verschlusslaut [t] (*was –> wat*; *es –> et*)
4. Monopthongierung von /au/ zu [o:] (*auch –> ooch*; *auf –> uff*)
5. Monopthongierung von /ei/ zu [e:] (*mein –> meen*)[19]

Auch die Romanfiguren geben sich primär gerade durch ihren Sprachgebrauch zu erkennen. Je nach Figur und Situation sprechen sie ein mehr oder weniger stark akzentuiertes gesprochensprachliches Berlinisch. Bei ihnen lassen sich – verstärkt oder abgemildert – dieselben Merkmale erkennen, die auf allen Sprachebenen anzutreffen sind. Dazu sind auf der lexikalischen Ebene auch Konstruktionsbrüche zu verzeichnen.

Im Folgenden werden einige Textbeispiele geliefert, bei denen auf die kommunikative Verwendung des Code-Wechsels (also das Umschalten von einer Sprache auf eine andere, oder von einem Sprachgebrauch auf einen anderen) eingegangen wird.

Die Figur, die am meisten „berlinert", ist Tante Hete, wodurch deren Mangel an Bildung, ihre Ortsgebundenheit und ihre Naivität unterstrichen werden soll (die in der folgenden Passage direkt von ihr selber thematisiert wird):

„Was sollten wir denn machen?" fragte Tante Hete, ohne Edith böse zu sein. „Maria ging noch auf Schule, Antje war *man* erst *fuffzehn*, und *ick* bin für so *'ne* Sachen einfach zu *dußlig*, Frau Jakobs. Wenn mir einer erzählt, im Himmel *is* Jahrmarkt, *ick gloobe det ooch*. Ich bin da nicht pfiffig genug, und mal ehrlich – was hätten wir denn machen können? Was *wär* uns denn damit gedient gewesen, wenn wir das, was Sie jetzt erzählen, schon vorher gewußt hätten? Wir hätten ja

---

[16] Bieler: Maria Morzeck, S. 5, 7, 21, 104.
[17] Beispiele für Anglizismen und sonstige Fremdwörter, die Marias Redeweise (sowohl als Ich-Erzählerin als auch als Romanfigur) kennzeichnen, sind u.a. *cleversten* (S. 34), *Beau* (S. 71), *Friseur* (S. 72) *Lover* (S. 123). Ferner verweist sie auf die schon im Titel durch westliche, und zwar angelsächsische, Kultur beeinflusste TV-Sendung: *Seventy-Seven-Sunset-Strip* (S. 149), die in der DDR sehr populär war.
[18] Ausnahmen, die im Roman anzutreffen sind: „nicht" wird zu „nischt".
[19] Androutsopoulos: Intermediale Varietätendynamik, S. 9.

doch *keenen* Gebrauch davon machen dürfen, sonst hätten wir wieder *'n* andern ins Unglück gestürzt. Woher sollten wir denn das überhaupt wissen?"[20]

Die Passage weist Beispiele für die oben dargelegten (und nummerierten) lautlichen Phänomene auf: 2. (*ick*), 3. (*det*), 4. (*uff*), 5. (*keenen*). Außerdem kommen Merkmale der Alltagssprache vor (*man*: Umgangssprache mit norddeutscher Färbung; vgl. auch *fuffzehn, dußlig, is, wär*). Überraschend ist das Fehlen von Beispielen für 1., obwohl der Text durchaus passende Wörter enthält (*gedient gewesen, gewusst, Gebrauch, Unglück, gestürzt*). Das kann vielleicht als partieller Code-Wechsel von Berlinisch zu einer neutraleren Alltagssprache gedeutet werden: Tante Hete setzt sich mit einem ernsten Thema auseinander und gibt sich Mühe, verstanden zu werden (und ihr Gesicht zu schonen). Sie bemüht sich entsprechend – im Rahmen ihrer Fähigkeiten – um eine korrektere, „der Standardsprache nähere" Ausdrucksweise. Der von der jeweiligen Figur verwendete Soziolekt [21] wird nämlich bekanntlich durch den Handlungszusammenhang, die Sprachteilnehmer, den Ort sowie ggf. weitere außersprachliche Faktoren bestimmt. Hier spielt z.B. das Gesprächsthema die wichtigste Rolle.

Die nächste Passage, die nur nach wenigen Zeilen folgt, kann als Bestätigung dieser Vermutung betrachtet werden, denn sie weist deutlich verstärkt dialektale Züge auf:

„*Jebense* mal her, *det Pampelchen, jebense* mal her!" [Tante Hete zu Edith] [...] „Das ist ja *ooch Natür*", sagte Tante Hete auf französisch, „und Natur muß riechen. Da beißt die Maus *keen'* Faden ab. Was *meinste* denn, Kind, woraus Creme gemacht wird? Alles Schweineschmalz, *nischt* als Schweineschmalz, bloß die kippen noch *'n Troppen* Rosenöl *rin*, im Verhältnis: ein *Troppen Parföng* – eine Tonne Schmalz, das duftet dann so *'n* bißchen, und die Dose *kost'* nachher zehn Mark. Bei mir *nich*! *Nu mal* das andere Füßchen?"[22]

Diese Passage kreist inhaltlich um unwesentlichere Themen (Fußsalbe, Parfum...) als die vorherige; nicht zufällig weist sie auch Beispiele für Punkt 1. (*jebense*) auf. Außerdem kommen 3. (*det*), 4. (*ooch*), 5. (*keen'*),[23] sowie die Verwandlung des Affrikatlauts *pf* (Tro*pf*en) in den Okklusivlaut *p* (Tro*pp*en) vor.[24] Lexikalisch fällt

---

[20] Bieler: Maria Morzeck, S. 161.
[21] Vgl. Löffler: Germanistische Soziolinguistik, S. 114.
[22] Bieler: Maria Morzeck, S. 161.
[23] Dieselbe Variation betrifft das Diphthong „ei" bekanntlich nicht in anderen lautlichen Kontexten: Vgl. im selben Redebeitrag, „meinste". Im selben Dialog verwendet Tante Hete übrigens zwei unterschiedliche Substandard-Varianten für „nicht": „nischt" und „nich".
[24] Diese Verwandlung ist übrigens typisch für die norddeutschen Dialekte, die meist mit der unscharfen Bezeichnung „Platt" identifiziert werden.

Pampelchen auf, sowie die „phonetische Transkription" von Tante Hetes unkorrekter Aussprache französischer Wörter (*Natür, Parföng, Pangsion*).[25]

Maria, die einen ausgesprochen starken Sinn für metasprachliche Reflexion zeigt,[26] indem sie die Menschen gerade in Hinsicht auf deren Sprachverwendung zu beurteilen scheint, bekennt sich zu ihrer Generation, indem sie ihre Sprache mit westlichen Wendungen spickt und beweist, die damaligen kulturellen Erscheinungen zu kennen (vgl. die Erwähnung der Halbstarken, des Existenzialismus, sowie die Verweise auf die Kino-Kultur). Sprachlich gibt sie sich weiterhin als „Berliner Göre". Es lässt sich eine „positiv-aufwertende Haltung zum Berlinerischen" erkennen.[27]

Dargestellt wird eine Skala von Sprachgebräuchen, an deren äußersten Polen die berlinische Alltagssprache und die offizielle Sprache stehen.

1. Die – berlinisch gefärbte – Alltagssprache erweist sich als die höchste Stufe der Sprache der Nähe, d.h. der kollaborativen Kameradschaft (mit den Kollegen im Café *Clou*), der Familie (mit Tante Hete und dem Bruder), aber insbesondere auch der Liebe (z.B. im Dialog mit dem Freund Ulli, und später mit Paul) und der Freundschaft.
2. Die offizielle, in öffentlichen Kontexten verwendete Sprache erweist sich hingegen oft als Sprache der Falschheit, der Heuchelei oder der verständnis- und mitleidlosen Regeldurchführung.
3. Die Standardsprache erweist sich als Sprachgebrauch der Mitte: In den persönlichen Gesprächen wird sie verwendet, wenn zwischen den Partnern eine gewisse Entfremdung entsteht.

Beispiele für Gespräche, die meist in der Standardsprache geführt werden, sind die Dialoge zwischen Gudrun Deister und Maria bzw. zwischen Paul Deister und Maria.[28] In beiden schaltet Maria auf Berlinisch um, sobald sie die Notwendigkeit fühlt, sich auszusprechen, die ganze Wahrheit zu erzählen. Berlinisch konstituiert sich mithin als Sprache der Nähe, der Gefühle, der Unmittelbarkeit, das Standard-Hochdeutsch als Sprache des Verstands, der rationalen Erklärungen.

Maria erkennt sich im berlinisch gefärbten alltagssprachlichen Sprachgebrauch wieder und will nicht zuletzt aus diesem (sprachlichen) Grund Ostberlin nicht verlassen. [29] Auch Maetzigs filmische Hauptfigur hegt keinerlei Wünsche, Republikflucht zu begehen, denn ihre Identität ist stark ostberlinisch geprägt. Marias

---

25 Bieler: Maria Morzeck, S. 218.
26 Maria versteht die soziale Bedeutung (als einzige ihr zur Verfügung stehende Aufstiegsmöglichkeit) der Bildung und der Bildungssprache, obwohl sie sich über deren Besonderheit auch lustig macht, z.B. verwendet sie lustvoll den Ausdruck „Schatzkammer menschlichen Wissens" als Beispiel des einen Lehrer kennzeichnenden Sprachgebrauchs (S. 57).
27 Vgl. Androutsopoulos: Intermediale Varietätendynamik, S. 9.
28 Bieler: Maria Morzeck, S. 256-66.
29 Bieler: Maria Morzeck, S. 64f.

Liebes- und Leidensgeschichte entwickelt sich ganz in der DDR, und zwar zwischen Ostberlin und Brandenburg.

Die Sprache der Autorität wirkt kalt und distanziert, die Kommunikation mit deren Verwaltern erweist sich als schwierig: Hauptbeispiele dafür sind der Staatsanwalt und der Richter im Prozess gegen Dieter sowie der Schuldirektor von Marias Gymnasium; weitere Beispiele sind der Wachtmeister im Brandenburger Gefängnis[30] und die jungen FDJ-Genossen, die sich untereinander als „verehrte Jugendfreunde" ansprechen. Das wird im Folgenden anhand einiger Textpassagen dargelegt.

Beispiel 1

[Der Richter] setzte eine Brille auf und sagte, daß wir den siebenundzwanzigsten hätten und Dieter Morzeck wegen Staatsverleumdung und planmäßiger Hetze angeklagt sei. [...] Der Staatsanwalt erhob sich und verlangte, im Interesse der Geheimhaltung von Staatsgeheimnissen die Öffentlichkeit von der weiteren Verhandlung auszuschließen. [...]. Dem Antrag des Staatsanwalts wurde stattgegeben, und der Grüne, der an der Tür stand, winkte uns beiden, mir und Tante Hete, damit wir den Saal verließen. [...] Komischerweise waren wir die einzigen, die rausmußten.[31]

Die Passage berichtet über den Verlauf des Prozesses gegen Dieter Morzeck. Dabei wird die mangelnde Kommunikation zwischen den Vertretern der staatlichen Autorität (dem Gericht) und den Angehörigen des Angeklagten hervorgehoben, die all die kleinen Leute darstellen, von denen erwartet wird, dass sie den Gesetzen gehorchen, ohne Fragen zu stellen. Die Äußerungen sind durchaus gesichtsbedrohend,[32] denn – anders als alle weiteren sich im Gerichtsraum befindenden Zuschauer, die über „Einladungen" verfügen – dürfen Maria und Tante Hete nicht einmal der ihre Familie direkt betreffenden Verhandlung beiwohnen.

Beispiel 2

„Setzen Sie sich", sagte er freundlich, und als ich mich hingesetzt hatte, stand er auf und lief ein paar Schritte über das Parkett.

---

[30]   Der Wachtmeister zeichnet sich dadurch aus, dass er eine sehr offizielle Sprache verwendet. Insbesondere zeigt er eine Vorliebe für Passivsätze, was Maria gleich unangenehm berührt (S. 102-07).

[31]   Bieler: Maria Morzeck, S. 17ff.

[32]   Erving Goffmann: On Face-Work. An Analysis of Ritual Elements in Social Interaction. In: Erving Goffman: Interactional Ritual. Essays on Face-to-Face Behaviour. London: Penguin 1972, S. 5-46: „Face is an image of self delineated in terms of approved social attributes – albeit an image that others may share, as when a person makes a good showing for his profession or religion by making a good showing for himself" (S. 5).

„Wie lange muß Ihr Bruder noch dort bleiben?"

„Dreieinhalb Jahre," sagte ich.

„Sagen Sie mal, Morzeck – warum hat er das eigentlich getan?"

„Ich weiß nicht, Herr Direktor. Wie sie bei Gericht darauf zu sprechen kamen, mußten wir raus." [...]

„Verstehe," sagte er. „Aber Sie verabscheuen doch seine Tat, nicht wahr?"

„Ich weiß gar nicht, was er gemacht hat."

Er drehte sich auf dem Absatz um und sah mich sprachlos an.

„Na ja," sagte ich.

„Aber Kind – das stand sogar in der Zeitung!" [...]

„Mir wär es angenehmer, wenn ich's von ihm selber gehört hätte," sagte ich.

„Haben Sie denn kein Vertrauen zu unseren Gerichten?"

„Wie man's nimmt," sagte ich. „Ich finde eher, unsere Gerichte haben kein Vertrauen zu mir. Sonst hätten sie mich doch dringelassen bei der Verhandlung."

„So dürfen Sie das nicht sehen," sagte der Direktor. „Es gibt gewisse Dinge, die man der Öffentlichkeit im Augenblick noch nicht mitteilen kann. Wer garantiert uns denn dafür, daß diese Sachen nicht weitergetragen werden? Was?"

„Jaja," sagte ich, „aber wer garantiert mir dafür, daß mein Bruder wirklich was verbrochen hat?" [...]

„Morzeck, Morzeck," sagte er und massierte sich die Schläfen, „wie wollen Sie mit einer solchen Haltung weiterkommen? Wohin? Wohin geraten Sie damit eines Tages? Es war doch in der Presse!"[33]

Das Gespräch wird fast durchweg in Standardsprache geführt, denn der Direktor gibt darin den Ton an. Er erwartet von Maria, dass sie sich auf der Grundlage eines absoluten Vertrauens zu den Gesetzen der sozialistischen Republik von ihrem Bruder distanziert, der wegen staatsgefährdender Hetze verurteilt worden ist. Er spielt seine Autorität als Schuloberhaupt auch szenisch aus, indem er aufsteht und von dieser Position aus zu der sitzenden Maria redet. Seine Worte sind gesichtsbedrohend für Maria.[34] Die Gymnasiastin reagiert aber als gleichberechtigter Gesprächspartner, lässt sich nicht von der offiziellen Sprache einschüchtern und weist die Drohung zurück, indem sie auf ihre Erfahrung zurückgreift. Diese Haltung wird vom Schuldirektor gleichzeitig als gesichtsschonend für Maria selbst (sie akzeptiert die Kritik an ihrer Familie nicht, sie verlangt Beweise) und als

---

[33] Bieler: Maria Morzeck, S. 43f.

[34] In dieser Szene ist die Gesichtsbedrohung besonders stark: Vgl. Benjamin Stoltenburg: Was wir sagen, wenn wir es ‚ehrlich' sagen. Äußerungskommentierende Formeln von Stellungnahmen am Beispiel von ‚ehrlich gesagt'. In: Susanne Günthner und Jörg Bücker (Hg.): Grammatik im Gespräch. Konstruktionen der Selbst- und Fremdpositionierung. Berlin: de Gruyter, 2009, S. 249-81. „Die Gesichtsbedrohung einer Handlung lässt sich nach der universalen Formel errechnen: Die Schwere einer Gesichtsbedrohung ergibt sich aus der Kombination der Faktoren ‚soziale Distanz', ‚Macht' und der ‚Bedrohung/Zumutung' für das *negative face* (Selbstbestimmung, Freiheit) oder *positive face* (Anerkennung)" (S. 265).

gesichtsbedrohend für die DDR-Gerichte (Maria kritisiert deren undurchsichtige Vorgehensweise) interpretiert. Er wird später dafür sorgen, dass die begabte Gymnasiastin – im Unterschied zu all ihren Schulkameraden – keinen Studienplatz bekommt.

Im gesamten Roman fungiert der Dialekt nicht primär als „Stimme des einfachen Mannes", [35] sondern eher als Stimme des authentischen Menschen und als Hervorhebung der eigenen Identität. Die häufig mit dialektalen Zügen versehene Umgangssprache wird alles in allem positiv konnotiert und spielt eine wichtige Rolle bei der Herstellung und Mitteilung der sozialen Identität. Die grammatisch korrekte Standardsprache wird im Roman oft in der Distanzkommunikation (vgl. das oben angeführte Beispiel für Code-Wechsel) verwendet. Sie eignet sich ferner zum Schwindeln und zur Manipulation. Am entgegengesetzten Pol steht der offizielle Sprachgebrauch, der sich als bedrohliche Sprache der staatlichen Gewalt erweist.

Maetzigs Filmadaptation: Schauplätze und Handlung

Kurt Maetzig entschloss sich mit dem Film *Das Kaninchen bin ich* im durch Chrustschow gerade eingeleiteten Prozess „zur Demokratisierung und zu größerer Rechtssicherheit", der „auch in der DDR einen entsprechenden Reflex fand[...]", selbst einen Beitrag zu liefern. Er wollte dadurch insbesondere „die Möglichkeit der Abhaltung von Gerichtsverhandlungen in Betrieben oder Dörfern unter Mitwirkung von gesellschaftlichen Verteidigern" unterstützen. [36]

Der Regisseur entschied sich deshalb dafür, im Film eine im Roman nicht vorhandene Episode einzubauen, die den zweiten Teil des Films dominiert: den Fall des Fischers Grambow und des darauf folgenden öffentlichen Prozesses im Dorf.[37]

---

[35]   Androutsopoulos: Intermediale Varietätendynamik, S. 2.

[36]   Christiane Mückenberger: Interview mit Kurt Maetzig zu *Das Kaninchen bin ich*. In: Mückenberger (Hg.): Prädikat: besonders schädlich, S. 319.

[37]   Die Filmhandlung unterscheidet sich von der Romanhandlung dadurch, dass Maria, um besser von einer leichten Erkrankung (Spondylosis) zu genesen, sich mehrere Monate auf dem Land in Pauls Datscha im Berliner Umland (in Breganz) aufhält. Der Geliebte besucht sie jedes Wochenende. Maria arbeitet zwischendurch als Kellnerin in der Gaststätte des Wirtes Beetz. An einem Abend, als Maria und Paul im Lokal tanzen, kommt plötzlich der betrunkene Fischer Grambow in den Saal. Er teilt mit, dass er die ertrunkene Leiche eines Unteroffiziers gefunden habe und beschimpft anschließend die Armee. Die Anwesenden machen daraufhin Anstalten eine Schlägerei zu beginnen. Paul gibt sich als Richter zu erkennen und bittet den Wirt, die Polizei zu rufen. Da sich diese nicht erreichen lässt, schaltet sich der Bürgermeister ein: Im Unterschied zu Paul ist er dagegen, die Bezirksautorität zu verständigen, und lässt Grambow nach Hause gehen. Am selben Abend begibt sich der Bürgermeister zu Pauls Datscha, um mit ihm über den Vorfall zu reden. Die beiden legen grundlegend verschiedene Einschätzungen der Rechtsprechung an den Tag. Der Bürgermeister setzt sich durch und beruft eine offizielle Dorfversammlung ein.

Er wollte sich nämlich mit seinem Film nicht auf die Kritik beschränken, sondern auch ein positives Beispiel geben:

[Es ging] mir gleichzeitig um die Unterstützung der Demokratisierung [...]. Das bedingte eine Umarbeitung des Stoffes. Der ganze Komplex der Gerichtsverhandlung auf dem Dorf, der so augenscheinlich kontrastiert zu der ersten Gerichtsverhandlung, bei der die Öffentlichkeit ausgeschlossen wurde, kam hinein. Manfred Bieler fand sich zu dieser Veränderung bereit, weil er hoffte, dadurch den verbotenen Roman für die damalige DDR annehmbar zu machen.[38]

Der Schritt vom Roman zum Film [39] erforderte notwendigerweise gründliche Variationen des Stoffs, die Figurenkonstellation (1), Schauplätze und Handlungsräume (2) sowie Handlungsinhalte und Reihenfolge der Ereignisse (3) betrafen.

Was die Figurenkonstellation (1) angeht, so ist das Drehbuch durch eine deutliche Reduzierung gekennzeichnet, indem einige als unwesentlich betrachtete Romanfiguren getilgt werden. Andererseits kamen im Drehbuch die Figuren aus dem Breganz-Aufenthalt (einschließlich des Prozesses) hinzu.

Bei den Schauplätzen und Handlungsräumen (2) gibt es neben einigen Auslassungen auch Abwandlungen. Die grundlegendsten Veränderungen bestehen im Weglassen der moralisch durchaus anfechtbaren Wohnung in der Ackerstraße[40] und im Streichen von Marias Besuch in Pauls Wohnung (wo sie dessen Frau trifft).

In Bezug auf die Handlungsinhalte und die Reihenfolge der Ereignisse (3) folgt das Drehbuch der Reihenfolge des Romans. Unterschiede bestehen in den Auslassungen und im Schluss: Im Roman wohnt die Hauptfigur mit der Freundin Edith zusammen, arbeitet im Café *Clou* weiter und weiß noch nicht, was aus ihr werden wird, während im Drehbuch Maria sich – anscheinend mit guten Chancen – um einen Studienplatz bewirbt und auf ,ein Zimmer für sich allein' im Sinne von Virginia Woolf Aussicht hat.

Maetzigs Filmadaptation: Die Sprache, zwischen Off-Stimme und In-Dialogen

Dass der Film *Das Kaninchen bin ich*, der sich als Beitrag zur Gestaltung eines „Sozialismus mit menschlichem Antlitz" verstand, [41] von einigen Parteifunktionären

---

38 Mückenberger: Interview mit Kurt Maetzig, S. 319f.
39 Im Folgenden wird auf die veröffentlichte Drehbuch-Version aus dem Jahr 1965 Bezug genommen. Vgl. Manfred Bieler: Kurt Maetzig, „Das Kaninchen bin ich". In: Mückenberger (Hg.): Prädikat: Besonders schädlich, S. 23-177. Der Text erweist sich bis auf einige Ausnahmen als identisch mit dem Filmtext. Im Folgenden wird deshalb aus dem Drehbuch zitiert, das als „Das Kaninchen bin ich" abgekürzt wird.
40 Sie wird dramaturgisch geschickt durch die dank der Präsenz der Landschaft „moralisch" rehabilitierte Breganzer Datscha ersetzt.
41 Auszug aus einem Filminterview von Ralf Schenk mit Kurt Maetzig aus dem Jahr 1999 (Video). Vgl. auch Ingrid Poss und Peter Warnecke (Hg.): Spur der Filme. Zeitzeugen

als solcher auch interpretiert wurde und schon die unterschiedlichen Prüfungsstadien passiert hatte, letztlich doch im Dezember 1965 im Laufe des 11. Parteikomitees verboten und aus den Kinosälen zurückgezogen wurde, ist nicht zuletzt auf die unkonventionelle Sprachbehandlung der Figuren zurückzuführen, die die Ablehnung des sozialistisch „politisch korrekten" Sprachmodus zum Ausdruck brachte.

Wie dargelegt zeichnet dieser Aspekt sehr deutlich schon Bielers Roman aus, kommt aber im Film dank der diesem Medium eigenen Unmittelbarkeit – und trotz der Veränderungen, Auslassungen und Hinzufügungen, die im Laufe der Arbeit am Drehbuch auch in Absprache mit Parteifunktionären beschlossen wurden – noch stärker zum Ausdruck. Bild, Musik[42] und Ton werden auf sehr moderne Weise verkoppelt. Der Film unterstreicht dabei ferner die Präsenz der amerikanisch-angelsächsischen Kultur. In der Handhabung der filmtechnischen Mittel kommen allerdings auch der Einfluss der *Nouvelle Vague* und des italienischen Neorealismus zur Geltung (z.B. im gekonnten Umgang mit den Schwarz-Weiß-Gestaltungsmöglichkeiten, in den vielen Naheinstellungen, im direkten Blick der Protagonistin ins Objektiv und in der steten Bewegung der Kamera). Der Rhythmus des Films wird durch die in den 1960er Jahren hoch in Kurs stehende Beat-Musik deutlich mitbestimmt.[43] Dies stellte eine subtile und daher von den Autoritäten umso entschiedener zurückzuweisende Kritik am öffentlich propagierten und gepriesenen sozialistischen Kommunikationsmodus dar.

Was die Figurensprache angeht, so zeichnet sich der Film durch die medien-wirksame Unmittelbarkeit der – notwendigerweise schriftlich konzipierten – Dialoge aus, die sehr überzeugend authentisch klingen.[44] Sie sind also ein gutes Beispiel für gelungene fingierte Mündlichkeit.

Sprachlich sind im Film (sowohl ansatzweise in der Off-Stimme als auch verstärkt in der Figurensprache) dieselben Phänomene zu erkennen, die im Roman beobachtet wurden, und zwar: häufige Parataxe, Pausen und Wiederholungen sowie Konstruktionsbrüche auf der syntaktischen Ebene, reduzierter Wortschatz

---

über die DEFA, S. 202, und Wolfgang Gersch: Film in der DDR. Die verlorene Alternative. In: Wolfgang Jakobsen, Anton Kaes und Hans Helmut Prinzler (Hg.): Geschichte des deutschen Films. 2. Auflage. Stuttgart und Weimar: Metzler 2004, S. 357-404, hier: S. 382. Vgl. ferner Bernard Eisenschitz: Le cinéma allemand. Paris, Armand Collin 2005.

[42] Die Filmmusik wurde von den bekannten Komponisten Gerhard Rosenfeld und Reiner Bredemeyer verfasst. Letzterer avancierte zum bedeutendsten Komponisten seiner Zeit; er gehört zur Komponistengeneration, die sich vom Sozialistischen Realismus löste und an der westlichen Avantgarde orientierte. Er ließ sich u.a. von der Musik von John Cage und Morton Feldman inspirieren.

[43] Vgl. Benoit Blanchard: *Das Kaninchen bin ich* oder die Ästhetik des Neuen Films. Verfügbar unter: http://www2.hu-berlin.de/francopolis/films/Kaninchen.htm (konsultiert am 10.04.12).

[44] Vgl. Peter Koch und Wulf Österreicher: Sprache der Nähe – Sprache der Distanz. Mündlichkeit und Schriftlichkeit im Spannungsfeld von Sprachtheorie und Sprachgeschichte. In: Romanistisches Jahrbuch 36 (1985), S. 15-43.

(lexikalische Ebene); viele Abtönungen, Ansätze von Dialekt oder Merkmalen einer regionalen Umgangssprache, phonetische Sprecherleichterungen und Verschleifungen (phonetische Ebene). Dazu kommt der verstärkte Einsatz von nonverbalen und paraverbalen Mitteln anstelle von verbalen Äußerungen.

Aus dem Romanmonolog wurde ein „zupackend[er] [Film]dialog mit dem Zuschauer".[45] Das Einbeziehen des Publikums konnte weitreichendere Folgen bei diesem bewirken, da es sich unmittelbarer in dem auf dem Schirm dargestellten Schicksal involviert fühlte, wie das folgende Beispiel zeigt:

5. Bild […]

Maria (K):
Das ist so meine Welt... […] das „Alt-Bayern". Hier bin ich Serviererin von acht bis drei. Um acht bin ich noch *flott*, um elf bin ich müde, um eins *marode* und um drei kaputt. […] Aber ich hab's wenigstens nicht weit nach Hause. Ich wohne am Oranienburger Tor – oder denken Sie etwa, ich bin in diesem Laden geboren? *Nee, ich hatte große Rosinen im Kopp.* Wollte Slawistik studieren. Ging zur Oberschule und lernte alles, was man dazu braucht […], aber das reichte nicht, *kam was dazwischen* […].[46]

Das Publikum wird direkt – als Voyeur – angesprochen und seine erwartbaren negativen Urteile (über die Anfechtbarkeit des Lokals und womöglich der Sprecherin) werden Stück für Stück widerlegt.[47] In dem für sie charakteristischen Ton, der alltagssprachlich ist (*flott*, *marode*), Phraseologismen aufweist (*Rosinen im Kopp*) und berlinisch gefärbt ist (*Nee*, *Kopp*), beginnt Maria ihre Geschichte zu erzählen. Dabei schützt sie ihr Gesicht ([…] *ich hatte große Rosinen im Kopp. Wollte Slawistik studieren. Ging zur Oberschule und lernte alles, was man dazu braucht […], aber das reichte nicht, kam was dazwischen*). Zugleich beruhigt sie die Zuschauer dahingehend, dass ihnen nichts Unmoralisches dargeboten wird. Dabei wird auch auf das Gesicht des Publikums Rücksicht genommen.

Wie im Roman wird auch im Film die Sprache der Autorität als problematisch dargestellt (Richter, Schuldirektor…). Im Mittelpunkt des Films steht die Gegenüberstellung von zwei Prozessen, die sich durch Situation, Teilnehmer, Durchführung, Ergebnis und Sprache unterscheiden. In der Fischerepisode wird diese Spannung zwischen berlinisch gefärbter Alltagssprache und Sprache der

---

45. Mückenberger: Interview mit Kurt Maetzig zu *Das Kaninchen bin ich*, S. 320f: „Das Drehbuch […] ließ […] *Schärfe des Ausdrucks, berlinischen Witz und treffende Auseinandersetzungen* erkennen." (Dezember 1989; Kursivschrift der Verfasserin)

46. „Das Kaninchen bin ich", S. 26f.

47. Vgl. auch Joshua Feinstein: The Eleventh Plenum and *Das Kaninchen bin ich*. In: Joshua Feinstein: The Triumph of the Ordinary. Depictions of Daily Life in the East German Cinema 1949-1989. Chapel Hill, NC, und London: University of North Carolina Press, 2001, S. 151-75.

Autorität aufgehoben: Da findet eine positive, die Wahrheit suchende Kommunikation statt (seitens des Richters und später seitens des Bürgermeisters).

Paul Deister als Richter in der Strafsache Dieter Morzeck[48]	Der Richter in der Strafsache Grambow – Dorfprozess[49]
22. Querfahrt (mit den beiden)	**268. Total**
Maria und Tante Hete betreten den Sitzungssaal und nehmen in einer der vorderen Stuhlreihen Platz. Etwa zehn andere Zuhörer sitzen bereits im Saal und weitere kommen nach und nach herein; sie bewegen sich sachlich, kühl, selbstverständlich, geschäftlich. Ihre Nüchternheit steht im krassen Gegensatz zur Aufregung Marias und Tante Hetes. […] Am Schluss des Kommentars, den wir auf den Gesichtern von Maria und Tante Hete erleben, erheben sich die Zuschauer. Auch Maria und Tante Hete.	Der Saal ist voller Menschen. Alle sehen mit Spannung nach vorn. Grambow hat auf einem Stuhl Platz genommen, der vor der ersten Reihe steht. Dabei hören wir den letzten Satz von Pauls Erinnerungsstimme: Ich bitte, daß die betreffenden Personen den Saal verlassen. […] Der Saal ist übervoll, auch an der Tür drängen sich die Leute, und ein paar Kinder drücken von außen ihre Nasen an der Fensterscheibe platt.
23 Langsame Anfahrt – Total – Nah (auf Paul Deister) An den Tischen haben der Staatsanwalt (Hoppe), der Verteidiger und eine Protokollantin Platz genommen. Sie stehen jetzt. Auch Dieter steht vor der Anklagebank neben dem Volkspolizisten. Das Gericht, bestehend aus Paul Deister, einer Beisitzerin und einem Beisitzer, ist erschienen und nimmt Platz. (Danach hört man, daß sich auch das Publikum wieder setzt.) Der Vorsitzende, Paul Deister, eröffnet die Verhandlung:	

---

48 „Das Kaninchen bin ich", S. 32f.
49 „Das Kaninchen bin ich", S. 116f.

Der zweite Strafsenat des Berliner Stadtgerichts hat heute, am 18. Juni 1961, zur Verhandlung die Strafsache Dieter Morzeck, Aktenzeichen römisch zwei Strich 364 aus 59. die Anklage lautet auf staatsgefährdende Hetze. Als Richter fungiert Paul Deister. Zu Beisitzern wurden bestellt: Renate Heber und Wolfgang Bechler. Die Anklage vertritt Staatsanwalt Hoppe, die Verteidigung Rechtsanwalt Krüger. Ich erkläre die Verhandlung für eröffnet. Gibt es irgendwelche Anträge?

Der Staatsanwalt erhebt sich sehr schnell.

Staatsanwalt: Ja!

Paul Deister: Bitte, Herr Staatsanwalt.

Staatsanwalt: Im Interesse der Sicherheit des Staates beantrage ich, die Öffentlichkeit von der weiteren Verhandlung auszuschließen.

Für den Staatsanwalt ist dieser Antrag eine Routineangelegenheit, genau wie für Paul Deister, der nur einige Worte mit den Beisitzern wechselt und dann mit Routinestimme bekannt gibt:

Gibt es Einwände? Gegenanträge? Das ist nicht der Fall. Dem Antrag der Staatsanwaltschaft wird stattgegeben. Damit wird die Öffentlichkeit von der weiteren Verhandlung ausgeschlossen. Ich bitte die betreffenden Personen, den Saal zu verlassen.

Der Bürgermeister hebt die Hand und sagt:

Ich bitte, doch das Rauchen einzustellen.

Zigaretten und Zigarren werden ausgedrückt. der Bürgermeister fährt sachlich fort:

Es geht um das, was letzten Sonntag hier passiert ist, und wie ihr wißt, kommt deshalb heute das Gericht zu uns.

Bild 73A, Dorfkrug-Küche, Innen-Tag-Sommer, 269 Total-Nah
 	
Maria trocknet einen großen Haufen Messer ab. Sie ist erregter, als sie es zugeben will. Man merkt es an dem heftigen Klappern des Geschirrs. Die Kochfrau öffnet neugierig die Tür zum Saal, blickt hinaus und winkt Maria zu:
 	
    Hör uff zu klappern, komm
    mal ran, das Gericht ist
    schon da. […]
 	
    Die Kochfrau stößt Maria
    an:… und so viel Leute, alle
    sind da.
 	
    Maria zur Kochfrau: *Paß uff,*
    die müssen gleich wieder
    raus.

In Dieters Prozess wird die Distanz des Gerichts zu den „nicht eingeladenen" Zuhörern, die die einzige – nicht zugelassene – Öffentlichkeit darstellen, hervorgehoben. Die vom Richter und Staatsanwalt verwendete Sprache ist offiziell, ihre Gesten routinemäßig. In der Szene wird die Theatralität des Geschehens betont, dem jedoch das einzige authentische Publikum (Maria und Tante Hete) fehlt. Dadurch wird das Gesicht der beiden gefährdet, denn sie werden nicht als Teilnehmer (d.h. als Adressaten) im Kommunikationsakt anerkannt.

Die Szene des Dorfprozesses, die durch Marias Erinnerung an den Prozess des Bruders und dann durch den berlinisch gefärbten Dialog mit der Kochfrau eingeleitet wird, konstituiert sich als exaktes Gegenbeispiel dafür: Sie zeichnet sich durch die geräuschvolle Anwesenheit des Publikums (es wird mehrmals betont, dass alle Dorfbewohner gekommen sind) und den demokratischen Umgang der Machtvertreter (des Richters und des Bürgermeisters) mit der zu beurteilenden Tat aus. Diese äußern sich in der Standardsprache, zeigen den Zeugen gegenüber Respekt und gewähren ihnen genügend Raum, sich zu äußern. Es ist Maria, die in diesem Kontext Grices Maxime der Qualität[50] verletzt, indem sie absichtlich lügt.

---

[50]   H. Paul Grice: Logic and Conversation. In: Peter Cole und Jerry L. Morgan (Hg.): Syntax and Semantics, vol. 3. Speech Acts. New York: Academic Press 1975, S. 41-58:

Sie erwartet keine ehrliche Kommunikation und keine faire Rechtsprechung und hofft deshalb, durch eine Lüge Grambow vor dem Gefängnis zu retten. Maria wird aber vom Richter (wie später erneut vom Bürgermeister) wegen ihrer falschen Aussage gescholten.[51]

272 Schwenk Total-Nah

Der Vorsitzende des Gerichts sagt gerade: Wir beginnen mit der Vernehmung der Zeugen. Zeugin Maria Morzeck, bitte, treten Sie vor. [...]

274 Schwenk-Halbtotale

Der Vorsizende: Beginnen Sie, bitte.

Maria glaubt, Grambow durch einen Schwindel vor dem Zuchthaus retten zu können. [...]

280 Nah

Der Richter, ernst und nüchtern, jedoch sympathisch: Ich weiß nicht, warum Sie uns beschwindeln.

281 Groß

Maria will protestieren: Ich...

282 Nah

Der Richter: Nein! Glauben Sie denn, hier sind hundert Leute zusammen-gekommen, weil einer verlangt hat, daß alle nach Hause gehen?
(Milder) Wissen Sie denn überhaupt, warum wir hier sind?
(Ehrlich und eindringlich) Damit wir die Wahrheit finden, die ganze Wahrheit, nichts als die Wahrheit. Merken Sie sich das, bitte.
(Nebenbei) Und jetzt können sie gehen.

Diese positiven Züge, die im Film extra hinzugefügt wurden, um der Autorität ein menschlicheres Gesicht zu verleihen, konnten aber letzten Endes die auf dem Bildschirm besonders ausdrucksvoll wirkende Desillusionierung Marias nicht konterkarieren.

---

[51] „Under the category of QUALITY falls a supermaxim – ‚Try to make your contribution one that is true' – and two more specific maxims: 1. Do not say what you believe to be false."
„Das Kaninchen bin ich", S. 124f.

Die für das Filmthema – aber auch für die im Film erfolgende Sprachreflexion – zentrale Auseinandersetzung findet zwischen Paul und dem Bürgermeister in Anwesenheit Marias statt. Paul plädiert für die harte Linie, möchte, dass Grambow, den er für einen Feind hält, einen richtigen Prozess vor dem Bezirksgericht bekommt. Der Bürgermeister ist der Meinung, dass zuerst eine Dorfversammlung einberufen werden sollte. Dabei schützt der Bürgermeister sein Gesicht, indem er den pompösen Sprachgebrauch Pauls ablehnt, der auf den lateinischen Spruch „Ignorantia non est argumentum" zurückgegriffen hat.[52] Der junge Bürgermeister zeigt Maria, dass es auch verantwortungsbewusste Verantwortungsträger gibt. Er unterscheidet sich von Paul nicht zuletzt durch eine verständliche, alltagssprachliche Ausdrucksweise.

Dieser Erfahrung wird das aufgeweckte Mädchen Rechnung tragen, als sie Paul geradezu zu einer Erklärung des Vorgefallenen zwingt und er versucht, seine Vorgehensweise bei Dieters Verurteilung durch immer abstruser werdende Argumentationen zu verteidigen und sein Gesicht zu schützen, indem er sie des Unverständnisses beschuldigt. Sie lehnt sich in einem Monolog leidvoll gegen diesen Sprachgebrauch auf:

Maria (K):
Paul, du darfst mit mir nicht so reden. Mit jedem Wort gehst du von mir weg. Ich kann dich nicht unterbrechen. Ich hab' nicht die Kraft dazu. Ich müßte aufstehn und sagen: *Paul, du redest dir was ein.*
Ende der Anfahrt.
Du willst dich frei machen, aber du machst dich unglücklich, Paul, wenn du ein Zufall wärst… Aber du bist kein Zufall. Du bist der Mann, den ich liebe. Immer wenn ich an dich denke, sehe ich dein Gesicht über dem blauen Pullover, *höre ich deine Stimme, wenn sie nachts vorm Einschlafen sagt: Rike…*[53]

Maria weiß nun aus Erfahrung, dass es durchaus möglich ist, auf verständliche Weise über grundlegende (Justiz)fragen zu reden. Sie durchschaut endgültig Pauls falsche Argumentation, die darauf zielt, ihr Gesicht als gescheite junge Frau zu bedrohen, um sein eigenes zu wahren. Sie kann nun in der Person von Paul den Verantwortungstragenden von dem Geliebten trennen, dessen (auch sprachliche) Liebkosungen sie vermissen wird. Diese durch die geschilderte Ausdrucksweise gekennzeichnete Sprache kann Maria nicht mehr gelten lassen. Sie hat ausgedient.

310 Schwebefahrt

Maria legt Paul die Hand auf den Mund und sagt:
Hör auf. Ich verstehe kein Wort…

---

[52]   „Das Kaninchen bin ich", S. 111f.
[53]   „Das Kaninchen bin ich", S. 133.

[…] [Paul:]
Wir müssen am Sonnabend nochmal über alles reden…
Maria sagt abwesend und tonlos:
Es hat keinen Zweck, Paul…
Sie geht allein den Flur hinunter, während Paul ratlos stehenbleibt.[54]

Schlussfolgerung

Der vorliegende Aufsatz hat versucht zu zeigen, dass der Film als eine Reflexion über den Sprachgebrauch interpretiert werden kann, an deren Ende – Joshua Feinsteins Band paraphrasierend – der „Triumph of ordinary Speech" steht. Die vom einzelnen zu eigenen, egoistischen Zwecken verwendete Autoritätssprache wird als solche entlarvt, wodurch das Gesicht des Sprechers (z. B. Pauls) einen großen Schaden erleidet. Dieses Umstands gewahr werdend, ist Maria am Ende des Films in ihrer persönlichen Suche nach der Konstitution einer reiferen sozialen Identität ein Stück weiter gekommen. Diese soziale Identität, die sich primär durch den Sprachgebrauch konstituiert, ist zwar eindeutig ostberlinisch, aber nicht, wie in Pauls Fall, explizit sozialistisch. Es handelt sich ferner um eine Identität, die realistischer und konkreter – d.h. illusionsloser und weniger idealistisch – als von der Partei erwünscht zu sein scheint:

> […] Maria's most impressive qualities are self-assurance, candor, and confidence. Her tale is one of growing personal autonomy. […] *Maria's sexuality is openly admitted. [Maria's] sarcasm and wit in discussing such matters underline the discrepancy between societal norms and life's complexity.* By extension, this attitude calls into question the all-too-neat moral universe inherent to the Party's worldview.[55]

Einerseits kann behauptet werden, dass die Botschaft des Films im Kern utopisch-sozialistisch ist. Von dieser Grundüberzeugung ausgehend, nimmt der Film andererseits bestimmte unerwünschte Erscheinungen (Bürokratismus, Karrieredenken) aufs Korn. Zudem ist er formal-ästhetisch von westlicher Kultur durchtränkt, wie Einstellungen, Kameraperspektiven und -bewegungen, Tonbehandlung und musikalische Untermalung zu erkennen geben, die häufig auf westliche Traditionen (u.a. auch Ingmar Bergmans Filme) zurückgreifen.[56] Diese Aspekte wurden von der politischen Partei-Elite sehr kritisch betrachtet.

---

[54] „Das Kaninchen bin ich", S. 134.
[55] Feinstein: The Triumph of the Ordinary, S. 175.
[56] Vgl. Blanchard: *Das Kaninchen bin ich* und Die Ästhetik des Neuen Films.

Da bei der Fertigstellung des Drehbuchs die Hardliner wieder das große Wort führten,[57] wurde der Film nach kurzer Zeit für antisozialistisch und staatsfeindlich befunden und verboten. Danach musste der Regisseur Selbstkritik üben, was für ihn „eine scheußliche, moralische Selbstbeschmutzung" und eine schmerzhafte Etappe in seinem Leben war. [58] Durch die von den Parteifunktionären verlangte Selbstbeschimpfung – und den dadurch bewirkten Gesichtsverlust seitens des Filmemachers – wurde der Fall (vorübergehend) erledigt. Erneut erwies sich die Sprache als mächtiges Argument (in den Händen der Macht). Glücklicherweise nicht für immer.

Claudia Buffagni teaches German Linguistics in the Department of Human Sciences at the Università per Stranieri, Siena.

---

[57]   Außerdem wurde darauf Wert gelegt, dass der Jugend keine falschen Vorbilder gezeigt werden. Insbesondere nach einigen Zwischenfällen, in deren Mittelpunkt gerade die kritische Jugend gestanden hatte, vgl. Feinstein: The Triumph of the Ordinary, S. 171ff.

[58]   Kurt Maetzig: Filminterview mit Ralf Schenk, 1999 (Video). Vgl. dazu auch Ingrid Poss und Peter Warnecke (Hg.): Spur der Filme. Zeitzeugen über die DEFA, S. 202ff.

Bernadette Cronin

POLA: Adaptation as Process and Product

This article will discuss adaptation as process and product in the context of a theatre
project entitled *POLA* realized by the Viennese free theatre company, *Projekttheater
Studio*, performed in Vienna in November / December 2002 and in Krakow in May
2003. A piece of bi-lingual (German/Polish) theatre, *POLA* drew on two main
literary sources. The first source is the short story *Pola*[1] by Polish author and
journalist Hanna Krall (1937) from her collection entitled *Tam juz nie ma zadnej
rzeki / Da ist kein Fluss mehr / There, There Won't be Another River*, for which she
was awarded the *Leipziger Buchpreis* in March 2000. A main point of interest in
Krall's work is the disappearance of the Jews in Europe and the after-effects in the
present of the Second World War. She interviews survivors of the Holocaust in
Europe, North America, Canada, and Israel, creating literary documents out of the
material gathered. For *Pola* Krall drew on Christopher Browning's and Daniel
Goldhagen's historical accounts of the Nazis' so-called 'final solution' in Poland,
both of which accounts refer to the true story of Apolonia Machczyńska, the main
protagonist in Krall's story. The second source that Krall adapted was Beckett's
dance or movement piece for television, the "Fernsehballett" *Quad* or *Quadrat 1 +
2*, in its original German title. Haunted by Kasimir Malevich's revolutionary
painting of 1918 *White Square on White Background*, *Quad*, like much of Beckett's
work, represents a central tension between the futility of human existence and
endeavour, on the one hand, and the imperative to persist, on the other. Each of the
sources drawn on for the theatre adaptation could be said, therefore, to be
adaptations in themselves: Krall's text a literary re-working of oral and written
history, translated from Polish into German, and Beckett's *Quad*, a re-mediation and
re-interpretation of Malevich's representation of modernity, translated from visual
art into performance mode.

Created by a multidisciplinary team of collaborators that crossed national,
linguistic, socio-historical and -cultural borders, *POLA*, it could be argued, is a case
that forces us to question the status quo that privileges the author and the literary
text whereby the adapted text is seen as primary and the adaptation as secondary.
POLA instead emphasizes a polyphony of contributing voices and personal artistic
filters – including the translator of Krall's text – engaging with each other in an anti-
hierarchical mode. The other point of focus in this discussion is the specific
challenges that the theatre adaptation process entails. These involved in this case, on
the one hand, the remediation from literary prose text to performance, the shift from

---

[1]   For clarity sake, I will use upper case for the performance piece and lower case for the
short story.

telling to showing, the "leap from imagined and visualized literary text to the 'directly perceived,'"[2] and, on the other, the question of representing in the performance medium material relating to the Holocaust. Following Claude Lanzmann's principle that it is impossible to take an illustrative approach to representation in the case of the Holocaust, central questions that informed the dramaturgy, as outlined by director Eva Brenner in interview, included:

> Wie verhält man sich performativ rund um das Thema, ohne es zeigen zu müssen, ohne auch in die Versuchung zu geraten, und trotzdem eine Nähe zu behaupten zu dem Thema? Wie halte ich mich fern und lasse trotzdem das Bild leben?[3]

What emerged in the process of devising an adaptation, I will be arguing, is a piece of theatre that resists the conventions of a dramatic theatre engaged in "the representation of a closed-off fictional cosmos, the mimetic staging of a fable."[4] Instead, what we have here is a kind of theatre that is not spectatorial, but rather "a reversal of the artistic act towards the viewers."[5] This, I will be arguing, entails modes of theatrical representation which invoke Lanzmann's guiding principle of a "blind gaze," the "refusal of psychological understanding"[6] in his film *Shoah*, resulting in the creation of a medium through which memory-work, the subtleties of damage and the inexpressible, and the difficult task of re-claiming the past can be explored. Such modes ultimately allow for a more meaningful and currently missing representation of the collapse in Western civilization that found its ultimate expression in the Nazis' "final solution." In my discussion of the dramaturgical choices made in the adaptation process, I will mainly draw on Hans-Thies Lehmann's seminal work *Postdramatic Theatre*, which theorizes developments in Western theatre in the second half of the twentieth century. Central to these developments, as Lehmann shows, is the drifting apart of theatre and drama, the shift away from the totality of the *logos* to new kinds of "text" or performance writing,[7] whereby the (dramatic) text "is considered only as one element, one layer, or as 'material' of the scenic creation, not as its master,"[8] and the performers are not merely the agents of the discourse of a director who remains external to them but rather "act out their own corporeal logic within a given framework."[9] In his

---

2   Linda Hutcheon: A Theory of Adaptation. London: Routledge, 2006, p. 42.
3   Eva Brenner: Interview with Bernadette Cronin. Vienna: 2005.
4   Hans-Thies Lehmann: Postdramatic Theatre. Trans. Karen Jürs-Munby. London: Routledge, 2006, p. 3.
5   Lehmann: Postdramatic Theatre, p. 106.
6   Claude Lanzmann: The Obscenity of Understanding. In: Cathy Caruth (ed.): Unclaimed Experience: Trauma, Narrative, and History. Baltimore, MD: John Hopkins University Press, 1996, p. 200-20, here p. 204.
7   Lehmann: Postdramatic Theatre, p. 4.
8   Lehmann: Postdramatic Theatre, p. 17.
9   Lehmann: Postdramatic Theatre, p. 32.

discussion, Lehmann considers a broad panorama of heterogeneous theatre and performance genres: "'devised' experimental performance art and 'new writing,' as well as innovative stagings of classical drama that push this drama into the postdramatic (by directors such as Einar Schleef, Robert Wilson and Klaus-Michael Grüber)."[10]

In the following, the material chosen for adaptation will be examined in terms of the process of transcoding literary texts into the different set of conventions associated with the performance medium. This reading will also consider the socio-historical, political and cultural context that informed the work, and will consider how the dramaturgy was shaped both in response to the adapted sources and in accordance with the artistic, aesthetic and political concerns of the team of adapters.

Adapted Sources

Central to Krall's short story, *Pola*, and based on historical facts taken from Browning's *Ordinary Men: Reserve Police Battalion 101 and the Final Solution in Poland*[11] and Daniel Goldhagen's *Hitler's Willing Executioners*,[12] is the eponymous protagonist Pola, or Apolonia Machczyńska, a Polish woman who conceals twenty-five Jews under the floorboards of her house on the outskirts of Kock (Siedlecki district, north of Lublin) in the spring of 1943. Pola is betrayed by a Jewish neighbour, who hopes thereby to save herself and her children's lives, hunted down by members of Police Battalion 101, and shot together with some of the Jews she had been sheltering. The German policeman, ordered at gunpoint to shoot Pola, is her lover, by whom she was pregnant at the time of her execution. The Reserve Police Battalion 101 consisted of middle-aged family men of working- and lower-middle-class backgrounds from the city of Hamburg. Considered too old for the Wehrmacht, they had been drafted instead into the Order Police [the *Ordnungspolizei* or *Orpo*]. Most were raw recruits with no previous experience in German occupied territory.[13] They were first sent to Poland in 1939 as part of Himmler's scheme to 'Germanize' the occupied regions. By 1942, the year in which the (hi)story is set, Himmler's 'final solution' was being implemented, and Battalion 101 was given the task of rounding up the Jews in their villages in the district of Lublin and shooting them in nearby woods in killing sessions that sometimes lasted up to seventeen hours.

Pola might best be described as episodic in structure, a montage consisting of fifteen brief chapters in seventeen pages, drawing together several strands of

10   Lehmann: Postdramatic Theatre, p. 2.
11   Christopher Browning: Ordinary Men. Reserve Police Battalion 101 and the Final
      Solution in Poland. London: Penguin, 2001.
12   Daniel Goldhagen: Hitler's Willing Executioners. Ordinary Germans and the Holocaust.
      London: Abacus, 2003.
13   Browning: Ordinary Men, p. 1.

narrative in a non-linear mode. All of the motifs that are central to Krall's prose work can be found in this short text: the persecution of the Jews, the roles played by Poles, Jews and Germans during and after the war, crime and its origins, resistance and collaboration, love and the quotidian. Krall writes about the horrors of the crimes of National Socialism with a marked economy and simplicity of language and in a tone that is almost laconic, the writing style blending a mixture of journalism, documentary and poetry. The narrative voice, which includes abrupt shifts to the present moment with interpolated references to Browning and Goldhagen's texts, could be said to possess something of the quality of Lanzmann's "blind gaze" rejecting any psychological insight or "understanding."[14] As the dramaturge notes in the production's PR material, "Sie belässt ihren Figuren das Geheimnis und versucht so, das Unbegreifliche begreifbar zu machen."

Although there is a clear story-line, the fragments of the text somehow resist integration creating in the reader the impulse to revisit it, to pick up the threads and attempt somehow to piece it all together. This effort evokes, as it were, the greater effort of trying to come to terms with the Holocaust and the central – and for Lanzmann, obscene – question: Why were the Jews killed? This question is reframed in the narrative, reformulated to reflect the context of the ordinary, middle-aged policemen from Hamburg who came to massacre thousands of innocent victims in the woods of Poland: "Warum waren normale Hamburger Bürger, zu alt für die Front, zu Mördern geworden?" The narrator then leaves the reader suspended between the polarized viewpoints of Browning and Goldhagen:

> Weil sie Deutsche waren, und den Deutschen wurde der Hass gegen die Juden jahrhundertelang beigebracht, gibt Daniel Goldhagen in seinem Buch zur Antwort.
> Weil sie Menschen waren, und jeden Menschen kann man zum Mörder machen, antwortet Christopher Browning.[15]

A dialectic is established here which invokes the ethical imperative of remembrance, articulated by Primo Levi, Adorno and others: the imperative to acknowledge that human beings are all somehow implicated in each other's tragedies, or as Julie Salverson expresses it, that "[p]ersonal narratives of crisis are never merely personal."[16] If the reader is left struggling to take a position on the central question, out of the centre of the "magnetic field" of the text emerge two vivid, poetic images that also function – and were read by the company – as metaphors in the text: the

---

[14] Lanzmann: The Obscenity of Understanding, p. 204.
[15] Hanna Krall: Pola. In: Da ist kein Fluss mehr. Frankfurt a.M.: Verlag Neue Kritik, 2001, p. 18-32, here p. 23.
[16] Julie Salverson: Performing Emergency: Witnessing, Popular Theatre, and the Lie of the Literal. In: *Theatre Topics* 6/2 (1996), p.181-91, here p. 182. Available online at: http://muse.jhu.edu/journals/theater_topics/v006/6.2salverson.html (last accessed 25.07.2012).

first image is that of the twenty-five Jews concealed in Pola's cellar, seen through a gap in the floor boards by Pola's young sons: "Unter unserm Fußboden sitzen irgendwelche Leute…"[17] This glimpse of subterranean persecuted Jews offers a ready metaphor for repressed memories and the refusal of many to engage at all with the traumatic past. The second image is of the heart of a Jew, discovered under the melting ice by children playing by the lake in the springtime following the murder of Pola and the Jews. One of the Jewish victims was buried on this spot after first being dragged behind the sledge that conveys Pola and the others to their place of execution:

> In der Grube erblickten sie Teile eines menschlichen Rumpfes.
> "Das sind Rippen" sagte der Fischer.
> Daneben lag etwas Längliches, Rötlichblaues, das aussah wie zwei gefaltete Hände.
> "Das ist ein Herz," sagte der Fischer. "Wem mag das gehören?"
> "Einem Juden" sagte einer der Jungs. "Dem, den sie vom Schlitten abgeschnitten haben."
> "Das Herz von einem Juden," sagte der Mann, hob den Sack an und schüttete die toten Fische in die Grube.[18]

The heart of the Jew, re-emerging, returning unexpectedly from a hole in the earth, preserved by the ice, serves as a metaphor for the traumatic wound left behind by the annihilation of Eastern Europe's Jews. Here we can invoke Freud's writing on trauma and the associated idea of the *return*, and his interpretation of the parable of wound: the idea that trauma "is always the story of a wound that cries out, that addresses us in the attempt to tell us of a reality or truth that is not otherwise available."[19]

The literary tropes identified above suggest that Krall's text might lend itself well to a shift from the "telling to showing mode"[20] inasmuch as the text is not characterized by features that pose particular challenges in the transcoding process from prose to performance such as interior monologue, point of view, reflection, comment, irony, ambiguity. The very clear images and figures that emerge from the fifteen brief chapters suggest that this text is "adaptogenic"[21] for performance mode. Furthermore, the detached character of the narrative voice, the economy of language – creating a sense of an author getting out of the way, removing herself – would suggest that the source material lent itself to adaptation in accordance with the

---

[17]   Krall: Pola, p. 19.
[18]   Krall: Pola, p. 27.
[19]   Cathy Caruth (ed.): Trauma. Explorations in Memory. Baltimore, MD: John Hopkins University Press, 1995, p. 3.
[20]   Hutcheon: A Theory of Adaptation, p. 38.
[21]   Hutcheon: A Theory of Adaptation, p. 15.

company's stated intention: to maintain a distance while allowing the images to resonate.

Beckett's *Quad*, the other main source drawn on by the adapters, first transmitted in Germany in 1982 by Süddeutscher Rundfunk under the title *Quadrat 1 + 2*, is a piece for four players, light and percussion. To quote from the outline offered in *The Faber Companion to Samuel Beckett*:

> Four figures, each in pastel djellabas, appear to describe a quadrangle to a rapid, polyrhythmic percussion, then depart in sequence. Each describes half the quad, but abruptly avoids the centre, turning to the left, like Dante's damned. The action first seems comic, as characters rush toward a central collision, avoided by abrupt turns, but 'something terrifying' emerges. The pattern repeats, from one to four participants, then back to one, then none in an oscillation, crescendo, and diminuendo that shatters whatever comic possibilities were anticipated. The effect is of prescribed, determined, enforced, motion.[22]

This describes the original *Quadrat 1*. *Quadrat 2* is of a considerably slower tempo and monochrome in colour. Written in 1981 by the then 75-year-old Beckett at a time in his life when his mistrust of language had become heightened and the visual image, which had always been important to him, became paramount,[23] *Quadrat 2* came about almost by accident: when the producer, Reinhart Müller-Freienfels, took Beckett home to dinner after the shooting he told him how impressive the piece had looked in black and white on the monochrome monitor in the production box. Beckett, fascinated, asked if they might record a second black and white version in a slower speed the next day. The fast percussion beats were also removed, and all that could be heard "were the slower, shuffling steps of the weary figures, and, almost inaudible, the tick of a metronome."[24]

Adaptation Context

Every adaptation has a context, or, as Hutcheon puts it: "[a]n adaptation, like the work it adapts, is always framed in [...] a time, a place, a society and a culture."[25] *POLA* was devised and performed in the context of "Polish year in Austria" (April 2002-2003), building up to the EU-accession of ten new member states including Poland (1 April 2004), and was designed to highlight Poland's contribution to global

[22] C.J. Ackerly and S.E. Gontarski (eds.): Faber Companion to Samuel Beckett. London: Faber and Faber, 2004, p. 472.
[23] James Knowlson: Damned to Fame. The Life of Samuel Beckett. London: Bloomsbury Paperbacks, 1997, p. 673.
[24] Beckett was delighted at this second version, commenting that it took place "ten thousand years later." Knowlson: Damned to Fame, p. 674.
[25] Hutcheon: A Theory of Adaptation, p. 142.

and European culture as well as the shared history between Poland and Austria. In terms of the political climate in Austria in the early years of the twenty-first century, the rise to power of the extreme right-wing Freedom Party, which managed to secure an alarmingly high percentage of votes (27%), was a source of considerable concern to many in the "green" 7th District of Vienna. In the microcosm of the company, Eva Brenner, the director, planned *POLA* as a precursor to a larger project relating to her own family's troubled history with National Socialism and the family's lost eastern European Jewish roots. A key concern for the ensemble as a whole,[26] and central to the piece of theatre they were creating, was what Brenner identified in interview as "the act of looking away," denial of the part played by Austria in the Third Reich which was something that they perceived to be characteristic of Austrian families:

> Wir wollten versuchen dieses Wegschauen, das gerade in Österreich und Wien eines der Übel ist, als sehr bekannt in allen Familien [zu zeigen], das kam in den Erzählungen mit den Schauspielern immer wieder vor, wie setzen wir das um?[27]

Umsetzung / Adaptation

While the work was led by the artistic director of the company, emphasis was placed on process-led ensemble collaboration. Furthermore, and as is often the case with Austrian – and in the wider context, European – theatre companies operating within what is varyingly known as the "free," "fringe," "freie Theaterszene," "OFF-Theaterszene" or "independent theatre scene," the company in question does not make theatre that serves the literary (dramatic) 'source' text in a conventional sense, but rather breaks with the conventions of naturalism, the mimetic representation of a fable, characteristic of the European drama after Ibsen,[28] conventions which continue to influence much mainstream, state-funded theatre in the western world. As Lehmann writes, "[i]n postdramatic forms of theatre, staged text (*if* text is staged) is merely a component with equal rights in a gestic, musical, visual, etc., total composition."[29] Such elements as dance, gesture, and music, which characterized theatre before the advent of writing, either completely vanished in the bourgeois literary or dramatic theatre, or became relegated in a cultural hierarchy in

---

[26]   The team of collaborators at the Projekttheater Studio included, in the case of this project, two Polish performers (Jan and Susanna Tabaka), one Austrian (Clemens Matzka) and two Germans (Maren Rahmann and Anna Wiederhold), ranging in age from mid-twenties to mid-fifties. Lighting and set design were created by sculptor and video artist Walter Lauterer.

[27]   Brenner: Interview with Bernadette Cronin. Original grammatically incomplete.

[28]   Raymond Williams: Drama from Ibsen to Brecht. Harmondsworth: Penguin, 1981, p. 317.

[29]   Lehmann: Postdramatic Theatre, p. 46.

which the written text – literature – as "as an offer of meaning" took on the lead role, with all other theatrical means employed to serve it and "rather suspiciously controlled by the authority of Reason."[30] While avant-garde movements such as Expressionism, Theatre of Cruelty, Symbolism, Epic Theatre, Happenings, Theatre of the Absurd, and Theatre of Images, some of which date back to the earlier part of the twentieth century, broke with the naturalistic mode of representation characteristic of dramatic theatre, the literary text retained its status in some of these as the primary "offer of meaning," including, for example, in Brecht's Epic Theatre. Today, however, as Florian Malzacher writes, theatre-makers outside the establishment no longer need to liberate themselves from the literary text or the conventional representational system of the drama – previous generations of theatre makers have done that. Now they play rather on the borders of associated conventions, emphasizing their fundamental doubts:

> Wie viel Narration erträgt das Theater noch, an wie viel Kausalpsychologie können wir noch glauben, wo wir doch seit über hundert Jahren lernen, dass wir nicht die Herren im eigenen Haus der Psyche sind? Und wo das Kino doch ohnehin viel besser ist im Behaupten großer Geschichten – weil es perfekter lügen kann als das Theater, das bei aller Technik immer durchschaubar bleibt: viel mehr Medium zum Denken als zum Glauben.[31]

Theatre as a medium for thought and reflection, memory-work, as a means of exploring the core concerns of how to represent the "act of looking away" and reclaim the past were ideas central to the devising and rehearsal process of *POLA*. Pearson and Shanks define the dramatic structure of such "devised performances" as:

> constituting a kind of stratigraphy of layers: of text, physical action, music and/or soundtrack, scenography and/or architecture (and their subordinate moments). Dramatic material can be conceived and manipulated in each of these strata which may carry different themes or orders of material in parallel.[32]

Any one of these layers may be the starting point in the devising process and any one may from time to time bear principal responsibility for carrying the prime narrative meaning while the others are turned down in the composition. In the case of *POLA*, the principal layers, elements, and rehearsal techniques identified in interview with members of the team were as follows: the spatial / choreographic work on Beckett's *Quad*, Krall's prose text, either grafted onto the *Quad*

---

30   Lehmann: Postdramatic Theatre, p. 47.
31   Florian Malzacher: Ein Künstler, der kein Englisch spricht, ist kein Künstler. In: Theater Heute 10 (2008), p. 8-13, here p. 8.
32   Mike Pearson and Michael Shanks: Theatre/Archaeology. London: Routledge, 2001: p. 24-25.

choreography or worked into scenic representation sequences, the live music (led by classically trained violinist Susanna Tabaka-Pillhofer, with contributions by each of the other four performers and the dramaturge on accordion, guitar, cello, clarinet), and the *Erinnerungsgestus* or attitude of remembering. Described in the company's PR material as "ein Projekt gegen das Vergessen," the central thematic concerns underlying the project are encapsulated in the binaries: remembering/forgetting, proximity/distance, and refuge/returning home. As part of the adaptation and devising process (defined by Heddon and Milling as "a process for creating performance from scratch, by the group, without a preexisting script"),[33] the five performers were invited by the directorial team, director Eva Brenner and dramaturge Axel Bagatsch, to weave into the performance work elements of their personal biographies that were relevant to the central thematic concerns of the piece, an approach that Brenner characterizes as "the emancipation of the actor."[34] Ultimately, only two of the five performers chose to act on this invitation, an element to which I will return later. In terms of rehearsal techniques and approaches to devising work as an ensemble in a given site,[35] the company drew heavily on the "Viewpoints of Performance," first developed in the 1970s and 80s as a postmodern approach to generating performance by dance choreographer Mary Overlie, and further developed by Ann Bogart and Tina Landau for theatre.[36]

Dramaturgical Choices

The work did not find its starting point, therefore, in a pre-prepared script adapted from Krall's text and filtered through a playwright's personal artistic choices, but

---

[33]   Deirdre Heddon and Jane Milling: Devising Performance. A Critical History. Basingstoke: Palgrave Macmillan, 2006, p. 3.

[34]   "Ich suche jetzt seit Jahren die Möglichkeit, wie ich erstens rauskomme aus dem reinen Rollenspiel des Theatralischen und was wir die Emanzipation des Schauspielers nennen, dass der Schauspieler sich aktiv in den Prozess einbringt. Also, dass ich als Regisseurin eine Spielleiterin bin oder Animateurin oder Dinge ermögliche oder zur Verfügung stelle, entwickele aber nicht sage, was nicht passiert, ich wähl dann aus, oder wenn Angbote kommen, leite ich oder lenke ich das, aber ich glaube nicht dran, dass ich den Leuten, gerade bei so einem sensibelen Thema, vorschreiben sollte oder könnte: sag das oder jenes oder zeig das oder jenes. Und eine Form der Emanzipation im Theater, glaube ich, ist schon dieses radikale sich-in-Beziehung-Setzen persönlich zu einem Text." Brenner: Interview with Bernadette Cronin.

[35]   The former premises of the Projekttheater Studio at Burggasse 38, in Vienna's 7th district, consisted of a large, ground-floor apartment, an open-plan rectangular space, the floor and walls painted white, with sliding doors in one wall, leading into a 'backstage' area.

[36]   The nine viewpoints, as developed by the Ann Bogart and Tina Landau, are subdivided into the following categories: Space (architecture, spatial relationship, topography), shape (shape and gesture: behavioural, cultural, expressive), and time (tempo, kinaesthetic response, and duration).

rather in the search for a form that could represent the "act of looking away." In the early phases of the devising and rehearsal process, it was decided that the choreographic structure of *Quad* could provide answers to this central thematic question on the one hand, and the mass murder on an industrial scale of innocent victims on the other. The company came up with the idea of adapting Beckett's *Quad* into a constant structure in the piece, which could be broken away from periodically for scenic representation of elements of the story, and then returned to. To this end, the performance space was divided into two playing areas – a quad in the centre of the space created by four rows of seats for spectators, forming a square but positioned facing outwards. The other playing area was formed by the remainder of the rectangular room in front of the audience, an oval, as it were, subtending the square. Gaps were left at the corners of the square to enable the performers to move between the two areas. The audience was seated, consequently, with their backs to the quad, separating the two playing areas, and if they wanted to see what was happening in the central space they had to turn around in their seats. The precise choreography of Beckett's piece was adhered to, but the tempo varied, a slowing of the tempo signalling a breaking out of the structure in the inner performing area, created by the seats, to move into the memory-work and scenic representation of fragments of Krall's text in the outer performing area. Overall, it corresponded more to *Quadrat 2*, both in terms of tempo and colour scheme. In terms of the rest of the set, Krall's prose text, printed in its entirety in blocks of type script on a continuous narrow band of white paper, was mounted at eye-level along the four walls of the space, including on the sliding doors in one of the walls, with the result that the spectator was always confronted with a section of the "source" text. The final set element consisted of eight iron frames, two suspended at two sides of the space, in the outer playing area and two mounted on each of the other two remaining walls in front of sections of the text. The performers were costumed in generic, grey pinstripe suits, the women in long skirts and the men in trousers. The effect was neutral, contemporary, without the literal referencing of Nazi uniforms or other period costume.

As the audience entered the performance space, the adapted version of *Quad* was already being performed. The spectators were therefore immediately confronted with the dilemma of whether to take a seat, which would place them with their backs to the action. As the performers in turn broke away from the quad, shifting to another mode of performance in the outer performing area, the spectators had again to turn around in their seats to experience representations of scenes from Krall's text. The adapted *Quad* was kept going, however, for the most of the 70-minute piece as the performers shifted between the two areas. The central point of the Quad, designated as: "E," "a supposed danger zone,"[37] which the performers avoided by a

---

[37]   Knowlson: Damned to Fame, p. 673.

sharp turn to the left,[38] became the point of silence and avoidance that was central to Krall's text and one of the key thematic concerns of the ensemble:

> [Es ging] um eine Choreographie einer immer wiederkehrenden Bewegung, die sich auf das Zentrum zubewegt aber immer das Zentrum vermeidet, was irgendwie dieser Punkt des Schweigens und des Ausweichens war in/mit dem Text von Hanna Krall.[39]

In this dialogue between Krall's text and Beckett's *Quad*, the latter becomes a death machine evoking the industrial-scale extermination of Hitler's victims in the concentration camps. By virtue of their positioning in the space, the spectators performed the act of not looking at what was behind them, representing Austria's failure to deal with its National Socialist past. In the act of turning around to look behind them, they performed a conscious engagement with the past and with the act of remembering. In this sense the theatrical performance became a social situation emphatically unlike the more traditional dramatic mode in which (fictionalized) reality is represented end-on behind an invisible fourth wall. *POLA* might also be described an "event" in the way that Lehmann uses the term: "a provocative situation for all participants," "a reversion of the artistic act towards the viewers [...] [who] are made aware of their own presence and at the same time are forced into a virtual quarrel with the creators of this theatrical process: what is it they want of them?"[40] Needless to say, audience reactions varied at each performance forcing the performers to improvise and adjust their performance accordingly. In this sense, the audience members became co-creators of the piece, "active witnesses who reflect on their own meaning-making."[41]

Text fragments from Krall's text – the terser elements of the narrative such as dates, figures, and statistics – were grafted onto the "death machine," sometimes enunciated in chorus and sometimes solo, marking a further divergence from or grafting onto Beckett's script. The tone of the delivery in the inner space was devoid of colour and expression. This space represented the dark world of suppressed memories, caught up in the relentless machine. We could invoke here Primo Levi's portrayal of prisoner life in Auschwitz and the impossibility of acquiring "an overall vision of his universe": "[i]n short he felt overwhelmed by an enormous edifice of violence and menace but could not form for himself a representation of it because his eyes were fastened to the ground by every single minute's needs."[42] In the scenic representations of passages from Krall's text, performed in the outside playing area,

---

[38] Beckett explained to his Polish translator that Dante and Virgil in Hell always turn to the left (the direction of the damned), and in Purgatory always to the right. Knowlson, p. 673.

[39] Brenner: Interview with Bernadette Cronin.

[40] Lehmann: Postdramatic Theatre, p. 106.

[41] Jürs-Munby. Introduction. In: Lehmann: Postdramatic Theatre, p. 1-15, here p. 6.

[42] Primo Levi: The Drowned and the Saved. London: Abacus, 2008, p. 6.

Pola and her lover were represented by two of the performers, the remaining three performers taking on a variety of roles: Pola's neighbours, who choose not to see from behind their curtains, her sons, who are left orphaned, and her father, who when forced to choose between his own life or his daughter's, surrenders his daughter.

It could be argued that this adaptation allowed the text as a material object to become a performer in the piece: it was not just drawn upon for elements of dialogue and narrative, but was, as mentioned above, an integral part of the set, physically present. The audience was confronted throughout with the visual, paratextual effect of the prose text *itself* running around the four walls of the performance space. Going beyond the visual impact, the performers occasionally interacted through a language of gesture with the text: when, for example, Plebanki, the site of the executions, was described, one of the performers pointed to what first seemed to indicate an imaginary place, saying: "Da ist Plebanki," but as he moved towards that place, arm and forefinger extended, the gesture was completed by his forefinger making contact with the word "Plebanki" in the text mounted on the wall. A shift took place in the arc of this one gesture, between a traditional dramatic form and what could be described as a more postdramatic mode of performance: the spectator is first required to suspend disbelief – the actor pointing to a place he sees in his imagination, conjuring it up for the spectator – and, as the performer's finger makes contact with the word in the text, the spectator is brought back to the here and now of the performance, their own material presence as a "reader" in the space, of the text, the performance, their role in the event, and also to the ethical imperative of remembrance. The aesthetic distance between the spectator and the performance, characteristic of dramatic theatre, is broken down by this gesture. In a later sequence, some of the performers positioned themselves behind the iron frames suspended in the space and enunciated in turn that section of Krall's text that relays the account from Browning's book of the activities of Police Battalion 101 in Lublin. The performers read the text in the style of machine-like dictation, including even the diacritical marks, again drawing attention to the materiality of the text. Towards the end of the performance, four of the five performers literally exited the text, pulling back the sliding door in the back wall of the space on which part of the text was mounted, and closing it again behind them. This had the effect of leaving the fifth character, representing Pola's lover and assassin, locked inside the text. He ran at the door, trying in vain to break out of the text, then proceeded to run along the walls from one word or phrase to the next, beginning to enunciate the text, words which, however, seemed to get stuck in his throat. The text as an agent, as material evidence of the facts, became an actor in the piece, a force that refused to give way to any pleas or explanations or excuses; the text, it could be argued, enacted "a refusal of psychological understanding."[43]

---

[43]   Lanzmann: The Obscenity of Understanding, p. 204.

The multi-layered and non-linear quality of Krall's text was reflected in the performance through ruptures: between the performance mode in the inner space and that in the outer space; between performers inhabiting roles of figures in the story (both victim and perpetrator), and becoming epic-narrator figures, as well as acting as 'themselves' in order to include an element from their personal histories. Maren Rahmann, a German actress, for example, chose a moment during the performance to take an old family photograph of her grandmother from where she had inserted it in a gap in the wall of the set, explaining that she had only recently discovered that her "Oma Gertrude" had been in a concentration camp during the war because she had hidden Jews from the Nazis in her house. In interview, Brenner compared these ten- to twenty-second elements of the performance to lightning flashes: "[e]s war so wie ein Blitz, der plötzlich auftaucht, und das war sehr überraschend und sehr interessant."[44] The shifts between different modes of enunciation contributed to the fragmented, multi-layered quality of the performance: from monotone, to expressivity, to dictation, to chorus, to chant, to song.

In a video-recording of the performance,[45] there was no applause at the end of the performance. This is possibly because the performers were not making the usual shift at the end from "a closed-off fictional cosmos,"[46] dissolving a "fourth wall" to encounter the audience in the present. The audience members had been invited to position themselves in the performance space, to perform their bodies in response to what was happening in the piece, and applause might have signalled a distance between the audience and the performers that would have been at odds with the involved, engaged nature of the theatrical event. The five performers stood in silence before the audience, returning the audience's gaze as though not expecting to receive applause. Here again, the spectators did not know what was expected of them. It was unclear whether the performance was over, or whether this was yet another rupture, signalling a departure into another phase of the piece. Above all they were made acutely conscious of their own material presence in the here and now of the shared time and space of the theatrical event, and of their involvement in the work's core concerns of remembrance and engagement with the past.

Although the company was keen to remain faithful to Krall's text in its adaptation, the adaptation was not faithful in any conventional sense – although in a sense it was ultra-faithful as the text intact was re-presented by literally sticking it *qua* text to the walls of the performance space. Selected elements of the narrative were represented scenically by the actors, who were, however, multiple agents, shifting constantly between different roles and functions in the composition of the performance. Translated also were themes such as the reader's accountability, the refusal of psychological understanding, the central images – the return of the heart

---

44   Brenner: Interview with Bernadette Cronin.
45   The recording in question is a video-documentation of one of the Vienna performances (November-December 2002), made available to the author by the director. It is not in general circulation.
46   Lehmann: Postdramatic Theatre, p. 3.

of a Jew, a metaphor for the trauma of Eastern Europe's lost Jewry, and the twenty-five Jews hidden under Pola's floorboards, standing in for repressed memories. Formal features of the text that were translated included the shifts and ruptures between textual elements, including interpolations of Goldhagen's and Browning's texts. Playwright Thomas Kilroy argues that a "good adaptation is always a substantial tribute to its original and it should send us back to that original with an enhanced view of it."[47] Projekttheater Studio certainly paid tribute to the 'original' by having the text in its entirety feature as a set element; but, interestingly, the text arguably also acted as a 'performer' or collaborator in its own adaptation, physically entrapping one of its characters within itself. This physical presence of the source also offered the spectator the possibility of reading the whole text after the performance, a text filtered now in their minds through the rich "palimpsestuous intertextuality"[48] created by the multilayered adaptation they had just seen. The company invited the author Hanna Krall to attend one of the performances of *POLA*, and were gratified by the author's reception of their work, one of her comments being: "Das Theater fügt dem Text etwas hinzu."[49] As an enhancement of the original, by Kilroy's criterion this was "a good adaptation." Of course, had the audience already been familiar with the source text before the performance, this new "palimpsestuous reading" would have offered quite a different experience. As Hutcheon writes, "what is intriguing is that, afterward, we often come to see the prior adapted work very differently as we compare it to the result of the adapter's creative and interpretive act."[50] Rather than reading this adaptation as second or secondary, however, we might rather read it as an anti-hierarchical conversation between an extensive list of authors, Krall, Beckett, Malevich, Goldhagen, Browning, Roswitha Matwin-Buschmann (who translated Krall's text into German),[51] the ensemble of collaborators at the Projekttheater Studio Wien and, not last or least, the spectators, active meaning-makers in the live theatre event.

To conclude, I would argue that modes of performance that we might characterize as postdramatic, that relate to but break with classically dramatic principles such as unity, wholeness and sense, provide a more appropriate 'container' within which theatrical expression can be given to experiences relating to the Holocaust. In the context of his work with victims of the Hiroshima bombing, psychoanalyst Robert J. Lifton speaks of the shattering of prior forms as a prerequisite for new insight. Where existing forms or systems do not allow the re-

---

[47] Thomas Kilroy: The Seagull. Loughcrew: The Gallery Press, 1993, p. 12.
[48] Hutcheon: A Theory of Adaptation, p. 21.
[49] Brenner: Interview with Bernadette Cronin.
[50] Hutcheon: A Theory of Adaptation, p. 121.
[51] Karen Jürs-Munby refers in the introduction of her English translation of Lehmann's book to Benjamin's "Art des Meinens," how translation "is a curious activity of moving from one 'way of meaning' to another" and how the translation can tend to become invisible, "not unlike the performance dimension in Naturalist plays the translation." Lehmann: Postdramatic Theatre, p. 15.

creation of unprecedented experience, new forms are required. As he says in interview, "we never receive anything nakedly, we must recreate it in our own minds."[52] Likewise, Shoshana Felman writing about the poetry of Holocaust survivor Paul Celan, talks about "[t]he breakage of the verse," which "enacts the breakage of the world."[53] In relation to a theatre that seeks to explore events representing the collapse of Western civilization, we could assert that the breakage of the forms offers a possibility for the enactment of the breakage of the world. Sutured together from fragments of other works, and involving, in its brokenness, the uncanny intact physical presence of the source text, itself a collage of history and story, the collaborative devised performance POLA, manages to be simultaneously excessively faithful to 'originals' and to constitute a rupture.

Bernadette Cronin teaches Drama and Theatre Studies in the School of Music and Theatre at University College Cork.

---

[52] Caruth: Trauma, p. 135.
[53] Caruth: Trauma, p. 32.

Nadine Nowroth

Authentizität inszenieren? Remediatisierung im Zeitzeugentheater: Anmerkungen zur filmischen Umsetzung der *Staats-Sicherheiten* nach dem Konzept von Lea Rosh und Renate Kreibich-Fischer

Einleitung

Ein Konvolut von Literatur, musealen Präsentationen und kulturellen Darstellungsformen ist rund um den zwanzigsten Jahrestag der deutschen Wiedervereinigung erschienen. Zu den regional erfolgreichsten Darbietungen gehörte in Berlin und Brandenburg das Theaterstück *Staats-Sicherheiten*, das im Oktober 2008 am Potsdamer Hans Otto Theater uraufgeführt und als „beste Aufführung 2008 in Berlin und Potsdam" mit dem Friedrich Luft Preis der Berliner Morgenpost ausgezeichnet wurde.[1] In *Staats-Sicherheiten* erzählen ehemalige politische Häftlinge aus den Stasi-Gefängnissen in Potsdam und Berlin-Hohenschönhausen ihre Geschichte. Aufgrund des großen Erfolges wurde die Inszenierung noch einmal in einer 90-minütigen filmischen Darstellung auf DVD produziert. Die mitwirkenden Darsteller sind, sowohl in der Theaterversion als auch in der später folgenden Filmfassung, allesamt ehemalige Häftlinge. In beiden Fassungen treten dieselben Personen auf.

„Wir suchten [...] nach ‚echten' Betroffenen"[2] – so beschreibt die Publizistin Lea Rosh, die zusammen mit Renate Kreiblich-Fischer für die Dramaturgie und das Konzept des Theaterstückes *Staats-Sicherheiten* und die für den ZDF Theaterkanal erschienene gleichnamige Filmfassung des Stückes verantwortlich zeichnet, die Idee zu dieser Inszenierung. Wie das Zitat bereits deutlich macht, war der Gedanke zentral, möglichst unmittelbar und originalgetreu die Erlebnisse der Opfer der zweiten deutschen Diktatur zu schildern; darüber hinaus sind auch die Zweifel der Dramaturgin an der Authentizität von melodramatischen Spielfilmdarstellungen über Regimekritiker der DDR und die Hinterlassenschaften der ehemaligen sozialistischen Diktatur als die Initialzündung zu dem Theaterstück zu sehen. Der Wunsch nach „Echtheit" und Authentizität in der Darstellung der Betroffenen führte schließlich dazu, dass man ehemalige Häftlinge der Stasi-Gefängnisse in Berlin

---

[1] Stefan Kirschner: Luft-Preis für *Staats-Sicherheiten*. In: Berliner Morgenpost, 20.02.2009.

[2] Lea Rosh: "Anfrage zur Dokumentation *Staats-Sicherheiten*". Message to the author. 3.03.2012. E-mail.

Hohenschönhausen und Potsdam Lindenstraße auswählte und anhand von Gesprächen und Notizen das Stück erarbeitete.

Dieser Artikel will die Inszenierungsformen in dem Theaterstück und der daraus hervorgegangenen Filmfassung untersuchen und dadurch gängige Theorien von Adaption hinterfragen und auf ihre Grenzen überprüfen. Als zentral erweist sich hier das Konzept der Remediatisierung, also der Wiederverwendung von mediatisierten Geschichten und Narrativen in einem neuen Medium. Des Weiteren soll untersucht werden, ob und wie in dieser Art der Inszenierung Konzepte von konstruktivistischer Authentizität umgesetzt werden und inwiefern die Berichte der Zeitzeugen und die Art der filmischen Inszenierung diese Formen der Authentizität unterstreichen oder vermindern. Besondere Beachtung soll dabei der These zukommen, dass „Medien [...] keine neutralen Träger von vorgängigen, gedächtnisrelevanten Informationen [sind]. Was sie zu enkodieren scheinen – Wirklichkeits- und Vergangenheitsversionen, Werte und Normen, Identitätskonzepte – erzeugen sie vielmals erst".[3]

Staats-Sicherheiten ist nicht die erste Produktion, die das Leid und die Traumata politischer Häftlinge in den Haftanstalten der DDR thematisiert. Es ist aber die erste Produktion, die mehrere ehemalige politische Häftlinge, zum Teil auch in Interaktionen oder Rollenspielen, zusammen bringt und sich dabei vielfältiger Darstellungsformen bedient, um eine vermeintliche Authentizität zu erreichen. Die Untersuchung konzentriert sich in erster Linie auf die aus dem Theaterstück entstandene gleichnamige filmische Aufzeichnung *Staats-Sicherheiten*, die im Jahr 2009 im Auftrag der ZDF Theateredition in einem Studio in Berlin aufgenommen wurde, zieht aber das ursprüngliche Theaterstück zum Vergleich heran, um die medienspezifischen Darstellungsformen, die zur Konstruktion der Authentizität beitragen, deutlicher herauszustellen.

Abschließend sei an dieser Stelle angemerkt, dass in diesem Artikel Zitate, die sich auf den reinen Textkorpus des Stückes beziehen, aus Gründen der Zitierfähigkeit mithilfe der filmischen Variante belegt werden, da der reine Text in den beiden Darstellungsformen nahezu deckungsgleich ist. Differenzen ergeben sich in erster Linie aus der jeweiligen Inszenierungform beider Varianten.

Theoretische Grundlagen

Die vorliegende Studie stützt sich auf neue Erkenntnisse der kultur- und medienwissenschaftlichen Gedächtnistheorie. Zentral ist hier der Begriff des prosthetischen Gedächtnisses, wie er von Landsberg geprägt wurde. Das ‚prosthetische Gedächtnis' ist als eine neue Gedächtnisform zu verstehen „that emerges at the interface between

---

[3]   Astrid Erll: Kollektives Gedächtnis und Erinnerungskulturen. Stuttgart: J.B. Metzler, 2005, S. 124.

a person and a historical narrative about the past, at an experiential site, such as a movie theatre or museum".[4]

Indem Filme und Museen die Besucher sowohl körperlich als auch kognitiv involvieren, ermöglichen diese Medien dem Individuum an einem historischen Narrativ teilzunehmen. Das Individuum bekommt nicht nur ein besseres Verständnis für die Geschichte, sondern auch Erinnerungen an Ereignisse präsentiert, die er oder sie selber nicht erlebt hat. Nach Landsberg können die auf diese Weise erzeugten Erinnerungen sich auf die Subjektivität und Politik des Individuums auswirken und als Grundlage für unerwartete Allianzen fungieren.[5] Im Mittelpunkt der Debatte um die Erfahrbar- und Erlebbarkeit solcher historischen Ereignisse, zu denen auch ein Theaterstück oder eine filmische Darstellung mit historischen Zeitzeugen zu zählen ist, steht immer wieder die Frage der Authentizität. Nicola Macloed beschreibt verschiedene Deutungen des Begriffes in der wissenschaftlichen Literatur, unter anderem ‚konstruktive Authentizität', wonach die Authentizität kein statischer Begriff, sondern relationell und konstruiert ist – und ‚existentielle Authentizität', wonach das Individuum das Gefühl der Authentizität herstellt, das er oder sie erlebt.[6] Für die Kulturwissenschaftlerin Aleida Assmann ist die „Inszenierung [...] Schlüsselbegriff eines konstruktivistischen Weltverständnisses, demzufolge Wirklichkeit nicht vorfindlich existiert, sondern performativ hergestellt wird".[7]

In diesem Artikel wird der Begriff der Authentizität entsprechend des letztgenannten Zitats verwendet: Authentizität als Teil der Inszenierung der Geschichte. Die Frage ist, wie Authentizität in den hier untersuchten Darstellungsformen konstruiert wird, welche spezifischen medialen Effekte verwendet werden, und welche Rolle die Zeitzeugendarstellungen bzw. Zeitzeugenberichte in diesem Zusammenhang spielen. Den Narrativen der Zeitzeugen wird – und diese Feststellung trifft hier unabhängig von der medialen Darstellungsform zu – generell eine zentrale Rolle im Hinblick auf die Authentizität zugesprochen. Grundsätzlich haben Zeitzeugenberichte, besonders Opfer-Narrative, einen besonderen Stellenwert in der Aufarbeitung traumatischer Geschichte, denn es werden ihnen oft besondere Glaubwürdigkeit und Legitimität zugeschrieben, so konstatiert Jeffrey Wallen: „Eyewitness testimony contains an imperative – you too must know, must remember, must bear the marks of the past."[8] In der museologischen Gedenkstättenarbeit, in der oft Zeitzeugen Führungen oder

---

[4] Alison Landsberg: Prosthetic Memory: The Transformation of American Remembrance in the Age of Mass Culture. New York: Columbia University Press, 2004, S.2.

[5] Vgl. dazu Landsberg: Prosthetic Memory, S. 2 f.

[6] Vgl dazu: Nicola Macleod: Cultural Tourism: Aspects of Authenticity and Commodification. In: Melanie K. Smith und Mike Robinson (Hg.): Cultural Tourism in a Changing World. Politics, Participation and (Re)presentation. Clevedon: Channel View Publications, 2006, S. 177-90.

[7] Aleida Assmann: Geschichte im Gedächtnis. München: C.H. Beck, 2007, S. 162.

[8] Jeffrey Wallen: Narrative Tensions: The Archive and the Eyewitness. In: Partial Answers 7/2 (2009), S. 261-78; hier S. 262.

Diskussionsrunden leiten, wird ein ähnliches Phänomen beschrieben: „In der Regel hinterlässt der Bericht von Zeitzeugen einen tieferen Eindruck als der Vortrag von Personen, die nicht selbst betroffen waren", befindet etwa Sascha Möbius, Leiter der Gedenkstätte Moritzplatz in Magdeburg.[9] Auch bei der Inszenierung von *Staats-Sicherheiten* wird, bis auf wenige Ausnahmen, in denen sich die Zeitzeugen beispielsweise gegenseitig aus ihren Stasi-Akten vorlesen, vollständig auf die Narrative der Zeitzeugen gesetzt, um der Darstellung eine besondere Glaubwürdigkeit, Unmittelbarkeit und Echtheit zu verleihen. In darstellerischer Hinsicht ist anzumerken, dass der Ablauf grob unterteilt ist. So gibt es verschiedene Sequenzen, in denen die Zeitzeugen sich äußern. Welches Moment innerhalb des Ablaufes gerade thematisiert wird, erfährt der Zuschauer durch eine mediale Einblendung von Schlagworten, die wie eine Art Kapitelüberschrift fungieren. Diese Schlagworte lauten: Festnahme, Transport, Untersuchungshaft, Prozess, Strafvollzug, Entlassung und Hinterlassenschaften und lassen sich als narrative Schwerpunkte erkennen, zu denen sich dann jeweils verschiedene Zeitzeugen in einem offenbar zuvor festgelegten Ablauf äußern. Die vorgetragenen Texte sind im Theaterstück und in der filmischen Fassung weitestgehend identisch. Auch die Unterteilungen in die genannten Sequenzen sind sowohl im Theaterstück als auch im Film zu finden, werden allerdings aufgrund der unterschiedlichen räumlichen Gegebenheiten in unterschiedlichen Varianten dargestellt. Auf der Theaterbühne werden die ‚Kapitelüberschriften' mit einem Beamer auf die Bühne projiziert, in der Filmversion hingegen vor Beginn der jeweiligen Sequenz im Bild eingeblendet. Auch weitere begleitende Medien, welche auf der Bühne oder im Film eingesetzt werden, um die Zeitzeugenberichte zu untermalen oder zu kommentieren, werden an die Rahmenbedingungen der jeweiligen Darstellungsform logistisch und technisch angepasst.

Erzählform, Darstellbarkeit und Perspektivenwechsel im Theater und Film

Der größte Teil der inszenierten Zeitzeugenberichte ist als Erzählung in der ersten Person gestaltet, wodurch das Moment der subjektiven Empfindung des Berichtenden noch erhöht wird. Die Narrative sind in erster Linie als Rückblick gestaltet – dennoch ist das Tempus, in dem diese wiedergegeben werden, zum größten Teil im Präsens gehalten um den Effekt der Unmittelbarkeit zu steigern. Unterstrichen wird diese Rückschau noch durch die Einblendung von Fotos aus der Vergangenheit der Zeitzeugen. Die Bilder werden in der Theaterfassung auf die Bühne projiziert, auf der gleichzeitig der Darsteller steht. Diese Koppelung unter-

---

[9]   Sascha Möbius: Überlegungen zur historisch-politischen Bildung in der Gedenkstättenarbeit. In: Sascha Möbius und Annegret Stephan (Hg.): Erinnern: Forschung, Bildung und die gesellschaftliche Auseinandersetzung mit politischer Verfolgung in der SBZ/DDR. Berlin: Metropol Verlag, 2009, S. 189-212, hier S.208.

streicht wiederum die Glaubwürdigkeit der Erzählungen. Mithilfe des medialen Zusammenspiels wird somit eine Authentizität generiert, die durch den Bericht des Zeitzeugen direkt übertragen wird, gleichzeitig lässt sich eine solche Szene aber auch als inszenierte Authentizität entlarven, denn der Bericht aus der Gegenwart zielt in die Vergangenheit ab, und natürlich ist der Zeitzeuge zum Beispiel heute nicht mehr in der Situation, gerade verhaftet zu werden. Das Bühnenbild suggeriert dem Rezipienten eine stimmige Situation, die im Gesamtkontext inszeniert ist, vom Rezipienten aber aufgrund der beglaubigenden Requisiten wie Originalfotos und Zeitzeugennarrativen als stimmig, beglaubigend, echt und in diesem Sinne auch authentisch angenommen wird. Diese Erzählform der individualistischen Rückschau bestimmt und prägt den größten Teil der Inszenierung. Durch die Interaktion auf der Bühne werden die Individuen für den Rezipienten als Erlebnisgemeinschaft erkennbar, wodurch den individuellen Berichten noch einmal eine besondere gegenseitige Beglaubigung zuteil wird. Auch in der filmischen Fassung wird mit Fotos gearbeitet, hier wird die Simulanität allerdings durch typische filmische Kunstgriffe wie beispielsweise eine Überblendung von Foto und Erzählung der betreffenden Person erreicht. Die verwendeten Erzählstränge sind also zwar in Bühnen- und Filmversion inhaltlich gleich; das Beispiel macht aber deutlich, dass die Authentizität der Zeitzeugenberichte in den beiden Fassungen auf unterschiedliche Arten gesteigert wird.

Die Narrative beschränken sich nicht ausschließlich auf individuelle Rückschauen, auch wenn diese den größten Teil der Erzählstruktur ausmachen; es sind auch Perspektivenwechsel erkennbar: Im Kapitel zur Untersuchungshaft imitieren mehrere Zeitzeugen in einer Formation die Gefängniswärter. In einem dialogischen Wechsel werden die Zuschauer zeitweise direkt angesprochen. Darsteller 1: [imitiert die Stimme des Gefängnisaufsehers]: „Kommen se, gehen se" – Darsteller 2: „Sie werden allein durch den langen Gang geführt – bei ihnen nur Wachpersonal. Sonst sehen sie keinen Menschen" – Darsteller 1: „Gehen se" Darsteller 2: „Man bringt sie in die Einlieferungszelle" [...] Darsteller 1: „Ausziehen!"[10] Hier gestaltet sich die Darstellung als Inszenierung, als deren Teil sich auch die Zuschauer betrachten können.

Bereits dieser kurze Ausschnitt macht deutlich, wie mithilfe verschiedener medialer Darstellungsformen bestimmte Eindrücke von Authentizität vermittelt werden, was hier erneut an das von Landsberg beschriebene prosthetische Gedächtnis erinnert. Durch kognitive Involvierung der Zuschauer wird den Rezipienten ermöglicht, an einem historischen Narrativ teilzunehmen, das sie selbst so nicht erlebt haben. Dadurch, dass die Zuschauer direkt vom Zeitzeugen angesprochen werden, entsteht eine inszenierte dialogische Situation, die im Falle der Bühnenfassung, durch die physische Anwesenheit des Zeitzeugen noch verstärkt

---

[10] Staats-Sicherheiten. Clemens Bechtel [dir.] Die Theater Edition, 2009. Digital Versatile Disc. 0:13:52. [Im Folgenden abgekürzt mit Staats-Sicherheiten und der vereinheitlichten Zitierweise Stunden: Minuten: Sekunden]

wird. In der filmischen Fassung stehen zwar wiederum dieselben Textfragmente im Mittelpunkt, da die physische Anwesenheit des Zeitzeugen hier jedoch nur medial gegeben ist, wird mit Zooms auf Gesichter gearbeitet um die oben erwähnte Atmosphäre zu generieren. Das inszenierte Zwiegespräch, das zwischen dem Zeitzeugen und den Rezipienten gehalten wird, kann so jeweils als Grundlage für eine Allianz zwischen dem Rezipienten und den Darstellern fungieren. Es kann jedoch nicht nur das inszenierte Zwiegespräch zu solchen Allianzen führen, wie im Folgenden zu sehen sein wird.

Theaterstück versus filmische Darstellung

Die filmische Inszenierung – wohl in erster Linie Ergebnis des großen Erfolges des Theaterstücks – lässt sich, wenn man den Fokus ausschließlich auf den Text und den inhaltlichen Ablauf legt, unter Gesichtspunkten der Adaptionstheorie eher als Replikation denn als Adaption interpretieren. Diese Einschätzung ist in erster Linie der Ähnlichkeit von Text und Ablauf zwischen dem Theaterstück und der filmischen Fassung geschuldet. Die von den Darstellern vorgetragenen Texte wurden beispielsweise im Film nicht verändert. Oberflächlich stellt sich so beim Rezipienten das Gefühl einer großen Ähnlichkeit zwischen den beiden Darstellungsformen ein, was sich ja auch in den bisher angestellten Beobachtungen zu bestätigen scheint. Bei genauerem Hinsehen wird jedoch deutlich, dass der Begriff der Replikation nicht ausreichend ist, um die Relation zwischen dem Theaterstück und der filmischen Inszenierung zu beschreiben, und dass trotz der vermeintlich großen Ähnlichkeit der beiden Darstellungen wesentliche Merkmale einer Adaption auszumachen sind, die in erster Linie aus dem Wechsel von einem Medium zu einem anderen resultieren und durch diesen Prozess zu gestalterischen und dramaturgischen Unterschieden zwischen den beiden Fassungen führen. Linda Hutcheon beschreibt Adaptionen als „an announced and extensive transposition of a particular work or works. This 'transcoding' can involve a shift of medium [...] or a change of frame and therefore context."[11] Ein Wechsel des Mediums zieht einen „change of frame" in diesem Fall automatisch nach sich und ermöglicht so den Einsatz differenzierter dramaturgischer und genrespezifischer Elemente.

Besonders gravierend wirkt sich der mediale Wechsel im Hinblick auf atmosphärische Momente aus: Die Erzählungen der Zeitzeugen auf der Theaterbühne zeichnen sich durch eine physische Nähe zwischen dem jeweiligen Darsteller und dem Rezipienten aus. Die physische Anwesenheit der Zeitzeugen macht die Erzählungen unmittelbar und direkt. Die konstruierte Unmittelbarkeit ist bei der filmischen Aufzeichnung schon allein durch den physischen Abstand des Rezipienten zum Medium des Bildschirmes verringert und muss durch filmtechnische Kunstgriffe wie besonder nahes Heranzoomen eines individuellen

---

[11]　Linda Hutcheon: A Theory of Adaptation. New York: Routledge, 2006, S.8.

Charakters oder Überblendungen sowie besondere Schnitt-Techniken simuliert werden.

Die Ähnlichkeiten in Bezug auf die Texte deuten aber bereits an, dass die filmische Fassung trotz aller darstellerischen Unterschiede als eine Variation des gezeigten Theaterstücks verstanden werden soll. Ähnlichkeiten gibt es auch in der Gestaltung des Bühnenbildes: Die Kulisse ist, sowohl in der Theater- als auch in der Filmfassung in schlichtem Grau gehalten, als sollte sie eine Imitation der grauen Gefängnismauern darstellen. Auch das sehr reduzierte Bühnenbild – mit einer weitestgehend freien Fläche, die im Hintergrund Platz für ein paar Schemel bietet, um denjenigen Zeitzeugen einen Sitzplatz zu bieten, die gerade nicht im Scheinwerferlicht stehen und ihre Erinnerungen erzählen – ist in den beiden Darstellungen gleich. Die Sequenzen, in denen mit originalgetreuen Möbeln, Akten des Ministeriums für Staatssicherheit und anderen originalen Requisiten gearbeitet wird, sind weitestgehend vom Theaterstück in die filmische Darstellung übertragen worden.

Dennoch eröffnet sich dem Rezipienten im Wiedererkennungsmoment dieser Requisiten einer der signifikantesten Unterschiede zwischen der Bühnen- und der Filmfassung: Während in der Theaterfassung die Nachbildung einer Gefängniszelle am rechten Rand der Bühne aufgebaut ist, in der im Verlauf Szenen nachgespielt werden, ist diese Zellen-Sequenz im Film an Originalschauplätzen gedreht und anschließend mithilfe der Schnitttechnik in den Verlauf des Filmes eingefügt worden. Während die Bühnenfassung aus platz- und zeittechnischen Gründen nur mit recht reduzierter Requisite auskommen muss, arbeitet die filmische Fassung bei sich anbietenden Momenten mit mediumsspezifischen dramaturgischen Eingriffen. So wird die Sequenz in der Gefängniszelle tatsächlich in einer solchen filmisch festgehalten – der Zeitzeuge rezitiert dabei denselben Text wie auf der Theaterbühne, wodurch sich auf der rein textlichen Ebene die Ähnlichkeit zwischen beiden Stücken weiterhin verdeutlicht – es werden die Gefängnisvorschriften vorgelesen.[12] Dennoch ist die Szene im filmischen Bewegungsablauf sehr viel eindrücklicher darstellbar als auf der Theaterbühne, da man sich filmtechnischer Kunstgriffe bedient, um die Szene dramaturgisch zu untermalen. So wird zum Beispiel der Gang des Zeitzeugen in die Zelle mit der Kamera eingefangen, ebenso wie der angsterfüllte Blick des Inhaftierten, der die Zellenwände mit den Augen absucht. All dies wird mit einer sehr verlangsamten Bewegung eingefangen, als wolle man die Eindrücklichkeit und Bedrohlichkeit der Situation noch unterstreichen. Zudem wird die Szene mit spannungsfördernder Musik untermalt. Als die Gefängnistür hinter dem Inhaftierten zuschlägt, wird durch den Schlitz in der Tür ein Zettel mit den Gefängnisvorschriften durchgereicht, den der Inhaftierte anschließend am Tisch sitzend laut vorliest.

Es kann festgestellt werden, dass in den beiden Versionen der *Staats-Sicherheiten* jeweils eine adäquate medienspezifische Dramaturgie eingesetzt wird,

---

[12] Staats-Sicherheiten, 0:16:45.

um die gewünschte Authentizität zu transferieren: Die Bühnendarstellung ist eine real und in Echtzeit stattfindende Inszenierung, die somit auch weiteren Einflüssen unterworfen bleibt, wie etwa der darstellerischen Tagesform der Zeitzeugen. So kann der Zuschauer beispielsweise erkennen, dass die Darsteller auf der Bühne den Text beim Sprechen geringfügig variieren: durch hinzugefügte Nebensätze, Gedankenpausen oder Ähnliches wirken die Darstellungen frei interpretiert, obwohl der Ablauf und die Rahmenhandlung feststehen. „Replications – like adaptations – are never without variations",[13] konstatiert Linda Hutcheon in Bezug auf dieses Phänomen die Tatsache, dass jede Wiederholung, auch eines vermeintlich festgelegten Mediums, stets geringfügigen Änderungen unterworfen wird.

Die filmische Darstellung hingegen stellt eine bereits abgeschlossene und nicht mehr veränderbare Version des Theaterstücks dar. Die Inszenierung von Authentizität lässt sich also nicht durch die reale physische Anwesenheit eines Zeitzeugen generieren. Daher werden, wie am Beispiel der kurz zuvor erwähnten Zellen-Sequenz verdeutlicht wurde, bestimmte Kameraführungen, sowie die Untermalung mit dramatischen Geräuschen und Perspektivwechsel, und eine sehr ausgeprägte Darstellung der Mimik des Zeitzeugen gezeigt, alles wird sehr verlangsamt dargestellt. Die Filmszenen, die an den Originalschauplätzen gedreht werden, wirken in dieser Variation ebenfalls authentisch. Die zuvor genannten verwendeten medialen Elemente können auch in dieser Darstellung nicht isoliert voneinander betrachtet werden, sondern funktionieren im Zusammenspiel miteinander. Ein direkter Blick auf die Vergangenheit wird simuliert, auch die bereits thematisierten filmischen Effekte fungieren als dramaturgischer Kunstgriff, der Unmittelbarkeit suggerieren soll und ein Hilfsmittel darstellt um den Rezipienten das Medium als solches vergessen zu lassen. Zusammenfassend lässt sich im Hinblick auf die Darstellungsformen konstatieren, dass die Inszenierung der Authentizität in erster Linie durch genrespezifische dramaturgische Kunstgriffe des jeweiligen Mediums erreicht wird. Dies gilt sowohl für die Bühnen- als auch für die Filmfassung des Stückes.

Vom Theater zum Film – und zuvor?

Bei der Wahrnehmung der Zeitzeugenberichte spielt nicht nur die unmittelbare Rezeption im Theater oder Film eine Rolle. In vielen Fällen ist die Wahrnehmung bestimmter Narrative von Medien beeinflusst, die den Rezipienten bereits vor der Inszenierung bekannt waren. Je nachdem wie die zurückliegende Rezeption ausfiel, kann die Wahrnehmung bestimmter Darstellungsformen schon im Vorfeld an entsprechende Erwartungen geknüpft sein, denn einige der Zeitzeugen sind auch unabhängig von ihrer Mitarbeit an diesem Projekt in der Öffentlichkeit zum Thema Vergangenheitsaufarbeitung tätig: sie halten beispielsweise Besucherführungen in

---

[13]   Hutcheon: A Theory of Adaptation, S.173.

spezifischen musealen Gedenkstätten ab oder haben über ihre traumatischen Erfahrungen mit dem SED-Regime geschrieben. Wie eng die einzelnen Narrative dabei ineinander greifen und was dies für das Moment der Authentizität bedeutet, möchte ich im Folgenden am Beispiel von Vera Lengsfeld, einer Darstellerin in den *Staats-Sicherheiten* und ehemaliger DDR-Bürgerrechtlerin erläutern. Vera Lengsfeld zählt außerdem zu den Gründungsmitgliedern des Fördervereins der Gedenkstätte Hohenschönhausen e.V., die im ehemaligen Untersuchungsgefängnis Hohenschönhausen in Berlin untergebracht ist. Sie hat bereits mehrere Autobiographien veröffentlicht, in denen sie an ihren Lebensweg erinnert, wobei die Verhaftung und die folgenden Repressionen durch das Regime der Staatssicherheit eine wichtige Rolle spielen.

Als zentral erweist sich bei den folgenden Überlegungen das bereits erwähnte Konzept der Remediatisierung, das heißt der Wiederverwendung von mediatisierten Geschichten und Narrativen in einem neuen Medium, wobei die verschiedenen Medien sich in einem kontinuierlichen Wechselspiel befinden und dabei Wirklichkeits- und Vergangenheitsversionen, Werte, Normen und Identitätskonzepte vielfach erst erzeugen.[14] Um das Zusammenspiel sowie die wechselseitige Beeinflussung der Medien und somit auch deren Auswirkung auf die Rezipienten zu verdeutlichen, möchte ich einen autobiographischen Text von Vera Lengsfeld aus dem Jahr 2002 der filmischen Inszenierung der *Staats-Sicherheiten* gegenüber stellen. Lengsfeld schreibt darin über die Situation der Verhaftung:

Als wir uns dem Frankfurter Tor von der Rückseite der Häuser näherten, sah ich, dass dort etliche Überfallwagen der Polizei bereitstanden. Außerdem waren schon im Hinterhof so viele Uniformierte und Zivile, dass ich merkte, wie schwierig es werden würde, überhaupt den Demonstrationszug zu erreichen. Ich bedauerte, dass wir uns nicht schon, wie ich spontan vorgeschlagen hatte, in der Storkower Straße in die Massen eingereiht hatten. Ich hatte ja vorgehabt, möglichst unbemerkt mitzugehen und das Transparent erst auf dem Bahnhof Friedrichsfelde, vor den Repräsentanten der Partei- und Staatsführung zu entrollen. Schon während wir uns den Arkaden näherten, die zur Frankfurter Allee führten, wurden wir angerufen: ‚He, was wollt ihr da?‘ ‚Ich will auch demonstrieren‘, antwortete ich. Dieser Satz sollte mir noch Ungelegenheiten bereiten – er wurde vor Gericht zu einem ‚Hauptbeweisstück‘. Ich bemerkte, dass die Stasileute Miene machten, uns festzunehmen, und rannte los, in der Hoffnung, ihnen in der Menge zu entkommen. Nach 100 Metern merkte ich, dass Herbert nicht mehr neben mir war. Er stand bereits an eine Hauswand gedrückt, umringt von Zivilisten. Ich ging zurück, um zu fragen, was los sei, als mich zwei Männer von hinten packten: ‚Komm mit.‘ Ich registrierte noch, dass sie sich nicht ausgewiesen hatten, es also kein ‚Widerstand gegen die Staatsgewalt‘ war, wenn ich mich weigerte. So mussten mich die beiden Herren die 100 Meter Allee zurück – und durch die Arkaden bis zu einem bereitstehenden Lastwagen

---

[14] Erll: Kollektives Gedächtnis und Erinnerungskulturen, S. 124.

schleifen. Einem von ihnen war es offensichtlich peinlich, er beschwor mich immer wieder, doch ‚ordentlich zu laufen'. Aus meiner Froschperspektive sah ich die teils ungläubigen, teils erschrockenen Gesichter der Demonstranten mit ihren ‚Winkelementen' in den Händen.[15]

Dieses Narrativ wird in abgewandelter Form und unter Nutzung spezifisch filmischer Inszenierungsstrategien in den *Staats-Sicherheiten* remediatisiert. Die folgende Beschreibung bezieht sich, in erster Linie aus Gründen der Zitierfähigkeit, auf die filmische Darstellung; es sei der Vollständigkeit halber erwähnt, dass der Text in der Bühnenfassung derselbe ist – auch die Darstellungsform ist ähnlich, den räumlichen und logistischen Gegebenheiten der Theaterbühne angepasst.

Bereits als die Darstellerin Vera Lengsfeld mit anderen Darstellern die Szene betritt, fängt die Kamera sie im Laufen ein. Als Lengsfelds Erzählung einsetzt, dreht sie sich mit Schwung in die Kamera. Sie spricht ihren Text, während die Kamera in der Frontale auf ihr Gesicht gerichtet ist. Neben dem Kopf wird in weißer Schrift der Name Vera Lengsfeld eingeblendet. Sie spricht in die Kamera: „17. Januar 1988, Berlin Friedrichshain, vormittags"[16] – bei dem Wort „vormittags" findet ein Schnitt auf ein Schwarzweißfoto statt, das die Darstellerin auf einer Demonstration zeigt. Dieses Foto ist als Abbildung auch in der Autobiographie Lengsfelds zu finden.[17] Es füllt in der Filmversion den kompletten Bildschirm aus. Zu sehen ist darauf Vera Lengsfeld in einem hellen Hemd, sie trägt ein Transparent auf dem zu lesen ist: „Abrüstung auch in Schule und Kindergarten." Die Darstellungen werden kommentarlos überblendet. Aus dem *Off* ist die Stimme der Darstellerin zu hören, die in der ganzen Szene fortlaufend über die verschiedenen Kamera-Einstellungen spricht: „Ich bin auf dem Weg zur Demonstration. Zu dieser Demonstration hat die Sozialistische Einheitspartei Deutschlands aufgerufen." In der nächsten Einstellung ist wieder Vera Lengsfeld zu sehen, frontal gefilmt, die Augen sind nicht in die Kamera gerichtet. Sie spricht weiter: „Ich habe ein Transparent bei mir, darauf steht: Jeder Bürger der DDR hat das Recht seine Meinung frei und öffentlich zu äußern. Ich habe mich extra fein gemacht im Pelzmantel meiner Mutter. Ich will nicht gleich als Bürgerrechtlerin erkannt werden. Ich weiß, die Staatssicherheit hat ein Feindbild von Bürgerrechtlerinnen in Sackkleidern und alles verhüllenden Tüchern." Zwischen dem gezeigten Bild und dem gesprochenen Text besteht also keine Übereinstimmung. Nun wird wieder ein Schwarz-Weiß Foto eingeblendet, auf dem Lengsfeld von der Seite zusammen mit einem Mitdemonstranten aufgenommen ist. Parallel dazu spricht die Darstellerin ihren Text weiter: „Ich nähere mich dem Frankfurter Tor. Ich kann schon von Weitem die Demonstration sehen." Die Szene ist nur durch den aus dem gesprochenen Text gegebenen Kontext und nicht durch das fotografische Bild selbst als Demonstration zu erkennen. Auch dieses Foto

---

[15]   Vera Lengsfeld: Von nun an ging's bergauf... mein Weg zur Freiheit. München: Langen Müller Verlag, 2002, S. 223.

[16]   Staats-Sicherheiten, 0:02:00-0:4:23.

[17]   Lengsfeld: Von nun an ging's bergauf, S. 296f.

wurde bereits, ebenso wie das zuerst gezeigte, in der Lengsfeld Biographie *Von nun an geht's bergauf* verwendet.[18] Es folgt wieder ein Schnitt auf Lengsfelds Gesicht, wieder frontal, der Ausschnitt ist allerdings größer und im Hintergrund kann man noch sehr unscharf andere Darsteller erkennen. Lengsfeld spricht folgenden Text:

„Dann höre ich eine Stimme: Was willst du hier? Ich will hier demonstrieren rufe ich und beschleunige gleichzeitig meine Schritte, denn ich hoffe meinen Häschern im Demonstrationszug zu entkommen". Die Kamera zoomt nun langsam auf das Gesicht, die Darstellerin spricht weiter: „Aber bevor ich mich einreihen kann, werde ich von hinten gepackt. ‚Komm mit'. Ich realisiere in Sekundenbruchteilen: Die beiden jungen Männer sind in Zivil", in diesem Moment stoppt der Zoom. Lengsfeld spricht weiter: „sie haben sich nicht ausgewiesen und ‚Komm mit' ist keine Verhaftung. Ich weigere mich." Es wird dann auf das Gesicht eines weiteren Darstellers geschwenkt, sein Gesichtsausdruck ist betreten, er schaut nach unten. Die Kamera schwenkt in der Halbtotalen weiter nach rechts, jedoch unscharf, zur nächsten Darstellerin – als das Gesicht eingefangen ist, wird die Kameraeinstellung auf scharf gestellt. Lengsfeld spricht dazu den Text: „Sie schleifen mich weg. Im Weggeschleift-Werden sehe ich die entsetzten Gesichter der schwenkenden Demonstranten mit den Wink-Elementen in ihren Händen."

Die Kamera fängt wieder das Gesicht von Lengsfeld ein. Sie spricht:

Sie schleifen mich bis zu einem LKW. Dort sind noch andere Stasi-Leute. Was wollt ihr mit der Dame? Dame? Das ist eine der schlimmsten sagt einer meiner Häscher. Sie durchsuchen mich. Ich muss meinen Ausweis abgeben, dann soll ich auf den LKW klettern. Ich bin elegant gekleidet, der LKW ist hoch. Ich weigere mich. Tu's lieber, sonst müssen wir dir an den Arsch greifen. Die Situation wird gerettet von zwei frisch verhafteten Bürgerrechtlern, die mir auf den LKW hinaufhelfen. Oben sitzen schon andere Bürgerrechtler. Nach einer Weile wird eine Plane über den LKW gespannt und wir fahren los.[19]

Die Szene, in der Lengsfeld auftritt, ist ungewöhnlich lang und ist die erste Sequenz in dieser filmischen Darstellung, die mit der Montage von Fotos arbeitet. Dass zwischen der Erzählung der Darstellerin und den dargestellten Fotos keine faktische Kohärenz besteht, wird nicht weiter kommentiert. Das mediale Zusammenspiel wirkt in dieser Szene sinnbildend: Die einzelnen Medien werden nicht als einzelne gestalterische Elemente wahrgenommen, sondern als ein stimmiges Gesamtkonzept. Bei einem punktuellen Abgleich fällt zudem auf, dass die Darstellung in der Inszenierung vor allem dramatisch abgerundet wurde. Während es in der Inszenierung heißt: „Oben sitzen noch andere Bürgerrechtler",[20] kann man in der Autobiographie lesen, dass die anderen Verhafteten „meist Unbekannte" gewesen

---

[18] Lengsfeld: Von nun an ging's bergauf, S. 296f.
[19] Staats-Sicherheiten, 0:02:00-0:4:23.
[20] Staats-Sicherheiten, 0:04:13.

seien.[21] Dieses Beispiel zeigt deutlich, dass mit der Wiederholung der Narrative auch eine Veränderung einhergeht, dass die Narrative nicht statisch, sondern inneren und äußeren Einflüssen unterworfen sind.

Theoretische Erklärungsmuster zu Medien in Interaktion

Dieses Phänomen der Veränderung lässt sich als ein typisches Merkmal der Remediatisierung erklären, wenn man die hier beschriebene Wiederverwendung von schon mediatisierter Erinnerung als eine Inszenierung der Geschichte begreift. Erll und Rigney sprechen in diesem Zusammenhang von einem „„repurposing [...] taking a ‚property' [in our case a memory matter] from one medium and re-using it in another. In this process, memorial media borrow from, incorporate, absorb and refashion earlier media".[22] Begründen lassen sich diese Veränderungen mit Theoremen der Gedächtnisforschung. Nach Harald Welzer ist „die Autobiographie als situationsabhängige, asoziale, ‚wirklich' gelebte Lebensgeschichte [...] ja nichts als eine Fiktion, in der autobiographischen Praxis selbst realisiert sie sich nur als jeweils zuhörerorientierte Version, als aktuell angemessene Montage lebensgeschichtlicher Erinnerung".[23] Auch Zierold weist darauf hin, dass wir in unserer Analyse des sozialen Gedächtnisses die Frage nach der Rezeption mediatisierter Erinnerungen nicht unbeachtet lassen können: „Im Zusammenhang von Medien und Erinnerung ist die Rezeptionsseite von entscheidender Bedeutung, denn erst in der Rezeption entscheidet sich, ob ein Medienangebot als potentieller Erinnerungsanlass auch tatsächlich für einen entsprechenden Anschluss genutzt wird."[24] Es lässt sich auch hinzufügen, dass es sich erst in der Rezeption entscheidet, ob ein Medienangebot als ‚authentisch' anerkannt und entsprechend wahrgenommen wird. Astrid Erll und Ann Rigney beschreiben in Anlehnung an Jay David Bolter und Richard Grusin in diesem Kontext die „double logic of remediation"[25]: Nach dieser doppelten Logik streben Gedächtnismedien nach immer höherer „Unmittelbarkeit". Das Ziel ist, uns ein Fenster auf die Vergangenheit anzubieten, bei dem wir die Anwesenheit des Mediums vergessen sollen. Dieser Effekt wird normalerweise zustande gebracht, indem man verschiedene Medien wieder-verwendet und multipliziert.[26] Die Berichte der Zeitzeugen und die Erinnerungen an

---

21   Lengsfeld: Von nun an ging's bergauf, S.224.
22   Astrid Erll und Ann Rigney: Introduction. Cultural Memory and its Dynamics. In Astrid Erll und Ann Rigney (Hg.): Mediation, Remediation, and the Dynamics of Cultural Memory. Berlin: Walter de Gruyter, 2009; S. 1-15, hier S. 5.
23   Harald Welzer: Das kommunikative Gedächtnis. Eine Theorie der Erinnerung. München: C.H. Beck, 2002, S.213.
24   Martin Zierold: Gesellschaftliche Erinnerung. Eine medienkulturwissenschaftliche Perspektive. Berlin: Walter de Gruyter, 2006; S. 161.
25   Erll und Rigney: Introduction. Cultural Memory and its Dynamics, S.5.
26   Vgl. dazu Erll und Rigney: Introduction, S.4.

die Repressionen, die sie erlebt haben, werden demnach nicht nur in den Narrativen der ehemaligen Gefangenen remediatisiert. Im medialen Zusammenspiel von individuellem Narrativ, Requisiten und einem atmosphärischen Moment, das sich durch die Anwesenheit der Zeitzeugen generiert, wird in der Bühnenfassung diese Doppelung der Medien angestrebt; in der Filmfassung geschieht dies auf andere Weise, nämlich durch die Darstellung der originalen Schauplätze im Zusammenspiel mit einer akustischen Kulisse und einer entsprechenden dramatischen Kameraführung, die den jeweiligen Zeitzeugen entsprechend in Szene setzt. Für beide Darstellungsformen gilt: obgleich jeder der ehemaligen Häftlinge seine individuelle Geschichte vorträgt, scheinen die verschiedenen Erinnerungsfragmente miteinander zu korrespondieren.

Im Kontext des kommunikativen Gedächtnisses bemerkt Assmann, dass Erinnerungen nicht isoliert produziert werden, sondern mit anderen Erinnerungen vernetzt: „Durch ihre auf Kreuzung, Überlappung und Anschlussfähigkeit angelegte Struktur bestätigen und festigen sie sich gegenseitig. Damit gewinnen sie nicht nur Kohärenz und Glaubwürdigkeit, sondern wirken auch verbindend und gemeinschaftsbildend."[27] Die Bildung einer Erinnerungsgemeinschaft in diesem Sinne geschieht nach Assmann im Prozess des kommunikativen Erinnerns, des „conversational remembering".[28] In den *Staats-Sicherheiten* wird diese Erinnerungsgemeinschaft unter anderem in der mündlichen Kommunikation entwickelt, die Zeitzeugen erinnern sich ja nicht im Gespräch miteinander, sondern anhand der Medien. Die Medien generieren auf diese Art und Weise ebenfalls eine Erinnerungsgemeinschaft. Auch wenn die Zeitzeugen sich in der Inszenierung nicht gemeinsam erinnern, so teilen sie ähnliche Schicksale und interagieren auf der Bühne oder im Film entsprechend. In der filmischen Fassung wird dem Zuschauer die vermeintliche Erinnerungsgemeinschaft durch die eingeblendeten thematischen Überschriften suggeriert; in der Bühnenfassung wird der gleiche Effekt, wie bereits erwähnt, durch das Projizieren der einzelnen Themenabschnitte auf eine Bühnenleinwand erreicht. Durch Einzelaussagen werden die Zeitzeugen als Mitglieder einer Erlebnisgemeinschaft erkennbar, die alle ein ähnliches Schicksal erlitten. Die Erinnerungsgemeinschaft ist dabei bereits in der Einleitung durch den Schriftzug „15 Schicksale aus dem Gefängnis – ehemalige Häftlinge berichten"[29] als solche ausgewiesen.

---

[27] Aleida Assmann: Der lange Schatten der Vergangenheit: Erinnerungskultur und Geschichtspolitik. München C.H. Beck, 2006, S.24.

[28] Assmann: Der lange Schatten, S.54.

[29] Staats-Sicherheiten, 0:00:06.

Grenzen der Darstellbarkeit?

Da die Inszenierungen hauptsächlich auf die Narrative von Zeitzeugen in Wechselwirkung mit anderen Medien wie Fotos oder originalen Requisiten oder Schauplätzen setzen, gestalten sich manche Passagen als schwierig darstellbar. In dem Kapitel *Prozess* wird mitunter aus den Akten des Ministeriums für Staatssicherheit vorgelesen. Auch hier möchte ich wieder beispielhaft die Darstellung Vera Lengsfelds aufzeigen. Die Szene wird als klassischer Dialog aufgeführt. In einer abgedunkelten Halbtotalen sind hier im hinteren Teil der Bühne mehrere mit Akten gefüllte Regale zu sehen. Die Darsteller haben sich zwischen den Regalen positioniert, manche hocken auch auf dem Boden. Die vordere Hälfte der Bühne ist leer, lediglich ein Lichtkegel strahlt auf eine Stelle, in die die Darsteller treten, nachdem sie ein anderer Darsteller aufgerufen hat. In dieser Interaktion, die ähnlich wie ein Rollenspiel aufgebaut ist, tritt Vera Lengsfeld zusammen mit dem Journalisten Gilbert Furian auf. Lengsfeld sitzt rechts im Bild, sie ruft Furian mit den Worten: „Gilbert Furian"[30] auf, dieser lässt eine Akte, in der er offenbar gerade gelesen hatte, aus der Hand auf den Boden fallen und tritt nach vorne ins Scheinwerfer-Licht. Die beiden halten folgenden Dialog:

Lengsfeld: Angeklagt wegen?
Furian [spricht]: Anfertigungen von Aufzeichnungen, die geeignet sind, den Interessen der DDR zu schaden mit dem Zweck der Verbreitung im Ausland in Tateinheit mit öffentlicher Herabwürdigung der staatlichen Ordnung.
Lengsfeld: [ist nun sitzend zu sehen im Portrait, wie sie aus der Akte vorliest] Der Angeklagte hat insgesamt eine ablehnende Haltung zu Teilbereichen der Entwicklung der DDR. Er versuchte sich seit Jahren von der DDR-Gesellschaft abzugrenzen und wandte sich insbesondere Erscheinungen destruktiven Charakters zu. Er nahm an Zusammenkünften verschiedener Jugendlicher teil, die sich an westlichen Punkgruppen orientierten. Sein Ziel war es, daraus ein Material herzustellen, um es seinem Bekannten in der BRD zuzuleiten. Er stellte die Schrift: ‚Erinnerung an eine Jugendbewegung Punk' her und wählte Stimmen aus, nach denen man sich drehen und wenden könne wie man will, wenn man nicht so nach der Pfeife tanzt dann wird man irgendwie fertig gemacht. Die objektiv hohe Schwere der Straftat hat gesellschaftsgefährliche Auswirkungen und das Verhalten des Angeklagten qualifiziert sich zum Verbrechen. Der Angeklagte wird zu einer Freiheitsstrafe von zwei Jahren und zwei Monaten verurteilt.[31]

Furian tritt ab. Bevor ein anderer Darsteller auftritt, gibt es eine kurze Zäsur, in der die Darsteller im Hintergrund zwischen den Aktenregalen hin- und her gehen, die Akten nehmen und in ihnen lesen. In die Pause hinein wird in regelmäßigen

---

[30]   Staats-Sicherheiten, 0:47:37.
[31]   Staats-Sicherheiten, 0:48:52.

Abständen wieder mit der Maultrommel gespielt und die Stimme Stephan Krawczyks spricht hart darüber: „Die Partei, die Partei, die hat immer recht".[32] Als Vera Lengsfeld in das Spotlicht tritt und ein Zeitzeuge aus dem Hintergrund ruft: „Vera Lengsfeld. Angeklagt wegen"? – antwortet diese: „Rowdytum".[33] Die Stimme aus dem Hintergrund setzt nach: „Verurteilt zu?" Lengsfeld antwortet wiederum: „Sechs Monate wegen versuchter Zusammenrottung".[34]

Die Inszenierung der Verurteilungen und Prozesse als klassisches Rollenspiel ist ein Teil der Dokumentation, in dem die ehemaligen Häftlinge auch in die Rolle ihrer Widersacher schlüpfen. Das Einnehmen der „Täter"-Rollen bzw. die Imitation des Stasi-Deutsch ist zwar in der literarischen Aufarbeitung von Fällen innerfamiliärer Bespitzelung in Schriftstellerfamilien ein häufig anzutreffendes sprachliches Mittel der Darstellung – und auch in Führungen von Gedenkstätten wie beispielsweise in der ehemaligen Haftanstalt Hohenschönhausen in Berlin, wo Zeitzeugen häufig historische Führungen dokumentieren, ist zu beobachten, dass die ehemaligen Häftlinge auf den Rundgängen die Rollen ihrer ehemaligen Vernehmer oder Aufseher einnehmen, um den Besuchern ein Gefühl für die ehemalige Häftlingsrolle zu geben und so eine möglichst hohe Authentizität zu erzeugen. Diese Vermittlung von Authentizität lässt sich aber an einem historischen / museologischen Ort leichter erzeugen, da sich eine Wechselwirkung zwischen konstruktiver und existenzieller Inszenierung der Geschichte besser generieren lässt als in einer Darstellungsform eines Dokumentationstheaters, das bei der Inszenierung vorwiegend auf Opfernarrative als Einzelschicksale setzt. Da die Rezipienten von *Staats-Sicherheiten* die politischen Häftlinge aufgrund der vorgetragenen Opfernarrative in erster Linie als vom Regime Verfolgte ausmachen, ist die Inszenierung der Häftlinge als vermeintliche Richter oder Staatsanwälte, die Urteile verlesen, insofern problematisch, als es schwer ist, diese ‚Spielart' in ihrer Darstellungsform als ebenso authentisch zu werten wie die anderen durch die Zeitzeugen vorgetragenen Texte. Diese Schwierigkeit der Darstellung Authentizität zuzuschreiben resultiert meines Erachtens nach aus der Tatsache, dass der größte Teil der Inszenierung darauf abzielt, die Zeitzeugen anhand ihrer Narrative als „echte" Betroffene zu inszenieren. Wie bereits zuvor angemerkt, wird den Opfernarrativen eine besondere Glaubwürdigkeit zugeschrieben, so dass die Imitation eines Anderen für die Rezipienten ein Rollenspiel bleibt, das in seiner Inszenierung eher unbeholfen wirkt. Die Vertauschung der Täter /Opfer Rollen in dieser spielerischen Form erweist sich hier als schwierig, da die gesamte Darstellung sehr auf die Opfer-Narrative der Zeitzeugen konzentriert ist. So bleibt der Versuch, die ‚Täterseite' durch die Zeitzeugen darzustellen, ein Unterfangen, bei dem die sonst durchgängige Authentizität an ihre Grenzen stößt. Es fällt dem Rezipienten schwer, den Wechsel der Erzählstrukturen nachzuvollziehen und als authentisch einzustufen. Diese

---

[32] Staats-Sicherheiten, 0:46:58.
[33] Staats-Sicherheiten, 0:49:31.
[34] Staats-Sicherheiten, 0:49:36.

Problematik löst sich jedoch durch das anschließende Wiederaufgreifen der Zeitzeugennarrative, so lässt sich für die gesamte Inszenierung ein Spannungsbogen beobachten, der mit dem Niedergang der DDR und damit auch des totalitären Regimes endet. Die Inszenierung bietet aber nur ein vornehmlich versöhnliches Ende an – auch wenn die DDR nicht mehr existiert, hat die Zeit in der Haft doch Fragen, psychische Wunden und Traumata hinterlassen, die bis in die heutige Zeit fortwähren, und mit denen sich jeder auf seine Art und Weise arrangieren muss.

Im Kapitel „Entlassung" hat Vera Lengsfeld noch eine längere Passage, die sie direkt in die Kamera spricht.

Am Tage meiner Entlassung wurde ich in ein sehr vornehmes Haus am Rande von Ostberlin gebracht. Dort eröffnete mir ein heute sehr bekannter Rechtsanwalt, dass ich in den Westen abgeschoben werden würde. Auf alle meine Forderungen sei eingegangen worden. Ich könnte mit DDR Pass gehen, meine Kinder mitnehmen und nach einem Jahr in die DDR zurückkehren. Danach ging es zum letzten Mal auf Transport – bei Nacht und Nebel an die Westgrenze bei Herleshausen. Am anderen Morgen hab ich die erste Pressekonferenz meines Lebens gegeben. Und was für eine. Über hundert Journalisten waren da. Und da wurde mir zum ersten Mal klar, warum ich Bedingungen stellen konnte, denn an jedem Tag an dem die verhafteten Bürgerrechtler im Gefängnis waren, fanden in den mehr als 30 Gemeinden und Städten der DDR allabendlich Protestveranstaltungen statt, solange bis Partei- und Staatschef Honecker gezwungen war, auf einer internationalen Pressekonferenz zu versprechen, dass alle Bürgerrechtler entlassen werden würden. In Leipzig haben sich die Menschen allabendlich in der Nikolaikirche versammelt. Nach unserer Abschiebung haben die aktivsten von ihnen den Montagskreis gegründet. Aus diesem Montagskreis gingen anderthalb Jahre später die Montagsdemonstrationen hervor, die innerhalb kürzester Zeit die Mauer zum Einsturz und die DDR zum Verschwinden gebracht haben. Man kann also mit Fug und Recht sagen, dass die Massenverhaftungen am 17. Januar 1988 der erste Nagel zum Sarg der DDR gewesen sind. [Geht ab][35]

Unter dem Kapitel „Hinterlassenschaften" spricht Vera Lengsfeld dann, zusammen mit allen anderen Häftlingen in einer Stuhlreihe sitzend, als letzte den vermeintlich wohlmeinenden Satz: „Es bleibt die Genugtuung, dass wir heute die Schlüsselgewalt über die Stasi-Knäste haben"[36] und gibt der Inszenierung trotz aller dunklen Seiten ein versöhnliches Schlusswort.

---

[35]   Staats-Sicherheiten, 1:22:28.
        Staats-Sicherheiten, 1:26:52.

Fazit

Die filmische Aufarbeitung von *Staats-Sicherheiten* stellt eine Adaption dar, deren Produktion offenbar dem großen Erfolg des Theaterstückes geschuldet ist. Obschon beide Fassungen sich durch einen hohen Ähnlichkeits- und Wiedererkennungswert auszeichnen und die in den beiden Versionen verwendeten Texte übereinstimmen, wählen sie aufgrund der medialen Rahmenbedingungen in Schlüsselszenen verschiedene Darstellungsformen. Das trifft besonders auf den Prozess der Remediatisierung zu, durch den in dem dokumentarischen Theaterstück und dessen filmischer Aufarbeitung ein möglichst hohes Maß an Authentizität erzeugt werden soll. Die Darbietung so zentraler Bestandteile wie der Zeitzeugen-Narrative und der originalen Requisiten wird jeweils den medienspezifischen Gegebenheiten angepasst, um als insgesamt authentisches Rezeptionsangebot wahrgenommen zu werden. Während in der Theaterfassung in erster Linie durch die physische Anwesenheit von Zeitzeugen und entsprechende Narrative im Zusammenspiel mit Bildern Authentizität erzeugt und ein stimmiges Bild von der Vergangenheit konstruiert wird, generiert sich die Authentizität in der filmischen Fassung zwar ebenfalls durch die Narrative als solche, jedoch sind die Zeitzeugen nicht physisch sondern medial zu sehen. Die Erzeugung einer besonderen und authentischen Atmosphäre wird daher in diesem Fall durch spezifisch filmische Kunstgriffe erreicht, als Beispiele wurden in der Untersuchung die Untermalung von Szenen mit dramatischer Musik, das Drehen von Filmsequenzen an Originalschauplätzen sowie eine spezielle Kameraführung genannt.

Aufgrund des großen Erfolgs der *Staats-Sicherheiten* stellt sich die Frage, ob das Stück in seiner dokumentarischen Darstellungsform noch ähnliche Inszenierungen nach sich ziehen wird und wie diese möglicherweise dem Anspruch an Authentizität gerecht werden.

Nadine Nowroth is a Postgraduate Student in the Department of Germanic Studies at Trinity College Dublin.

GENERAL CONTRIBUTIONS

Una Carthy

Attitudes to Language Learning in Letterkenny Institute of Technology: Some Recent Findings

The issue of language provision in Ireland has been the focus of many studies in the last decade.[1] The lack of an overarching language policy at national level, it has been argued, has led to a decrease in the numbers of students studying foreign languages in both second- and third-level education. As it is one of the leading educational providers in the Northwest Region and one of fourteen Institutes of Technology nationwide, Letterkenny Institute of Technology (LyIT) provides the setting for an interesting case study, described here, on attitudes to language learning in Ireland.[2]

In order to contextualize this study, it will be necessary to outline briefly the history of language provision in LyIT. Languages have been part of mainstream programmes since the late 1970s. The eighties and early nineties saw a relatively high number of students taking foreign languages due to the fact that languages were a mandatory element of some programmes. In addition to the core language programme (Commercial Translators / Applied Languages / European Languages and Business), there were four other programmes for which students had to take either French or German language: the Certificate in Business Studies and Secretarial Studies (now redenominated as BA in Administrative Management), the Diploma in Marketing, and the Certificate in Electronics. Towards the end of the 1990s it became apparent, however, that students who demonstrated lower language aptitude were disadvantaged by compulsory language courses. When these were no longer mandatory parts of the programmes, there was a concomitant fall in overall numbers learning languages. French and German language, which had been eliminated from the Diploma in Marketing, now became elective elements in both the Business Studies and Office Information Systems programmes. An optional

---

[1]   See, for example, David Little: Languages in the Postprimary Curriculum. A Report for the NCCA. Dublin: NCCA, 2003; Pól Ó Dochartaigh and Miriam Broderick: Language Policy and Language Planning in Ireland. A Report from the Royal Irish Academy for Modern Language, Literary and Cultural Studies. Dublin: Royal Irish Academy, 2006; Heidi Zojer: When the Celtic Tiger Roared, Foreign Modern Languages Whispered: Modern Languages in Ireland 1998-2009. In: Germanistik in Ireland 5 (2010), p. 177-87.

[2]   The Institutes of Technology (IoTs) are often compared to the former Polytechnics in the United Kingdom, or the *Fachhochschulen* in Germany, because of the applied focus in their suite of programmes. Letterkenny Institute of Technology (formerly Letterkenny Regional Technical College) was founded in 1971 to serve the training needs of the local community, with a particular emphasis on vocational education and practical skills for the workplace.

language component, which had been part of Engineering from the late nineties until 2008, was completely removed.

A similar trend can be observed in the School of Tourism in Killybegs, which became a constituent School of LyIT in 2007. Here there was greater emphasis on language provision in the past, with mandatory elements in the majority of programmes. Over the past five years, however, language learning has gradually become elective.[3] Despite the gradual erosion of modern languages' mandatory status, however, it seems that learners at the School of Tourism in Killybegs have greater access to language electives than learners on the main campus in Letterkenny.

Each IoT has its own unique School structure overseen by Academic Councils. In LyIT, there are four Schools: Business Studies, Tourism, Engineering and Science. Traditionally, modern languages have belonged to the School of Business Studies and Tourism and, while the links between these specialisms are perhaps apparent, this categorization has prevented students from other disciplines from acquiring language skills of equal importance to their careers.

In a period of severe economic recession which has led to widespread unemployment and high levels of emigration among recent Irish graduates, understanding patterns of language learning becomes a matter of acute importance. The prevailing funding model in the IoTs is demand driven, which has major implications for modern languages. Because of dwindling student numbers, many language lecturers have found themselves redeployed, often struggling to adjust to new roles in a fast-changing educational sector.[4] Paradoxically, despite diminishing prestige within academia and falling student numbers,[5] job opportunities for graduates with language skills have never been more plentiful.[6]

When the issue of language provision was first raised at LyIT's Academic Council in 2006, a proposed Language Policy was rejected on the assumption that students were simply not interested in studying modern languages. In order to challenge this belief, an institute-wide survey of all first-year students was launched to determine what students' attitudes towards learning languages actually were.

---

[3]   Of the seven programmes on offer in the Department of Hospitality and Tourism, five have a modern language elective, while two have mandatory language elements. Of the seven programmes on offer in the Department of Gastronomy and Culinary Arts, two offer language electives and one has a mandatory language element.

[4]   Susan O'Shaughnessy: All Change? Professional Identities of German Language Lecturers in a Changing Structural Field. In: Germanistik in Ireland 6 (2011), p.179-201.

[5]   See Zojer: When the Celtic Tiger Roared.

[6]   Providing Multilingual Communication Skills for the Labour Market. Brussels: European Commission, 2011. http://ec.europa.eu/languages/pdf/languages-for-jobs-report_en.pdf (last accessed 27 July 2012); A Report by the Expert Group of Future Skills Needs. Dublin: Forfás, 2011. www.egfsn.ie/newsevents/news/title,7647,en.php (last accessed 27 July 2012); See also: Employers' Perception of Graduate Employability. Brussels: European Commission, 2010.
http://ec.europa.eu/public_opinion/flash/fl_304_en.pdf (last accessed 27 July 2012).

In 2008, while this research was still being carried out, a Language Strategy was finally approved, and an ad hoc committee including representatives from all Schools was set up by Academic Council to oversee its implementation.[7] This strategy document outlined the history of language provision in LyIT, revealing some interesting trends (see above). Drawing on the mistakes of the past, the Strategy proposed a roadmap for the future which would harness the new modular semester structure to allow students from all disciplines to acquire the linguistic skills demanded by a competitive global work market.

This local initiative was mirrored at national level with the establishment of an IoT Language Policy Network in 2006.[8] This Network provided a collaborative framework for language lecturers across the IoT sector. More recently at European level, the Molan report has challenged higher-education institutions to integrate language learning into 'non-linguistic' disciplines.[9] The report's findings, based on a review of forty-one case studies from thirty-eight higher-level institutions across Europe, provide interesting examples of best practice for motivating students to study languages.

Both the IoT Network and Molan Report provide an interesting context to the research undertaken in the study described here, demonstrating that these local findings are not only of relevance to language provision at LyIT, but are also crucial to the successful development of language teaching across the IoT sector and further afield, including at European level.

Methodology

It is generally accepted that the validity of research findings is greatly enhanced by choosing more than one method of data gathering.[10] More traditional approaches tended to apply individual methods, but it is preferable to have a mixture, provided, of course, that they are used in a complementary manner.[11] Other reasons for combining methods include that it allows the researcher to arrive at a better

---

[7] Una Carthy: Language Strategy. [Unpublished. Approved by Academic Council of Letterkenny Institute of Technology, 2008.]

[8] http://www.languagesinireland.ie/ (last accessed 27 July 2012).

[9] http://www.molan-network.org/docs/impact_reports_document_0.pdf (last accessed 1 August 2012).

[10] Maire Messenger Davies: Practical Research Methods for Media and Cultural Studies. Edinburgh: Edinburgh University Press, 2006; N.K. Denzin: The Research Act. A Theoretical Introduction to Sociological Methods. Englewood Cliffs, NJ: Prentice Hall, 1988; Thomas Ricento (ed.): An Introduction to Language Policy. Oxford: Blackwell, 2009; Ruth Wodak: Linguistic Analysis. In: Thomas Ricento (ed.): An Introduction to Language Policy, p. 346-361; Susan Canagarajah: Ethnographic Methods. In: Thomas Ricento (ed.): Introduction to Language Policy, p. 153-169.

[11] Zoltan Dornyei: Research Methods in Applied Linguistics. Oxford: Oxford University Press, 2007.

understanding of the target phenomenon and to verify one set of findings against another.[12] With regard to the investigation at hand, the use of two methods had a developmental function: qualitative and quantitative methods were used in succession, so that the results obtained by the first method could inform the development of the second approach applied.[13] Interviewees for the qualitative (second) phase were selected on the basis of the data sets which emerged from the quantitative (first) phase.

A vital element of the quantitative phase was the questionnaire which was rigorously designed to elicit relevant responses from participants. In this first phase of data collection (September 2007), a two-page questionnaire was circulated to all first-year students, with the exception of the Tourism College Killybegs (TCK), during Induction. Learners were asked to fill out the questionnaire on the spot for immediate collection. An on-line questionnaire was also made available to facilitate off-site TCK learners and those who had missed the opportunity to take part during Induction. In total, 539 questionnaires were completed during Induction, while a further 48 were completed on-line, and 34 completed in TCK, giving a sum total of 622 respondents (a response rate of approximately 76%). The findings from the first phase were presented in both local and national colloquial where it was suggested that further research was needed to reinforce the quantitative findings. A series of semi-structured, face-to-face interviews followed in 2009, using some of the same respondents (now second-year students) who had participated in the first phase. In total, thirteen interviews were recorded, each of approximately fifteen minutes in duration.

The interviewees came from all four Schools of the Institute: four from the School of Engineering, three from the School of Business Studies, three from the School of Science, and three from the Tourism College Killybegs. The research questions were similar to those asked in the first phase and were also informed by the recent Molan Report, mentioned above.[14] Issues such as accredited language modules, the integration of language modules into 'non-linguistic' academic programmes, and student mobility were explored in these interviews. Experts had specifically recommended the methodological approach used in this phase, as it allowed interviewees to volunteer information that may not have been anticipated by the interviewer: The strength of the semi-structured interview is that it allows the interviewer to use some predetermined questions, but also permits him / her to change and modify them, as appropriate.[15]

---

[12]   Margarete Sandelowski: Tables or Tableaux? The Challenges of Reading and Writing
       Mixed Method Studies. In: A. Tashakorri and C. Teddlie (eds.): Handbook of Mixed
       Methods in Social and Behavioural Research. Thousand Oaks, CA: Sage, 2003, p. 321-
       54.
[13]   Jennifer Greene: Toward a Conceptual Framework for Mixed-Method Evaluation
       Designs. In: Educational Policy Analysis 11/3 (1989), p. 255-74.
[14]   See footnote 9.
[15]   Colin Robson: Real World Research. Oxford: Blackwell, 2002.

Summary of Quantitative and Qualitative Findings

- Approximately one third of respondents would opt to learn a language if it were an integral part of their main programme of study.

- The majority of these students came from the Schools of Business, Science, and TCK.

- While two thirds initially ruled out taking a language module, 58% would take a language module if it were offered in conjunction with a period abroad.

- All respondents felt that institute-wide language modules should be available to students from all disciplines.

- All respondents felt that language skills were important, particularly in the current economic climate.

- Of the thirteen students interviewed, ten expressed interest in a study semester / work placement abroad.

Details of Quantitative Findings

The questionnaire was divided into two sections: a 'Demographic' section (questions 1-5) which sought data relating to age, gender and previous language-learning experiences, and an 'Attitude' section (questions 6-13) which sought data specifically related to the research question(s). Both the demographic and attitude sections used a combination of multiple-choice and tick boxes, allowing respondents to answer quickly while not necessarily assuming the mutual exclusivity of different answers. While the questionnaire was essentially a quantitative tool, it also incorporated qualitative elements. Question 14, for example, asks how language teaching could be made more attractive to students. And a Comment Box section provided room for other feedback not directly elicited by the questionnaire.

Demographic Section

The majority of respondents (81%) were native speakers of English, with 12% giving Irish as their native language, and 3.2% indicating Irish and English jointly as their mother tongues. 3.5% were native speakers of other languages including Lithuanian, Polish, Edo, French, Spanish, Russian, Latvian, Finnish, Tagalog, Romanian, Igbo, Slovakian and Chinese dialect. The majority of respondents (76%) were between the ages of 17 and 25, while the remainder could be classified as mature learners (over 25). Most respondents (almost 59%) were female. Figure 1 below shows the language(s) which respondents took in their Leaving Certificate examination, the overwhelming majority taking either Irish and French (46%) or Irish only (33%), when compared to the percentages taking other languages: German and Irish (11%), Spanish and Irish (4.4%). 40% of respondents were registered in Business Studies, 29% in Science, 25% in Engineering and 6% in the School of Tourism. This is proportionate to the size of each School in terms of student numbers.

Prior Knowledge of Languages

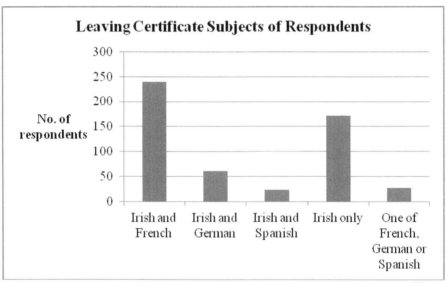

Fig. 1

Attitude Section

The following questions were asked in this section:

- Would you take a language as an integral part of your programme?
- Would you take a language as extra to your programme?
- What is your preferred language module?
- Reasons for not taking a language module
- Reasons for taking a language module
- Would you take a language if there were a period abroad?
- What type of period abroad would you prefer?
- How could language modules be made more attractive?

Q. Would you take a language module as an integral part of your programme?

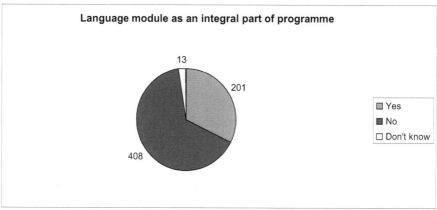

Fig. 2

Figure 2 illustrates the responses to question 6. The majority of respondents (66%) indicated that they would not take a language module if it were integrated into their course of study, while approximately a third (33%) indicated that they would.

Q. Would you take a language module as extra to your programme?

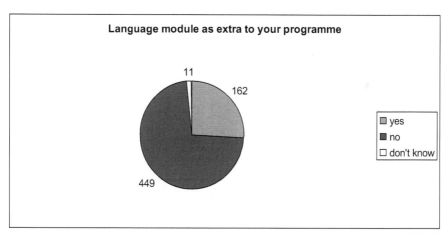

Fig. 3

Figure 3 shows the responses to the idea of studying a language as part of an extra workload, additional to the core programme of study as opposed to integral to it. Here even more students (83%) were opposed to taking language modules, while, conversely, even fewer (26%) were in favour. Nonetheless, over a quarter of students from all Schools indicated a willingness to learn a language in addition to their main workload.

Correlations

A correlation between attitudes and School emerges upon closer examination of these findings: The majority of learners who indicated a preference for language modules were from the Schools of Business Studies, Science and TCK, whereas proportionately more learners from Engineering ruled out a language option. A correlation between attitudes and gender also exists. Those who were in favour of language modules were more likely to be female, while those who ruled out a language option were more likely to be male. While this may not be of central importance to this particular investigation, it is certainly worth mentioning in the context of other studies on gendered attitudes to language learning.

Q. 8: Preferred Language Module

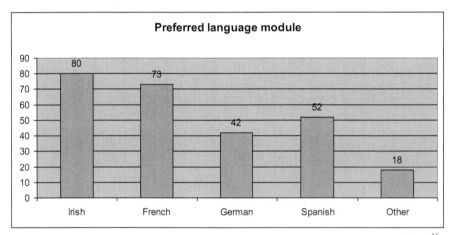

Fig. 4[16]

Figure 4 above shows the language preferences of respondents (in other words, the languages the respondents would prefer to learn), the majority indicating Irish (30%), French (27%), German (16%), Spanish (20%), and the remainder opting for other languages. These preferences reflect respondents' previous language-learning experiences (see fig. 1 above). In other words, students are more inclined to choose languages to which they have already been exposed at secondary-school level where Irish and French dominate the curriculum. It is worth noting, however, that Spanish

---

[16]   Other here = English as a Foreign Language (EFL), Japanese, Polish, Turkish, Arabic

is more popular at undergraduate level than German, even though fewer students have had exposure to it at secondary school (see fig. 1). Overall, figure 4 shows that by widening the foreign language provision to include all Schools, viable student numbers for all language classes could be generated.

Q. 9: Reasons for not taking a language module

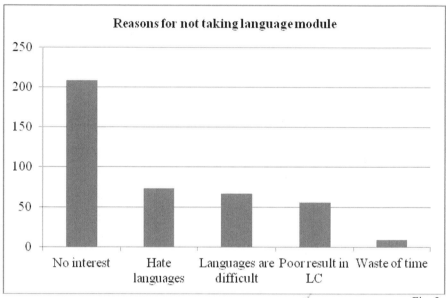

Fig. 5

Figure 5 above gives some insights into respondents' negative attitudes to learning languages. Approximately half of all respondents indicated that they had no interest in taking a language module, with almost one fifth (18%) indicating that they "hated" languages, while 16% viewed language learning as "difficult." A further 13% of respondents stated that their attitudes had been influenced by poor Leaving Certificate examination results. Interestingly, only 2% found learning languages to be a waste of time. So, it appears that even those who would not opt to take a language module themselves still consider language learning as such worthwhile.

Q. 10: Reasons for taking a language module

The table in figure 6 below contains information on respondents' positive attitudes to language learning. The overwhelming majority (83%) believed that languages were beneficial for travelling, with career prospects (71%) cited as the second most important reason for learning another language. 23% mentioned a love of languages, while 8% felt that languages were beneficial to their main programme of study.

Interestingly, fewer than 3% of respondents found languages easy. (It is important to note that the percentages do not add up here because students were invited to tick as many boxes as they felt were applicable.)

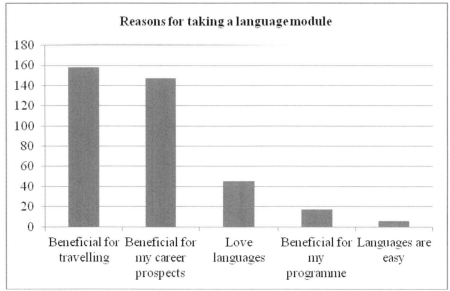

Fig. 6

Q. 11: Would you take a language module if associated with a period abroad?

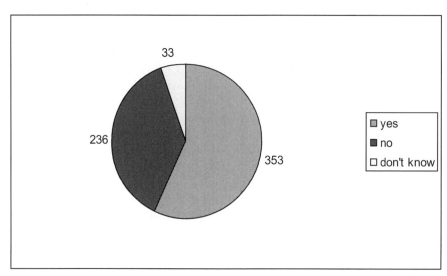

Fig. 7

As figure 7 above shows, over half of the respondents would take a language module if it were linked or led to a period abroad. However, almost 39% would still not opt to study a language under these circumstances.

Q. 12: Which type of period abroad would you prefer?

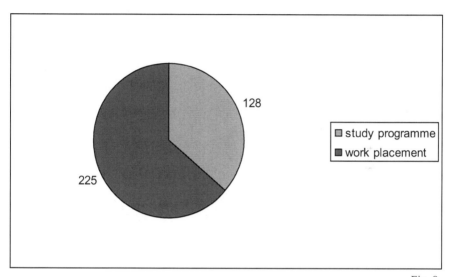

128

□ study programme
■ work placement

225

Fig. 8

The majority of respondents (64%) favoured work placement over a study semester (36%) for the period abroad, as shown in figure 8 above.

Q. 13: How could language modules be made more attractive?

Figure 9 below indicates the responses to this question. The majority (41%) felt that offering a work placement or study semester abroad would make language modules more attractive to students. The second most popular suggestion was "more interaction with international students" (17%), followed by enhancing students' awareness of the importance of language skills (16%). Next in importance was the provision of greater background knowledge of the target country (9%), linking language learning to business skills (8%), more language learning choices (7.8%), and, finally, more e-learning opportunities (3%).

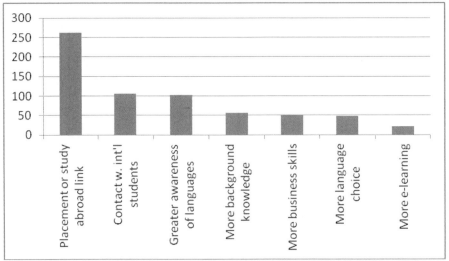

Fig. 9

Details of Qualitative Findings

As mentioned above, the interviewees came from all four Schools of Letterkenny Institute of Technology. They were also selected on the basis of datasets that emerged from the first phase:

Datasets:

1.   'No' to integral language modules
      'Yes' to work placement / study abroad
2.   'No' to integral language modules
      'No' to work placement / study abroad
3.   'Yes' to integral language modules
      'Yes' to work placement / study abroad

The semi-structured interviews of the second phase allowed several issues to be explored in greater depth. In keeping with the basic line of enquiry of the questionnaire, specific information was sought about attitudes to language learning, international mobility, programme-integral language modules etc. Almost a year had elapsed since respondents had filled out their original questionnaires, and it was necessary to establish whether their attitudes had changed in the interim. The qualitative method both reinforced and complemented the approach taken in the first phase. In order to illustrate this point, let us consider the question relating to institute-wide language modules. Students who took part in the quantitative phase were asked if they would opt for a language module, if it were available to them. Two datasets emerged from the responses: those who ticked 'yes' in response, and those who ticked 'no'. Both groups were subsequently represented in the qualitative phase, i.e. the 'yes' and the 'no' respondents. Interestingly, all interviewees, both from the yes and the no datasets, felt that language modules should be offered, even if they would not opt to take them themselves. This finding would never have emerged had the research been confined to the quantitative method, as the original questionnaire did not include this specific question.

Rather than give a detailed account of each interview, the most salient aspects that emerged in this phase will be highlighted in the following. Four of the selected respondents had ticked 'no' initially when asked if they would opt for a language module, but had subsequently ticked 'yes' if language were offered in the context of a semester abroad. These respondents were from Bioscience, Civil Engineering and Graphic Design, in other words from very diverse academic backgrounds. Nonetheless, there is a marked similarity in the views expressed.

> Interviewee 1 (Bioscience) explained that he initially failed to see how languages could be relevant to a science student, but if language learning led to a period abroad he could see the point of it.

> Interviewee 2 (Civil Engineering) felt that she had been weak at languages in secondary school, and had ticked 'no' initially because she had a more mathematical background. However, she responded that if she were going to work abroad she would feel compelled to learn a language.

> Interviewee 8 (Graphic Design) saw the importance of languages for travelling. She expressed her love of languages and stated that she would like to travel and spend time studying and working abroad.

> Interviewee 9 (Graphic Design) did not see the relevance of a language module until it was associated with spending a semester abroad. He felt that it would be much easier to learn a language abroad than to learn it in Ireland. This is why he had initially ticked 'no' and then 'yes.'

Another aspect that was explored in more detail in the second phase was the prior language-learning experience of interviewees. Only one respondent had not gone through the Irish secondary school system; all other 12 respondents had some experience of learning languages at secondary school in Ireland. Two had had to abandon their study of French because of timetable restrictions in their schools. Two had found French difficult to learn, but one of these had found Spanish easy to learn when exposed to it during Transition Year (optional fourth year at secondary school that allows students to acquire skills outside the set curriculum). While perceptions of individual languages is not the main focus of this study, it is interesting to note that this correlates to the findings in figure 4 where Spanish fared well as a preferred language module. Two respondents were critical of the teaching approaches used in language classes: one respondent blamed poor teaching approaches for lack of curiosity among Irish students about other countries; another felt that teaching approaches needed to be altered.

Additional Questions Arising from First Phase

In addition to these core questions, two further questions were asked to see if respondents would make conscious connections between language learning and mobility (both in the form of foreign students coming to Ireland on mobility schemes, and Irish students going abroad). In figure 7 above, over a third (39%) of respondents had indicated that not even a semester abroad would motivate them to learn a language. The semi-structured interview presented the ideal opportunity to investigate further what the perceived obstacles to mobility and, relatedly, language learning might be, in the form of the question:

> I: Currently, a disproportionately low number of Irish students avail of Erasmus mobility schemes, compared to other European countries. Why do you think so few Irish students go abroad?

In figure 9 above, when respondents were asked to propose ways of making language modules more attractive, "more interaction with international students" was the second most popular suggestion. In other words, the desire to have contact with visitors from abroad seems to be a motivating factor in learning languages. It was necessary to investigate this further and to see how the presence of so many international students on campus could be connected with the attractiveness of language modules. This idea was pursued in the additional question:

> II: We have over a hundred international students studying at LyIT at the moment. Do you have any contact with them? What could be done to help them to integrate into college life?

Rather than list all responses in numerical order, they will be grouped into categories for closer analysis.

> Question I: Three interviewees were unable to explain why so few Irish students availed of Erasmus mobility schemes, while three felt that it was simply too challenging for them because of poor linguistic skills. Three interviewees attributed the low up-take of Erasmus places to a lack of awareness and felt that more should / could be done to promote and advertise these schemes. Financial constraints were cited by two interviewees as the main deterrent, while one interviewee attributed the lack of interest in mobility to the poor teaching approach at secondary-school level. Finally, one interviewee felt that Irish

students lacked the necessary confidence, attributing this to the teaching approaches adopted at primary- and secondary-school levels.

Question II: Ten interviewees felt that more could / should be done to help Erasmus students to integrate, as they tended to hang around together in groups, while two thought that the language barrier was simply too great and nothing could be done to overcome it. Six suggested that social events such as dancing classes or other cultural activities could be organized to facilitate their integration. One expressed the view that visiting Erasmus students were intimidated by the Irish "drink culture," and that efforts should be made to show them other aspects of the Irish lifestyle.

Of the six respondents with positive attitudes to languages, one shared accommodation with a French student, while another two socialized regularly with Erasmus students. While it is difficult to draw conclusions from such a small sample, it seems likely that favourable attitudes towards languages correlate to interaction with people from other linguistic cultures.

Analysis of Quantitative and Qualitative Findings

These findings shed some light on the lack of up-take in foreign languages in LyIT. In figure 2, the majority of respondents (66%) indicated that they would not take a language module as an integral part of their study programme. Figure 5 allows some insight into the negative attitudes to languages, with the majority indicating that they had no interest. Other reasons cited were perceived difficulty and poor final examination results in secondary school. However, only a small percentage felt that language learning was a complete waste of time. Nevertheless, the fact that two thirds of respondents would not take a language option, while recognizing the importance of language-learning, sends a clear message about how important prior language-learning experiences are in terms of determining future attitudes to languages. Further insights into this issue were obtained in the qualitative phase in which individual respondents referred to the teaching approaches used at secondary school level. Previous studies have also identified these teaching methodologies as a cause for concern. In response to David Little's NCCA Report which criticized teaching approaches in mainstream Irish language classrooms, Muiris O'Laoire conducted a qualitative study of twenty-one students learning Irish in an English-language school. He observed that the new Irish syllabus which emphasizes communicative proficiency, cultural awareness, and language awareness, presented a wonderful opportunity to teachers wishing to motivate and engage pupils who were learning Irish. However, it also presents enormous challenges, and the language-awareness component in particular requires "more pedagogical testing and exploration, research and documentation."[17] Institutes of Technology and other third-level institutions might have a role to play in this process.

While secondary-school language provision is not the main focus of this study, the languages offered at this level and the mode of their delivery did impact on the language-learning attitudes of respondents in this survey. The fact that the majority of respondents had only been exposed to French and Irish (see fig. 1) to the exclusion of other languages, limited their language horizons. There is nothing new in this finding. Already in the 1980s studies drew attention to the imbalance in language provision at secondary-school level in Ireland.[18] At the time, a survey of employers revealed that the vocational need for German was much greater than for French.[19] While some improvements have been made in recent years, language provision at secondary-school level still has a long way to go in terms of diversification, as shown in David Little's NCCA report. Indeed, a recent survey of local secondary schools in the North West revealed that eight times as many students take French as German, with just under half of schools not offering German at all.[20] Limited language choice and limited exposure to languages in secondary schools appear to be a major deterrent to the take-up of languages at third level.

The semi-structured interviews also highlighted some of the obstacles associated with the relatively low level of participation in international mobility among Irish students, namely financial issues and lack of awareness. Data from the quantitative phase also reinforces this finding: figure 9 illustrates that 'work / study placements' and 'creating a better awareness' are seen as the two most important factors in making language modules more attractive. A recent study commissioned by the European Parliament looking at barriers to participation in international mobility schemes also established that financial hardship experienced by students from certain socio-economic backgrounds was the biggest obstacle to mobility.[21] Other reasons cited in that study include: lack of awareness, family circumstances and poor language skills, all of which have featured in our findings too. Some students simply did not know that it was possible for them to avail of mobility schemes;

---

[17]   Muiris O'Laoire: An Approach to Developing Language Awareness in the Irish Language Classroom. A Case Study. In: International Journal of Bilingual Education and Bilingualism 10/4 (2008), p. 454-70.

[18]   Mary Varilly: The Eighties. Towards Diversification in Language Learning. In: German in Ireland. A Complete Survey on Learning German in Ireland. Dublin: Goethe Institut, 1991, p. 5-9; Fionnuala Kennedy and Konrad Schröder: Foreign Language Learning Experience, Foreign Language Learning Motivation and European Multilingualism. In: German in Ireland, p. 16-29.

[19]   Konrad Schröder: The Vocational Need for German and other Foreign Languages. A Look at the Irish Scene. In: German in Ireland, p. 10-15.

[20]   Una Carthy: Survey of Post-Primary Schools in the North West [Unpublished, 2004].

[21]   Hans Vossensteyn et al.: Improving Participation in the Erasmus Programme. Brussels: European Parliament 2010. http://ec.europa.eu/education/erasmus/doc/publ/parlreport_en.pdf (last accessed 30 July 2012).

others cited personal circumstances, particularly mature learners many of whom may have dependants. Other respondents felt that they lacked the confidence to go abroad, linking this to poor language skills. All of these issues need to be addressed if learners are to consider international mobility. With regard to financial constraints, some EU countries provide bursaries based on academic achievement and / or socio-economic background. In the case of LyIT, the number of students availing of study-abroad schemes could be increased by providing financial support to students who demonstrate a commitment to international mobility. Greater awareness of the possibilities for participation in and benefits associated with mobility should be fostered at an early stage in all programmes of study. Widening the scope of language provision to include more academic disciplines would be another way of addressing the issue of poor language skills; as already mentioned, language learning in LyIT has traditionally been confined to two Schools of the Institute. Finally, the fact that some learners are unable to participate for personal reasons could be addressed by promoting greater interaction between visiting Erasmus students via tandem partnerships and other social extra-curricular events. This would serve the dual function of enhanced integration of Erasmus students in Institute activities and increased intercultural awareness among native students who are unable to go abroad.

With regard to the quantitative findings, it is interesting to note that the demand for language modules increases when these modules are integral to a programme of study and accredited, as opposed to optional and extra (see figs. 6 and 7). The data collected by the Molan Report, which was primarily a qualitative investigation, also highlighted the importance of accredited modules in motivating learners to take language options.[22] This is also borne out by the experience of language teaching in the School of Engineering in LyIT. Mandatory language-learning had been a feature of the Electronics programme in the eighties and nineties, until it became completely optional in 2005: students could continue to take either French or German, but this was not seen as an integral part of their programme. Some motivated students opted initially to take the optional language component, but numbers eventually waned to such an extent that the optional element was entirely abolished in 2007.

One of the most striking findings of both quantitative and qualitative methods is to do with what motivates people to learn languages in the first place. Do people learn languages because it will improve their career prospects, or because they wish to identify themselves with the target culture? Precisely this question was the object of earlier linguistic investigations of language-learning motivations, going back to the 1970s when Gardner and Lambert came up with the notion of integrative and

---

[22] "The data [...] strongly suggest that the ECTS crediting of language learning, potentially in combination with other, parallel forms of creditation, plays a powerful role in motivating students for language learning." Ian Tudor: Promoting Language Learning in European Higher Education. European Journal of Language Policy 1/2 (2009), p. 188-205, here p. 191-92.

instrumental motivation.[23] Instrumental motivation is at work when people study languages because they believe that it will enable them to find employment; integrative motivation, on the other hand, is related to the learner's desire to become part of the culture and society where the language is spoken. In this context, it is interesting to note that in two of the cases explored in the Molan Report where student participation had been successfully increased, special emphasis had been put on the vocational benefits of language learning. These institutions (Berlin and Salford) packaged their language modules into an overarching programme designed to improve the employability of their future graduates.

The responses in the quantitative phase show clearly that motivation to take language modules increases when linked to a semester abroad. While two thirds of respondents ruled out a language module initially, 58% said they would take a language module if it were offered along with a period abroad. The qualitative phase enabled a deeper exploration of this apparent contradiction. Four of the interviewees had ticked the 'no' box when asked if they would opt for a language module, but went on to tick the 'yes' box indicating that they would take a language module if it was associated with a study semester or work placement abroad. All four explained in interview that they had initially failed to appreciate how a language module would be relevant to their programme; however, once it was offered in the context of a period abroad, it was perceived in a completely different light. These responses are of particular relevance when one considers the level of participation of Irish students in Erasmus mobility programmes in recent years. The statistics show a slow decline in student involvement over the past decade, up until as recently as 2007-2008. In that academic year, the total number of Irish students availing of Erasmus study programmes continued to fall. This decline is in sharp contrast to the trend in other mainland European countries where the number of participating students has been consistently rising over the past decade. The Socrates / Erasmus programme, which dealt with study mobility only, was replaced in 2007 by the European Commission's new Lifelong Learning Programme: Subprogramme Erasmus which includes work placements. A turning point in the level of participation among Irish students occurred in 2007-2008 when the combined figure (study and placement mobility) showed a slight increase.[24] While the overall level of participation remains relatively low when compared with other European countries, it is interesting to note that this turning point coincided with the introduction into the scheme of the work placement in 2007. This is in keeping with our findings: Figures 12 and 13 above show clearly respondents' preference for such placements. These findings send out a clear message to policy makers regarding international mobility. Indeed, the recent National Strategy for Higher Education to 2030 has highlighted the need for higher

---

[23]   Robert Gardner and Wallace Lambert: Attitudes and Motivation in Second Language Learning. Rowley, MA: Newbury House, 1972.

[24]   European Commission: Annex 1: Outgoing Erasmus students from 2007/08 to 2009/10 under the Lifelong Learning Programme. Brussels: European Commission, 2011. http://ec.europa.eu/education/erasmus/doc920_en.htm (last accessed 30 July 2012).

education institutions to internationalize their programmes further, and has called upon the HEA to explain the reluctance of Irish students to avail of Erasmus mobility opportunities.[25] Our survey has established that the majority of respondents would consider a semester or placement abroad, a finding that appears to challenge the common perception that Irish students are reluctant to spend a period abroad.

It is clear from these findings (fig. 2 as compared with fig. 7) that the appetite among respondents for international mobility is much greater than the appetite for language modules. There is a growing trend in IoTs and other third-level institutions engaged in Erasmus mobility to partner colleges with an implicit or explicit policy of English as the language of instruction. While it is laudable that the level of participation in Erasmus schemes is increasing, the impact on linguistic skills will be minimal if there is no prior linguistic preparation in the target language, and if non-English language partner institutions are (therefore) sidelined. The link between mobility and language learning needs to be highlighted and used strategically by programme designers. As these findings show, international mobility, if integrated into programmes, could act as a motivator for language learning.

At the time of writing, the "Periodic Programmatic Evaluation" process is drawing to a close at LyIT. This process, which takes place every four years, presented an ideal opportunity to implement the goals set out in LyIT's Language Strategy. The obstacles to implementation cited are, among other things, constraints set by external accreditation bodies and concerns among non-language lecturers about poor native language skills among learners. Further research is now needed to investigate attitudes among lecturers towards language learning, and establish whether languages are perceived as a core activity which should be embraced across all disciplines, or as something which should be confined to an interested few.

On a more positive note, LyIT's Language Strategy has not been ignored, with some discernible progress within the Department of Law and Humanities. Learners on the new BA in Criminal Justice have the option of taking a language minor and availing of an Erasmus semester abroad, and languages will be offered as electives on the proposed BSC in Sports Performance and Coaching. While integral language electives may not be offered outside of the Schools of Business and Tourism, international mobility is now encouraged in the School of Science where some students have already availed of mobility schemes. These are steps in the right direction, albeit baby ones. It should be noted, however, that the link between language learning and mobility may be severed if these placements / study visits are to study destinations where English is the lingua franca. Indeed the intercultural benefit of these visits may also be lessened.

This study focused on the attitudes of first-year students in LyIT to learning languages, and how these attitudes have been affected by their prior learning

---

25   Colin Hunt: National Strategy for Higher Education to 2030. A Report from the Strategy Group. Dublin: Department of Education and Skills / Government Publication Office, 2011.

experiences and their views of international mobility. Further research is required to investigate why so many disengage from the language-learning process prior to entering third level, and what can be done to improve teaching methodologies at secondary-school level. Future research could expand the scope of this study to include other IoTs, and refine the instrument used in the quantitative phase by employing Likert Scales and providing more scope for qualitative responses in the questionnaire.

Conclusion

The findings of this research, albeit confined to one IoT, shed some light on the current crisis in foreign language provision in Ireland. Language learning is perceived as a hugely challenging activity by learners, but one that is nonetheless worthwhile and beneficial for career prospects. There is a demand for language modules across all disciplines in LyIT, and this demand could be met using existing human resources. What has emerged from these findings is that programme designers could use the prospect of Erasmus mobility as a way of motivating students to take language modules. Financial assistance could be given to those from disadvantaged socio-economic groups, as is the case in other EU countries. As regards the wider implications of this research, IoTs have a responsibility to 'package' languages in a way that will motivate learning and nurture an interest in international mobility. Integral language modules that reward learners for their effort and commitment to learning a language should be offered. For those who are unable to avail of international mobility schemes, alternative ways of promoting languages should be explored, including harnessing the on-campus linguistic resource of visiting Erasmus students. These and other strategies to promote and encourage language learning need to be put in place in order to raise awareness of the benefits, both interpersonal and intercultural, of language study and international mobility, and to raise the participation levels of Irish students in mobility schemes to European levels.

Una Carthy teaches German in the Department of Law and Humanities at the Letterkenny Institute of Technology, Co. Donegal.

Antje Hartje

William Butler Yeats and Stefan George: Hermetic Texts as Ritualistic Texts

The respect that has been paid to William Butler Yeats' oeuvre in the history of English and Irish literature reflects the degree of attention paid to it at universities and in cultural life in general. Despite striking parallels in their work and their involvement in the Symbolist movement, the poetry of Yeats' contemporary Stefan George (1868-1933) is, however, read and discussed almost exclusively by an in-crowd of scholars of German literature.[1]

If George is remembered at all, the focus lies on his connections with Claus Schenk Graf von Stauffenberg who, famously, made an attempt on Hitler's life in July 1944. Indeed, the debate on whether Stauffenberg's last words immediately before his execution were "Long live our holy Germany!" or "Long live the secret Germany!" has not lost momentum, and people who favour the latter version consider this exclamation to be a direct connection to Stefan George's circle of disciples and friends whose central aim was the formation of a secret nucleus of renewed German culture which George saw as his goal. The publication of several new monographs about George's life, work and famous 'circle' has revived interest in his oeuvre. These recent publications include the biographies by Robert Norton (2002) and Thomas Karlauf (2007), and Ulrich Raulff's book (2009) which analyses the history of the 'circle' after George's death in 1933.

Despite their different cultural and religious backgrounds (Yeats was born in Ireland into a Protestant family engaged in an ongoing struggle between mercantile and artistic aspirations, whereas George had a typically German Catholic bourgeois background), both writers are deeply rooted in French Symbolism. Interestingly enough, both were guests at Stéphane Mallarmé's Tuesday meetings, but apparently never met.[2] The impulses they received from the Aestheticist / Symbolist movement are condensed in their early work of the late-nineteenth century, with Yeats

---

[1]   However, some works need to be cited here that do compare Yeats and George. These include Cecil Maurice Bowra: The Heritage of Symbolism. London: Macmillan, 1943; Hellmut Salinger: William Butler Yeats. Seine Gedichte und Gedanken. Bern: A. Francke, 1983; Haskell M. Block: Some Concepts of the Literary Elite at the Turn of the Century. In: Mosaic. A Journal for the Comparative Study of Literature and Ideas 5 (1971-72), p. 57-64; Jutta Elgart: Das mythische Bild in den Werken von Stefan George und William Butler Yeats. Wesen, Stellung, Funktion. In: Wolfgang Braungart, Ute Oelmann and Bernhard Böschenstein (eds.): Stefan George: Werk und Wirkung seit dem 'Siebenten Ring.' Tübingen: Niemeyer, 2001, p. 411-30.

[2]   Jutta Elgart: Das mythische Bild, p. 411.

exploring the richness of Irish mythology and George creating fantastical worlds with aestheticized settings.

At the beginning of the twentieth century, they turned to contemporary topics such as the Irish independence movement or the devastation of World War I. Apart from these parallels, however, the most striking feature they have in common is their extensive use of textual strategies aimed at the creation of hermetic poems. These strategies are clearly visible in the two poems *Gratitude to the Unknown Instructors*,[3] first published in 1932, and *Ob deine augen dich trogen*, published in 1897 in what many claim is George's best-known volume, *Das Jahr der Seele*.[4]

Gratitude to the Unknown Instructors	Ob deine augen dich trogen
	Durch fallender äste hauf?
What they undertook to do	Treiben die kämpfenden wogen
They brought to pass;	Den strom hinauf?
All things hang like a drop of dew	
Upon a blade of grass.	Du jagest nach und die steigen
	Von fremden kräften erfasst
	Wirbelndem rieselndem reigen
	Folgt die begehrende hast.
	Hüte dich! führe nicht weiter
	Das spiel mit schwerem kauf –
	Ziehen nicht deine begleiter
	Schon ihren alten lauf?[5]

Gratitude to the Unknown Instructors seems to have a logical structure, with Peter Allt reading it in the context of Yeats' wife's attempts at automatic writing.[6] However, the poem is made hermetic through various referential gaps. The text neither enables the reader to find out who or what exactly is meant by "they," nor does it propose any unambiguous interpretation of the line "they brought to pass," not least because it plays with the variety of connotations the verb "pass" offers. Though probable, there is no certain connection between the instructors in the title and the "they" of the second line. A connection might exist between "what," which represents a noun we cannot name, and "All things," but this too cannot be verified. The precarious image invoked by "hang like a drop of dew" seems to exist in tension with a title that expresses a positive feeling, and which is itself a conundrum

---

[3]   William Butler Yeats: The Poems. In: Yeats. The Collected Works of William Butler Yeats. Ed. by Richard J. Finneran. Vol I. 2nd edn. New York: Scribner, 1997, p. 258.

[4]   Stefan George: Das Jahr der Seele. 2nd edn. Stuttgart: Klett-Cotta, 2005, p. 113.

[5]   A significant number of George's poems, including *Ob deine augen dich trogen*, do not bear a title.

[6]   Peter Allt: Yeats, Religion, and History. In: The Sewanee Review 60 (1952), p. 624-58, here p. 644.

because "Unknown Instructors" constitutes a paradox: under normal circumstances, the term 'instructors' implies that the person who instructs and the one who is instructed know one another. All these referential gaps force the reader to read and re-read the text in order to fulfil the readerly desire for some kind of coherence.

Ob deine augen dich trogen is dominated by a variety of as yet unanswered questions which lack obvious connections to one another. The identity of the addressees remains obscure. Its waves ("wogen") which go upstream ("den strom hinauf") go against every known physical law. However, as they are part of a question and not a statement, and the first question in the poem implies the possibility of a hallucination, their existence cannot be verified or indeed challenged. The fact that waves can neither fight ("kämpfenden") nor climb ("steigen") compounds the difficulty, while "steigen" is also ambiguous because its other possible meaning is 'to rise.' The expression "Das spiel mit schwerem kauf" is obdurately enigmatic as its components do not form a homogenous metaphorical whole; a game or play ("spiel") about a difficult or heavy ("schwerem"; which of these it is cannot be determined) purchase ("kauf") does not make any sense in itself, and even less in a text that seems to deal mainly with water. The "Begleiter" (companions) und "alten lauf" (old route) of the last two lines cannot be located in any meaningful contextual framework.

A statement by one of George's friends, Carl Rouge, displays how much George must have enjoyed confusing his readers with such truncated, decontextualized references. Rouge complained about this in regard to the volume *Hymnen, Pilgerfahrten, Algabal*:

> Vor allem im Detail hatte Rouge vieles zu bemängeln. Manches verstand er nicht – so etwa den Titel des Gedichts "Neuländische Liebesmahle" –, anderes empfand er als gewollt. Er tadelte unklare Bezüge, äußerte sich befremdet über die "romanesken Velleitäten" und bemängelte die spärliche Zeichensetzung.[7]

What purpose is served by publishing poems the core meaning of which, if there is any, does not reveal itself to the reader? Two theoretical starting points offer the reader a way of escaping the dilemma of being torn between hermeneutics – the legitimate wish to understand a text – and deconstruction – a position that questions whether the text has meaning at all. The first is Moritz Baßler's view that the search for hermeneutic access to a text is a legitimate enterprise, but only up to the point at which meaning in the conventional sense cannot be found.[8] This point is reached when the text resists any kind of paraphrase. Texts repudiating any kind of hermeneutic access create an "Oberflächen-Ästhetik,"[9] which roughly translates as

---

[7]   Thomas Karlauf: Stefan George. Die Entdeckung des Charisma. Munich: Karl Blessing Verlag, 2007, p. 114.

[8]   Moritz Baßler: Die Entdeckung der Textur. Unverständlichkeit in der Kurzprosa der emphatischen Moderne 1910-1916. Tübingen: Max Niemeyer Verlag, 1994, p. 6.

[9]   Baßler: Die Entdeckung der Textur, p. 176.

an 'aestheticism of the textual surface.' This occurs when the elements of a text refer "nicht auf eine symbolische Ebene, sondern auf ein weiteres Element der Textoberfläche."[10]

The second possible approach is offered by the Constance School branch of reception aesthetics founded by Wolfgang Iser and Hans Robert Jauß. Iser is not predominantly reader-oriented, unlike Jauß, but does emphasize the structures embedded in the text to guide reader reception.[11] The central concept of Iser's theory is built around the analysis of gaps between textual elements (syntagmatic gaps), and also between the text and its context (paradigmatic gaps). According to this model, the interpretation of a text is a constant balancing act between textual structures which help the reader perceive the text and readers' individual acts of realizing the text. In this process, the reader is forced to give the text coherence. And since each reader is unique, the ways in which a text is read by different readers can never be exactly the same. In this context, and as a counterweight to the entirely subjective readerly experience, Iser developed the concept of an implied reader, or an inherent textual structure, albeit one which is realized differently by different readers.

Brian Richardson proves especially helpful in the analysis of Yeats' and George's poems. He develops Iser's idea of the implied reader into a concept he calls "Multiple Implied Readers."[12] According to this model, a text can have several implied readers which are placed in hierarchical order based on the degree of assumed previous knowledge. "Private readers"[13] are able to perceive all layers encoded in a text, whereas the "ordinary reader"[14] is granted access only to a limited number of textual codes.

Both Yeats and George use the idea of a 'private reader.' This takes the form of an elite, which, unlike the 'ordinary reader,' is able to read the secret signs embedded in the enigmatic texts. 'Secret signs' can, for example, take the form of biographical references that only a small number of people or only the addressee can read. The basic distinction between the elite and those left outside the circle, however, lies in the emphasis on the poem as structure, which makes hermeneutic access less important than recognition of formal elements. Aesthetic writing focuses on the materiality of language rather than what language is able to express. Moritz Baßler calls it a "Verschiebung des Form-Inhalt-Gleichgewichts in Richtung Form."[15] In Yeats and George's case, agreement about the 'right' way of writing

---

[10]   Moritz Baßler et al. (eds.): Historismus und literarische Moderne. Tübingen: Niemeyer, 1996, p. 176.
[11]   On Iser's theory see: Wolfgang Iser: Der Akt des Lesens. Theorie ästhetischer Wirkung. Munich: Wilhelm Fink, 1976.
[12]   Brian Richardson: Singular Text, Multiple Implied Readers. In: Style 41 (2007), p. 259-74, here p. 259.
[13]   Richardson: Singular Text, p. 267.
[14]   Richardson: Singular Text, p. 267.
[15]   Baßler et al. (eds.): Historismus und literarische Moderne, p. 200.

poetry – copying the structure of chanted magic formulae[16] as opposed to composing easily understandable, mimetic poems – is the secret nucleus that holds the elite together. Adorno, for example, says of George's circle that anyone willing to enter it had to be "fähig oder willens […], ein Dichtwerk als Gebilde zu begreifen."[17]

Two poems that present an interplay of comprehensibility and inaccessibility while seeming to offer some deeper revelation to the shrewd reader are *The Phases of the Moon*,[18] first published in 1919, and *Der Teppich*, first published in 1900. In the first thirty lines of *The Phases of the Moon* we encounter Michael Robartes and Owen Aherne, two characters who start a dialogue within the text. They make various appearances in Yeats' poems, in his epic work *Rosa Alchemica* and in the 1937 version of *A Vision*. Generally speaking, they function as representations of Yeats' esoteric concepts. In *The Phases of the Moon* they also introduce the implicit reader in the form of the character (as opposed to the actual poet) Yeats:

> He wrote of me in that extravagant style
> He had learned from Pater, and to round his tale
> Said I was dead; and dead I choose to be

In the poem, Robartes drafts a concept that is not readily – if at all – accessible, drawing parallels between the phases of the moon and the stages of human life.[19] Youth, for example, is equated with the appearance of the first crescent after new moon:

> From the first crescent to the half, the dream
> But summons to adventure, and the man
> Is always happy like a bird or a beast

However, 'revelations' about the course of life such as "All dreams of the soul / End in a beautiful man's or woman's body," need to be treated with the utmost care. The reader may be entrapped by the seeming consistency of the poem and try to see in it a rule or instruction that might be followed if he or she could only find the deeper

---

16 In Lenoski's opinion, Yeats subjects his poems to a certain degree of monotonous rhythm reminiscent of a ritualistic magical chanting: the "magical word was the chanted word." Daniel Lenoski: The Symbolism of Sound in W.B. Yeats. An Explanation. In: Etudes Irlandaises 3 (1978), p. 47-55, here p. 48. This is supported by one of Yeats' essays in which he says: "A poem and an incantation were almost the same." William Butler Yeats: Bardic Ireland. In: Yeats: Early Articles and Reviews. Uncollected Articles and Reviews written between 1886 and 1900. Ed. by John P. Frayne and Madeleine Marchaterre. Vol. IX: Early Articles and Reviews. New York: Scribner, 2004, p. 110.

17 Theodor W. Adorno: Noten zur Literatur. Frankfurt a.M.: Suhrkamp, 1974, p. 526.

18 As it is about 140 lines long, the poem cannot be reproduced here in its entirety.

19 While parallels between the phases of the moon and the stages of human life may seem straightforward enough, the line "His body moulded from with the body / Grows comelier" demonstrate the more obscure thrust of the poem.

meaning. Yet, what is in store for the first kind of implicit reader – the Yeats figure here – is also waiting for every other reader:

> I'd stand and mutter there until he caught
> 'Hunchback and Saint and Fool,' and that they came
> Under the three last crescents of the moon,
> And then I'd stagger out. He'd crack his wits
> Day after day, yet never find the meaning.

The poem can therefore be said to operate with a twofold implicit reader, one of whom is embedded as a character in the poem. The second type of implicit reader, who is not represented by a character but is inscribed in the text nevertheless, is also only offered limited insight. However, the poem suggests to him that the answer is at hand:

> And then he laughed to think that what seemed hard
> Should be so simple.

Yet, for the reader trying to find his way through the esoteric jungle the poem presents, nothing is really this simple.[20] The poem operates with two different kinds of hermetic strategies: first, the esoteric content which presents itself as nearly impenetrable, and, second, the concept of a twofold implicit reader, the tangle of which also presents difficulties.

Der Teppich

> Hier schlingen menschen mit gewächsen tieren
> Sich fremd zum bund umrahmt von seidner franze
> Und blaue sicheln weisse sterne zieren
> Und queren sie in dem erstarrten tanze.
>
> Und kahle linien ziehn in reich-gestickten
> Und teil um teil ist wirr und gegenwendig
> Und keiner ahnt das rätsel der verstrickten..
> Da eines abends wird das werk lebendig.
>
> Da regen schauernd sich die toten äste
> Die wesen eng von strich und kreis umspannet
> Und treten klar vor die geknüpften quäste
> Die lösung bringend über die ihr sannet!

---

[20]   However, two works which try to pin down the sources Yeats may have used need to be mentioned here: James Lovic Allen: Life as Art. Yeats and the Alchemical Quest. In: Studies in the Literary Imagination 14/1 (1981), p. 17-42, and Shalini Sikka: Indian Thought. In: David Holdeman and Ben Levitas (eds.): W.B. Yeats in Context. New York: Cambridge University Press, 2010, p. 256-65.

Sie ist nach willen nicht: ist nicht für jede
Gewohne stunde: ist kein schatz der gilde.
Sie wird den vielen nie und nie durch rede
Sie wird den seltnen selten im gebilde.[21]

The title of *Der Teppich* immediately draws the reader's attention to the fabric-like structure, the text-ile, that awaits him, with lexemes such as "schlingen," "franze" and "geknüpften quäste" intensifying this effect. The lack of punctuation, the missing distinction between subject and object in line three, and line five with its incomplete syntax, create the impression that the words "refer to the carpet which refers back to the words."[22] Strathausen very clearly describes here the sort of self-referentiality that is the basic characteristic of *Der Teppich*. After the first two lines, there is a semantic caesura in the text as the carpet comes to life and the ornaments begin to move about. This caesura allows parallels to be drawn between *Der Teppich* and *The Phases of the Moon*. Where in Yeats' text the word "simple" is used, George's poem speaks of "klar," suggesting a secret lying hidden in plain sight for the initiated reader to see. What the two poems hint at here is described by Strathausen as a "secret of life allegedly hidden within or behind linguistic structures."[23]

In her work on literary aestheticism, Annette Simonis talks of a division within the "Rezipientengruppe entlang der Esoterik-Exoterik-Differenz," which creates an "inneren [...] Kreis," in which "strukturelle Affinitäten" act as "Solidaritätsmomente."[24] So, by means of structural affinities, a common identity among an inner circle of initiated readers is created. Of course, this process must be seen in the context of the paradigmatic turn caused by the rise of aestheticism at the turn of the twentieth century. Pierre Bourdieu provides one way of understanding this paradigmatic turn: He coins the term "literarisches Feld" which he defines as "ein Feld von Kräften, die sich auf all jene, die in es eintreten, und in unterschiedlicher Weise gemäß der von ihnen besetzten Stellung ausüben [...], und zur gleichen Zeit ein Feld der Konkurrenzkämpfe, die nach Veränderung oder Bewahrung jenes Kräftefeldes streben."[25] At the turn of the century, the majority of writers within the 'Feld' rejected commercial success and popularity, pursuing instead the goal of independence, which meant that they began writing for each

---

[21]   Stefan George: Der Teppich des Lebens und die Lieder von Traum und Tod mit einem Vorspiel. Stuttgart: Klett-Cotta, 1984, p. 36.

[22]   Carsten Strathausen: Of Circles and Riddles. Stefan George and the "Language Crisis" around 1900. In: The German Quarterly 76/4 (2003), p. 411-25, here p. 415.

[23]   Strathausen: Of Circles and Riddles, p. 415.

[24]   Annette Simonis: Literarischer Ästhetizismus. Theorie der arabesken und hermetischen Kommunikation der Moderne. Tübingen: Niemeyer, 2000, p. 267.

[25]   Pierre Bourdieu: Das literarische Feld. In: Louis Pinto and Franz Schultheis (eds.): Bourdieu. Streifzüge durch das literarische Feld. Konstanz: UVK, 1997, p. 33-147, here p. 34.

other or for more exclusive groups of recipients. This manifests itself in a "Rückgriff auf eine teilweise vormodern anmutende, hermetische Kommunikationsform,"[26] with literature becoming increasingly autonomous and shielding itself from the intrusions of the 'ordinary' reader. *The Phases of the Moon* and *Der Teppich* mock the ignorance of this common-or-garden reader.

Within the literary elite thus created, hermetic poems are used for ritualistic purposes that further reinforce the group's identity. Yeats and George not only appreciated ritualistic texts, but rituals in all their forms, including those Yeats would have encountered in the 'Hermetic Order of the Golden Dawn' with its "rituals of ceremonial magic."[27] Similarly, George's meetings with the so-called 'Kosmiker' circle would have introduced him to their particular set of ritualistic performances. George was especially good at shaping his own life and the gatherings of his circle into a ritualistic form in which the consumption of bread, wine and fruit and the choice of simple but elegant clothes played a major role. Language and texts form, of course, an intrinsic part of this system.

The following poems are particularly relevant examples of Yeats' and George's efforts to create a magical ritualistic language: *The Cap and Bells*, first published in 1894, and *Verwandlungen*, written in 1890. Both poems use the same combination of carefully designed structure and obscure colour symbolism to create what Yeats called "wavering, meditative, organic rhythms."[28]

In Yeats' poem, certain arrangements of lexemes, in lines one and two, and also in four and five (soul – heart, window-sill – door, owls – owls, blue garment – red and quivering garment) give the poem a netlike structure, which is further reinforced by various repetitions both in rhythm and rhyme. The poem could easily be counted as one of that group of formulae that aim to create magical effects while refusing questions about deeper meaning.

The same is true for *Verwandlungen*. Complaining about the text, Carl Rouge wrote: "Sinn mir vorläufig insofern unverständlich, als das Subject nicht ermittelbar scheint, wenn man nicht den Dichter fragt."[29] The poem blocks hermeneutic access in a variety of ways. First of all, the introductory part of each stanza seems to contain or allow no reference to the rest. But most interesting is the fact that the order in which the lines appear suggests some kind of inner logic, the secret progression of which towards a violent end can be described, but not explained.

---

[26]   Simonis: Literarischer Ästhetizismus, p. 239.

[27]   Ronald Schuchard: The Last Minstrels. Yeats and the Revival of the Bardic Arts. Oxford: Oxford University Press, 2008, p. 19.

[28]   William Butler Yeats: Early Essays. Ed. George Bornstein and Richard J. Finneran. New York: Scribner, 2007, p. 120.

[29]   Cited after Stefan George: Hymnen, Pilgerfahrten, Algabal. Stuttgart: Klett-Cotta, 1987, p. 104.

The Cap and Bells

The jester walked in the garden:
The garden had fallen still;
He bade his soul rise upward
And stand on her window-sill.

It rose in a straight blue garment,
When owls began to call:
It had grown wise-tongued by thinking
Of a quiet and light footfall;

But the young queen would not listen;
She rose in her pale night-gown;
She drew in the heavy casement
And pushed the latches down.

He bade his heart go to her,
When the owls called out no more;
In a red and quivering garment
It sang to her through the door.

It had grown sweet-tongued by dreaming
Of a flutter of flower-like hair;
But she took up her fan from the table
And waved it off on the air.

'I have cap and bells,' he pondered,
'I will send them to her and die';
And when the morning whitened
He left them where she went by

She laid them upon her bosom,
Under a cloud of her hair,
And her red lips sang them a love-song
Till stars grew out of the air.

She opened her door and her window,
And the heart and the soul came through
To her right hand came the red one,
To her left hand came the blue.

They set up a noise like crickets,
A chattering wise and sweet,
And her hair was a folded flower
And the quiet of love in her feet.

Verwandlungen

Abendlich auf schattenbegleiteten
wegen
Über brücken den türmen und mauern
entgegen
Wenn leise klänge sich regen:

Auf einem goldenen wagen
Wo perlgraue flügel dich tragen
Und lindenbüsche dich fächeln
Herniedertauche
Mit mildem lächeln
Und linderndem hauche!

Unter den masten auf rüstig furchendem
kiele
Über der wasser und strahlen
schimmerndem spiele
In glücklicher ferne vom ziele:

Auf einem silbernen wagen
Wo lichtgrüne spiegel dich tragen
Und schaumgewinde dich fächeln
Herniedertauche
Mit frohem lächeln
Und kosendem hauche!

Lang ist nach jauchzendem tode die
sonne verschollen
Mit den planken die brausenden wogen
grollen
Und dumpfe gewitter rollen:

Auf einem stählernen wagen
Wo lavaschollen dich tragen
Und grell lohe wolken dich fächeln
Herniedertauche
Mit wildem lächeln
Und sengendem hauche!

Such texts are suited to ritualistic performance in the sense of being read aloud in a monotonous, chant-like voice. For both Yeats and George, reading poems aloud in a group (for Yeats, the Rhymers' Club and the Abbey Theatre, for George his 'circle') was an important element of the aesthetic experience. The aim was to ensure an interaction between text and reader, allowing the text in its pure material form to become performative; in other words, event rather than meaning: "Das auf diese Weise und in diesem Rahmen rituell gesprochene Wort ist Wirkung, nicht Mitteilung, es ist 'Geschehen'."[30] Thus, another kind of 'meaning' is created which is independent of the more traditional understanding of semantics; as Sven Reichardt puts it, the intention is "dass Rituale, Aufführungen, Inszenierungen, Sprechakte oder Verhaltensformen nicht bloß aufgeführt werden und etwas abbilden, sondern ihrerseits erstens im Zusammenspiel aller Beteiligten vom Produzenten bis zum Rezipienten Bedeutungen hervorbringen und Realität setzen."[31] The more hermetic texts are, the more they allow the reader to read and reread them, which is a desirable basis for an interaction of this kind with its mutual search for meaning. Annette Simonis says that "die Verrätselungsstrategien [...] dem kommunikativen Interesse letztlich weder gegenläufig noch abträglich [sind], da die hermetischen Strukturen in höherem Maße als vergleichbare nicht chiffrierte Texte in der Lage sind, ästhetische Beobachtungen auszulösen."[32]

This interpretation supports Iser's concept of the literary text, whereby gaps constitute the "elementare Kommunikationsbedingungen des Textes, die eine Beteiligung des Lesers am Hervorbringen der Textintention ermöglichen."[33] This idea of the text requiring the active engagement of the reader also offers insight into George's view of recitals as educational occasions: "George betrachtete sein für den Kreis verpflichtendes Lesen als ein dichterisches Erlebnis und als wirksames, psychisches wie physisches Erziehungsmittel."[34] Yeats also saw this process of understanding and learning as something more than just cerebral, entailing rather a connection between body and spirit: "We only believe in those thoughts which have been conceived not in the brain but in the whole body."[35] Thus the physical aspect of poetry recital is given priority over the semantic dimension. To use Bourdieu's terminology, this practice forms a common 'Habitus' which both creates and strengthens the identity of the initiated literary group.[36]

---

[30]   Wolfgang Braungart: "Durch Dich, für Dich, in Deinem Zeichen." Stefan Georges poetische Eucharistie. In: George-Jahrbuch 1 (1996-97), p. 53-79, here p. 74.

[31]   Sven Reichardt: Praxeologische Geschichtswissenschaft. Eine Diskussionsanregung. In: Sozial.Geschichte 22 (2007), p. 52.

[32]   Simonis: Literarischer Ästhetizismus, p. 248.

[33]   Iser: Der Akt des Lesens, p. 45.

[34]   Martin Roos: Stefan Georges Rhetorik der Selbstinszenierung. Düsseldorf: Grupello, 2000, p. 36.

[35]   William Butler Yeats: Essays and Introductions. London: Macmillan, 1961, p. 235.

[36]   This idea of the creation and strengthening of the identity of the initiated literary group goes back to Jan Assmann: Das kulturelle Gedächtnis. Schrift, Erinnerung und politische Identität in frühen Hochkulturen. 6th edn. Munich: C.H. Beck, 2007, p. 57.

Unfortunately, there are no recordings of George's recitals, but descriptions of his way of reading poems to an audience do exist: "Kassner erinnert sich an eine Lesung Georges wie an einen magisch-rituellen Akt: 'murmelnd Wort an Wort reihend, jedes Pathos vermeidend, als läse er Zauberformeln, Gebete vor in einer Sprache, die niemand zu verstehen brauche, weil sie heilig und zu rein magischen Wirkungen bestimmt sei.'"[37] Some of Yeats' recitals, however, were recorded, and are a vivid demonstration of his conviction that a "poem and an incantation were almost the same."[38]

Both Yeats and George saw themselves as priest-poets, called to form and minister to a religious community gathered to practice an aesthetic religion based on beauty. Yeats talked about the dramatist as a "priest initiating his rapt audience into the new religion,"[39] while George was interested in the Eucharistic, transformatory quality of poetry created by self-referentiality: "Diese grundsätzliche Selbstbezüglichkeit der Poesie ist auch für George und für den Symbolismus überhaupt kennzeichnend. Gerade aber als solche selbstbezügliche Poesie [...] soll sie verwandelnde, sakramentale Kraft haben, weil sie nichts anderes will, als unmittelbar sinnhaft und in ihrem Sinn unausschöpfbares Geheimnis zu sein. Darum kann, was symbolistische Poesie sagt, nur durch sie selbst gesagt werden. Sie ist, wie die Eucharistie für den Gläubigen, unhintergehbar."[40]

Poems such as *Litanei* from *Der Siebente Ring* (1907), and *Long-legged Fly*, first published in 1939, manage to combine this 'aestheticism of the textual surface' that returns us to the materiality of the text with a ritualistic and religious dimension.

Litanei

Tief ist die trauer	die mich umdüstert•
Ein tret ich wieder	Herr! in dein haus..
Lang war die reise•	matt sind die glieder•
Leer sind die schreine•	voll nur die qual.
Durstende zunge	darbt nach dem weine.
Hart war gestritten•	starr ist mein arm.
Gönne die ruhe	schwankenden schritten•
Hungrigem gaume	bröckle dein brot!
Schwach ist mein atem	rufend dem traume•

37 Wolfgang Braungart: Ästhetischer Katholizismus. Stefan Georges Rituale der Literatur. Tübingen: Niemeyer, 1997, p. 166.
38 William Butler Yeats: Early Articles and Reviews, p. 110.
39 Daniel Lenoski. W.B. Yeats and Celtic Spiritual Power. In: Canadian Journal of Irish Studies 5/1 (1979), p. 26-51, here p. 42. Although he is speaking about drama, this view equally applies to poetry.
40 Braungart: "Durch Dich, für Dich, in Deinem Zeichen," p. 61.

Hohl sind die hände   fiebernd der mund..

Leih deine kühle•   lösche die brände•
Tilge das hoffen•   sende das licht!

Gluten im herzen   lodern noch offen•
Innerst im grunde   wacht noch ein schrei..

Töte das sehnen•   schliesse die wunde!
Nimm mir die liebe•   gib mir dein glück!

Long-legged Fly

That civilisation may not sink
Its great battle lost,
Quiet the dog, tether the pony
To a distant post.
Our master Caesar is in the tent
Where the maps are spread,
His eyes are fixed upon nothing,
A hand under his head.

Like a long-legged fly upon the stream
His mind moves upon silence.

That the topless towers be burnt
And men recall that face,
Move most gently if move you must
In this lonely place.
She thinks, part woman, three parts a child,
That nobody looks; her feet
Practise a tinker shuffle
Picked up on the street.

Like a long-legged fly upon the stream
Her mind moves upon silence.

That girls at puberty may find
The first Adam in their thought,
Shut the door of the Pope's chapel,
Keep those children out.
There on the scaffolding reclines
Michael Angelo.
With no more sound than the mice make
His hand moves to and fro.

Like a long-legged fly upon the stream
His mind moves upon silence.

In both texts, the speaker addresses pleas to a second person, possibly a divinity given the prayer-like quality of the two poems.

The most striking features of *Litanei* are its monotonous rhythm (dactyls and trochees) and the fact that its structure resembles that of a prayer uttered by a prayer-leader and congregation alternately. Its eight stanzas consist of two lines each which show a distinct caesura after one sequence of a dactyl and a trochee, followed by another sequence of the same kind. The ending of a line thus sounds like the echo of its first part. *Litanei* implies a religious context, but while the form of the poem is fully in tune with what the title promises, the content forms a sharp contrast. Phrases such as "Leer sind die schreine," "Tilge das hoffen," "Töte das sehnen," or "Nimm mir die liebe," express the speaker's deep mourning and his rejection of love, life and hope. Therefore, the poem can only be seen as a litany in terms of its structure, whereas its content diverges utterly from the standard Christian position: "Diese Litanei ist ganz und gar kein christlicher Text. Für jede christliche Position ist sie reine Häresie."[41] The poem does not work with syntagmatic as much as with paradigmatic gaps, with the incongruity between form and content. According to Braungart, this is the source of the text's sadness: "Darum bleibt die 'trauer' in dieser Litanei, weil sie weiß, daß sie sich als Litanei-*Text* selbst genug sein muß."[42]

Like *Litanei*, *Long-legged Fly* expresses a series of different requests or wishes: "That civilisation may not sink / Its great battle lost," "That the topless towers be burnt / And men recall that face," "That girls at puberty may find / The first Adam in their thought." These are followed by instructions about how these requests might be accomplished: "Quiet the dog, tether the pony / In this lonely place," "Shut the door of the Pope's chapel, / Keep those children out." All of these instructions aim to overcome a state of lifelessness and immovability. *Long-legged Fly* is designed as a prayer of intercession in which the three lines "To a distant post," "In this lonely place," and "Keep those children out" separate the request from the rest in each stanza. The refrain "Like a long-legged fly upon the stream / His[43] mind moves upon silence" sounds like a conclusive formula. The refrain especially makes clear the incongruity between form and content that can also be found in *Litanei*. In spite of the fact that what the poem is saying shares no common ground with Christian belief, and even ladles on the irony (Caesar is unable to act, Helena is happy with a simple dance, and Michelangelo provokes no more of a sensation than a rodent), the poem aims at a religious appearance or form, and this is how the paradigmatic gap is created. Michael Zink sees in the material aspect of prayer its suitability for ritualistic performance: "Da man den Gedanken abweist, daß es eine notwendige Form des Gebetes oder gar einen Zwang der Worte auf Gott geben könnte […], rechtfertigt die christlich-religiöse Praxis prinzipiell einen ästhetischen Umgang mit dem Gebet, vor allem mit dem liturgischen Gebet […]. Damit aber veschiebt sich

---

[41]   Braungart: Ästhetischer Katholizismus, p. 216.
[42]   Braungart: Ästhetischer Katholizismus, p. 215.
[43]   'Her' instead of 'his' in the second stanza.

der Stellenwert der Materialität des Gebets. Nicht mehr auf Wörtlichkeit als Vorbedingung für Wirksamkeit kommt es an, sondern auf die Materialität der Wörter [...]."[44]

A significant number of Yeats' and George's poems feature syntagmatic and / or paradigmatic gaps, in other words, gaps within the textual structure or within their contextual framework. In this sense, they can be seen as hermetic poems, designed to shield themselves from attempts at comprehension, while inviting deeper understanding from those-in-the-know. In other words, they encourage different readers to read them differently. Using Wolfgang Iser's concept of the implied reader, Brian Richardson distinguishes between initiated readers and so-called ordinary readers. The ordinary reader is not granted access and is not allowed to decipher the full meaning of the texts. The initiated reader, on the other hand, has come to accept the fact that it is the underlying structure which makes a hermetic poem usable (as opposed to decipherable). A hermetic poem is designed to resemble a magic formula and adopts the structure of religious texts used for incantatory recitals in a small group of initiates. These ritualistic practices were intended to address the participants physically or viscerally, rather than by their intellect. Through the creation of an initiated readership through ritualistic practices, a literary elite was formed as part of an exclusive avant-garde literature that emerged at the turn of the twentieth century. The proximity of hermetic texts to religious texts is also evidence of the fact that Yeats and George were attempting hereby to create an aesthetic religion.

Antje Hartje teaches Anglo-Irish modernist poetry in the Department of English at Ruprecht-Karls-Universität Heidelberg.

---

[44] Michel Zink: Materialität und Literarizität des Gebets. Beispiele aus dem französischen Mittelalter. In: Hans Ulrich Gumbrecht and K. Ludwig Pfeiffer (eds.): Materialität der Kommunikation. Frankfurt a.M.: Suhrkamp, 1988, p. 161-77, here p. 163.

Buchbesprechungen / Book Reviews

Joachim Fischer and Gisela Holfter (eds.): Creative Influences. Selected Irish-German Biographies. *Trier: Wissenschaftlicher Verlag Trier, 2009 (= Irish-German Studies / Deutsch-Irische Studien 4). 197 pp. €20.00. ISBN 978-3-86821-158-0.*

The feeling is mutual! Originally based on an interest in the Celtic roots of Irish culture, Germany's love of everything Irish dates back centuries, and any dent this affection may have suffered during the island republic's recent financial crisis, which was seen as an outbreak of irresponsibility and megalomania, betrays German disappointment at the fact that the Irish had veered from certain preconceptions about them by enjoying themselves too much for a short decade, and in the process littering the countryside so beloved by their German visitors with ghost estates and shiny empty business parks. Conversely, the Irish love of Germany and the Germans is rather newer and is closely linked to the formation of nation states on either side; and the recent hardening of attitudes towards German banks as holders of Irish debt and towards Germany as the strict taskmaster of the EU is but an acknowledgment of this mutual dependency. However, sweeping generalizations such as these, in their positive as well as negative manifestations, have never captured the richness, the uniqueness and the complexity of Irish-German inter-cultural relations, and the images each culture has of the other. The volume reviewed here is a reminder that relationships between cultures are negotiated by a multitude of individual mediators as agents of reciprocal influence. The fifteen articles contained in this work are devoted to fifteen people of Irish and German backgrounds who, in very distinct ways, fields of activity and historical periods, have acted as conduits for something German, introducing it into Irish culture, or (in two instances) Irish people who moved to Germany and worked there. The designation "creative" is used here in the broadest sense since the activities of the figures, though often involved in the arts, music and literature, extended into other walks of (public) life (science and engineering, constitutional law), and, as a whole, impacted on Irish society in a meaningful way.

In the first article, Michael Cronin describes John Anster (1793-1867), a translator of Goethe, more particularly the first translator of selected scenes from *Faust* (1820/1835), and one of the first practitioners to reflect on the processes of translation. Significantly, Cronin sees Anster's translational exploits as part of a wider process of positioning in culturally European, but politically unionist contexts. Not pursued in any depth is the question of how exactly the engagement with German writing (Schiller and some Romantics also attracted Anster's attention) functioned as an alignment with continental greats that was meant to demonstrate cultural affinities and provide evidence of superiority. But the realization that publishing world literature (together with the individual's own poetic attempts) offered a means of social advancement to the Protestant elite, both in Dublin and in

Britain, in itself offers an insight into Irish culture during the first half of the nineteenth century. A generation later, in a bid to promote national awakening and Catholic cultural emancipation, Canon Patrick Augustine Sheehan (1852-1913) infused his novels and journalistic writings with ideas derived from German sources, including the Humboldtian concept of education, the practice of a 'scientific' religious training for candidates for the priesthood, and a national literature that could help to develop a mature sense of Irishness.

The role played by musicians from German backgrounds in shaping the musical life of Ireland is the subject of four contributions. Hans Conrad Swertz (b. 1858), one of about twenty-five German-born organists working in Ireland around 1900, his son-in-law Aloys Georg Fleischmann (1880-1964), and his son Aloys Fleischmann (1910-1992) shaped musical life in Cork for over a century. The articles on these figures afford insights into the musical infrastructure, music education, and role played by music in public life, including the foundation of the Cork International Choral Festival in the 1960s. The compositional and theoretical output of Aloys the younger, Professor of Music in UCC, poses questions regarding the position of Irish folk music in historical European musical traditions, and the renaissance of "Gaelic art-music," which was rooted in but also transcended the generic conventions of folk song. The contributions by Joseph Cunningham, Ruth Fleischmann and Michael Murphy relating to this dynasty, all members of which received some training in Germany, whetted this reader's curiosity about specific German influences in areas like repertoire, composition, and the position of music in national life. Dresden-born Hans Waldemar Rose (1922-1994) contributed to Irish cultural life as choir conductor in RTÉ (from the late 1940s to 1974). From 1923 until his death in 1940, Fritz Brase (b. 1875 near Hannover) was in charge of Military Music in the Irish Free State. The articles devoted to these two prominent figures (by Margaret O'Sullivan Farrell and Garth Cox/Joseph J. Ryan) do not discuss the reasons why Germans took on these official and representative musical positions, nor do they address the impact that their German background may have had on shaping Irish musical life, but they pave the way for investigations into such inter-cultural questions.

Inextricably linked to the darkest period of twentieth century German history are the careers of Bauhaus-trained textile designer Margaret Leischner (1907-1970), who from the late 1950s worked in carpet design for Irish Ropes Ltd in Newbridge, Co. Kildare, and that of John Hennig (1911-1986), the eminent scholar who lay the foundations of Irish Studies as a distinct discipline: both were refugees from the Nazi regime. Irish writer Francis Stuart (1902-2000), however, moved in the opposite direction: Hermann Rasche's discussion of Stuart's time in Berlin as a teaching assistant, and his contribution to German international broadcasting in the early 1940s, does not perhaps offer any new position on the controversy surrounding Stuart, but it does highlight the complexities of Stuart's involvement with the propaganda machinery of the Third Reich. Sculptor Imogen Werner (b. 1927) followed fellow arts student, Ian Stuart, son of Francis Stuart, to Ireland in the early

1950s and made a name for herself producing religious and public art for Irish patrons. Her statue of Pope John Paul II on the campus of St Patrick's College, Maynooth reveals the influence of Ernst Barlach. Study periods in Germany influenced the professional activities of two further Irishmen: During a sojourn at Berlin's Humboldt University in the early 1920s, engineer John McLoughlin (1896-1971) found inspiration for the hydro-electrical scheme on the Shannon, and became convinced that German firm Siemens should implement the ambitious plans. Lawyer, academic and politician, John Maurice Kelly (1931-1991) studied in Heidelberg for a time during the 1950s; among the more curious ideas inspired by his German experiences was the proposition that the cooperation between the CDU and CSU parties in post-War Germany might provide the model for a merger between Fianna Fáil and Fine Gael in Ireland.

The last two contributions of the volume return to contemporary literary figures. Rüdiger Imhof looks at some of the influences at work in John Banville's "science trilogy" (*Birchwood*, 1972; *Doctor Copernicus*, 1976; *Kepler*, 1981), seeing there traces of German thought from Goethe and Schiller to Rilke, Wittgenstein, Nietzsche and Adorno. Eoin Burke, finally, summarizes conflicted multi-cultural identities in the writings of that poster child of Irish-German hybridity, writer Hugo Hamilton. In the works of these two contemporary writers we see the very different results of extra-cultural influences: on the one hand, abstract literary engagement with European intellectual traditions, and, on the other, (occasionally painful) lived experience of in-betweenness and the negotiation of belonging. A little-known episode illustrates the migration of influence and expertise in the other direction: William Thomas Mulvany's (1806-1885) involvement in Shannon drainage schemes and other hydro-engineering projects enabled him, after his retirement from the civil service in Ireland, to go on to establish mines in the Ruhr valley region during Germany's rapid industrialization. Hibernia, Shamrock and Erin, the names of pits in Herne, Castrop-Rauxel and Gelsenkirchen, are testimony to this Irishman's role in the development of Germany's industrial heartland.

The assembled articles provide biographical sketches of varied, sometimes remarkable, always interesting cases of German-Irish cross-pollination, shedding light on an ongoing process of German-Irish interrelationship. They do not, however, enter into the (potentially controversial) debates raised by some of these exemplary careers, but do avoid engaging in generalizations about intercultural dynamics or patterns of influence. In this respect, the volume as a whole and in its constituent parts make one hungry for more: more detail, more contextualization, more conceptualization, both in the historical field of concrete encounters between the cultures as well as in the theoretical field of intercultural studies. From a cultural point of view, the volume highlights certain elements in a rich and complex tapestry; from a scholarly point of view it offers the raw material for further investigation and theorization.

Florian Krobb (NUI Maynooth)

Stephen Boyd and Manfred Schewe: Welttheater übersetzen, adaptieren, inszenieren. Thomas Hürlimanns *Das Einsiedler Welttheater*, nach Calderón de la Barca, und in englischsprachiger Fassung: *Cork's World Theatre* / World Theatre. Translation, Adaptation, Production: Thomas Hürlimann's *Das Einsiedler Welttheater*, after Calderón de la Barca, and Its English-Language Version: *Cork's World Theatre*. Berlin: *Schibri Verlag, 2011 (= Edition Scenario: Performative Sprach-, Literatur- und Kulturvermittlung 1). 184 pp. € 14.00. ISBN 978-3-86863-083-1.*

Stephen Boyd and Manfred Schewe both teach at University College Cork. The result of their collaborative work is volume one of a new bilingual book series *Edition Scenario* edited by Manfred Schewe and Susanne Even. The subtitle defines the series' purpose as a forum for fostering and disseminating research in drama in education: "Performative Sprach-, Literatur- und Kulturvermittlung: Eine Buchreihe zur Förderung des interkulturellen Dialogs in der Drama- und Theaterpädagogik / Performative approaches to language, literature and culture: A book series for the promotion of intercultural dialogue in drama and theatre pedagogy." Judging by the present volume, the series promises to add exciting new perspectives to both German Studies and Theatre Studies in Ireland.

The somewhat larger than normal format indicates that this is an unusual book: offering the complete text of Hürlimann's work in parallel English and German translation, it is impossible to tell, given the authors' backgrounds, which one is the original and which the translation. As with the series title, readers may initially baulk at the rather wordy, Baroque title of the present volume, covering, as it does, nearly the full title page. However, one can easily argue that in this particular case this is not at all inappropriate; the book, after all, leads us right back to the great Baroque dramatic masterpiece of the Spanish Jesuit Pedro Calderón de la Barca, *El gran teatro del mundo* (c. 1636). Like many other publications of that period, Boyd and Schewe's volume, too, consists of several related but distinct parts.

Part I contains a scholarly introduction to the concept of *Welttheater* and to Calderón's original *auto sacramental*, its background and reception. We are also given a close analysis and interpretation of Swiss writer Thomas Hürlimann's two 2000 and 2007 adaptations of the Spanish classic for the *Welttheater* production in the Swiss town of Einsiedeln where a German-language version of Calderón's play has been performed at irregular intervals since 1924. This is followed by a detailed account of the intentions behind the authors' own adaption of Hürlimann's play, *Cork's World Theatre*, and of its first performances 29 November-1 December 2010 in the Aula Maxima of University College Cork. A summary of reactions ranging from the learning diary of a student of German to reviews in the local press give an insight into the local reception of the play and its effectiveness on the stage (96ff.). Part II of the volume contains the German and English texts of the adaptation. The programme of the play and a bibliography are provided in an appendix. Full-colour illustrations of the Cork and Einsiedeln performances are included in the volume.

In the scholarly introduction of Part I one may quibble a little with the all-too-brief discussion of the term *Welttheater*. Here the authors seem to assume that *Welttheater* and *World Theatre* are exact equivalents. That Calderón's play is invariably translated into English as *The Great Theatre of the World* is an indication that this is not the case. Rather than inferring its German meaning from Goethe's concept of *Weltliteratur*, a look in Gero von Wilpert's still widely used classic *Sachwörterbuch der Literatur* (5th edn. Stuttgart: Kröner, 1969, p. 848) shows that in German literary scholarship the term is restricted to a "Vorstellung vom Welttreiben und Menschenleben als einem großen, vorüberziehenden Schauspiel, in dem jeder seine Rolle zu spielen hat, bis der Tod sie ihm abnimmt," and thus applies to plays like Calderón's, von Hofmannsthal's and indeed Hürlimann's. The wider "quantitative meaning" (p. 21) evident in book titles such as *The Cambridge Guide to World Theatre* may in fact have come into German more recently through its usage in English. Curiously, neither the text nor the bibliography mention the most recent and easily accessible German translation by Hans Gerd Kübel and Wolfgang Franke of Calderón's play, *Das große Welttheater* (Zurich: Diogenes, 1981), all the more curious as this translation, unlike Eichendorff's which is frequently referred to, was explicitly written for lay actors and with Einsiedeln in mind, and would therefore would have seemed particularly useful for the authors' own purposes.

But these are minor points. The introduction combines scholarship and the experiential, performative and visual nature of the theatre in a convincing and engrossing fashion. Calderón's *auto sacramental* is a theocentric play, and yet it believes in the free will of human beings to influence their own fates and that of the world as a whole: "[T]he Law of Grace will always be available to help them to give a good performance" (p. 71). In Hürlimann's modern version, on the other hand, "the world is not created or ruled by a supreme being [...] rather, human beings are caught up in an endless, impersonal and incomprehensible cosmic cycle of coming into and passing out of being" (p. 71), "choice is limited and [...], no matter what choices are made, the inexorable processes of existence will continue to work themselves out in endless cycles of creation and destruction" (p. 85). The interaction between the local and the universal (global) is central to both Hürlimann's and Calderón's plays, as it is to the Cork adaptation. The authors make the interesting observation that its easy transfer to Cork may have been facilitated by the fact that both Calderón's original and Hürlimann's adaption were created within a consciously Catholic framework. (p. 95)

Overall, the adaptation *Cork's World Theatre* in Part II of the volume sticks quite closely to Hürlimann's original. The play is a vibrant mixture of philosophical musings, clever witticisms, local allusions, and much humour, political and otherwise. In the play, the good burghers of Cork do not heed Father Wise's exhortation: "woe to those who add house to house says the prophet" (p. 137), inevitably leading to "Anglo Nama fluctuality" (p. 163). Catholic devotion comes in for a few jibes too: "This way to the Grotto, / We've tranquilizers and Video-Cams / And raffle tickets / For the Pilgrim's Lotto." (p. 134) Still, a group of German tourists insists that everything is "Ja, sehr schön, sehr schön" (p. 131). As in Hürlimann's play, much is made of wind turbines as harbingers of a new world, which in Ireland controversially, as in Switzerland and Germany, are starting to adorn or spoil the landscape, depending on one's aesthetic sensibilities. In clever ambiguity, their sustainable energy production is dependent on the Endwinds which in the play threaten the earth seven times. The last lines "And since all of life / Is but partaking in a play / May we and you be pardoned / For our performance of each day. Finis" (p. 175) highlight that all human existence is performance and the world a stage, thus linking the Cork play once again closely to the central idea of its seventeenth-century predecessor, and making it true *Welttheater* in the narrower German sense of the word. Even in is printed form one gets a good sense of how well *Cork's World Theatre* must work on stage; the photographs provide further visual proof.[1] We also learn that the original idea of the authors/directors was a larger-scale open-air production in the Einsiedeln tradition with the stronger involvement of the community, but in the end only a studio version in UCC could be realized. Rather than divine intervention or "cosmic cycles," it was the financial crisis that limited the exercise of (the authors') free will in post-crash Ireland.

The wonderful cover image notwithstanding, I feel that the slim, rather flimsy brochure-like format, partly the result of the thin low-grade paper used, does not do justice to the book's profoundly engaging content, neither to the witty play nor to the imaginative and intelligent scholarship underpinning it. Often, there also seems to be just too much text on the page. While the price may make the book eminently affordable, for future volumes in the series a different presentation and lay-out might be considered.

Joachim Fischer (University of Limerick)

Gisela Holfter: Heinrich Böll and Ireland. *Newcastle upon Tyne: Cambridge Scholars Publishing, 2011. 200 pp. € 48.99. ISBN 978-1-4438-3195-6.*

This is *the* definitive book on the subject of Heinrich Böll's long-standing relationship with Ireland, arising from Gisela Holfter's well-known dedication over the years not only to German-Irish Studies in general but also to research on Böll. For this undertaking, indeed, there is hardly anyone better placed in the field of letters than she, given the fact that she wrote her dissertation on German travel writing in Ireland in the twentieth century for the university of Böll's beloved Cologne, has lived and worked in Ireland since St. Patrick's Day (!) 1996, co-founded and still co-directs the highly successful Centre for Irish-German Studies in

---

[1]   A film version of the performance is available on *youtube* at: http://youtu.be/sEBX1-lB6Ak.

the University of Limerick, and sees Böll quite rightly as the twentieth-century epitome of German-Irish interaction on a literary and creative level, a reciprocity exemplified by Böll's *Irisches Tagebuch* but also borne out by the numerous articles, reviews and comments by Böll on Ireland as well as the impressive number of translations of Irish literature by him and his wife Annemarie. Indeed, the strands of Holfter's career, the focal points of her past research, as well as her vast knowledge of Irish history, her close acquaintance with Heinrich Böll's son René, and with the Achill-born poet John F. Deane, seem inevitably to lead to a career climax in this study, much of which, fittingly enough, she completed in what she aptly calls "a truly magical place": Heinrich Böll's cottage in Dugort, presumably in that very room described so lovingly by Deane, "with the window looking down over Nangle's valley to the sea at Dugort [...] while great fuchsia bushes hang their flowers drenched with mist before the window. Deora Dé, the Tears of God. Time stands cautious, and the act of writing becomes a great labour of love."

This book, too, is a labour of love. The author's affection for her subject is made everywhere evident, even in the book's cover picture, which speaks volumes about how at home Böll felt on Achill. He poses for a snapshot on the road with his hands in the pockets of his baggy trousers, a cigarette dangling from his mouth, while his beret, rather than at a rakish French tilt, is pulled unceremoniously but realistically on both sides down to his ears as protection against Irish rain and wind. On encountering him like this, one would be forgiven for taking him to be a local farmer and asking him for directions to the nearest pub.

On the other hand, Holfter's treatise is rigorously scholarly, taking us through Böll's biography, his early links to Ireland, his first trip there in 1954, his discovery of Achill Island in the following year, an in-depth and lengthy analysis of *The Irish Journal* covering all of its most important aspects, from its structure, its treatment of time, its characteristic blend of fact and fiction to Böll's discrete handling of poverty, emigration and religion. As regards Irish Catholicism, Böll, who in his own German context was a severe critic of his own Church, gives a somewhat blue-eyed view of its Irish manifestations. This, too, is treated by Holfter. She quotes a private letter of Böll's to Georg Rosenstock defending his lack of criticism of Irish clericalism, of which he was very aware, as the wish not to get involved as a foreigner in domestic problems. To this one could say that his discretion sometimes went too far and blunted the potential thrust of his depiction of the Ireland of the 50s.

Holfter includes very interesting chapters on the comparative reactions to the book in Germany, where it was and is Böll's best-selling book, and Ireland, where it came in for both praise and criticism. Another important chapter looks at Böll's 45-minute black-and-white film *Children of Éire*, the comparative reception of which was far more polarized. Screened on German television on 8 March 1961, it was viewed by an amazing 47% of all potential viewers, and was received extremely positively because it showed a society in which money was not the be-all and end-all of life. In Ireland it caused huge controversy, John O'Donovan calling in the *Sunday*

Press for the immediate withdrawal of "that disgraceful production" which exhibited the Irish "as the most hapless and hopeless race in the northern hemisphere," and outraged letters to the editors of the major newspapers signed with noms-de-plume such as "Annoyed," "Angry," and "Disgusted." When Böll next visited Achill, a neighbour asked him – whether in jest or earnest is not made clear – if he was not afraid of being stoned. But in 2010 Fintan O'Toole, with his usual perceptiveness, called the film a "prescient vision of Ireland, through a 1960 lens" that made uncomfortable viewing after the collapse of the Celtic Tiger because of its focus on emigration.

Eoin Bourke (NUI Galway)

Anna Nunan: Autobiographical Progression in the Writings of Christa Wolf. *Nachdenken über Christa T.* (1968), *Kindheitsmuster* (1976) and *Ein Tag im Jahr* (2003). With a foreword by Caitríona Leahy. *Lewiston: The Edwin Mellen Press, 2011. 276 pp. £ 94.95. ISBN: 978-0-7734-1541-6.*

Central themes of recent scholarship on autobiography and life writing – from the difficult imperative to represent the everyday, to the relationships between individual and cultural memory, to the *auto*biographical investments involved in biographical representation – speak clearly to the three texts by Christa Wolf that are the main focus of this book. Through detailed discussions of *Nachdenken über Christa T.* (1968), *Kindheitsmuster* (1976), and *Ein Tag im Jahr* (2003), Nunan's study charts the progression of the autobiographical in Wolf's writing over several decades. The complex interplay of experience, reflection, context, and form that constitutes autobiography or 'self-writing' is carefully considered, and each of the texts is discussed with reference to ongoing debates around subjectivity, personal criticism, female/feminist aesthetics, and life writing.

The time is ripe for a re-evaluation of Wolf's works in terms of current theories of life writing. As the immediate political context of their initial reception begins to recede, the extent and nature of Wolf's commitment to, or disillusionment with, the 'real existing socialism' of the German Democratic Republic can increasingly be seen within a longer historical view as one important, but not the sole or even dominant question that her books might continue to pose. Feminist approaches inform the readings offered here, reflecting not only the explicit, if tempered, feminist commitment of many of Wolf's writings, but also the highly productive dialogue between theories of autobiography/life writing and feminist/gender-aware perspectives that has developed in recent decades. Autobiography, in its evolution from the fact-bound, retrospective and more or less coherent narrative of an identifiable subject who seems in firm command of an 'I,' towards more fragmented, self-reflexive, and experimental forms (Nunan references landmarks in the tradition from Augustine and Teresa of Avila through Virginia Woolf to Roland Barthes), proves fertile terrain for feminist and gender-theoretical interrogations of subjectivity, textuality and representation. Intersubjective and relational models of selfhood; impatience with received distinctions between personal and political, public and private spheres; a keen awareness of the critical potential of 'disruptive epistemologies' which trouble the boundaries of fact and fiction: all of these central concerns of feminist theory are, as Nunan shows, anticipated and elaborated in Christa Wolf's texts. Whether through their barely fictionalized reminiscence, their self-critical attempts at biographical portraiture, or their unabashedly mundane diaristic detail, the works of Wolf dramatize many of the problems surrounding the attempt to write of self and other.

Nunan's thorough exposition mediates successfully between the various strands in the text corpus that seem to pull in different directions. These include awareness of the limitations of language and the fallibility of memory; acknowledgement of the intractable relationship between individual experience and historical moment; and, through and despite all this, the desire for, and claim to, 'subjective authenticity' (*subjektive Authentizität*, Wolf's term, which is given a central place in the discussion). Wolf's ongoing quest, as Nunan tells it, is the quest for an 'I' that could continue to write itself in full knowledge of the difficulty of doing so.

Nunan's approach to the material is, perhaps, not as reader-friendly as it could be; in places, this is due to a somewhat deferential over-reliance on critical and theoretical sources which, while they provide theoretical weight, are not always woven seamlessly into the discussion of Wolf. The above-mentioned autobiographical tradition is one significant frame of reference; another is provided by poststructuralist perspectives on writing and authorship, such as those of Barthes, Foucault, Derrida and Paul de Man. More recent work on life writing, and particularly on women's autobiography (Laura Marcus, Linda Anderson, Sidonie Smith, Estelle Jelinek), is well mined for relevant insights, as is the conceptual and definitional ground broken by Philippe Lejeune. What emerges, then, is a variegated landscape of autobiographical theory and practice, an effective background against which to read Christa Wolf's 'progression' from novelist to life-writer. The book's final chapter is particularly effective in its negotiation of the issues surrounding Wolf's status as public intellectual and 'cult figure' from the 1990s on; *Ein Tag im Jahr*, with its deliberate focus on the often-banal details of domestic life, is read as an effort to counteract the tendencies towards canonization visible in the biographies of Wolf that began to appear late in her lifetime (Jörg Magenau's 2002 biography is singled out in the discussion, and Sonja Hilzinger's 2007 study is also referenced). Nunan thus highlights some interesting contrasts between the agenda of the biographer and that of the diarist and seemingly reluctant cult figure; and these issues are well contextualized with reference to the 1990 *Literaturstreit*, without being reduced to its mere aftermath.

It is in mapping the field of tension between biography and autobiography that the study makes some of its most valuable contributions. Nunan reminds us that it is not, or not only, through the attempt to write the self that Christa Wolf's endlessly self-questioning yet committed poetics are forged; the difficulty of saying 'I,' (*die Schwierigkeit, 'ich' zu sagen*, a Wolfian motif to which Nunan often recurs), is at its most acute in the 'quest' for the *du* and the *sie* of *Christa T*. The tensions in autobiographical theory between expressive and constructivist models of self-writing (put simply, is the self represented in the writing, or does the writing process in fact produce the self?) gain a further level of complexity when confronted with the task of representing and remembering an *other*. The crucial first steps in the 'autobiographical progression' that Nunan sketches here are in fact biographically motivated.

Nunan's clearly defined focus on a single writer, and indeed on a selection from this writer's works, is balanced by a breadth of conceptual scope that allows for coverage of a range of thematic and formal issues. The chapter on *Kindheitsmuster*, for example, covers the death of the mother, humour, sexuality, the question of generations and the inheritance of guilt, all in a fairly short space of time; while such rapid coverage can sometimes create the impression that the material, rather than the argument, is dictating the course of the discussion, Nunan manages to bring all the strands together to create a narrative of autobiographical progression that establishes clearly the compelling relevance of Christa Wolf's work to current theorizations of autobiography and life-writing.

Caitríona Ní Dhúill (University of Durham)

Caitríona Ní Dhúill: Sex in Imagined Spaces. Gender and Utopia from More to Bloch. *Oxford: Legenda, 2010. 190 pp. £ 45.00. ISBN 978-1-906540-41-8.*

Textual utopias always serve a double function: both vision and critique, they construct alternative imaginary worlds while also criticizing actual historical practices. It is precisely this dual role that Caitríona Ní Dhúill explores in her excellent monograph *Sex in Imagined Spaces: Gender and Utopia from More to Bloch*, which engages with utopian writings from the nineteenth and twentieth centuries and includes detailed analyses of works by Gerhart Hauptmann, Charlotte Perkins Gilman and Frank Wedekind, among others. Ní Dhúill understands utopia both as a literary topos and as a form of historically contingent critical-imaginary practice. It is in the deliberate divergence from socio-historical reality that she locates the utopian text's political potential: each utopian vision is shown to engage directly with the socio-historical reality to which it responds – be that in a critical, a subversive or a nihilistic manner. The utopian text is, then, marked above all by its *alterity*, "its deviation from historical reality, and by its *indebtedness* and *referentiality* to its real context" (p. 7).

Ní Dhúill's more specific and original contribution to utopia studies, however, is her investigation of the role of sex-gender systems in the utopian societies represented in literary texts. These sex-gender systems are manifest in conceptions of masculinity, femininity and sexual identity, the social organization of sexual desire, the division of labour between the sexes, and a society's technologies of reproduction. As Ní Dhúill rightly argues, the "re-imagining of social structures and collective practices can entail a corresponding reinvention of gender identities and gender relations; or the alterity of the utopian society can call forth a compensatory intensification of existing discourses, received wisdoms, and contemporary practices" (p. 54). In her perceptive analyses of individual texts, Ní Dhúill investigates what happens to specific socio-historical gender arrangements, sexual identities, and sexual practices in imaginative utopian spaces, and reads the utopian re-imaginings as forms of commentary on these arrangements and norms.

The focus on questions of sex and gender in narrative utopias is further justified by the fact that they became increasingly central to literary discourse around 1900, primarily as a result of secularization and the emergence of sexology and Freudian psychoanalysis in the later decades of the nineteenth century. The sexologists and Freud instigated a paradigmatic shift in the wake of which sexuality was no longer debated in terms of sin and virtue, but under the signs of pathology and normality. Moreover, particularly in the writings of Freud and Nietzsche, sexuality ceased to be considered as a subsidiary matter and took on existential importance – not least as an expression of a longing for a lost unity and for overcoming specifically modern forms of alienation. However, as Ní Dhúill points out, the sexological enterprise itself, characterized primarily by its taxonomical impulse, seems motivated by a desire that is essentially utopian in nature, namely the desire for a rationally regimented, "controlled and legible world" (p. 71).

One of the many strengths of Ní Dhúill's lucid study is the way in which she shows how various non-literary discourses impacted on the utopian conceptions of the authors she discusses. These include diverse strands of *fin-de-siècle Lebensreform* discourse, such as maternalist feminism, eugenics, body culture and new developments in the realm of pedagogy. Frank Wedekind's incomplete utopian text *Die Große Liebe* (parts of which were published as the novella *Mine-Haha oder Über die körperliche Erziehung junger Mädchen* in 1903), for example, is read primarily as a critical intervention in then-dominant discourses on pedagogy, sexuality, and gender relations. Gerhart Hauptmann's novel *Die Insel der großen Mutter oder Das Wunder von Île des Dames: Eine Geschichte aus dem utopischen Archipelagus* (1924), in contrast, engages among other sources with Bachofen's theories on matriarchy. Ní Dhúill convincingly proposes that the notion of 'essentialist complementarity' resides at the very heart of Hauptmann's utopian vision, that is, the idea that masculinity and femininity are transhistorical, universal essences, but are also complementary, in that "the ideal state is one in which these essences coexist in a harmonious and balanced relationship" (p. 76).

Charlotte Perkins Gilman, too, embraces essentialist concepts of masculinity and femininity in her novel *Herland* (1915). In contrast to Hauptmann, however, she advocates maternalist feminist doctrines based on the idea that the 'feminine' nurturing, altruistic values of motherhood can act as a positive alternative to an alienating, coldly intellectual, and technology-obsessed 'masculine' culture, and can therefore be mobilized to instigate social reform. "Gilman's narrative steers a risky course between reducing women to their maternal function and expanding the idea of the maternal so that it becomes all-encompassing" (p. 80), Ní Dhúill writes, yet in *Herland*, motherhood is elevated from a domestic to a social quality, as "the cycle of reproduction and child-rearing [is] elevated to the status of a religion, an end itself, indeed the entire purpose of existence" (p. 79).

While other writers tend more towards the constructivist side of the argument, rather than the essentialist one embraced by Hauptmann and Perkins, Ní Dhúill also rightly reminds the reader that the very "notion of a 'truth' of gender, an authentic way of living one's sex and sexuality freed from the corrupting distortions and repressions of civilization, is itself utopian" (p. 71). In a similar vein, she reveals the utopian element present in eugenic discourse, and analyses the ways in which eugenicist ideas have infiltrated utopian fictions: "the eugenic dream of a beautiful, 'fit,' healthy population, fully in control of its own reproduction, continues to haunt utopian thought even today" (p. 83).

Ní Dhúill's study shines a bright light on the hitherto neglected importance of sex and gender questions in utopian societies. *Sex in Imagined Spaces* is a cogently argued, beautifully written, and highly original contribution to knowledge in utopia studies and beyond; it not only mobilizes important wider cultural developments for the analysis of literary texts, but also gives a brilliant gender-theoretical spin to the double function of utopian texts as vision and critique.

Anna Katharina Schaffner (University of Kent)

John Ward: Jews in Business and their Representation in German Literature 1827-1934. *Oxford: Peter Lang, 2010 (= British and Irish Studies in German Language and Literature 53). 250 pp. € 46.30. ISBN 978-3-0343-0126-8.*

Jews in business is a challenging topic because it brings together socio-historical realities with the realm of stereotype and downright prejudice. Yet precisely because it is so steeped in ideology, the theme lends itself so well to evaluating the position of Jews in a predominantly non-Jewish society such as Germany. The question of Jewish presence in the economic realm is thus of interest to historians, sociologists, and literary critics, among others, who want to know how Jews fared within a rapidly modernizing society and under the influence of the socio-economic changes that drove this development. Ward's book, which analyses the depiction of Jewish business men (there are no female figures under consideration here) in works by Jewish and non-Jewish writers from the early nineteenth to the twentieth century right up to the beginning of the Nazi reign, makes a contribution to this larger area, tracing a historical pathway that could perhaps have led to the acceptance of Jews into German society, but of course did not.

When dealing with a topic pertaining to Jews in Germany, it is a particular challenge for the researcher to look at the evidence in a way that does justice to the historical context. Ward's study places the texts under consideration between the twin poles of embourgeoisement, meaning the arrival of Jews in German middle-class society through participation in economic life, and decomposition, referring to the belief that Jews destroyed the fabric of German society and its values through their corrupt and corrupting business practices. This analytic structure runs through the entire book and informs discussions of the individual texts, resulting in an interpretative trajectory from emancipation to the Nazis that comes across as somewhat mechanical because it is highly focused on the outcome. For its historical background, the book relies on the classic studies about Jews in eighteenth- and nineteenth-century Germany and the question of their position within German society by authors such as Selma Stern, Monika Richards, and Jacob Toury. While these are fundamental works, they are also somewhat dated at this point, and, as a result, Ward's analysis to some degree lacks innovativeness. The other structuring element at work in this study is the juxtaposition between Jewish and non-Jewish authors, a model that is certainly legitimate, but also runs the risk of conflating an author's social identity with the characters and plots he created.

Texts analysed include several versions of the Jud Süß material from the Romantic Wilhelm Hauff's anti-integration story to Leon Feuchtwanger's famous novel and Paul Kornfeld's 1929 politicized drama; the book also contains interpretations of Gustav Freitag's *Soll und Haben*, Heinrich Mann's early novella *Schauspielerin*, Lothar Brieger-Wasservogel's lesser known story *René Richter* and Hermann Bahr's *Die Rotte Kohras*, as well as Georg Hermann's two-part novel *Jettchen Gebert* and *Henriette Jacoby*. Chapters and chapter sections include foci like city literature versus *Heimatkunst*, but also historical treatments of the theme of the *Hofjude* – the quintessential "Jew in Business" – or an analysis of historian Heinrich von Treitschke's well known anti-Semitic statements about Jews. The study thus usefully combines readings of literary texts with discussions of historical themes and contexts.

Ward's book offers competent close readings of these works, which is especially welcome in the case of lesser known texts. For example, Brieger-Wasservogel's novel *René Richter: Die Entwicklung eines modernen Juden* (1906) tells the story of a young man who overcomes the alienation from modern society he experiences in turn-of-the-century Berlin by adopting Zionist views and by suggesting that Jews might be better off leaving modernizing Germany for a Jewish state. In this case, a Jewish character (and a Jewish author) subscribe to the wide-spread assumption that modern Germany is a corrupt and corrupting place, but suggests that Jews are the victims rather than the cause of this. Another interesting example is Fritz Mauthner's *Der neue Ahasver* (1881), a novel whose Jewish main character discovers his fundamental Germanness during an extended stay in Africa, only to realize that there is no place for him in Germany as a German and a Jew. The sections on Theodor Fontane and Heinrich Mann address anti-Semitic qualities in the works of canonical German authors. Ward is not the first one to point out such traits, but those are important arguments to make. One might have wished for further-reaching analyses of the "ambiguous" (p. 129) stances these two writers expressed towards Jews as middle-class entrepreneurs. Finally, the study includes a number of outright anti-Semitic depictions of Jewish businessmen such as Wilhelm von Polenz' *Der Büttnerbauer* (1895) and Felix Nabor's Nazi-piece *Shylock unter Bauern* (1934). In sum, the texts compiled and discussed here show a range of approaches from cautious optimism for Jewish integration into German society (Hermann's *Jettchen Gebert*-novels are the prime example here) to unabashed anti-Semitism, and a number of positions in between.

Overall, Ward's study makes for somewhat unsatisfying reading because it does not go much beyond the well-known story of the complexities that accompanied Jewish attempts at assimilation into German society and its disastrous end. The texts under consideration confirm an established pattern, making the outcome of the study rather predictable. In the end, the book seems less interested in literary representation in all its nuanced and often contradictory traits than in determining whether or not a text is indeed anti-Semitic and thus a step toward the Nazi regime and the Final Solution. The relationship between Jews and modernity could have been explored in a more productive fashion, placing, for instance, the socio-economic changes of the nineteenth and twentieth centuries into a larger framework. Nevertheless, the book offers good close readings of important texts and is thus well worth reading for anyone interested in the figure of the Jew in business and his representations in German literature.

Katharina Gerstenberger (University of Utah)

Elaine Martin: Nelly Sachs. The Poetics of Silence and the Limits of Representation. *Berlin: De Gruyter, 2011. 190 pp. ISBN 978-3-11-025672-7.*

As the death of Margarete Mitscherlich is announced, there is an added aptness to the reading of Elaine Martin's fine study of Nelly Sachs' poetry. The delusions and denials of the Adenauer era diagnosed so famously by the Mitscherlichs as underpinning a national 'inability to mourn,' and defining in some measure the repressive climate of post-war Germany, play a substantial role in Martin's book. Not that it is the psychoanalytical that is the focus of attention here; on the contrary, here the literary is emphatically historical. But the political forces that shape this history, are themselves the products of profoundly psychological stances, and it is what Martin terms "the changing relationship between memory and politics" that determines not just the German public sphere between the late 1940s and the late 1960s, but also the seemingly erratic reception of Sachs' work during this period.

This is the starting point of this book, in which the first of three sections is dedicated to tracing the roots of Sachs' "tumultuous" reception history. This section offers above all, and in the best sense of the word, an orderly illustration of how Sachs' critical reception is politically determined by the narratives, myths and truisms of the day. In the West, Herbert Marcuse's myths of German victimization, ignorance and resistance hold sway, and not just in the political sphere. Here Martin's narrative is illuminating and skilful as she weaves a storyline that moves between politics and culture. Thus Adenauer's declared intention in 1949 "Vergangenes vergangen sein zu lassen" (p. 19) is set alongside an account of the cultural projects of the Goethejahr 1949, which served to reconnect with 'authentic' pre-Auschwitz German culture and erase the memory of recent 'abberations.' Examples such as the reconstruction of the Goethehaus in Frankfurt exemplify Martin's claim that culture became one important tool in the state's reinvention of itself and the concomitant silencing of voices that bore witness to a different version of that self.

Nelly Sachs was one such voice, and so, in the state which is itself "built on a culture of 'Verdrängung'" (p. 14), her poetry must bide its time. That time comes with the political shifts of the Cold War, the Ulm Task Force trial, the Eichmann trial, the Auschwitz trials, and the establishment of diplomatic relations with Israel. In this environment, Sachs finds herself suddenly lauded and prized – literally, repeatedly – as a living embodiment of German-Jewish reconciliation. Martin's account of the hijacking of Sachs' poetry for deeply problematic political purposes is sensitive to the bitter irony that now her 'success' is as wrong-headed as her boycotting had been in the previous decade. It amounts to memory suppression by other means – "an attempt to have Sachs perform the task of mourning on behalf of the German people, to applaud her for doing so and to return to 'business as usual'" (p. 47).

The second section of the book turns to Adorno, specifically to the infamous 'barbarity of poetry after Auschwitz' reference. Martin patiently and thoroughly shows the error of so many readings of this line, by placing it alongside its companion comment from *Negative Dialektik*, contextualizing both instances and subjecting them to closer readings than most commentators have bothered to do. For those (and there are surely many of us!) who have often been exasperated at the sheer laziness of the 'poetry is barbaric' shorthand, this strong refutation is welcome indeed. In terms of the broader function of Adorno for Martin, her argument is clear and controversial: "Sachs is [...] not only a test-case for Adorno, she is engaged in the same debate as Adorno: her writing is a reflection on the act of writing" (p. 183).

Some readers will doubtless take issue with the notion that poetry might be a 'test-case' for thought, or a thinker; others will find the notion of self-reflection too generally drawn here to address the specificity of Sachs' aesthetic. But Martin's argument for reading Sachs in the light of Adorno's struggle to perform an act of thinking that would at once be adequate to the ethical imperatives of bearing witness and the choked possibility of expression is well made. Moreover, the juxtaposition of two very different kinds of silencing – one to do with publishing and politics, the other with the philosophy of the sayable and unsayable – means that each approach is balanced by the other, and a more rounded and grounded Sachs emerges.

The final section of the book features a series of close readings of Sachs' poems under headings inspired by the general context of 'the limits of representation after Auschwitz' debates, and specifically arguing that Sachs develops what can be termed 'a poetics of disfiguration.' These readings will be enlightening, not just to Sachs readers, but also to those of Celan and Bachmann, of Blanchot, Jabès and many others. For what emerges in Martin's detailed analyses is not just a nuanced sense of Sachs' own poetic project, but also a broader sense of how her 'undoing' of representational devices, indeed, her dismantling of language itself, echoes the struggle of others to perform that now quintessentially post-Auschwitz task: by disfiguring, to reconfigure the possibilities of representation.

Celan fans may find themselves hankering for more acknowledgment here. And, certainly, there is more that might be said about the correspondences that reverberate between the works of the two poets. But one of the many strengths of Martin's excellent study is that it will attract many different audiences and leave each of them wishing for more. Literary historians, I think, would welcome a reception history that extended the memory politics approach to Sachs from the late 1960s to the present, while theorists will want more intertextuality, and more lines of comparison between Sachs' language and thinking and that of her contemporaries. This is no criticism, but rather a tribute to Martin's authority, and to the considerable achievement of making difficult material accessible without destroying its complexity and richness.

Caitríona Leahy (Trinity College Dublin)

Eoin Bourke: "Poor Green Erin." German Travel Writers' Narratives on Ireland from Before the 1798 Rising to After the Famine. Texts Edited, Translated and Annotated by Eoin Bourke. *Frankfurt am Main: Peter Lang, 2011. 773 pp. € 83.20. ISBN: 978-3-631-61369-6.*

In his satirical short story, *Die Emanzipation der Dienstboten* (1840), the German writer Otto Ludwig (1813-65) has his narrator look forward in 'this age of emancipation' to the coming liberation of a whole series of traditional 'underdogs': domestic servants, Jews, negroes, women – and even the Irish. The plight of Ireland and her people had gradually established itself during the previous years as a topic popular among the editors and publishers of liberal media for its capacity to engage public interest. Ireland appealed in particular to radical younger writers, born during the Napoleonic era and politicized by the 1830 Revolution. Since these writers were prevented by a harsh and vigilant censorship, equipped with powerful sanctions, from writing overtly about political conditions in their country, the state of 'poor Erin' suffering under the yoke of her rulers provided a useful allegory for their own situation. It was through the vogue for travellers' tales that Ireland became a fashionable subject. In the stultifying atmosphere of Restoration Germany, the island on the western edge of Europe provided virtual experience of the wider world to those who could not afford to move far from home. Prior to 1830, German travellers to Ireland had, however, been a relatively rare phenomenon. Unlike Scotland, Ireland had produced no Walter Scott, widely translated and published in Germany, who might have excited the anthropological curiosity of the adventurous. True, Karl Jakob Küttner's four-volume *Letters about Ireland to his Friend the Publisher* which appeared in Leipzig in 1784, at the time effectively Germany's media capital, had provided a kind of blueprint for later writers in the form of "the first-ever extensive German eye-witness account of Ireland" (p. 13).[2] Over the next decades half a dozen visitors of varying ideological backgrounds recorded their desultory impressions of the country and its people. That landscape changed with the appearance in 1831 of a work entitled: *Letters of a Dead Man* which Goethe himself would greet as "a work of signal importance for German literature" (p. 189). Its author was the idiosyncratic but media-savvy Prince Hermann von Pückler-Muskau, who came to Ireland in (the vain) search for a rich bride who would invest in his run-down estates in distant Lusatia (*Lausitz*). Between the two Revolutions of 1830 and 1848 the success of his travelogue was instrumental in the Irish nation's acquiring its almost iconic status among politically conscious Germans as a byword for humanity's suffering under the yoke of the oppressor.

"Poor Green Erin" is a substantial volume, reflecting the number of those who came from Germany in these years and their capacity to write at considerable length of their sojourns. It also reflects the appetite of nineteenth-century German readers for the print media, and one which book publishers and newspaper editors in an era of low-cost labour and new, cheap methods of paper production proved eager to supply. From the period under review Bourke identifies some twenty-seven named authors (and two anonymous), devoting a section to each. He provides a succinct introduction (p. 1-12), organized chronologically, placing the authors in their age and analysing the reasons for their interest in Ireland. He makes the point that many of the most empathic (including Heinrich Heine, who never actually visited the country) were emancipated Jews, who could more easily identify with the social exclusion which they encountered among the native Irish. Among these was the democratic republican, Jakob Venedey (1805-71) who visited Ireland in 1843. His

---

[2]   All subsequent references to *"Poor Green Erin"* are included parenthetically in the flowing text.

extensive and highly informative, though not unprejudiced account was immensely influential in shaping the perception of Ireland among German liberals and democrats, most notably in the Rhineland and the south. Each of the texts included here is introduced by a brief biography of their authors; sub-sections of longer texts are provided to locate the events and impressions. Particularly useful is the extremely detailed table of contents, which with its some 450 separate section headings serves as a kind of subject index. In the case of the longer texts, several of which run to over fifty pages, the editor intersperses his text with further information on the particular circumstances or political context.

A first reading of their titles suggests widespread 'borrowings' by each traveller from his predecessors, an impression which most scholars working in this field would confirm. One such was Victor Aimé Huber, son of famous parents, whose *Sketches from Ireland* (1850)[3] was a selective and unacknowledged plagiarization of the well-known three-volume *Ireland: Its Scenery and Character* (London 1841-43) by the peripatetic English couple, Mr and Mrs S.C. Hall. However, in noting the regular recurrence of particular topics across the travelogues of ideologically diverse visitors, we need to remember that many of these German visitors, and indeed nineteenth-century European travellers more generally, were journalists who needed to finance their travels by what they wrote. Accordingly they wrote to satisfy their prospective publishers, who knew that – then as now – the average reader liked to read about what he or she had heard about before.

In a manner still characteristic of German travellers in our own time, their nineteenth-century predecessors did not confine themselves to the well-known sights but covered a wide geographical range across all four provinces. The contents section allows us to see at a glance which were the recurrent themes and impressions of these serious visitors. The texts themselves make clear that opinions were by no means uniform. To some as Küttner (1783/4) or Helfferich (1851) Dublin was a splendid city, "one of the loveliest cities of the world" (Hailbronner [1836?], p. 261), to others the very antithesis. Connaught was, in the view of the much-travelled Ida von Hahn-Hahn (1846/7), "the purest province" (p. 512), while to Helfferich, 'Galwegians' are "infamous for being particularly vindictive" (p. 590). A number of travellers were doughty apologists for Belfast or indeed Orangeism, excoriating 'native superstition,' while one of the best informed, the Prussian constitutional historian Friedrich von Raumer (1835), lamented what he saw as the flagrant misuse by Orangemen of the name of that apostle of religious toleration William of Orange, King William III of England. Invariably German visitors focused on poverty and beggary, drunkenness and landlordism, on the beauties of the Irish scenery and the impenetrable nature of the Irish language – "very guttural, even more so than the Zurich dialect, and quite unpleasant to the ear" (Küttner, p. 31). Confessional

---

[3]   Referred to on p. 3 and 757 (not 756 as in text), and rightly not included here. Huber's parents were the highly intelligent Therese Heyne, first married to Captain Cook's companion, Georg Forster, and subsequently to the writer Ferdinand Ludwig Huber (who published much of Therese's work under his own name).

difference fascinated most, although, as might be expected, attitudes were largely determined by the writer's own position. A handful take an independent line and can be thoroughly informative on subjects as diverse as the Belfast linen industry and the Irish rail system, at the time under process of construction, or the Trinity College honorary conferring.[4] Partly because only two German witnesses from the years 1846 to 1847 are recorded here – one of these, Lewald did not actually visit but wrote presciently about the Irish in England – there is less reference to the Famine than one might have expected. Of those recording their impressions in the 1850s, only Friedrich Engels gave the impact of the Famine the attention it deserved.

However by far the most favoured topic of German travellers in the inter-revolutionary years (1830-48) was that of Daniel O'Connell, on whose 'German persona' Bourke has already written.[5] Though Prince Pückler-Muskau could hardly be termed a political radical, it was he who first and successfully promoted the most prominent Irishman of his generation and author of Catholic Emancipation in Germany. O'Connell's legendary hospitality had been enjoyed by the prince in Derrynane, and subsequent German travel writers keen to reimburse their expenses through publication, always made sure to seek him out. O'Connell's attraction to the generation of Germans who had been politicized by the Revolution of 1830 lay not least in the universality of his emancipatory focus.[6] Thus only three weeks after his successful guidance of the bitterly contested Catholic Emancipation Bill through the House of Commons, O'Connell had written to Isaac Lyon Goldschmid, head of the Jewish community in Britain, promising his assistance in promoting the cause of Jewish emancipation both as his moral duty and as a matter of political logic.[7] O'Connell's campaign to win the repeal of the Act of Union (1801)[8] in the 1840s with his carefully orchestrated monster meetings and non-violent agitation, is well

[4] The renowned historian Ranke came to Ireland specifically to receive an honorary doctorate in 1865. His proposer was a Senior Fellow of the College, Charles Graves, whose sister Clarissa was Ranke's wife.

[5] Eoin Bourke: Daniel O' Connell. "Ein Riese unter Zwergen oder ein rechter Lump?" Der irische Agitator in Vormärzperspektive. In: Helmut Koopmann and Martina Lauster (eds): Vormärzliteratur in europäischer Perspektive I. Öffentlichkeit und nationale Identität. Bielefeld: Aisthesis (1996), p. 159-74.

[6] The radical Lutheran pastor Ludwig Uhlich, who in the mid-1840s formed a mass movement to evangelize and modernize his church, was familiarly known as 'the Saxon O'Connell.'

[7] Writing from Derrynane on 11 September 1829, O'Connell declared: "I think every day a day of injustice until that civic equality is attained by Jews. Command my most unequivocal and energetic exertions in parliament to do away with the legal forms and the laws which now ensnare or impede the conscientious Jew in seeking for those stations to which other subjects are entitled." He went on in this remarkable letter to advise Goldschmid on parliamentary tactics, offering practical assistance: The Correspondence of Daniel O'Connell. Ed. Maurice O'Connell. Vol. IV: 1829-1832. Dublin: Irish Manuscripts Commission, 1977, p. 95f.

[8] Campaign to repeal the 1801 Act of Union, the latter briefly addressed here by P.A. Nemnich (1806), p. 70.

documented here. It was the subject of considerable interest to some of the most intelligent of these travellers, among others Jakob Venedey and the Prussian senior civil servant Ernst Ludwig von Gerlach. Indeed at a dinner in Berlin prior to his departure Gerlach had been commanded by King Frederick William IV of Prussia to convey his personal greetings to O'Connell. How extraordinarily long the Irishman's reach in German socio-political history was destined to be, became evident only years later and even today is relatively little known to scholars of the period. In the late 1840s his Repeal campaign became the model for the emerging Catholic movement in Germany, initially styled the *Piusverein* (after Pope Pius IX who had then not yet shed his liberal credentials), but changing its name during the 1848 Revolution to the more programmatic First German *Katholikentag* or Catholic popular assembly. It was not, however, until the crisis between [Catholic] Church and state in Bismarck's Germany known as the *Kulturkampf* (1872-85) that O'Connell's policies of non-violent protest, coupled with nation-wide organization and sophisticated 'media-management' came into their own. At the close of the nineteenth century the million-strong *Deutscher Katholikentag*, with its characteristic mix of radical conservative policies and highly modern organization and propaganda techniques, could trace its origins directly to the Great Liberator.[9]

The particular merit of *"Poor Green Erin"* is to have assembled and edited in accessible form in English such a substantial number of 'witness statements' across a key stage in the history of modern Ireland and its awakening political consciousness. Eoin Bourke has been well served for much of his source material by mid- and late twentieth-century real and virtual travellers, duly acknowledged in the text. These include the pioneering John Hennig, refugee from Nazi Germany (1911-86),[10] and Karl Holl who as far back as 1959 wrote his Mainz doctoral thesis on German political journalists' critique of the 'Irish Question' in the O'Connell era. It was not, however, until the Irish-Canadian Patrick O'Neill published his *Ireland and Germany: A Study in Literary Relations* in 1985 with its substantial section on travel literature, that German travellers to Ireland became a popular research topic for scholars of German-Irish relations, among them Eda Sagarra (1992) and more particularly German graduate students, notably Andreas Oehlke (1991 and 1993), Doris Dohmen (1994), Gisela Holfter (1996) and Andreas Boldt (2007).

As always with the 'Eoin-and-Eva Bourke cottage industry,' the translations are both true to the originals, and highly readable and idiomatic. To quote just one example among many, namely the pen portrait of her host by Magdalene von

---

[9]   See Geraldine F. Grogan: The Noblest Agitator. Daniel O'Connell and the German Catholic Movement 1830-50. Dublin: Veritas, 1991, p. 59ff. O'Connell has the distinction, thanks to the initiative of an ambitious local parish priest and the intervention of Pope Leo IX (1878-93) who had witnessed his maiden speech in the House of Commons fifty years earlier, of being the only Catholic layman to have a church dedicated to him in his birthplace Cahirciveen, Co. Kerry.

[10] On Hennig, a member of the Royal Irish Academy, see Gisela Holfter and Hermann Rasche (eds.): John Hennig's Exile in Ireland. Galway: Arlen House, 2004.

Dobeneck, the twenty-six-year-old recent divorcée, painter, composer and sister of the 'philosopher of atheism' and mentor of Karl Marx, Ludwig Feuerbach. Dobeneck visited Dublin in 1832, and acted as governess for several months to the daughter of the Earl of Ranfurly, Thomas Knox, at his Dungannon castle. Knox, she writes to her father, offers 'copy' for her interest in physiognomy:

> [L]ean and agile as he is, every part of him quivers, indeed even the slightest movement of his little finger puts the whole entire person in motion. When he speaks, his mouth has the form of a triangle or spout [...]. He could be 36 years of age, is rather tall, has black hair, small, cunning, pale greyish green eyes, an oblong, almost regularly shaped face, no hips, a blue beard, good teeth (p. 181).

For whom is *"Poor Green Erin"* written? The author describes his work as a bridge "between academe and the general reading public" (p. 1). There is a substantial community of Irish readers at home and in the diaspora who are interested in and well-informed about Germany and German-Irish relations, but not sufficiently fluent in the language to read such texts. Moreover the bulk of these travellers' accounts are only available in Gothic script, which even advanced university students of German can, alas, no longer read. Yet the 'academic' reader asks her- or himself: is there sufficient context to enable the general reader to form a critical judgement about what is here presented? The broad question of reception is only addressed in terms of plagiarization from English sources: how far, for example, did individual writers, most of whom were journalists, actually copy from one another, how much was based on direct experience? We receive little information on how the work of these travellers impacted on the image of Ireland in Germany. It would, for example, have been useful to have had some editorial guidance to readers unfamiliar with the publishing scene in nineteenth-century Germany. The bibliography includes the names of the publishers, but nothing to suggest whether a particular publishing house had merely a local or rather a national outreach. Yet it is a fact that very many of these travellers' accounts were published in some of the most prestigious houses, and by publishers in key locations right across the German Confederation. They include Cotta in Tübingen and Stuttgart, Brockhaus in Leipzig, Hoffmann & Campe in Hamburg – Heine's publishers – Vieweg in Braunschweig, and Berlin's Julius Springer. Even as early as the mid-1840s these publishers were advertising their lists vigorously, and their authors could expect to be widely read. This was certainly also the case for those who, like Jakob Venedey or Adolf Helfferich, had access to the liberal *Augsburger Allgemeine Zeitung,* and could enjoy a captive audience. That the erstwhile feminist Ida Countesss Hahn-Hahn, described in 1846 by one of her London acquaintances as "a one-eyed man-eater," published her "Irish reminiscences," following her well-staged conversion, in one of the leading Catholic houses, Kirchheim and Schott in Mainz, ensured her presence for decades thereafter in (Catholic) school libraries, presbyteries and lending libraries. A long-seller, her romanticized portrait had a material impact on her readers' impression of 'Green

Erin.' Similarly, the rather 'folksy' image of Ireland in the latter decades of the century owed much to the influential position of one of the media moguls of the Berlin and German literary scene, namely Julius Rodenberg (1831-1914) who, following his visits in the late 1850s and early 1860s, had published a number of books on Ireland.

We owe Eoin Bourke a debt of gratitude for producing in his massive compendium such a rich and enjoyable source of information on how a diverse group of Germans across some three generations perceived Ireland at a particularly bitter period of her history. Equally, students working in the fields of Irish-German literary relations and of travel literature will find its comprehensive character and the accessibility of the accounts of otherwise lesser known figures of particular value. It will be important that future students working in this field position their own research centrally within the structures and techniques of the extraordinarily vibrant German media industry, in order to be able to evaluate critically the actual dynamics of its travel literature.

Eda Sagarra (Trinity College Dublin)

Konferenzberichte / Conference Reports

Friedrich Engels' "Geschichte Irlands" (1869/1870)
(Berlin-Brandenburgische Akademie der Wissenschaften, 11-12 August 2011)

A joint initiative of the Berlin-Brandenburg Academy of Science (BBAW) and the University of Limerick's Centre for Irish-German Studies, this two-day conference held in the Einsteinsaal of the Academy of Sciences at the Gendarmenmarkt, attracted an audience of over 120 people.

The topic of what was the thirteenth conference in Irish-German Studies (and the first to be held outside Ireland) was Friedrich Engels' attempted history of Ireland. In the end, he only completed two chapters, but in the course of his research filled more than 600 pages (mostly unpublished) with notes from over 150 books and manuscripts. Another little-known fact related to this episode in his life is that he even learned Irish and married an Irish woman. Conference organizers Jürgen Herres (BBAW) and Gisela Holfter (Centre for Irish-German Studies, UL) brought together ten speakers who looked at different aspects of Engels' (and Marx's) engagement with Ireland and the Irish cause, which in turn shed light on European discourses on "the Irish question." In other words, the focus was not only on contextualizing Engels' engagement with Ireland, but also on contemporary European perspectives on Ireland. Gisela Holfter's paper dealt with the background of the project as whole, and presented theoretical approaches to intercultural hermeneutics, while situating Engels' portrayal of Ireland and his interest in Irish history within Irish-German relations of the nineteenth century. Jürgen Herres introduced Engels' and Marx's writings on Ireland. Editor of the *MEGA* (Marx-Engels-Gesamtausgabe) I/21, which includes the two completed chapters of the *Geschichte Irlands*, "Naturbedingungen" and "Altirland," Herres is a leading authority on Engels' writing on Irish history. The organizers plan to publish and edit the copious notes Engels took for the rest of the unfinished work.

Other conference contributors included Regina Roth (BBAW) who discussed Engels' portrayal of Ireland in his first monograph *The Condition of the Working Class in England* (1845). She charted the origins of the stereotypes he used to describe the Irish in Manchester and the role they took on in his critical analysis. Sean McConville (Queen Mary, London) looked at the situation of Irish political prisoners in Great Britain 1865-67, and examined Engels' (and Marx's) views on Fenianism. He argued that they displayed a variety of attitudes to Irish nationalism, but that Fenianism and the situation of Fenian prisoners instigated considerable reflection and political activity on both their parts (although Engels clearly had the greater knowledge of Ireland). Detlev Mares (Darmstadt) discussed different attitudes to Ireland in the English workers' and reform movements, concentrating on popular radicals' stance towards Ireland and the Irish question in the late 1860s, a period in which Anglo-Irish tensions had culminated in the activities of the Fenians.

Eoin Bourke (Galway) spoke about German travel narratives of Ireland, mainly from the first half of the nineteenth century. Some German commentators happened more or less accidentally upon Ireland in their travels, going first to Britain to experience and describe for their readership that "cradle of democracy," which, in comparison to Germany at least, was greatly politically advanced in many respects. They then journeyed on to Ireland to see, as they thought, more of the same. Instead, they found they had moved from the richest country in the world to the poorest they had ever experienced, and suffered the shock of discovering a dark side to the British Empire. Other German commentators went out of curiosity, intent upon discovering a country associated with romantic fairy tales and (equally romantic) politicians such as Daniel O'Connell. O'Connell exercised the minds not only of travel writers, but also fascinated politicians, journalists, poets and diplomats, as James Brophy (University of Delaware) demonstrated in his paper on O'Connell's reception in German political circles and the media. Eberhard Illner (Wuppertal) gave an overview of working conditions in the textile factories established by Engels' father in Barmen and Manchester. Director of the Historisches Zentrum Wuppertal, which generously supported the conference, Illner provided extensive background information on life in both early-industrial Manchester and Germany.

Gisela Mettele (Jena) looked at the private Engels, specifically the role played in his life by Mary and Lizzie Burns. Not long after he arrived in Manchester, Engels struck up a relationship with Mary Burns, daughter of an Irish immigrant. She later joined him for a while on the continent. When he returned to Manchester, he set up two residences, one for his official business partners, and one where Mary and her sister Lizzie lived and where his socialist friends gathered. After Mary's death, he started a relationship with Lizzie, marrying her shortly before she died. This insight into Engels' private life triggered a particularly vigorous debate among participants and audience members, continuing a pattern of enthusiastic involvement in the discussion on the part of all attendees.

To conclude the event, the Irish Embassy, conveniently located opposite the Academy of Sciences, hosted an evening reception for participants. Irish Ambassador to Berlin, Dan Mulhall, had contributed a lively paper to the conference on other little-known links between Ireland and Germany in the nineteenth century, concentrating on Jemima Montgomery, Baroness von Tautphoeus, who wrote a number of well-received novels about English-speakers in Germany, but also mentioning other notable Irish figures in Germany such as Lola Montez.

The conference was widely reported in a number of high-profile German media outlets, including the *Frankfurt Allgemeine Zeitung* and the *Süddeutsche Zeitung*, with a report and interview on *Deutschlandfunk*. Due to the success of the event, the organizers were asked to edit the 2011 issue of the *Marx Engels Jahrbuch*, which will publish the proceedings of the conference.

Gisela Holfter (University of Limerick)

Weimar Colonialism
(NUI Maynooth, 12-14 April 2012)

The School of Modern Languages, Literatures and Cultures at the National University of Ireland Maynooth played host to an international conference on Weimar Colonialism from 12-14 April 2012. Organized by Florian Krobb and Elaine Martin (both NUIM), the main objective of the conference was to investigate the manner in which colonial losses found expression in the literary and public discourse of the Weimar period. Germany was entirely stripped of her colonial possessions at the Treaty of Versailles. Unlike other European nations, therefore, the country was faced with the end of empire well before the demise of the European colonial project as a whole. Strikingly enough, however, the colonial theme blossomed in German literature, culture and public discourse in the two decades following the confiscation of Germany's overseas territories, demonstrating the deep-rooted nature of the colonial imaginary in German society. The disparity between colonial imagination and reality, and the expression of desire and loss provided a starting point for the deliberations of the fourteen delegates who presented at the conference.

Following a welcome from Philip Nolan, President of NUI Maynooth, Heidrun Kämper (Mannheim) opened proceedings with her paper on linguistic representations of colonialism. She highlighted the binary order of discourse on colonialism, divided between a pro-colonial political right and an anti-colonial political left. Linguistically, pro-colonial discourse aimed at constructing a discourse of colonial mission through the use of terms such as "Lebensnotwendigkeit," "(geistige und sittliche) Hebung," and "Lebensraum." Meanwhile the anti-colonial left utilized the vocabulary of Marxism, using terms such as "kapitalistische Herrschaft," "Ausraubung," and "Ausbeutung."

Carolyn Birdsall's (Amsterdam) contribution focused on a very different aspect of Weimar colonialism, namely *Karneval* during the interwar period. Her talk demonstrated how the celebration of *Karneval* at this time served as a platform for marketing and consuming "otherness," and how exaggerated gendered, racialized and sexualized imagery was deemed acceptable within this temporary suspension of normal social relations.

Elaine Martin (Maynooth) addressed the issue of reverse colonialism in a paper entitled "'Die Bestien im Land': The 'Black Horror' in the Literary and Public Discourse of Weimar Germany." Based on an analysis of various newspaper and magazine articles, and the novel *Die Schwarze Schande: Grossstadt-Roman* (1921) by Rudolf Mavege, Martin described how a nationwide crisis was manufactured in interwar Germany using the participation of black soldiers in the occupation of the Rhineland. "Frauenehre" was connected to "Nationalehre," as fabricated reports of black debauchery and the rape of German women circulated and were linked metaphorically to the territorial invasion of Germany.

Continuing the theme of reverse colonialism, Cornelius Partsch (Washington) discussed two novels written during the interwar period: the novel *Der Neger Jupiter raubt Europa* (1926) by Claire Goll, and *Politische Novelle* (1928) by Bruno Frank. In both novels (African) American figures are crucially linked to jazz music and dance, and both texts portray the Rhineland occupation as shameful for Germany, with issues of race, gender and nation set against a backdrop of the "blackening" of Europe.

Catherine Repussard's (Strasbourg) paper looked at colonial booklets for young people from the Weimar period. These booklets, featuring regret-filled emotional story-telling, reject reality by re-telling and re-inventing Germany's colonial history. They feature an iconography in which the former African colonies are portrayed, on the one hand, in terms of a Garden of Eden, a lost, exotic but orderly paradise, and on the other hand, as wild nature, not yet tamed. Colonial culture held a specific attraction for interwar Germany, providing a way of re-imagining and re-building political life, and serving as a means of escapism for the middle classes in the unstable Weimar Republic.

Luke Springman (Bloomsburg) also focused on ambivalence towards colonialism in the Weimar Republic in his paper examining the representation of colonialism in films, texts and photography aimed at the Weimar youth. The works of Colin Ross, for example, depict Africans as indolent savages, debasing them in a sarcastic and derisive manner. Although advertised as documentary films, Springmann's analysis highlighted the fact that they were more projections than documentaries. In contrast to this, the work of Swiss aviator Walter Mittelholzer portrayed Africa as a pristine "paradise" from the air, depicting the beauty of the natives on the ground. By comparing the works of Colin Ross and Walter Mittelholzer, Springman showed that the colonizers created images of the colonized, whether as indolent savages or idealized children of nature, even before the first encounters.

Turning to the activities of colonial youth associations, Susanne Heyn (Frankfurt) examined the Weimar Colonial Youth Movement and its importance to the colonial revisionist agenda. Supporting the retrieval of the colonies, the youth movement also aimed at preparing members for a life as settlers in the colonies. Youth groups existed for both boys and girls, and events were organized to recruit new members and to fundraise for German schools in the colonies. Interestingly, these groups perpetuated ideas about gender, with groups for boys reading adventure magazines like *Jambo* and focusing on physical fitness, while the girls were taught about women's roles in Africa, focusing more on the domestic sphere, although they too took part in some physical activities.

Stefan Hermes' (Freiburg) paper analysed Hans Grimm's novella *Der Pavian* (1930). Broadening Homi Bhabha's concept of mimicry in his analysis, Hermes introduced the idea of inverted mimicry, whereby the colonizer imitates the colonized, also known as "going native" or "Verkafferung." Introducing this to the literary realm, he described as "inverted literary mimicry" cases in which a white author adopts the viewpoint of the natives. Hans Grimm's novella does just this, pretending to offer insights into the minds of the Africans and focusing on the black characters, while the white figures such as the "Polizist" are mere stock types rather than plausible individuals. However, the ironic tone of the narrator and insinuated inferiority of the Africans suggest that the novella is indirectly part of the German revisionist colonial project and is, essentially, a literary call to defy the geopolitical realities of the post-First World War period.

Brett Van Hoesen (Nevada) turned attention back to visual material and the artistic imagination with her paper on "Avant-Garde and Popular Press Photomontage in the Age of Weimar Postcolonialism," arguing that exoticized internationalism in the imagery of the interwar press served to sustain the myth that Germany still had a large overseas empire.

In her presentation Tara Windsor (Birmingham) examined Ernst Toller's anti-colonial links. Toller, well-known for his revolutionary socialism, pacifism and anti-fascism in the 1920s and 1930s, was also an outspoken anti-colonialist who challenged contemporary German colonial discourses and resisted demands for the recovery of Germany's overseas empire after the First World War. Windsor traced Toller's involvement in anti-imperialist organizations such as the League against Colonialism, pointing out that Toller inverted many ideas current in colonial discourse in his speeches, articles and literature from this period in an attempt to highlight the brutal realities hidden behind a rhetoric of benign and civilizatory colonialism.

A different geographical sphere of German colonial interest was introduced by Florian Krobb (Maynooth) in his contribution "Designs on Turkey: German Colonial Desire in the Middle East in World War I Memoirs." In comparison to German colonial fantasizing about the Middle East, which culminated in the period between 1914 and 1918, post-war attention to the Orientalist vision is remarkably restrained. However, non-fictional sources, such as military memoirs from 1918 until the late 1930s, constitute an exception to this rule. Although for the most part these writings cast a critical eye on German strategy during World War I, they simultaneously engage in nostalgic reliving of the colonial past, a moment when Germany could rival Britain for colonial space.

Kristin Kopp's (Missouri) paper looked at the issue of German colonization nearer home: in Eastern Europe. She demonstrated how maps and atlases published in Germany in the nineteenth and twentieth centuries, especially the *Deutscher Kolonial-Atlas* (1897), colluded in the colonial project by engaging in certain distortions, including the use of anachronistic representations of German "colonization" going back hundreds of years. During the Weimar period, Poland was regarded as a European space that had been "civilized" by Germany, not with the sword but by the plough. The German claim to Poland was lent weight by the idea that Germany had made Poland what it was, for example through "deutsche Kulturarbeit" in the realm of agriculture, an idea that was widespread during the Weimar period.

Jason Verber's (Tennessee) paper turned to colonialism post-1945. Although the official post-war position was that West Germany harboured no colonial interests, many West Germans hoped that the Bundesrepublik would pursue colonial interests in West Africa. Indeed far from vanishing after 1945, the colonial impulse remained, with many West Germans seizing upon and repurposing existing materials in an attempt to seek redemption in a mythologized version of the German colonial past. Interestingly, post-war narratives of German colonialism closely resembled those produced in the interwar period.

Dirk Göttsche (Nottingham) closed proceedings with another contribution that looked at colonialism beyond Weimar. In an analysis of the different ways in which contemporary literature engages with the aftermath of the colonial past, Göttsche examined a variety of texts from Stephan Wackwitz's novel *Ein unsichtbares Land* (2003), to Max Blauelich's *Menschenfresser* trilogy (2005-2008), Andreas Schmidt-Pabst's *Janus'lichte Seite* (2004) and Hans Christoph Buch's *Sansibar Blues* (2008). In conclusion, Dirk Göttsche made the important point that the Weimar period was very much a generational threshold, a transition from living memory of the German colonial past to history of the same.

Leesa Wheatley (NUI Maynooth)

'About Time': Women in German Studies Annual Conference
(University College Dublin, 28-30 June 2012)

The annual Women in German Studies conference took place on 28-30 June 2012 at University College Dublin. This was an open conference, organized by WiGS' Ireland representative, Gillian Pye, and supported by the Swiss and Austrian Embassies, as well as the Goethe Institute, Dublin. Turn-out was high, with almost fifty delegates from Germany, Switzerland, Austria, Ireland, Belgium, the US and the UK. There was a large postgraduate contingent, many of whom also presented their work.

The conference theme, „About Time," generated a rich variety of papers and approaches. In suitably chronological fashion, proceedings began with a medieval and early modern plenary session. The first speaker, Gráinne Watson (Stanford), highlighted the sophisticated narrative strategies employed in the twelfth-century *Kaiserchronik* and *Alexanderlied*, arguing for a revised understanding of medieval conceptions of temporality. Daniela Fuhrmann (Zurich) examined the influence of liturgical time on configurations of temporality in examples of late medieval *Offenbarungsliteratur*, while Lukas Werner (Wuppertal) sought to generate a model of historical narratology from an analysis of Grimmelshausen's *Simplicissimus* (1668).

The relationship between narrative temporality and identity construction was the focus of the first parallel session. Nadine Nowroth (Trinity College Dublin) noted the interplay between fragmented identity and place in the prose works of Susanne Schädlich, while Deirdre Byrnes (NUI Galway) explored the aesthetic representation of lost time and memory – and its subsequent recovery – in Kathrin Schmidt's 2009 novel, *Du stirbst nicht*. Emily Spiers (Oxford) compared progressive narratives of futurity in recent essayistic, popfeminist texts with two recent literary novels which disrupt linearity: Helene Hegemann's *Axolotl Roadkill* (2010) and Antonia Baum's *vollkommen leblos, bestenfalls tot* (2011). The parallel nineteenth-century panel included Erika Wickerson's (Cambridge) intertextual reading of time in Theodor Storm's *Immensee* (1848) and Thomas Mann's *Tonio Kröger* (1901), while Tracey Reimann-Dawe (Durham) explored the temporal marking of space in nineteenth-century travel writing. Tove Holmes (Colorado) examined destabilizations of linearity in Adalbert Stifter's *Die Narrenburg* (1844).

The conference then moved to the Goethe Institute, where author Angelika Overath gave a reading from her 'Senter Tagebuch,' *Alle Farben des Schnees* (2010). Overath's text moves between autobiography, chronicle and literary fiction as she depicts her family's experience of moving from Tübingen to the Swiss mountain village of Sent. The ensuing discussion ranged over several aspects of Overath's work, from the role played by the diary form in the construction of a suitable narrative temporality, to the role that writing poetry plays in language learning (in the author's case, learning Romansch). Overath also took part in the following morning's translation workshop, facilitated by Charlotte Ryland, editor of the journal *New Books in German*. Participants worked in small groups translating excerpts from *Alle Farben des Schnees*, and were subsequently treated to a translation 'slam' between professional translators Rachel McNicholl and Nick Johnstone, who had each translated one of Overath's renowned 'biographische Rätsel' for the event.

Cultural memory and the relationship between place and time were some of the main themes of the post-workshop plenary session. Samantha Fox (Columbia) undertook an anthropological analysis of nostalgia and cultural memory in Germany's "first socialist city," Eisenhüttenstadt. Anne Fuchs (St Andrews) argued that Wilhelm Genazino's prose narratives disconnect social time and social space, allowing the emergence of a model of temporality that challenges today's high-speed society. Elizabeth Boa (Emeritus, Nottingham) also considered the implications of accelerated and decelerated narrative time in the context of the Weimar Republic in her intertextual reading of Mann's *Der Zauberberg* (1924) and Vicki Baum's *Menschen im Hotel* (1929). In the second plenary session, Heike Polster (Memphis) identified critiques of linearity in key passages of Christa Wolf and Anna Seghers' works, while Georgina Paul (Oxford) considered how gradual shifts in Wolf's approach to narrative temporality corresponded with the author's shifting relationship to the State. Carolin Benzing (Ghent) focused on little-known

Swiss author Kurt Aebli's depictions of characters with ambivalent attitudes towards time.

The first plenary session on the final day of the conference focused on notions of interior and exterior time. Colin Benert (Chicago) explored the dynamic between these two modes in Goethe's *Wilhelm Meisters Lehrjahre* (1795-6), while Janet Pearson (Sunderland) offered an analysis of spiritual time in Hermann Broch's *Der Tod des Vergil* (1945). Kate Roy (Liverpool) argued for an understanding of time as duration in Emine Sevgi Özdamar *Das Leben ist eine Karawanserei* (1992) and Mariam Kühsel-Hussaini's *Gott im Reiskorn* (2010).

The subsequent parallel sessions centred on German-language literature by Swiss and Austrian writers. Thorben Päthe (Munich) explored the politically resonant uses of time in the work of Max Frisch; Katya Krylova (Vienna) offered a reading of Ingeborg Bachmann's *Malina* (1971) which focused on the collapsing of space and time within the narrative. Marcela Pozarek (Queen Mary, London) considered the interrelations between public and private time in Bachmann's poem, "Die gestundete Zeit" (*Die gestundete Zeit*, 1953) and Max Frisch's short story *Der Mensch erscheint im Holozän* (1979). The papers given in the concurrent session were clustered around the fin de siècle and early twentieth century. Simone Sauer-Kretschmer (Bochum) made the link between temporality and female corporeality in Franz Kafka's *Der Verschollene* (1927); Charlotte Woodford (Cambridge) explored time, creativity and maternal ambivalence in Helene Böhlau's *Der Rangierbahnhof* (1895) and Lou Andreas-Salomé's *Das Haus* (1904). Gilbert Carr (Trinity College Dublin) provoked lively discussion with his critique of Otto Weininger's conception of time, cognition and subject identity.

The final parallel sessions included a panel on film and poetry, in which the political implications of formal fragmentation emerged as a common theme. Leila Mukhida (Birmingham) explored Michael Haneke's politicization of the cinematic medium by means of aesthetic fragmentation, with particular reference to his 1994 film *71 Fragmente einer Chronologie des Zufalls*. Annja Neumann (Queen Mary, London) examined Paul Celan's treatment of historical time in "DAS GESCHRIEBENE" (*Atemwende*, 1967), arguing for the existence of lyric-specific temporality; finally, Johann Reißer (EUV, Frankfurt an der Oder) considered the way in which Ulrike Draesner and Barbara Köhler stage confrontations between the lyrical subject and rigid conceptions of time in their respective poems "ferngespräch" (*Gedächtnisschleifen*, 1995) and "Brechung" (*Deutsches Roulette*: *Gedichte 1984-1989*, 1991). In the concurrent parallel session, Francesca Goll (Nottingham) gave a reading of Werner Bräunig's *Rummelplatz* (2007) which focused on the interplay between depictions of time and space, while Jeanne Riou (UCD) considered temporality and energy in Freud's *Trauer und Melancholie* (1917), exploring, in particular, the relationship between grief, time, and 'normal' or pathological object-relations.

The conference successfully drew together a broad range of time-related topics, although it was perhaps unsurprising that the question of narrative time emerged as the dominant theme. Highlights of the event, which featured cutting-edge scholarly engagement with the multi-faceted topic of temporality in German-language literature, included the presence of author Angelika Overath and the translation workshop which gave participants insights into writing and translation as praxis.

Emily Spiers (Oxford)

GERMANISTIK
IN IRELAND

Jahrbuch der / Yearbook of the

German Studies Association
of Ireland (GSAI)

Die bisher erschienenen Bände können zum reduzierten Preis von € 8,00 pro Band bezogen werden.

Bestellungen bitte per Email an: r.magshamhrain@ucc.ie oder
strumper.krobb@ucd.ie

Vol. 1 (2006):   **Schiller: On the Threshold of Modernity**

Vol. 2 (2007):   **(Wahl-)Verwandtschaften**

Vol. 3 (2008):   **Weg   und   Bewegung: Medieval   and   Modern**
Encounters. Festschrift in Honour of Timothy R.
Jackson and Gilbert J. Carr

Vol. 4 (2009):   **Intercultural Encounters in the Classroom**

Vol. 5 (2010):   **Sexual-Textual Border-Crossings: Lesbian Identity in**
German-Language Literature, Film, and Culture

Vol. 6 (2011):   **After Postmodernism / Nach der Postmoderne**

Außerdem lieferbar:

GERMANISTIK IN IRELAND Schriftenreihe

Vol. 1:   **Jeff Morrison / Florian Krobb (eds.):**
Prose Pieces: Irish Germanists Interpret German
Short and Very Short Stories
1. Auflage 2008, 242 Seiten, € 20,00.